The Essential

JAMES BEARD

COOKBOOK

ALSO BY JAMES BEARD

Hors d'Oeuvre & Canapés

Cook It Outdoors

Fowl and Game Cookery

Beard on Birds

The Fireside Cook Book

Paris Cuisine (with Alexander Watt)

Jim Beard's New Barbecue Cookbook

James Beard's New Fish Cookery

How to Eat Better for Less Money (with Sam Aaron)

The Complete Book of Outdoor Cookery (with Helen Evans Brown)

The James Beard Cookbook

James Beard's Treasury of Outdoor Cooking

Delights and Prejudices

James Beard's Menus for Entertaining

How to Eat (and Drink) Your Way Through a French (or Italian) Menu

James Beard's American Cookery

Beard on Bread

Beard on Food

James Beard's Theory & Practice of Good Cooking

The New James Beard

Beard on Pasta

James Beard's Simple Foods

Love and Kisses and a Halo of Truffles: Letters to Helen Evans Brown

The Essential
JAMES
BEARD
COOKBOOK

450 Recipes
That Shaped the Tradition of
American Cooking

JAMES BEARD
EDITED BY RICK RODGERS

with John Ferrone, Editorial Consultant

ST. MARTIN'S PRESS ❈ NEW YORK

THE ESSENTIAL JAMES BEARD COOKBOOK. Copyright © 2012 by Reed College and John Ferrone. Foreword copyright © 2012 by Betty Fussell, adapted from her book *Masters of American Cookery*. All rights reserved. Printed in the United States of America. For information, address St. Martin's Press, 175 Fifth Avenue, New York, N.Y. 10010.

www.stmartins.com

Design by Ralph Fowler / rlfdesign

ISBN 978-0-312-64218-1 (hardcover)
ISBN 978-1-250-02788-7 (e-book)

First Edition: November 2012

10 9 8 7 6 5 4 3 2 1

CONTENTS

ACKNOWLEDGMENTS

I am grateful to Elizabeth Beier at St. Martin's Press, for asking me to take part in this celebration of James Beard's work, and for introducing me to John Ferrone, the charming and erudite executor of Beard's estate. Thanks also to Michelle Richter and Elizabeth Curione, for keeping the project on track. Copy editor Leah Stewart, proofreader Jane Liddle, and designer James Sinclair are consummate professionals, and their invaluable contributions show on every page of this book.

My partner, Patrick Fisher, and kitchen manager, Diane Kniss, took on the unenviable job of managing hundreds of recipes. The nuts and bolts of transcribing photocopies into Word documents fell to a dream team of food lovers, some of whom are also cookbook writers who brought their own appreciation of Beard to the chore: Peggy Fallon, Judy Kreloff, Johnisha Levi, Charles Pierce, Carl Raymond, Debbie Schulman, and Dédé Wilson.

—Rick Rodgers

COOKING WITH JAMES BEARD

"Don't gussy up spareribs with all that gunk," the chef boomed at us as we crowded around some naked ribs in the basement kitchen of his brownstone. "Just sprinkle with plain salt and pepper and half an acre of garlic." At 6 feet 4 inches and three hundred pounds, the chef seemed to take up half an acre himself. He certainly took up most of the kitchen. This was thirty years ago, in the now revered "James Beard House" on Twelfth Street in Greenwich Village, where the owner gave cooking classes to small groups of amateurs over the decades. I knew in 1981 how lucky I was to be among them.

Thirty years before that, I'd opened my very first cookbook, which happened to be *The Fireside Cook Book* of 1949. I was a newlywed and knew nothing. It was James Beard who taught me how to boil water, in my own language. He spoke to me directly. He gave me confidence. This was decades before Americans got all "gourmeticized" and learned how to cook French. Beard was as down-home American as "easy side up" and "a cuppa Joe." He taught us to cook American, in our own kitchens, with the simplest of foods, like garlic and onions, and lemons and parsley, and bread. He taught us how to bake our own bread. This was new!

He wasn't a schoolmarm like Fanny Farmer, uptight about thrift and nutrition. Nor a phony marketing brand like Betty Crocker. He was real, he was male, and he was big—he talked big, he thought big—American style. He spoke to guys outdoors at their grills and to gals indoors at their new electric stoves. He celebrated real food, what was fresh, and local, and growing anew after the deprivations of the Depression and the War. He celebrated our new sense of freedom, bounty, and largesse, both in his person and on the page. He was born to cook and to teach because he wanted to share his joy in being alive and savoring every sensuous moment, which is what food is for. Before Julia Child or Craig Claiborne or Jacques Pépin, or the hundreds of kitchen gurus who followed, Beard was the first to reshape the American palate at that moment of self-discovery when America found its new place in the world.

The place *he* came from mattered. Like Julia Child and M.F.K. Fisher, James Beard was a Westerner. Born thirteen and a half pounds on May 5, 1903, Beard learned to cook as he learned to breathe. His father, Jonathan, was "a Mississippi gambler type who wore a red carnation, smelled of fine soaps and colognes, and was loved by all the ladies," Beard wrote. His mother, Elizabeth Jones, was an English adventuress turned hotel owner, who paused briefly at age forty-two to birth a son. She brought her child up the same way she ran her hotel, which was sold a few years before James's birth. Beard described her as "That incredible woman who was my father."

That incredible woman had arrived in America at age sixteen, under the guise of governess, to travel through America and most of Europe and Central America before she settled in Portland, Oregon, and bought the Gladstone Hotel in 1896. Despite the hotel's dignified name, Beard remembers Portland as a raunchy port of waterfront hearties and sporting ladies with their pimps. There were plenty of French and Italian immigrants to hire as hotel cooks, but they would catch gold fever and head for the Yukon to leave Mother Beard fuming among her pots. She finally solved the help problem by hiring Chinese, men like Let, Gin, Poy, and Billy, immortalized now in Beard's recipes.

If hotel life was a natural theater, the landscape was a work of art. The waters teemed with Olympia oysters, Dungeness crab, razor clams, and Columbia River salmon. The woods were blue with huckleberries and blackberries. Tables were loaded with terrapin stew and chicken sautéed with wild mushrooms. The Yamhill Street public market offered seasonally white raspberries, husk tomatoes,

morels, lemon cucumbers, dozens of heritage apples. Italian truck gardeners brought in cardoons, fava beans, leeks, and Savoy cabbages.

With all this natural bounty at their command, Mother Beard and Let battled daily over the proper way to make aspic capon, or curries, applying the ancient arts of China, England, and France to the provender of western shores. Beard remembers Let brandishing a knife and Mother parrying with a stick of firewood. But such quarrels ended in laughter and renewed argument over the proper way to preserve a fig. They instilled in the wide-eyed child watching "a love for food . . . the most varied gastronomic experiences any child ever had." For an American child, it was a dream kitchen.

There was Let's Wonderful Sweet Cream Biscuit and My Mother's Black Fruitcake and My Father's Favorite Pear Preserves. It was the great American amalgam, where Mother imported the muffin and crumpet rings of her youth so that Chinese Let could make perfect English crumpets, "dripping with butter and daubed with our strawberry jam," as Beard wrote in his magnificent memoir, *Delights and Prejudices*. It was also a social amalgam of backyard, carside, and oceanside picnics. There were champagne parties, whist parties, bridge parties, fashionable luncheons and after-theater suppers. For a large fat boy, it was bliss.

He was so pampered, Beard recalls, that he became "as precocious and nasty a child as ever inhabited Portland." His lifelong friend Mary Hamblet agreed that he was a holy terror on occasion but always so generous that to admire a toy was to be given it to keep. She also remembers what may have been his first culinary dish, as they played on the beach at Gearhart and made a sand pie. They frosted it with a pink marshmallow whipped with salt water. "Eat it," said James. "And I did," said Mary. "Because I adored him—and he was big."

Gifted with a taste memory as acute as perfect pitch, Beard remembers his first gastronomic moment: after he'd crawled into a vegetable bin, he bit into a giant onion, eating it up skin and all. At three, sick with malaria, he remembers being fed a superb chicken jelly. At four, his father took him to dine out in Portland once a week so that he could begin to discriminate among restaurants. At five, his mother—in a lapse of discretion—took him to "a palace of high living" called the Louvre, where he sampled French cuisine in a burgundy boudoir setting. And at all ages, his Chinese godfather Let took him to eat in Chinatown.

Still, even as a child prodigy of gustation, his first love was not eating but acting. He advanced from charades in his mother's hotel to playing Tweedledum in the Red Lantern Players' production of *Alice in Wonderland* and Mr. Fuzzywig in their annual performance of *A Christmas Carol*. At nineteen, he set forth to be an opera singer, traveling by freighter *(The Highland Heather)* through the Panama Canal to London and Paris.

When a vocal ailment derailed that ambition, he sailed back to New York, played *Cyrano* and *Othello* at Walter Hampden's Theater, and went on to radio in San Francisco, broadcasting food commercials. But when it was clear, after more than a decade's trial, that he could not both act and eat, he chose to eat. He came back to Manhattan to become what he called a "gastronomic gigolo." In 1937 jobs were scarce but hunger was

not. So he cooked for his supper at the houses of friends, and still he went hungry. He went hungry until, with a pair of friends, he opened a catering shop on 66th Street and Park Avenue and went after the carriage trade. At last he had found his destiny. With his first book, *Hors d'Oeuvre & Canapés* in 1940, Beard spoke in a new voice for a new audience of both men and women. He revolutionized the feminine canapés of the time, those dabs and "doots" of cream cheese on soft white bread. Instead, he offered he-man highball stuff, like artichokes stuffed with caviar, smoked salmon rolls, brioche-onion rings. A year later, he hacked out the Real-Men-Eat-Good trail with *Cook It Outdoors* and later expanded it with cookery books on fowl and game, barbecue and rotisserie, and fish.

World War II interrupted his promising beginning with the draft. After a stint in a cryptography school, Beard was released from the Army to join the United Seamen's Service. It was back to the boards and he directed shows at USS clubs from Marseilles to Rio. "Get him to take his teeth out and sing 'Sylvie,'" said one of his oldest Portland friends, who remembered dying with laughter at Beard's tales of entertaining servicemen abroad. Veteran traveler that he was, Beard also picked up tips on food, like a dessert made with avocado, lime, and sugar whipped up by a cook in Brazil.

At the war's end, he found a new theater for food when NBC asked him to do the first major network cooking classes on television. "At last," he thought, "a chance to cook and act at the same time." Unfortunately, he had to share billing with a cow, fashioned by Bill Baird and produced by the Borden Company: *Elsie Presents James Beard in I Love to Eat.* A new medium inaugurated new "cuisines of advertisement" and a new age for the theater of food, but in 1946 Beard's cooking show was way ahead of its time. It would be decades before television's mainstream audience embraced the image of a man in an apron wielding an iron skillet and shouting, *Bam!*

Even without television, however, by the 1950s the Beard image of a bald man wearing a big grin and bow tie was as iconic as the ever-happy Green Giant. The Beard name branded American food the way *I Love Lucy* branded American comedy. In 1954 *The New York Times* dubbed Beard the "Dean of American Cookery," but that was too pompous a term for such a genial man with such a democratic message: "If I can cook it, you can too." His name became a household word through the continuous outpouring of his articles and books, and particularly his mass-market paperback in 1959, *The James Beard Cookbook.* It is still and forever my quick-reference kitchen bible, even though half the pages have fallen out. From then on he was the majordomo of the food establishment, a grinning Gargantua beaming over platters of fat sausages and hams and chops that fit the American mood in our heady decades of post-war affluence.

To those who carped that he worked too closely with the food industry promoting commodity products like Omaha Steaks and Camp Maple Syrup, Beard replied, "People take food too damn seriously. It's something you enjoy and have fun with, and if you don't, to hell with it." He expressed the same credo in his *Theory & Practice of Good Cooking* in 1977: "In my twenty-five years of teaching I have tried to make people realize that cooking is primarily fun and that the more they know about

what they are doing, the more fun it is."

Of course, like our other food mavens after the war, Beard spent a lot of time eating and drinking in France, soaking up the pleasures of French cuisine in Paris and Provence. But unlike many, he translated them fully into an American idiom and put them squarely on an American table. He reveled in the riches of America's cooking tradition when the French sniffed there was no such animal. In 1972, he revealed our riches like a horde of gold in his groundbreaking *American Cookery.* Knowing firsthand the power of women in the kitchen, he attributed the strength of America's culinary tradition to a trio of strong women in the nineteenth century: Mary Randolph of *The Virginia Housewife,* Miss Eliza Leslie of *Directions for Cookery,* and Mrs. Thomas Crowen of *Every Lady's Book.* "I would like to have known all three," he says. Like them, he understood the strength of American home cooking and the power of focusing on fresh ingredients, simply prepared, with flavor and fun first.

To learn from Beard is to toss diet books out the window as dreary and depressing and the wrong way to go about food. Forced into a no-salt, low-cal diet a few years before his death, Beard looked for new ways of flavoring that he hadn't imagined, just as he discovered new intensities of old friends like strong rooty vegetables, a saltless baked potato, a soothingly creamy yogurt.

To learn from Beard is to learn good cooking, whether its cultural roots are French, Italian, English, Asian, or just-folks American. In his recipes, as in his classes, he shows us the virtues of simplicity and the excitement of discovery. "Be bold," he tells us. "Taste for yourself. Taste things half-done, done—and overdone, if that happens; mistakes are to learn from, not to pine over."

Beard's voice is as American as Whitman's as he sings the body electric, knocks over old categories, and insists that we improvise, experiment, shake up old ideas to discover and to pleasure our own individual taste. Like Whitman, he celebrated America first. "I can assure you," he wrote, "that the smell of good smoked country ham sizzling in a black iron skillet in the early morning is as intoxicating and as mouthwatering as the bouquet of a fine Château Lafite-Rothschild or an Haut-Brion of a great year."

Like P. T. Barnum, he had the gift of gab and a sense of the grand gesture. Chicken with Forty Cloves of Garlic is an understatement compared to his Game-Stuffed Turkey, in which a turkey is stuffed with a goose, which is stuffed with a capon, which is stuffed with a partridge, which is stuffed with a quail. But his gamey version of "Turducken" is also thoroughly practical: fat birds baste drier ones as they cook, and with all the birds deboned, slicing and serving is a dramatic snap. "Put on a fine show!" he commands us. "Like the theater, offering food and hospitality to people is a matter of showmanship, and no matter how simple the performance, unless you do it well, with love and originality, you have a flop on your hands." Beard knows that imagination, rather than money, is the secret ingredient of a hit.

When Beard died in 1985 at age eighty-one, he had no idea that his house would be bought by friends like Julia Child and Peter Kump to provide a showcase for chefs from all over America in the continuing food revolution that he pioneered. He had no idea that his legacy would be maintained and honored by the vital work of the James Beard Foundation. But he surely saw that America was coming into its own in the kitchen and that in the twenty-first century cooking and eating and talking about it would connect young and old, celebrity chefs and novice bloggers, sports fans and video gamers, races and genders and classes and kinds as we sit together at the American Table and celebrate real food, food for flavor, food for fun. Thank you, Jim, for this great gift.

—Betty Fussell

The Essential
JAMES
BEARD
COOKBOOK

INTRODUCTION

AN AMERICAN ATTITUDE TOWARD FOOD

I grew up in a kitchen, and I guess the scent of food is like a perfume. It has stayed with me all my life. My mother ran a small residential hotel in Portland, Oregon, and eating was an experience in our family. We were three distinct personalities, my mother, my father, and I, and we all liked food cooked in a different way. Let, our Chinese cook, spoiled us, really, because he'd take a dish and do it separately for each of us.

Let was originally my mother's chef when she ran the Gladstone Hotel. At the turn of the century, she had an international approach to food that would be revolutionary even by the standards of the last ten years. She was of English and Welsh background, and the majority of her kitchen staff was Chinese, with intermittent French head chefs. Portland was clearly too small to contain the Gallic temperaments of the latter, so after a few months they'd leave, but their technique and style would have been perfectly mastered by the Chinese. The food was sort of the precursor of our "new cuisine," a combination of quick sautés, French sauces, and American ingredients.

My father loved food, too. His family, over a period of sixty years, had trekked from the Carolinas to Oregon, and he had what I think of as old southern—closely related to Scottish—ideas about food. He felt that spinach should cook for about four hours with a piece of hog jowl and that string beans needed about three hours of the same treatment.

But he also loved game, and among my earliest memories is the row of brilliantly colored ducks and pheasants that would hang in the larder. There were always teal, too, and I developed a great love for them because they are delicate and small enough to eat whole at one sitting.

When we had teal, it was always reserved for the household, never served to guests. These tiny members of the duck family are devastatingly good when roasted simply and quickly—basted with butter and seasoned with only salt and pepper—and like squab, eaten with the fingers. As an accompaniment, we often ate braised celery or tender raw celery, and potatoes cooked in the oven with broth. Several years ago, when I was staying in Yucatán, I had teal served to me—it migrates there from the Northwest—and it was the most sentimental meal I ever had eaten. I relished each bite. In France, too, one occasionally finds teal. It is called *sarelle* and it is as good there as it was in Oregon in my youth.

Little did I think, back in those days before the First World War, that food would become the foundation of my career. I started out wanting to be a singer and an actor—I'm not quite sure what kind of actor—and my family encouraged me to pursue these interests. For the most part, I'd have to say I succeeded. I got in at the beginning of radio, and I did a stint on the New York stage in the late thirties. To make ends meet, I taught at a country day school in New Jersey, where I got the first grade going on bread making.

It was around this time that I had a real identity crisis. I decided I was never going to earn enough money working in the theater and radio to keep my life going in the manner which I would have it. Noël Coward did not seem to be rushing to write plays for me, after all, and the only thing that matched my love of the theater was my love of food. I'd always been exposed to good food. My mother had several friends in the restaurant business who ran really excellent establishments, and I learned early in my life to appreciate them.

And then there was New York. New York in the late twenties and the thirties teemed with wonderful restaurants and restaurant chains— Schrafft's, Longchamps, and Child's—where a little bit of money bought a lot. At six foot four, I always had an appetite, and it usually took more than three "squares" to make a whole.

As luck would have it, around this time I met a man named Bill Rhode and his sister, Irma. As we were all in search of a career, we hit on the idea of capitalizing on America's mania for cocktails. The repeal of Prohibition had set the cocktail party into full swing, and in America the *cinq-à-sept*

was reserved for drinks and finger food. Something, we agreed, should be done about the food. We had eaten too many pieces of cottony bread soggy with processed cheese, anchovy fillets by the yard, and dried-up bits of ham and smoked salmon. The ghastly potato-chip dip invention had only begun to spread across the country. So we opened a small, exclusive catering shop called Hors d'Oeuvre, Inc.

There were, we gauged, at least 250 cocktail parties every afternoon on the Upper East Side of Manhattan, and we felt certain that all we needed was a better mousetrap. I remember Mother's saying that a good sandwich at teatime was hardly to be found anywhere. It would be a fine idea, I thought, to offer New York perfect tea sandwiches, also larger ones for evening entertaining— "reception sandwiches," I believe they are called officially. We called them "highball sandwiches."

Now we had to decide on our bill of fare. We discovered the trick of using various smoked sausages and meats as cornucopias and developed a dozen stunning ways to offer stuffed eggs. For the cornucopias, we used salami, bolognas, hams, smoked salmon, and the specially cured pork loin called *lachsschinken*. We also made rolls of salmon, tongue, and the rarest roast beef, and there were sandwiches of veal.

The fillings we created were appetizing and varied. For the most part, the base was a mixture of cream cheese and sour cream. This, with various additions, could be forced through a pastry bag, which speeded the work considerably. The salami filling contained *fines herbes,* with the addition of dill and sometimes a bit of garlic; the *lachsschinken* filling included horseradish and perhaps a little mustard, if customers liked their food piquant; the salmon filling was flavored with a combination of onion, capers, freshly ground black pepper, and a touch of lemon juice. For the rolls, the beef was spread with a very hot kumquat mustard and the ends dipped in chopped parsley, while the tongue was spread with a Roquefort or mushroom butter and sometimes garnished at either end with a sprig of watercress. Our veal sandwiches—two thin slices of veal cut in rounds—were filled with anchovy butter or a herring butter, both of which were tremendously popular.

Incidentally, I wrote my first cookbook, *Hors d'Oeuvre & Canapés*, during this time, and thirty years later, when I went back to revise it, I was surprised to see how little needed to be updated and by how many of our selections had become caterers' standbys. Not infrequently, when I'm at a cocktail party, a tray of canapés is passed before me, and I see old friends.

At this time, too, Americans were becoming more exposed to foreign foods, through luxurious ocean liners and the grand hotels that dotted the country. It was with the dawning of the New York World's Fair in 1939 that food in all its extraordinary variety was set before the American public in ways they had never seen before. A window opened on the food world that even the dreadful war could not close. The scents from those international kitchens—the Swiss Pavilion, the Belgian, the Italian, the Russian (where caviar cost practically nothing), the Swedish, and, of course Henri Soulé's French Pavillon—would eventually lead us to what we've come to know as the American attitude toward food. Even now it's not fully realized.

Well, when the war came I had to give up the catering business because rationing made it impossible. We couldn't buy enough butter or enough meat, but the incredible exposure to all those cuisines I'd sampled at the Fair sustained me through the bleak years until peace returned.

I have to say I was lucky, though, because I spent the war years working for the United Seamen's Services. Basically, we provided the same duties as the USO and the Red Cross, but entirely for the Merchant Marines. We had clubs all over the world, and given the circumstances, we served really top-notch food. I traveled a great deal for the USS, starting in Puerto Rico and going to Brazil, Peru, and the Canal Zone, then on to Morocco, Italy, and France. I never ceased to marvel at how people could make do. They learned to conserve and substitute—for example, making eggless, milkless, butterless cakes. Those were the years, too, when frozen foods began to take hold. They seemed like a miracle. (Mr. Birdseye, who had very particular ideas about food, would set his freezing equipment right out in the middle of acres of strawberries and freeze them on the spot.) And of course, all the meat and poultry that was served in Europe was shipped in refrigerated containers.

By the late forties, in a sprint to recoup all those lost years, people seemed to rush into the future, trying to rebuild their lives, their careers, and their families. Food reflected this sense of urgency. Along with frozen foods, there were fast foods in nascent form. Pizza was beginning—there were about three places in New York that were very good. Soda fountains everywhere produced milk shakes and malteds. Another staple of this time, still popular today, was the club-house sandwich, a meal in one course. I have particular ideas myself about this dish. To me, it's two slices of toast, not three; sliced breast of chicken, not turkey; bacon; sliced ripe tomato; and mayonnaise.

When you look back, you see periods of time inextricably linked with some person, some place, some thing. For me it was often food. The twenties, for instance, were the era of hot dogs and speakeasy food, some of it very good indeed. Hamburgers really didn't become popular until the forties and fifties, although I can remember being in Los Angeles around, oh, 1930, when there was a string of absolutely sensational hamburger stands. They would put everything on the burger, wrap it in a diaper of paper, and put it in a little bag. This magnificent construction cost fifteen cents. It was a full meal, because in addition to the hamburger, lettuce, tomato, onion pickle, mustard, and relish, this would be followed by a serving of hot apple pie with melted cheese. Deadly, when I think about it now, but good it seemed to me then.

By the fifties, there I was right in the midst of this burgeoning interest in food. People were taking the time to cook complex dishes, international dishes. Don't get me wrong—people had always taken the time to cook good food, but it was only now that the general public began to realize the varieties and possibilities of food. With this sophistication came a quest for diversity. No longer was eating simply a necessity; it became a pleasure. It seems at this time I found material for cookbook after cookbook and—wonder of wonders—people were buying them. Suddenly I was in demand to teach cooking classes (I was one of the first to do it—for NBC—on the infant medium television), and corporations sought me out as a consultant to elevate the quality of their goods for consumers who were more demanding than ever before. All this, combined with the boom in technology, helped to channel as well as unleash my own attitudes toward food in America.

In a way, though, it wasn't until the sixties that some of the jigsaw puzzle of my life came together. That was when I met Joe Baum, presi-

dent of Restaurant Associates. I worked with him, and the association, on a number of restaurant projects, but most of all on New York's the Four Seasons. It proved an ideal collaboration: my sixty years of experience, Joe's enthusiasm, and the excitement of using all-American seasonal products. Our ideas and approach seemed as fresh as the ingredients we sought out. For example, baskets of freshly picked vegetables would be brought to your table so you could pick out the ones you wanted. In asparagus season, there were perhaps twenty different ways you could have asparagus prepared. We had fiddleheads and wild mushrooms and many other things both weird and wonderful.

It was Joe Baum's premise that this was a restaurant for New Yorkers. Certainly it proved to be a complete change from everything we'd seen before. If for no other reason, the fact that our menus and format were copied so much convinced us we were right. We had an inimitable group, with Joe Baum, of course, Albert Stockli as executive chef, and Albert Kumin as first pastry chef. I worked a great deal at the Four Seasons. Apart from being consultant on the food, I did the wine list and held wine classes for all the captains every week for two or three years. I've gone through several beginnings in my life, and this is the one that I am most proud of.

I sometimes wonder if my being just one generation from the covered wagon makes me feel so allied to this country's gastronomic treasures. The pioneers lived off the land they traveled, and necessity sired invention. I'm always asked what the dominating factor in American cuisine is, and my reply is that it's the many ethnic groups, each of which brought its own ideas of food to this country. When they first settled here, they often could not find the ingredients they were used to, so they adapted their dishes and invented new ones, using whatever was available.

As people became neighborly and exchanged ideas about all sorts of things, they exchanged ideas about food, too. If you go back into the cookbooks written by the Ladies Aid Society of the Methodist Episcopal Church or the Hadassah, or by any such organization, you can almost trace the history of American food. In some books, you find a recipe done three different ways, and you can pretty well choose the original.

There are many dishes that could be considered completely American. Indian pudding is one, and it's coming into vogue again. Then we often forget that layer cakes—particularly baking powder layer cakes—are our invention. And while the Europeans have always had tarts, and the English originated apple pie and many deep-dish pies, the cream pies, and what I think of as "gooey" pies, along with a lot of fruit pies, were certainly developed in this country. And we have many hot breads, like muffins, biscuits, popovers, and baking powder coffee cakes.

Every country near an island developed a fish stew, and ours are New England clam chowder and California's cioppino. And what could be more American than a clambake? I remember splendid ones from my childhood, and you never see them in Europe.

Chili has become virtually an American creation. I don't think I could possibly choose just one kind, because part of the charm of this dish for me is that I can always make it differently, and it never disappoints. I must not forget to add barbecues either—the real southern kind that are smoke-cooked—for although they were first introduced by the French settlers in Louisiana, they are surely an American classic. The original idea was to feed a large outdoor gathering by roasting an animal, perhaps a whole sheep, goat, or pig, in front of an open fire on a homemade spit that pierced the tail from *barbe à la queue*—literally, from whiskers to tail. Thus the word barbecue came into our language and spread all over the world.

My father was able to tell me something of the pioneer culinary tradition, which he remembered from his trip in covered wagon from Iowa to Oregon. As a child of five or six, together with his brothers and other boys of the same age, he would shoot birds while his elders hunted small animals. These were usually cooked on wooden spits over a wood fire. According to my father, there was invariably a dispute among the members of the wagon train as to how the cooking should be done. I can only imagine that the dispute was settled by dividing the food so each group could cook in its own fashion—in other words, this was regional cooking standing up for its rights.

As outdoor cooking developed throughout the country, there were great chicken fries for church benefits, and in the South there were the famous fish fries, where the meals were prepared by servants or slaves after a hunting or fishing party returned to the plantation. Those fries were supplemented by enormous hampers of food from the main kitchen. Although lavish barbecues still flourish, outdoor cooking is generally done on a small scale these days. The custom has grown to the point where anyone driving through the suburbs on a summer weekend can smell more beef and chicken being charred, scorched, and burned than in all previous history.

—1983

NOTES FROM THE EDITOR

James Beard was a born cook who literally cooked at his mother's knee during his childhood in early twentieth-century Oregon. Yet his first book wasn't published until 1940, when he was thirty-eight years old, giving him plenty of time to soak up culinary experience around the world. His cookbook career spanned over forty years. Even in today's media-centric world, there are few food professionals who have constantly been in the public's consciousness for such an extended period. For many years, Beard was the only immediately recognizable face in American cooking. Did anyone know what Irma Rombauer (author of *The Joy of Cooking*) looked like? But Beard, with a figure nurtured by cream and butter, topped off with a jaunty bow tie, was the personification of an outsized chef, straight out of central casting.

The Essential James Beard celebrates this truly unique pioneer of American cuisine through more than four hundred of his best recipes, from the dishes that were served at his mother's Portland hotel to the ones that he shared with his coterie at his Greenwich Village row house. They are eclectic—French, Italian, Chinese, American, and even Persian—because Beard's curiosity about food was as insatiable as his physical appetite.

Imagine how much cooking evolved during the four-decade span of his cookbook writing, and then consider the enormous changes that have occurred since his death in 1985. In collecting the recipes for this book, the goal was to retain Beard's voice, exuberant and authoritarian in equal parts. However, I also made some changes for today's cooks. Chickens were much smaller then (just try to find a two-pound chicken at your local supermarket today), so some of the poultry recipes required adjustments. A meat thermometer was an oddity in many homes, and recipes gave other ways to test meat for doneness; I have provided temperatures where helpful. When the food processor was in its infancy, Beard was an early and quick convert to its conveniences. [My Editor's Notes to the reader are in brackets.]

Beard's Gargantuan life force of a personality illuminated everything he wrote, but he changed the format of the recipe depending on the venue. Teaching recipes, such as the ones in *Theory and Practice of Good Cooking,* were necessarily long and detailed, and reflect the influence of his good friend Julia Child's precisely tooled cookbooks. Especially when he was writing what one might call autobiographical recipes, Beard used a narrative form, and the formula is relayed as if he were speaking directly to the reader, without the benefit of an ingredient list at the beginning of the recipe. And there were recipes that were necessarily brief when he was writing for a newspaper or magazine article with limited space. Rather than force a universal style on all of the recipes, an effort was made to keep them as intact as possible, with a few words here and there to gently update, embellish, or clarify. Editor's Notes are there to give historical context or to elaborate when need be.

The historical reference is an important one. The James Beard Foundation confers awards of excellence to American culinarians in many fields from cookbook author to food writer to television cooking show host. Beard was all of these things, and more (you can add restaurant consultant and cooking teacher to the list), and whatever he tackled, it was with a joie de vivre that lives today in these marvelous recipes.

A Note on Ingredients

When Beard was writing, cooking oil was usually vegetable oil of some kind, flour was always bleached, and there was no such thing as reduced-fat milk (although skim milk was around, only the most desperate dieters bought it). We have many more choices today, and, based on Beard's opinions found in his books and anecdotally through his friends, the following ingredients are recommended.

OLIVE OIL: Extra-virgin olive oil was not readily available, although Beard certainly cooked with it during his many visits to Provence and would have been able to buy it around the corner from his house at that Manhattan bastion of midcentury gastronomy, Balducci's. Use high-quality French, Italian, or Spanish oil, but taste it first to choose one with a fruity flavor and not-too-heavy body so it can be used for a variety of cooking chores, from sautéing meat to making vinaigrette.

HERBS: Fresh herbs, beyond parsley and dill, were just beginning to be sold in specialty markets at the end of Beard's career. Until then, fresh herbs had to be grown in your backyard or on your windowsill. If you want to use fresh herbs, a general rule of thumb is to use twice as much chopped fresh herbs as dried herbs. But remember, dried herbs have their place, as the dehydration does intensify flavor. Basil, cilantro, and parsley, however, are always better fresh (although Beard does find a place for dried basil in some recipes). He preferred flat-leaf parsley, sometimes called Italian parsley, to the curly variety.

CANNED BROTH: Beard rarely (if ever!) uses canned broth in his recipes. During his lifetime, canned broths were clearly inferior, and just a step away from artificially flavored bouillon cubes. There are many good canned broths sold today, so if you want to use a brand that you like, go ahead. However, Beard also knew that there is something very satisfying and fun about simmering up a big pot of homemade stock, and Beard was all about having fun in the kitchen.

SALT: Beard lived in New York, and with its large Jewish community, he had easy access to kosher salt, which he appreciated for its purity and clean, unadulterated flavor. For most cooks, kosher salt was an oddity and most kitchens used iodized table salt laced with anti-caking agents. (Plain salt is fine-crystallized table salt without the added iodine.) In doughs and batters for baked goods, you may choose to use plain or fine sea salt, another additive-free salt, because these dissolve more readily than coarse kosher salt.

—Rick Rodgers
March 2012

FIRST COURSES AND COCKTAIL FOOD

FIRST COURSES AND COCKTAIL FOOD

CRUDITÉS WITH ANCHOVY MAYONNAISE

MAKES ABOUT 12 SERVINGS

For the Anchovy Mayonnaise

12 to 14 drained anchovy fillets in oil, drained and
　　coarsely chopped

2 garlic cloves, finely chopped

¼ cup chopped fresh flat-leaf parsley

¼ cup chopped fresh basil

1 tablespoon coarsely chopped capers

1 tablespoon Dijon mustard

2 cups Mayonnaise (page 355)

Thinly sliced cucumbers, sliced tomatoes, sliced onion,
　　whole scallions, match stick carrots, thinly sliced
　　raw beets, or other raw vegetables, for serving

To make the anchovy mayonnaise: Combine the anchovy fillets, garlic, parsley, basil, capers, mustard, and mayonnaise, and taste for seasoning. Use little salt in the mayonnaise; anchovies and capers have plenty. Arrange the vegetables on a platter; dunk in the anchovy mayonnaise.

CAPONATA

MAKES 6 TO 8 SERVINGS

While this Sicilian dish is traditionally served cold as part of the antipasto course, on its own it makes a zesty, refreshing appetizer for a summer meal.

3 globe eggplants, cut into 1-inch cubes, unpeeled

Kosher salt

1 celery heart (about 8 ribs), thinly sliced

½ cup olive oil

1 large yellow onion, sliced

5 large ripe tomatoes, peeled, seeded, and quartered,
　　or one 28-ounce can Italian plum tomatoes,
　　drained and coarsely chopped

1 or 2 pinches dried thyme

1 bay leaf

Freshly ground black pepper

6 to 8 anchovy fillets in oil, drained and chopped

1 cup pitted and coarsely chopped Mediterranean
　　black olives, such as Kalamata

3 tablespoons nonpareil capers

3 tablespoons sugar

2 tablespoons red wine vinegar

2 tablespoons chopped fresh flat-leaf parsley

Freshly grated zest of ½ lemon (optional)

Sprinkle the eggplant with 2 teaspoons salt and let it drain in a colander. Blanch the celery for 1 minute in a large saucepan of boiling water, then drain and plunge into cold water to stop it from cooking further. Drain and pat dry with paper towels.

Heat 2 tablespoons of the oil in a large saucepan over medium-low heat. Add the onion and cook, stirring often, until tender and golden, about 10 minutes. Add the tomatoes, thyme, and bay leaf, and season with salt and pepper. Cook until the tomatoes are tender and thickened into a sauce, about 20 minutes. Rub the mixture through a coarse-mesh wire sieve and discard the seeds and skin.

While the tomato mixture is cooking, rinse the eggplant cubes and pat them dry with paper towels. Heat the remaining 6 tablespoons oil in a large saucepan over medium-high heat until very hot but not smoking. Add the eggplant and cook, stirring occasionally, until the eggplant is browned, adding more oil as needed. They should just cook through. Add the tomato mixture, blanched celery, anchovies, olives, and capers. Dissolve the sugar in the vinegar and stir into the eggplant mixture. Add the parsley and lemon zest, if using.

CHILI CON QUESO

MAKES 8 TO 12 SERVINGS

Editor: When this recipe was first published in Menus for Entertaining *(1965), corn chips, such as Fritos, were the norm, and mass-produced tortilla chips were waiting in the wings. The truth is, you can dip just about anything crunchy (including the suggested bread sticks and celery) in chili con queso, and it would be addictive.*

For the Cream Sauce

2 tablespoons unsalted butter

2 tablespoons all-purpose flour

1 cup Chicken Stock (page 349), heated

½ cup heavy cream

One 28-ounce can Italian plum tomatoes

2 garlic cloves, finely chopped

Kosher salt and freshly ground black pepper

Two 4-ounce cans chopped green chilies, drained

1 pound shredded Monterey Jack or Cheddar cheese

Corn chips, bread sticks, and celery sticks,
    for serving

To make the cream sauce: Melt the butter over low heat in a heavy-bottomed medium saucepan. Mix the flour into the butter with a whisk or spoon and cook slowly, stirring all the time, for 2 to 3 minutes, or until the roux is well blended and frothy. Gradually stir in the stock. Increase the heat to medium and cook, whisking all the time, until the sauce is smooth, thick, and at the boiling point. Let the sauce simmer, stirring, for 3 or 4 minutes. Stir in the cream and simmer for a few more minutes.

Combine the tomatoes and garlic in a medium saucepan and season with salt and pepper. Cook down for 20 minutes over medium heat, stirring occasionally to break up the tomatoes. Add the chilies. Cook until the juices evaporate and the

Anchovy-Parsley Dipping Sauce

Makes about 2 cups

Editor: As with Anchovy Mayonnaise on page 13, serve this with raw vegetables.

1 cup extra-virgin olive oil

½ cup packed fresh flat-leaf parsley leaves

18 anchovy fillets in oil, drained

Freshly grated zest of 1 lemon

3 garlic cloves, crushed under a knife and peeled

1 teaspoon freshly ground black pepper

Kosher salt

Combine all of the ingredients in blender and whirl for 1 minute. Correct the seasoning with salt and more pepper.

mixture is thick and pasty, about 15 minutes. Add the cream sauce and cheese, and stir well until the cheese melts. Place in a chafing dish or electric skillet over warm heat. Serve with the chips, bread sticks, and celery.

SKORDALIA
(GREEK GARLIC SAUCE)

✐ MAKES ABOUT 1¾ CUPS

Skordalia is basically a mayonnaise with a great deal of garlic, further thickened by finely ground almonds (you can make these by chopping blanched almonds in a blender or food processor until they are pulverized to the consistency of very fine bread crumbs). Traditionally, the sauce is made with a mortar and pestle. First the whole garlic cloves are ground to a paste with the pestle, then raw egg yolks are pounded into the garlic with the pestle until thick and sticky, then the olive oil is pounded in drop by drop until it forms a mayonnaise. The other ingredients are then mixed into the mayonnaise.

I find it much easier to be less traditional and make the sauce in a blender or food processor. It is delicious with hot or cold poached fish, with fried fish, as a dip for shrimp, raw vegetables, or artichokes, and as a sauce for rather bland vegetables such as cauliflower and boiled potatoes.

4 to 6 garlic cloves, very finely chopped
2 large eggs
3 or 4 tablespoons freshly squeezed lemon juice
1 teaspoon kosher salt
1 cup olive oil or half olive oil and half peanut oil
½ cup finely ground blanched almonds
1 tablespoon finely chopped fresh flat-leaf parsley

Put the garlic (the amount depends on your taste), eggs, 2 tablespoons of the lemon juice, and the salt into a blender or food processor and blend or process until just mixed. Add the oil in a thin, steady stream, according to the directions for blender or food-processor Mayonnaise on page 355. Transfer to a bowl and stir in the ground almonds. Mix in more lemon juice to taste, and then the parsley. Chill before serving.

VARIATIONS

THICK SKORDALIA: For a thicker sauce, stir in 1 cup fresh white bread crumbs with the ground almonds.

POTATO SKORDALIA: Instead of ground almonds, mix 1 cup plain mashed potatoes (with no butter or milk added) into the sauce. After the mayonnaise is made, put the potatoes into the blender or processor and blend until just combined.

BRIOCHE EN SURPRISE
(ONION SANDWICHES)

✐ MAKES 24 SANDWICHES

Some famous French hostess supposedly started the fashion for the recipe below and created a sensation in her salon. I am sure a reputation and a leading position in any town can be built up if you serve enough of them for they are as contagious as measles. A good friend of mine can eat a dozen of them at one sitting.

Not only is this delicious, but it is one of the most decorative canapés you can make, for an edging of brilliant green enhances the golden yellow of the brioche and makes a most appetizing tidbit.

Twenty-four ¼-inch-thick brioche slices, cut into
2½-inch-diameter rounds
⅓ cup Mayonnaise (page 355), or store bought
2 small yellow onions, cut into 24 very thin rounds
Kosher salt
3 tablespoons finely chopped fresh flat-leaf parsley,
patted dry

Spread the rounds on one side with mayonnaise and place the rounds mayonnaise-side up on the work surface. On half of the slices place an onion round, just the size of the brioche, and salt it well. Top with the remaining brioche rounds, mayonnaise-side down. Roll the edges of each sandwich first in mayonnaise, and then in the chopped parsley.

VARIATION

ANCHOVY CANAPÉS: For a similar canapé, use the same process. Spread the brioche rounds with Fines Herbes Butter (page 17), and place fillets of anchovies on one half of the slices. Top with the remaining buttered brioche; roll the edges in mayonnaise and then in parsley.

Editor: Loaves of brioche bread are available at specialty bakeries. Or make your own (see recipe Brioche Bread, page 276). Use a sharp round biscuit or cookie cutter to cut out the rounds.

Sandwich Spreads

Editor: These sandwich spreads are a good indication of the creativity that Beard brought to his catering company in New York in the late 1930s. Sandwich the fillings on top-quality bread (firm white sandwich or brioche bread with a tight crumb work best, not sourdough breads with lots of air holes), and cut into fingers. Or cut into rounds with a biscuit cutter.

Chicken, Pimiento, and Pine Nut Spread

Chop together 1½ **cups of cooked chicken** and **2 drained canned pimientos**. Add ½ **cup of chopped pine nuts, 1 finely chopped shallot,** and **a few leaves of finely chopped fresh flat-leaf parsley**. Bind with **a few tablespoons of ketchup-style chili sauce** to make a firm paste. Season the spread with **kosher salt** and a **few grains of cayenne pepper**.

Ham and Pickle Spread

Finely chop **8 ounces (about 1½ cups) cold baked ham** with **3 sweet gherkins (small pickles)** and **1 teaspoon of dry mustard**. Moisten with **1 or 2 tablespoons of mayonnaise**.

Swiss Cheese and Olive Spread

Thoroughly mix **2 cups of grated Swiss cheese, 3 tablespoons of pitted and chopped green or black olives**, and **2 tablespoons of finely chopped green bell pepper**. Moisten this with enough **mayonnaise** to make a thick paste.

Compound Butters

The following basic butters here are useful for canapés and sandwiches, and they fill a need very often for snacks and sauces. [*Editor: They are also useful to have in the freezer to put on top of hot grilled steaks, chops, chicken breasts, and fish fillets, or to flavor boiled or steamed vegetables.*]

Chutney Butter

Cream **8 tablespoons (1 stick) softened unsalted butter** and add **2 tablespoons of finely chopped chutney**. This is improved by the addition of a little curry powder; the amount has to be left to your own taste. [*Editor: About ½ teaspoon of curry powder would tint the butter a vibrant orange-yellow and give it a brilliant flavor, too. Melt a pat on grilled chicken or pork chops.*]

Fines Herbes Butter

Chop together **1 cup packed fresh flat-leaf parsley leaves, ¼ cup each packed stemmed spinach and watercress leaves,** and **2 tablespoons coarsely chopped fresh chives**. Add a **tablespoon of chopped fresh chervil, tarragon, basil, dill, thyme, or sorrel** (either a single herb or in any combination) and chop again to blend the flavors. Put in a bowl and mix in **1 teaspoon salt** and **1 teaspoon anchovy paste**. Add **1 cup (2 sticks) softened unsalted butter** until the herbs have been thoroughly blended and the butter is completely green. [*Editor: Melt a tablespoon of this butter on top of grilled lamb chops or fish, or stir into plain cooked vegetables.*]

Garlic Butter

Crush **several cloves of garlic** through a garlic press and cream with **8 tablespoons (1 stick) of unsalted butter** and **½ teaspoon of salt**. This is a matter of "stop and go," for you know better than I your capacity for garlic flavor. So, let your own taste guide you.

Hazelnut Butter

Grind **1 cup (4 ounces) toasted salted hazelnuts** very finely. [*Editor: You can use a food processor for this.*] Mix with **8 tablespoons (1 stick) softened unsalted butter** to form a thick paste. This is delicious by itself or blended with ham or tongue for a canapé.

Mustard Butter

Cream **8 tablespoons (1 stick) softened unsalted butter** with **1 tablespoon Dijon mustard**. [*Editor: Serve this tossed with steamed asparagus, broccoli, Brussels sprouts, or cauliflower, or over grilled chicken or pork chops.*]

Roquefort Butter

Blend together **¼ pound room-temperature Roquefort cheese** and **8 tablespoons (1 stick) softened unsalted butter**. [*Editor: Serve a pat on grilled steaks or or mix with boiled new potatoes.*]

Cocktail Sandwich Fillings

America is a confirmed sandwich nation. Everywhere you go you find sandwich stands, sandwich shops, and nine out of ten people seem to stick to the sandwich-and-a-glass-of-milk or cup-of-coffee luncheon. America has developed variety in fillings, breads, and shapes, from the four-decker combination to the pale slab of white bread with a paper-thin slice of meat and much floury gravy poured over all to a vast array of really good sandwiches that distinguish our menus. It is no wonder, then, that the cocktail sandwich has come more and more into vogue.

First cousin to that aristocratic and refined member of the family, the English tea sandwich, the cocktail version should be commanding in appearance and richly attired in a simple way. The bread should be thin enough to be almost revealing, well filled, the sandwich large enough for only two bites, and tailored to the last degree of perfection. Stars, crescents, tigers, rabbits, and four-leaf-clover shapes may be acceptable for tea; but for cocktails—ah ha! Thin rectangular fingers or small squares, diamonds, and rounds should be the only shapes ever seen on a tray served with drinks.

Try to find the most interesting breads in your community and always use them for such sandwiches. In almost any town or city today, there is some semblance of variety offered by commercial bakeries; and there are many recipes for breads to be made at home for this service. I think the dark, heavier-textured breads are most desirable for the cocktail tray. There are many different types of pumpernickel and rye breads that are excellent. The Scandinavians, all of whom are sandwich lovers, have developed a dozen different types of dark, meaty breads; the Danish pumpernickel, dark and light; the Swedish rye breads; the coarse, very dark bread of the Russians. All these are remarkably good with drinks. There seems to be a renaissance these days in this country for the very close-grained homemade type of bread that we all knew as children. One energetic woman in the East perfected a firm white bread that sold over the entire seaboard, with the result that many commercial bakeries are now offering a loaf of this same type. [*Editor: Beard is very likely referring to Margaret Rudkin, the founder of Pepperidge Farm.*] The vogue is growing in every section of the country. Then, there is the delicious egg bread [*Editor: challah*] that is so much a part of the Jewish food tradition, and its cousin, the brioche.

Have bread cut very, very thin for cocktail sandwiches. If you have a very sharp knife and a good eye, you may be able to cut it at home; otherwise, ask your delicatessen manager to put it on his electric slicer and cut it as thinly as possible. Have him cut it the long way of the loaf, for that way you save labor and get more sandwiches per loaf. If bread is very soft and new, it should be placed in the refrigerator for an hour or two before slicing.

Have spreads ready and soft, meat sliced, knives sharp, and off you go. Pile the sandwiches on a tray as they are cut; cover them with waxed paper and a damp cloth, and give them at least an hour or two in the refrigerator before serving. Cut sandwiches in fingers, about 1 by 3 or 2 inches, or cut with a round cutter.

Here are some of the "regulars":

Anchovy fillets with chopped hard-boiled egg.

Thinly sliced avocado with Garlic Butter (page 17).

White meat of chicken or turkey with Chutney Butter (page 17).

Crabmeat mixed with chopped chives and mayonnaise.

Chopped ham and chopped chicken in equal parts and a few chopped, toasted Brazil nuts mixed with them. Season with prepared hot English mustard or horseradish.

Thin slices of baked ham and smoked salmon with plenty of unsalted butter; delicious on heavy black bread.

Chopped olives and nuts in equal portions bound with cream cheese.

Sliced onion marinated in Basic Vinaigrette Sauce (page 359) for several hours and drained.

Sliced salami with Fines Herbes Butter (page 17).

BUCKWHEAT BLINI

A sophisticated form of tiny pancake made popular by the Russians, eaten hot as a first course with quantities of melted butter, sour cream, and caviar (fine California caviar or Gold caviar from the Great Lakes), smoked salmon, or herring, according to the taste of your bank account.

One-and-a-half ¼-ounce packages (1 tablespoon
  plus ¼ teaspoon) active dry yeast
2½ cups warm (110° to 115°F) whole milk
1 teaspoon sugar
2 cups all-purpose flour
½ cup buckwheat flour
4 large eggs, separated, at room temperature
3 tablespoons sour cream
2 tablespoons unsalted butter, melted, plus more for
  cooking the blini
½ teaspoon kosher salt
Melted butter, sour cream, and smoked salmon,
  caviar, or herring, for serving

Sprinkle the yeast into the milk with the sugar in a large bowl. Let stand 5 minutes, then stir to dissolve the yeast. Add the all-purpose and buckwheat flours. Lightly beat the egg yolks and add to the flour mixture. Stir slowly, then beat vigorously until the batter is smooth—this can be done by hand, with an electric mixer, or in the food processor. If using a food processor, transfer the batter to a large bowl. Cover the bowl with plastic wrap and let rise in a warm, draft-free place for 1½ to 2 hours until doubled in bulk. Punch down the batter; stir in the sour cream and melted butter. Beat the egg whites with the salt until stiff but not dry, and fold into the batter.

Brush a hot griddle or heavy skillet well with melted butter and drop the batter on it by spoonfuls, enough to make pancakes 3 inches in diameter. When the bottom is lightly browned and bubbles have formed on the surface, flip them over and brown the second side. Keep warm in a 200°F oven, drizzled with a little more butter. Serve warm with more melted butter and the sour cream, accompanied with smoked salmon, caviar, or herring.

CARROT BLINI

A different and much simpler form of blini, basically a crêpe batter with shredded carrot added. They should be served with sour cream and red or black caviar. [*Editor: Beard developed these for a restaurant consulting job with L'Auberge in Philadelphia.*]

1 cup all-purpose flour, sifted
3 large eggs, lightly beaten
1 teaspoon kosher salt
3 tablespoons olive oil
¼ teaspoon freshly ground black pepper
1 cup whole milk, as needed
1 cup shredded raw carrot
3 tablespoons unsalted butter
Sour cream and red or black caviar, for serving

Put the flour in a bowl. Stir in the eggs, salt, oil, pepper, and just enough milk to make a thick batter. Stir in the shredded carrot. Heat enough butter in a heavy skillet to cover the surface, and drop the batter in by spoonfuls, enough to make pancakes about 3 inches in diameter. Cook on both sides until lightly browned, adding more butter to the pan as needed. Serve hot.

CREAM CHEESE-AND PISTACHIO-STUFFED BREAD RINGS

MAKES ABOUT 12 SERVINGS

For this process you need patience and determination, so don't try to perform it at the last minute and expect marvels. You will need **a very thin baguette known in the French bakeshops as French flutes**, **about 24 inches long.** [*Editor: These are also called ficelles.*] Cut the loaf in half lengthwise and scoop out the center so that only the crisp tubes of crust and a little of the white center for contrast in texture are left.

Cream **12 ounces of softened cream cheese with 3 tablespoons chopped fresh chives** and **1 tablespoon chopped fresh flat-leaf parsley**. Add **1 teaspoon Dijon mustard**, ½ **teaspoon of salt**, and ½ **cup of coarsely chopped pistachio nuts.** Spread the mixture into the bottom half of the bread (be sure that you pack the cheese in tightly so as to get even slices), and sandwich with the top half. Refrigerate for half an hour before slicing. Slice with a very sharp knife in slices ⅜- to ½-inch thick and arrange on a platter. [*Editor: The result is small rings of bread filled with the herbed cheese.*]

The Highball Sandwich

The highball sandwich is a coinage of my own, I believe. It has been the solution for many of my friends and pupils who wanted to know what to serve a group of men meeting for an evening of cards or talk, or to a mixed group that was to have highballs during an evening gathering.

It is the larger brother of the cocktail sandwich. It is thicker by an eighth of an inch or so and about three inches square. It fills in when a substantial snack is desired and where a buffet table would be a nuisance. Furthermore, such sandwiches may be prepared or ordered in advance and kept in the refrigerator until they are to be served.

The highball sandwich should be on dark, well-flavored bread and should be well filled and substantial in appearance. Chicken, meats, and cheese are the most acceptable fillings with plenty of spice and sauce. The mixtures welcome at cocktail time are not as desirable here nor are the very "gooey" fillings, which have a tendency to drip here and there.

Serve plenty of pickles with these snacks, additional mustard and horseradish, and some celery and radishes; usually scallions will be appreciated.

OLD-FASHIONED PICKLED EGGS

〰 MAKES 24 EGGS

Editor: There was a time when every picnic featured these magenta-colored eggs. Canned beets are fine. If you wish, roast the beets yourself. Wrap 2 scrubbed but unpeeled medium beets in aluminum foil and bake on a baking sheet in a preheated 400°F oven until tender when pierced with a knife, about 1 hour. Unwrap, cool, and slip off the skins before slicing.

2 dozen Hard-boiled Eggs (page 182), shelled

2 cups cooked beet slices

2 large yellow onions, very thinly sliced

2 tablespoons sugar

1 teaspoon plain salt

1 bay leaf

Cider vinegar, as needed

Place the hard-boiled eggs in a large jar or bowl. Add the beets, onions, sugar, salt, and bay leaf. Add just enough vinegar to cover all the ingredients and cap the jar or cover the bowl with plastic wrap. Allow to marinate in the refrigerator for at least 24 hours or up to 48 hours.

To serve, arrange the drained eggs, beets, and onions in a large bowl, moisten with some of the vinegar mixture, and serve as an accompaniment to meat salads, cold meats, and cheese. If you prefer, arrange the eggs in one bowl and the beets and onions in another.

CLAY'S DILL PICKLES

〰 MAKES ABOUT 2 QUARTS

Editor: Clay Triplette was Beard's housekeeper for decades.

For Clay's dill pickles, wash and dry **3 pounds of small pickling cucumbers,** the unwaxed kind, about 2½ to 3 inches long, that are in the markets in summer and early fall. Pierce each end of the cucumbers with a good-sized needle. This lets the pickling solution seep in and makes the pickles much crisper to the bite. Pack the cucumbers into a sterilized 2-quart canning jar with **1½ tablespoons of pickling spice, 1 teaspoon of plain (not kosher or iodized) salt, 3 unpeeled garlic cloves,** and **3 sprigs of fresh dill** arranging them neatly to make what Clay calls "a fine picture jar." Bring to a boil **5 cups of water** with **1 cup of white wine vinegar** and pour this over the cucumbers. Leave for 15 minutes before putting the lid on the jar. Store in a cool, dark place for 4 to 5 weeks before using.

Dill pickles are good to munch as a snack with cold foods and wonderful with *choucroute garnie* or any hot sauerkraut dish to which they give a pleasant zest. Thinly sliced dill pickles are marvelous tucked into a hamburger, and I also like to serve them, thinly sliced, with cold salmon or halibut or any other cold fish with which I'm serving a mayonnaise or dill sauce. You can make a quick tartar sauce for fish by chopping the pickles or putting them into the food processor with a little onion, garlic, parsley, and mayonnaise. In fact, you can make your mayonnaise in the food processor, then switch over from the blade to the shredder and shred the onion and pickle right into the mayonnaise.

COLD HAM MOUSSE

◦◦ MAKES 6 TO 8 SERVINGS

A savory mousse, with a béchamel sauce base, this is an easy and good way to use up leftover cooked ham. You might serve it for a summer luncheon party or as part of a cold buffet.

For the Ham Mousse

Vegetable oil, for the mold

4 tablespoons (½ stick) unsalted butter

4 tablespoons all-purpose flour

1 cup whole milk, heated

Kosher salt

Freshly grated nutmeg

Cayenne pepper

¼ cup Cognac

½ cup heavy cream

2 large egg yolks

1 envelope (2½ teaspoons) unflavored gelatin

½ cup cold water

½ cup Chicken Stock (page 349) or homemade
   ham broth (see Editor's Note), heated to boiling

2 cups very finely ground cooked ham

For the Cucumber Garnish

2 medium cucumbers, peeled, and very
   thinly sliced

1 teaspoon kosher salt

3 tablespoons white wine vinegar

2 tablespoons sugar

3 tablespoons finely chopped fresh flat-leaf parsley

2 tablespoons finely chopped fresh dill

To make the mousse: Prepare a 4-cup ring mold by generously brushing it with vegetable oil, then turning it upside down on paper towels to drain off any excess oil.

Melt the butter in a saucepan, blend in the flour, and cook over medium heat, whisking, until golden and bubbling. Slowly mix the milk into this roux, and continue to whisk over low heat, until very thick and smooth. Season to taste with salt (be sparing if the ham is salty), nutmeg, and cayenne. Stir in the Cognac. Mix the egg yolks and cream in a small bowl with a fork, then stir in a little of the hot sauce into them to warm up the yolks. Stir into the sauce in the pan and cook over low heat, whisking, until blended and thickened a bit more. Do not let the sauce get too hot or boil, or the yolks will curdle. Strain into a medium bowl.

Sprinkle the gelatin on the cold water in a small bowl. When softened, stir into the hot broth until thoroughly dissolved. Blend this into the sauce, then thoroughly mix in the ground ham. Fill the prepared mold with the ham mousse, smoothing it evenly with a rubber spatula. Cover the mold with plastic wrap and chill in the refrigerator until firm and set, at least 3 hours.

To make the cucumber garnish: Put the cucumbers into a bowl. Sprinkle with the salt, let stand 1 hour, then drain off the liquid. Return to the bowl. Stir the vinegar and sugar in a bowl until the sugar dissolves; mix with the parsley and dill; pour over the cucumbers and mix. Refrigerate until serving.

When ready to serve, remove the plastic wrap

from the mold; loosen the edges with a knife or spatula, dip the top of the mold in hot water for a second or two to release it, then invert onto a serving platter. Drain the marinated cucumbers. Put them in the center of the molded ring. Serve chilled.

Editor: Ham broth is simply a meaty ham bone, simmered in water to cover with 1 each chopped onion, carrot, and celery for a couple of hours until the broth is rich and flavorful, and strained. It can also be used as the cooking liquid for split pea soup.

PÂTÉ DE CAMPAGNE

〰 **MAKES 12 TO 16 SERVINGS**

A delicious country pâté, easy to make and always welcome.

2 pounds pork shoulder, well trimmed, very coarsely chopped

2 pounds trimmed and ground pork liver

2 pounds fresh pork fatback, cut into ½-inch dice

¾ pound ground veal

3 large eggs, beaten

⅓ cup Cognac or bourbon

6 garlic cloves, minced

1 tablespoon dried basil

1 tablespoon kosher salt, as needed

1 teaspoon freshly ground black pepper

⅛ teaspoon each ground cloves, ground ginger, freshly grated nutmeg, and freshly ground white pepper

1 tablespoon unsalted butter

1 pound sliced bacon or salt pork, for the baking dish

Sliced crusty bread, Dijon mustard, and cornichons, for serving

Combine all the pork shoulder, pork liver, fatback, veal, eggs, Cognac, garlic, basil, salt, black pepper, cloves, ginger, nutmeg, and white pepper in a large bowl. To check the seasoning, sauté a small patty—about 1 tablespoon—in hot melted butter in a skillet until cooked through. Cool and taste; you may want to add a bit more salt.

Line a good-sized straight-sided terrine with the bacon. A 2½-quart soufflé dish, heavy pottery dish, or a large round Pyrex dish are also ideal. Fill with the mixture and form a well-rounded top. Place a few strips of bacon over the top, and bake in a preheated 325°F oven for 2 to 2½ hours. I always cover it with a sheet of aluminum foil for the first hour or so of cooking. The pâté will pull away from the sides a bit when done.

Remove from the oven and let cool. After 30 minutes, put a foil-wrapped rectangle of wood or heavy cardboard cut to fit the inside of the terrine (or a plate or a baking dish) on the pâté, and weigh it down with a few heavy cans of food. Cover tightly with aluminum foil and refrigerate overnight on a plate. Serve from the terrine or dish cut in generous slices with a sharp, heavy knife.

Editor: When making pâté at home, the food processor will be your best friend. See the Note on page 26 for how to prepare the pork shoulder. Pork liver does not need to be frozen. It should be trimmed of any tough matter, cut into 1-inch chunks, and processed into a coarse purée.

CHINESE GINGER AND PORK BALLS

℘ MAKES 4 TO 6 SERVINGS

Editor: This recipe is from Helen Evans Brown, Beard's frequent collaborator. Serve these as an appetizer with drinks or a main course with rice and Asian greens. If you want a dip for these, go retro with soy sauce, hot Chinese mustard, and/or duck sauce.

1 pound ground pork

1/2 cup drained minced water chestnuts

2 tablespoons minced scallions, white parts only

1 large egg, beaten

1 tablespoon peeled and grated fresh ginger

1 tablespoon soy sauce

1/2 teaspoon kosher salt

1/4 cup dried cracker crumbs, as needed

Cornstarch, for rolling the balls

Vegetable oil, for deep-frying

Mix the pork, water chestnuts, scallion, egg, ginger, soy sauce, and salt in a bowl. Mix in enough cracker crumbs to make a mixture that can be easily shaped into balls. Form into walnut-size balls. Roll the balls in cornstarch. Pour enough oil into a large heavy-bottomed saucepan to come halfway up the sides. Heat over high heat until the oil registers 350°F on a deep-frying thermometer. Working in batches, add the pork balls and deep-fry until golden and cooked through, about 2 1/2 minutes. Using a slotted spoon, transfer to paper towels. Serve the pork balls hot on toothpicks.

RILLETTES OR RILLONS

℘ MAKES 8 SERVINGS

The difference between the two is that the rillettes are ground or pounded, the rillons left in small dice.

1 1/4 pounds fresh pork fatback, finely diced

1 pound pork shoulder, trimmed, finely diced

1 medium yellow onion, chopped

2 teaspoons kosher salt

1/2 teaspoon freshly ground black pepper

1/4 teaspoon freshly grated nutmeg

1/4 teaspoon ground cloves

1/4 teaspoon dried thyme

1 bay leaf

Toast or sliced crusty French bread, Dijon mustard, and cornichons, for serving

Mix the ingredients in a large heavy-bottomed saucepan and barely cover with water. Cook, uncovered, over medium-low heat until the water has evaporated and the meat is very tender and swimming in the melted fat, about 3 hours.

Remove the bay leaf. Strain off and reserve the fat. Return the meat to the saucepan and cook over medium-high heat until crisp and brown, 10 to 15 minutes. Rillons are left as they are. For rillettes, let the meat cool until tepid, and then grind in a food processor. Pack the meat into pots, bowls, or jars. Pour in the reserved melted fat to cover the meat by 1/2 inch. Refrigerate overnight. Serve cold with the bread, mustard, and cornichons.

Editor: Fresh pork fatback (not to be confused with salt pork) is available at Latino and Asian butchers.

You may be able to order it from your supermarket meat department because it is usually trimmed from the commonly available pork loin roast. To dice the pork and fatback in a food processor cut them into 1-inch pieces and freeze an hour or so, or until very firm. In batches, pulse until diced in a food processor fitted with the metal blade.

GRAMMIE HAMBLET'S DEVILED CRAB

〜 **MAKES 4 TO 6 SERVINGS**

This is far and away my favorite of the many versions of this most traditional of American dishes. I often serve a small helping as a first course before broiled or roast meats. [*Editor: Polly "Grammie" Hamblet was the mother of Beard's lifelong friend Mary Hamblet. His autobiography with recipes,* Delights and Prejudices, *was dedicated to Mary.*]

    2 pounds crabmeat, picked over for cartilage
        and shells
    2½ cups coarsely crushed cracker crumbs
    1 cup (2 sticks) unsalted butter, melted
    1 cup finely chopped celery
    1 large green bell pepper, seeds and ribs
        removed, finely chopped
    1 cup finely sliced scallions (white and
        green parts)
    ½ cup finely chopped fresh flat-leaf parsley
    ½ cup heavy cream
    1½ teaspoons dry mustard
    1 teaspoon kosher salt
    Dash of Tabasco

Combine the crabmeat, 1½ cups of the cracker crumbs, the butter, celery, bell pepper, scallions, parsley, cream, mustard, salt, and Tabasco in a large bowl and toss lightly. Spoon into a buttered baking dish, top with remaining 1 cup crumbs, and bake in a preheated 350°F oven for 25 to 30 minutes, or until the top is delicately browned. Serve at once.

VARIATION

DEVILED CLAMS: Substitute 2 cups steamed minced clams or drained chopped canned clams for the crabmeat.

GRAVLAX

〜 **MAKES ABOUT 12 SERVINGS**

For this dish, native to Scandinavia, the raw salmon is cured with salt and sugar, a process that, like the action of lime or lemon juice on fish, "cooks" the flesh and gives it a most exciting and interesting flavor.

    For the Gravlax
    Two 1½-pound center-cut salmon fillets
    ⅔ to ¾ cup kosher salt
    ¼ cup sugar
    1 to 2 tablespoons coarsely ground black
        peppercorns
    Large bunch of fresh dill, stems removed

    For the Sweet Mustard Sauce
    ⅓ cup vegetable oil
    4 tablespoons German-style prepared mustard
        (not hot, but very spicy)

3 tablespoons sugar

2 tablespoons white wine vinegar

1 teaspoon dry mustard

3 tablespoons finely chopped fresh dill

1 bunch fresh flat-leaf parsley, for garnish

1 bunch fresh dill, for garnish

Buttered pumpernickel bread slices, for serving

To prepare the gravlax: Using tweezers or pincers, remove all of the tiny pinbones from each fillet. Place one fillet, skin side down, in a large dish or casserole in which it can lie flat. Combine the salt, sugar, and peppercorns and rub the flesh of the salmon very well with half of this mixture. Place the dill sprigs on top. Rub the rest of the salt-sugar-peppercorn mixture into the flesh of the second piece of salmon and place over the dill, skin side up, sandwiching the fillets together. Cover the salmon with aluminum foil, then put a board or a large plate on top and weigh this down with canned goods. Refrigerate for 36 to 48 hours, turning the salmon over each day so that it cures evenly, and basting with the liquid that accumulates from the curing process. Each time, weigh it down again.

About 4 hours before the fish is done, make the sweet mustard sauce: Put the oil, German mustard, sugar, vinegar, and dry mustard in a small bowl and beat well with a whisk until it has the consistency of a thin mayonnaise (the mustard thickens the liquid). Mix in the dill and refrigerate for 3 to 4 hours before serving to allow the flavors to mellow.

At the end of the curing time, remove the fish from the liquid, scrape away the dill and seasonings, and dry the fillets well on paper towels. To

serve, place on a carving board (I like to put a bouquet of dill at one end, parsley at the other, as a garnish) and slice thickly on the diagonal, detaching the flesh from the skin as you do so. Serve with the sweet mustard sauce and buttered rye bread as an appetizer or a main course for luncheon or supper, or with other fish dishes on a cold buffet.

BRANDADE OF COD

 MAKES 6 SERVINGS

A specialty of Nîmes in Provence, this gloriously garlicky, creamy paste is without doubt one of the greatest and most exciting of all salt-cod dishes. Serve it warm in a mound and eat with fried toast as a first or main course.

1 pound poached salt cod (see instructions on
    page 177), finely flaked

2/3 cup olive oil

1/3 cup heavy cream

2 garlic cloves, crushed

1/2 teaspoon freshly ground black pepper

Fried toast, for serving

Remove any bits of bone from the flaked codfish. Heat the oil and cream separately in small saucepans. Pound or work the fish and the garlic to a paste, either with a mortar and pestle, a blender, a food processor, or a mixer fitted with the paddle attachment, adding the warm oil and cream alternately by the spoonful as you do so. When the oil and cream are completely absorbed and the mixture has the consistency of mashed potatoes, season with the pepper and heap in a serving dish. Serve warm, surrounded with triangles of fried toast (bread fried in olive oil).

SEVICHE

⤜ MAKES 4 TO 6 SERVINGS

This spicy Latin American dish of pickled fish "cooked" in lime juice is delicious served with cocktails or as a first course. If you wish, substitute tiny raw bay scallops, raw crabmeat, or raw red snapper fillets for the sole. You may also add slices of avocado and whole kernel corn (sliced from freshly cooked ears) to the sauce.

1½ pounds firm sole fillets, cut into thin strips about ½ inch wide

1 cup freshly squeezed lime juice

½ cup olive oil

¼ cup finely chopped scallions, white and green parts

¼ cup finely chopped fresh flat-leaf parsley

2 tablespoons finely chopped canned, peeled green chilies

1 garlic clove, finely chopped

1½ teaspoons kosher salt

1 teaspoon freshly ground black pepper

Dash of Tabasco

1 tablespoon chopped fresh cilantro

Arrange the fish strips in a baking dish and pour the lime juice over them. Refrigerate for 4 hours, by which time the citrus juice will have turned the fish opaque and made it firm. Drain off the lime juice; combine the remaining ingredients (except the fresh cilantro) and pour over the fish, tossing the pieces lightly in the mixture. Chill for a half hour, then sprinkle with the chopped cilantro and serve. [Editor: Substitute 1 tablespoon jalapeño or serrano chiles for the canned chiles, if you wish.]

SAUTÉED MARINATED FISH (ESCABÈCHE)

⤜ MAKES 4 TO 6 SERVINGS

Escabèche is the Spanish word for "pickled," and this is the kind of recipe where you start with a basic idea, then play around with your own variations, altering the flavors in the marinade as you see fit, perhaps adding 1 or 2 finely chopped garlic cloves, increasing the amount of mild green chilies or using a little hot chopped fresh jalapeño or serrano chile (in which case omit the Tabasco) or some freshly ground black pepper, and maybe some paper-thin slices of red onion. You can have it slightly on the sweet-sour side, or acid, or bland, or hot. Escabèche is ideal summer food, because of its refreshing quality, whether you serve it as a first course or as a main dish with a green salad or rice salad or onion and cucumber salad.

For the Fish

2 pounds firm fish fillets (sole, flounder, cod, or salmon), cut into even diagonal strips

All-purpose flour

4 tablespoons (½ stick) unsalted butter

2 tablespoons vegetable oil

Kosher salt

For the Marinade

1/2 cup olive oil

1/3 cup freshly squeezed orange juice

1 tablespoon red or white wine vinegar

1/4 to 1/3 cup thinly sliced canned,
   peeled green chilies

1/4 to 1/3 cup finely chopped onion or 1/2 cup
   chopped scallions (white and green parts)

Grated zest of 3 oranges

1 tablespoon freshly squeezed lemon or
   lime juice

1 1/2 teaspoons kosher salt

1/2 teaspoon Tabasco

For the Garnish

2 peeled and thinly sliced oranges

2 tablespoons olive oil

1 tablespoon freshly squeezed lime or lemon juice

Chopped fresh flat-leaf parsley or cilantro

To cook the fish: Dust the fillets lightly with flour and sauté them in the hot butter and oil in a heavy skillet over medium-high heat until delicately browned on both sides, turning them once and salting them lightly. As the fish browns, transfer to paper towels to drain and cool. Then arrange the fillets in a round or oblong serving dish that will look attractive on the table.

To make the marinade: Combine the ingredients and pour over the fish. There should be enough sauce to cover the fish, if there isn't, add more oil and orange juice. Let the fish marinate for 8 to 10 hours, or up to 24 hours.

A few hours before serving, marinate the orange slices in the oil and lime juice. Serve the escabèche garnished with the orange slices and chopped parsley or cilantro.

STUFFED OYSTERS

MAKES 2 SERVINGS

Editor: To broil the oysters, the broiler pan should be ridged to hold the oysters upright. Rock salt also works to keep the oysters in place, too, but so does aluminum foil crumpled into a large rimmed baking sheet; just nestle the oysters in the foil.

1/4 cup coarsely chopped shallots

1/2 cup finely chopped fresh flat-leaf parsley

1/4 cup finely chopped fresh chervil

6 tablespoons (3/4 stick) unsalted butter, at room
   temperature

12 oysters on the half shell

Rock salt for holding the oysters

Blend the shallots, parsley, and chervil well with the butter in a medium bowl. Spoon the herbed butter onto the oysters in their shells. Arrange the oysters in a broiler pan. (Or fill two individual casseroles with rock salt and place 6 oysters in each casserole.) Place under a hot broiler or in a preheated 500°F oven until the butter is melted and the edges of the oysters begin to curl, just a few minutes.

PÂTÉ OF PIKE
AND SALMON

Editor: This pâté is another classic of French cuisine that Beard encouraged his readers to make at home. Pike, a freshwater fish, is most commonly sold during Passover, as it is an ingredient in many gefilte fish recipes. Substitute any mildly flavored, firm white fish, such as flounder or halibut.

1½ pounds fillet of pike, finely ground and well
　　chilled

1½ cups heavy cream, well chilled

2 large eggs, plus 3 large egg whites, well chilled

3 tablespoons Cognac

Kosher salt

1 head romaine lettuce

Softened butter, for the mold

1 pound skinless salmon fillet, thinly sliced

Kosher salt and freshly ground black pepper.

¼ cup dry white wine

4 tablespoons (½ stick) cold unsalted butter,
　　cut into ½-inch pieces

Working in batches, process the pike, cream, eggs, egg whites, Cognac, and 1 teaspoon salt together in a food processor fitted with the metal blade until smooth. Transfer to a chilled bowl and combine well; refrigerate. Blanch the romaine leaves in boiling, salted water for 1 minute. Drain in a colander and rinse under cold running water. Pat the romaine leaves dry with paper towels. Trim off the thick central stems from the leaves.

　　Using half of the romaine, line a well-buttered, 2-quart pâté mold or terrine. Season the salmon slices with salt and pepper and arrange half of them over the romaine leaves. Spoon in the mousse and cover with overlapping salmon slices and the remaining romaine leaves. Pour in the wine and dot the top with the butter. Cover with aluminum foil and bake in a roasting pan half filled with water in a preheated 300°F oven for 1 hour, making sure that the water never boils. (If it does, add ice cubes to the pan.) Remove the mold from the pan. Chill thoroughly—at least a couple of hours. To serve, unmold and slice.

SALMON TARTARE

This unusual variation on steak tartare, made with raw salmon, became the rage of Paris a few years ago.

Editor: Beard wrote this in 1981 when some of the great chefs were evolving their French version of low-calorie cooking, or cuisine minceur, which owed more than a little to the Japanese. It is essential to buy fish that has been freshly caught because, like the Japanese sashimi and sushi, it is eaten raw. If you have a food processor, use it to separately chop the salmon, onion, and garlic and then mix them all together.

4 pounds very fresh salmon fillets

1 medium-large yellow onion, very finely chopped

2 or 3 garlic cloves, very finely chopped, or more
　　to taste

2 tablespoons Cognac

2 tablespoons finely chopped fresh flat-leaf parsley

1 tablespoon finely chopped fresh dill, or more
   to taste
1 tablespoon Dijon mustard
1 to 2 tablespoons freshly squeezed lemon juice
Kosher salt and freshly ground black pepper
Salad greens, for garnish
Firm white sandwich bread, cut into "fingers" and
   toasted, for serving

Remove the skin and every tiny bit of bone from the salmon (after filleting pull out any bones left behind with pincers of tweezers). Chop the salmon quite coarsely, using a very heavy chef's knife or a Chinese cleaver. Mix the onion and garlic well with the salmon, chopping it in with your knife, then mix in the Cognac, parsley, dill, and mustard; season with lemon juice, salt, and pepper. Keep tasting as you work and add whatever seasoning you think is needed. The amount depends on your personal taste. Pile the salmon tartare in a serving dish, garnish with greens, and chill for 1 hour before serving. Serve with freshly made toast fingers.

VARIATIONS

STURGEON TARTARE: Instead of salmon, use fresh sturgeon.

TUNA TARTARE: Instead of salmon, use fresh tuna.

STRIPED BASS TARTARE: Instead of salmon, use fresh striped bass or rockfish.

SOUSED SHRIMP

 MAKES ABOUT 20 SERVINGS

This keeps well and is good to have on hand for cocktails, so it is worth making in quantity—if affordable. The lemon slices must be cut paper thin.

5 pounds large cooked shrimp (preferably 15 count),
   shelled and deveined
3 medium red onions, thinly sliced
3 lemons, very thinly sliced
1 tablespoon finely chopped fresh rosemary or 1½
   teaspoons finely crushed dried rosemary
2 garlic cloves, finely chopped
Olive oil, as needed
Nonpareil capers, for garnish

Arrange layers of shrimp, onion, and lemon in a good-sized bowl, sprinkling each layer with rosemary. Add the garlic and pour in the oil to cover the shrimp. Cover the bowl with plastic wrap and let the shrimp marinate in the refrigerator overnight. Serve from the bowl.

VARIATION

TARRAGON SHRIMP: Substitute fresh or dried tarragon for the rosemary.

Cocktails

Editor: Seeing this list of alcoholic beverages from the 1963 edition of Hors d'Oeuvre & Canapés *illustrates how much drinking has changed in the intervening years. Vodka was a novelty liquor, and gin and whiskey ruled.*

Here are some good and truly basic recipes for cocktails and long drinks. You will find it helpful in planning your party to budget the liquor beforehand. Allow an average of thirteen drinks per bottle and you will be safe on all sides. Of course, with vermouth and liqueurs used for flavoring, you will get far more, but for rum, whiskey, gin, brandy, and applejack, thirteen drinks allows a safe margin.

Cocktail recipes are sometimes outlined in terms of parts—one part of A to two parts of B. However, it is more accurate to use a jigger (also a unit of 1½ fluid ounces) to measure liquor. The most useful jigger has both 1½ ounce and ¾ ounce (a half jigger) measures. And note that many drinks are stirred in a cocktail shaker, as shaking froths and clouds a drink, and there are some that should remain crystal clear. Stir or shake for about 8 seconds, as the slight dilution of the ice makes for a smoother, better-tasting drink. These recipes make 1 cocktail each, but they can be multiplied as needed.

My Favorite Bloody Mary

1½ ounces vodka

2 ounces canned tomato juice

Juice of ½ lemon

Dash of Tabasco

Dash of Worcestershire Sauce

Dash of salt

Shake vigorously in a cocktail shaker without ice. Pour over the ice into a large "on the rocks" glass.

The Bronx

⅓ gin (1 ounce)

⅓ French and Italian vermouth (½ ounce each dry and sweet vermouths)

⅓ freshly squeezed orange juice (1 ounce)

Shake well in a cocktail shaker and strain into a chilled cocktail glass.

The Daiquiri

Freshly squeezed juice from ½ lemon

2 ounces of silver rum, such as Bacardi silver

1 teaspoon of superfine sugar

Shake well in a cocktail shaker with plenty of ice. Strain into a chilled cocktail glass.

Dark Rum Cocktail

¾ Jamaica rum, such as Myers (2¼ ounces)

¾ teaspoon brown sugar

¼ freshly squeezed lime juice (¾ ounce)

Shake well in a cocktail shaker with plenty of ice and strain into a chilled cocktail glass.

Jack Rose

⅔ applejack (2 ounces)

⅓ freshly squeezed lemon juice (1 ounce)

Dash of Grenadine

Shake well in a cocktail shaker with plenty of ice. Strain into a chilled cocktail glass.

The Standard Manhattan

¾ rye whiskey (2¼ ounces)

¼ Italian (sweet or red) vermouth (¾ ounce)

1 dash of Angostura bitters per drink

Stir vigorously in the cocktail shaker with plenty of ice. Strain into a chilled cocktail glass. The maraschino cherry is the traditional addition to this drink.

The Martini—circa 1940

Put plenty of ice in your cocktail shaker. Add two or three strips of lemon peel. Add three parts of gin (2¼ ounces) and one part (¾ ounce) of French (dry) vermouth. Stir well, and strain into a chilled cocktail glass, garnished with tiny cocktail onions. [*Editor: These days, the cocktail onion garnish would render the Martini a Gibson.*]

The Martini—circa 1961

The modern Martini is made with nine parts of gin (3 ounces) now to one (1 teaspoon) of French (dry) vermouth. In other words, there's just a hint of vermouth as compared with its predecessor. Stir well in a cocktail shaker with plenty of ice. Strain into a chilled cocktail glass. [*Editor: Stuffed olive garnish, anyone?*]

Vodka Martini

Editor: The Martini originally had almost equal parts of gin and vermouth. Over the years, the amount of gin increased, and then changed to vodka as the Russian liquor's popularity increased. The "very dry" Vodka Martini with just a drop of vermouth didn't appear until the 1950s.

4 parts vodka (2 ounces)

1 part French-type vermouth (½ ounce)

Stir with ice as with a Martini. Strain into a chilled cocktail glass and serve with a twist of lemon peel.

Old-Fashioned

This is my own version of the Old-Fashioned, for I loathe "fruit salad" in a drink and all the decorations that usually accompany this simple cocktail. [*Editor: Beard means that many bartenders added maraschino cherries and orange slices to the original Old-Fashioned recipe, which never had fruit in it.*]

1 sugar cube

1 slice of lemon peel

2 dashes of Angostura bitters

3 ounces whiskey, rum, or brandy

(continued)

Mash the sugar, lemon peel, bitters in an old-fashioned glass (a.k.a. "rocks glass") with a muddler. Add the ice and the spirit and stir well.

The Screwdriver

2 ounces vodka

1 cup (8 ounces) freshly squeezed
    orange juice

Put several ice cubes into a 14-ounce glass, pour in the vodka and orange juice, and stir languidly.

Sidecar

⅓ freshly squeezed lemon juice (1 ounce)

⅓ Cointreau (1 ounce)

⅓ Cognac (1 ounce)

Shake well in a cocktail shaker with plenty of ice. Strain into a chilled cocktail glass.

Sour

2 ounces whiskey, rum, or brandy

1 teaspoon of superfine sugar

Freshly squeezed juice of 1 lemon

Shake well in cocktail shaker with plenty of ice. Strain into a small chilled cocktail glass.

Stinger

2 ounces Cognac

1 ounce white crème de menthe

Shake in a cocktail shaker with cracked ice. Strain into a chilled cocktail glass. [Editor: For a vodka stinger, substitute vodka for the Cognac.]

Tom Collins

The same recipe is correct for a rum Collins, substituting rum for gin. [Editor: Or use vodka for a vodka Collins.]

1½ teaspoons superfine sugar

1½ teaspoons water

Freshly squeezed juice of 1 lemon or 1½ limes

4 ounces of gin

Club soda, as needed

Stir the sugar and water in a cocktail shaker. Add the juice and gin and shake with ice. Strain into an ice-filled tall glass, then fill with club soda. Do not garnish with fruit.

VARIATION

FRENCH SEVENTY-FIVE: Substitute French champagne or domestic sparkling wine for the club soda.

Vermouth Cassis

4 ounces French (dry) vermouth

Crème de cassis liqueur

Club soda, as needed

Pour the vermouth over ice in a tall glass. Add crème de cassis to taste. Fill with club soda. Add a twist of lemon peel.

White Satin

½ gin (1½ ounces)

½ freshly squeezed grapefruit juice (1½ ounces)

Shake well in a cocktail shaker with plenty of ice and strain into a chilled cocktail glass.

SOUPS

SOUPS

BASIC CREAM OF VEGETABLE SOUP

✎ MAKES 4 SERVINGS

This is easy and quick because it consists of little more than puréed cooked vegetables and their cooking liquid (preferably homemade chicken stock, skimmed of all fat) mixed with cream, sour cream, half-and-half, or yogurt. If you have a food processor or blender, the puréeing is simplicity itself. If you use a blender, you will have to blend the vegetables with some or all of the cooking liquid, in batches; but unless the vegetable is very dense and starchy, like potatoes, or shell beans, this isn't necessary with the food processor.

The usual proportions for the soup are 1 cup uncooked chopped or cooked puréed vegetables and 2 cups stock to 1 cup cream, but the thickness of the soup depends on the vegetable you are using. Starchy root vegetables provide their own thickening. If you are using vegetables with a high water content, such as summer squash, cucumbers, or leafy green vegetables, you need a large quantity of the vegetable and added thickening. I find instant mashed potato, which cooks smooth and is comparatively tasteless, to be an excellent thickener. In fact, it is the best use I know for this "convenience" product. Use one of the 2-serving packages, or more if needed [see Editor's Note, page 38], and stir it into the reheated soup, cooking until you get the consistency you want.

For a more traditional and richer thickening, beat 2 egg yolks with the 1 cup cream before adding it to the soup, and cook gently, stirring, until thickened. [Editor: Do not let the soup boil.] However, I think you will find the all-vegetable thickening gives a better, purer flavor and a lighter result—with fewer calories.

The soup base of stock and puréed vegetables can be made in quantity and frozen, then thawed and reheated with the cream when you are ready to serve— and, of course, any of the soups may be served cold.

Once you start to play around with the basic recipe that follows, you can alter and adjust it to suit yourself, adding different flavoring herbs and experimenting with various vegetables and combinations of vegetables. For instance, a cut-up avocado put in the blender or food processor (not the food mill) with a zucchini, watercress, or cucumber soup will both thicken and give a lovely flavor and velvety texture.

> 2 cups Chicken Stock (page 349)
> 1 cup sliced or finely cut vegetable
> 1 small yellow onion, finely chopped
> 2 tablespoons chopped fresh flat-leaf parsley
> 1 tablespoon chopped fresh herb of your choice or
>   1 teaspoon dried herb
> Kosher salt and freshly ground black pepper
> 1 cup cream (heavy, light, sour), half-and-half, or
>   yogurt
> Instant mashed potato for thickening, if needed
>   [see Editor's Note, page 38]
> Chopped fresh parsley, dill, or chives, or a sprinkle of
>   paprika, for garnish

Put the stock, vegetables, and herbs in a saucepan and simmer until tender but not mushy. Purée the vegetables in a food processor or blender. [*Editor: Whenever you purée a hot mixture in a blender, vent the opening in the lid so the steam can escape. Otherwise, the steam will build up in the container and create pressure that splatters puréed food all over the kitchen walls—and you.*]

Return the vegetables and liquid to the pan and season to taste with salt and pepper, depending on how seasoned the stock is. Stir in the cream and re-heat. If using sour cream or yogurt, be sure to keep the soup under the boiling point, or it will curdle.

If the soup needs more thickening, stir in instant mashed potatoes and cook over medium-low heat, stirring, until thickened to taste. The amount will depend on the natural thickness of the vegetable used. Serve with a garnish of chopped parsley, chives, dill, or whatever herb is appropriate, or a dash of paprika. [*Editor: Add the instant potatoes by the tablespoon into the simmering soup until it reaches the desired thickness.*]

VARIATION

ARTICHOKE SOUP: Boil 3 or 4 large artichokes in a pot of lightly salted water until tender. Remove the bottoms, discarding the chokes. Scrape the artichoke meat from the leaves and discard the leaves. Purée the artichoke bottoms and meat; you should have 1 cup. Use in place of the sliced or chopped vegetable.

Vegetable/Seasoning Combinations for Basic Cream of Vegetable Soup

Jerusalem Artichokes/Fennel Seed

Parsnips/Cinnamon

Rutabagas/Rosemary

Pumpkin/Nutmeg

Salsify/Chervil

Summer Squash/Dill

Winter Squash/Ginger

BLACK BEAN SOUP

MAKES 12 SERVINGS

One of the greatest of all American soups, this version comes from Leon Lianides, owner of the Coach House Restaurant in New York, where it was a specialty of the house. Black bean soup freezes well and is worth making in quantity. Hot corn sticks (page 284) are wonderful accompaniments.

2 cups dried black beans

4 tablespoons (½ stick) unsalted butter

2 large yellow onions, coarsely chopped

3 leeks, white and pale green part only, well washed
    and coarsely cut

1 celery rib, coarsely cut

2 garlic cloves, crushed

2 bay leaves

2 or 3 whole cloves

1 ham hock, split, with bone and rind

3 pounds beef or veal bones

8 whole black peppercorns

2 tablespoons all-purpose flour

4 to 5 quarts water

½ cup Madeira wine

Chopped fresh flat-leaf parsley, 2 or 3 finely
    chopped hard-boiled eggs, thin slices of lemon,
    for garnish

Soak the beans overnight in cold water to cover. Meanwhile, melt the butter in a stockpot, add the onions, leeks, celery, garlic, bay leaves, and cloves. Sauté for 3 minutes. Add the ham shank and bones and cook for 3 or 4 minutes. Add the peppercorns and flour and blend well. Cook for 2 or

3 minutes, then add 4 to 5 quarts water and bring to a boil. Reduce the heat, skim off the scum, and simmer for 8 to 10 hours, covered, except for a small air space between the pot and lid. Strain the stock, discarding the bones, bay leaves, cloves, and peppercorns. Return the stock and remaining vegetables to the pot.

Drain the soaked beans, add them to the pot, and simmer a further 2½ hours, stirring occasionally. If the mixture gets too thick or if the beans are not completely covered with liquid, add more water. When the beans are soft, purée all the ingredients by processing in batches in a blender with the lid ajar or in a food processor. Reheat the puréed soup with the Madeira. Serve, sprinkling each serving with chopped parsley and hard-boiled egg, and top with a lemon slice.

Editor: Mario Batali's temple to Italian-inspired gastronomy, Babbo, is in the same location as the Coach House, passing the culinary torch.

BORSCH

∽ MAKES 6 TO 8 SERVINGS

There are many version of borsch. This one makes an excellent one-dish meal for supper or a winter lunch, when served with some good black bread and butter, and followed by cheese and fruit. There should be a balance of sweet and sour, so adjust the lemon juice and sugar to taste. If possible, add cooked meat from the stock for a heartier soup.

3 quarts Beef Stock (page 349)

4 or 5 small raw beets, shredded

4 baking potatoes, peeled and thinly sliced

2 medium yellow onions, coarsely chopped

2 cups finely shredded green cabbage

½ cup freshly squeezed lemon juice

2 or 3 tablespoons sugar

2 cups cooked beef (from the Beef Stock), diced

Bring the stock to a boil in a large pot. Add the beets and simmer 15 minutes, then add the remaining vegetables, and cook until the potatoes and cabbage are soft and sufficiently overcooked to give the soup body, about 40 minutes. Add the lemon juice and as much sugar as needed to augment the natural sweetness of the beets, adjusting the ratio to taste. Stir in the cooked beef and serve in large heated bowls or soup plates.

CALIFORNIA GAZPACHO

∽ MAKES 6 SERVINGS

The Spanish gazpacho had become one of the most universally popular uncooked, cold soups and, as was to be expected, variations have proliferated. Traditionally, the soup is a combination of puréed raw vegetables, garlic, bread crumbs, oil, vinegar, water, and seasonings—served well chilled with an ice cube in the soup plate and a garnish, passed in separate bowls, of the same vegetables, finely chopped, and sometimes small croutons. This version has more texture and needs no vegetable garnish.

For the Soup

2½ cups chilled tomato juice, as needed

3 pounds ripe tomatoes

2 cucumbers

½ cup finely chopped green bell pepper

½ cup finely chopped yellow onion

⅓ cup olive oil

3 tablespoons wine vinegar

2 garlic cloves, very finely chopped

¼ teaspoon Tabasco

Kosher salt and freshly ground black pepper

For the Croutons

1 cup diced (½-inch) day-old white bread

2 to 3 tablespoons olive oil

1 garlic clove, finely chopped

To make the soup: Pour enough tomato juice into an ice cube tray to make 6 cubes; freeze until solid, at least 4 hours.

Peel and seed the tomatoes and chop finely, saving as much of the juice as possible. Peel the cucumbers, split lengthwise, scoop out seeds with a teaspoon, and chop finely. Combine the tomatoes and their juice, 2 cups of tomato juice, the cucumbers, bell pepper, onion, oil, vinegar, garlic, and Tabasco in a large mixing bowl. Season with the salt and pepper. Stir well, cover with plastic wrap, and chill until very cold, 3 or 4 hours.

To make the croutons: Sauté the bread cubes in the olive oil with the garlic in a large skillet over medium-high heat until lightly browned on all sides, tossing them well. Do not let the bread or the garlic burn. Transfer to paper towels to drain and cool.

Taste the gazpacho for seasoning and add more salt, pepper, Tabasco, and garlic, if needed. Serve in chilled bowls or soup plates with a frozen tomato-juice cube in each and pass the croutons in a bowl.

MY FAVORITE CLAM CHOWDER

MAKES 4 TO 6 SERVINGS

Mother took a dim view of the average clam chowder. The one we loved was magnificently creamy and filled with the smokiness of bacon and piquancy of thyme. The clams and their juice were added at the moment of serving, and this timing, together with the seasoning, made it, we thought, better than any chowder on the beach in Gearhart.

2 dozen shucked razor, cherrystone, quahog, or littleneck clams; or about 1½ cups with liquid

3 thick slices bacon

1 medium yellow onion, finely chopped

2 baking potatoes, peeled and thinly sliced

2 cups boiling salted water

Kosher salt and freshly ground black pepper

3 cups half-and-half or whole milk

Unsalted butter, for finishing

Dried thyme, for garnish

Chopped fresh flat-leaf parsley, for garnish

Strain the clams over a bowl, reserving the liquid. With a sharp knife, finely chop the clams and set them aside. Cook the bacon in a skillet over medium heat until crisp and browned, about 10 minutes. Using a slotted spoon, transfer the bacon to paper towels. Pour out all but 2 tablespoons of the fat from the skillet. Sauté the onion in the bacon fat until lightly browned. Simmer the potatoes in a large saucepan in the salted water until tender, about 10 minutes.

Add the reserved clam liquid and bacon to the potatoes and their cooking liquid, and season with salt and pepper to taste. Simmer 5 minutes. Add the half-and-half, bring to a boil, and add the clams. Cook until they are barely heated through. Taste and correct the seasoning. To each serving, add a dollop of butter, a pinch of thyme, and a sprinkle of chopped parsley.

NOTE: Salt pork can be substituted for the bacon. Also, the size of the clams will determine the number. We used medium cherrystones at Gearhart.

COLD MINTED PEA SOUP

ᗡᗡ MAKES 8 SERVINGS

This is one of my favorite summer soups, which can be made with yogurt instead of cream if you like a tarter soup with fewer calories.

    6 cups Chicken Stock (page 349)
    3 pounds fresh peas in the pod (3¾ cups shelled
        peas) or 3¾ cups thawed frozen peas
    1 small yellow onion, stuck with 2 whole cloves
    1 garlic clove, crushed under a knife and peeled
    1 teaspoon dried tarragon
    Kosher salt and freshly ground black pepper
    3 cups heavy cream or yogurt
    Chopped fresh mint, for garnish

Put the stock in a large pot with the onion, garlic, tarragon, and peas. Cook until the peas are just tender. Remove and discard the onion. Add salt and pepper to taste and purée in a blender with the lid ajar or in a food processor. Combine with the cream or yogurt and refrigerate. Serve well chilled with a generous sprinkling of mint.

CREAM OF MUSHROOM SOUP

ᗡᗡ MAKES 6 SERVINGS

Editor: As the first course for a company dinner, or as a cold-weather lunch, cream of mushroom soup is very versatile. Cremini (baby portobello) mushrooms are more flavorful than white mushrooms, and can be used, but they make a darker soup.

    1 pound white mushrooms
    4 cups Chicken Stock (page 349)
    3 tablespoons all-purpose flour
    2 tablespoons unsalted butter, at room temperature
    2 cups heavy cream
    2 tablespoons sherry or Cognac (optional)
    ¼ teaspoon Tabasco
    Kosher salt

Wipe the mushrooms with a damp cloth and break off the stems. In a large pot, simmer the stems in the stock for 35 to 40 minutes, or until the mushroom flavor has thoroughly permeated the stock. Strain the stock through a sieve into a bowl; discard the stems. Return the stock to the pot. Mix the flour and butter into a paste, beurre manié, and roll into tiny balls. Bring the stock to a boil; drop in the balls of beurre manié and beat in with a whisk until the beurre manié is absorbed and the stock is slightly thickened. Slice the mushroom caps thinly and add them to the thickened broth. Simmer for 8 to 10 minutes. Meanwhile, heat the cream in another pan, stirring, until just at the simmering point. Add the sherry, if using, and stir in the cream. Stir in the Tabasco and season with salt. Reheat the soup until hot, but not boiling, and serve in heated soup plates or cups.

CREAM OF PEA SOUP

✎ MAKES 8 SERVINGS

Editor: If you make this with fresh peas, be sure that they are very fresh, sweet, and tender. Beard recommends frozen peas without reservations, knowing that they are sometimes more reliable than starchy, over-the-hill fresh peas. You may have to use more or less cream, depending on the thickness of the puréed peas.

  5 pounds fresh peas in the pod, shelled (6¼ cups) or
    use 6¼ cups thawed frozen peas
  1 medium yellow onion, sliced
  4 tablespoons (½ stick) unsalted butter

Kosher salt and freshly ground black pepper
3 cups light cream
Chopped fresh flat-leaf parsley, for garnish
Chopped fresh chives, for garnish

Cook the peas and onion in a large saucepan of boiling salted water until just tender. Drain, and purée in a blender with the lid ajar or in a food processor. Transfer to a saucepan over low heat, and stir in the butter and salt and pepper to taste. Slowly add the cream, and stir until well blended and very hot. Serve garnished with the chopped parsley and chives.

CREAM OF TOMATO SOUP

✎ MAKES 4 TO 6 SERVINGS

An easy soup that is distinctive enough to serve to company. This was the recipe used in the Beard household for many years.

  Two 28-ounce cans Italian plum tomatoes, drained
    (about 3 cups tomatoes)
  1 cup Beef Stock (page 349) or canned beef broth
  1 small yellow onion, stuck with 2 whole cloves
  1 teaspoon dried basil
  1 teaspoon kosher salt
  ½ teaspoon freshly ground black pepper
  1½ teaspoons sugar
  ¼ teaspoon baking soda
  1 tablespoon plus 1½ teaspoons all-purpose flour
  1 tablespoon plus 1½ teaspoons unsalted butter
  2 cups heavy cream

Chopped fresh basil or fresh flat-leaf parsley,
for garnish

Put the tomatoes, stock, onion, basil, salt, and pepper in a large saucepan. Cover and simmer over low heat for 30 minutes. Add the sugar, and cook for another 10 minutes. Remove the cloves from the onion, and purée the tomato mixture in a food processor. Return to the saucepan. Add the baking soda. Taste for seasoning. Blend the butter and flour together into a smooth paste, beurre manié, and whisk it, bit by bit, into the tomato mixture over medium heat. Cook until slightly thickened. Remove from the heat. In a separate saucepan bring the heavy cream almost to a boil. Gradually stir into the tomato purée. Bring nearly to a boil over low heat. Serve with a sprinkling of chopped basil or parsley.

FOUR-DAY VEGETABLE SOUP

✐ MAKES 8 SERVINGS

I happen to think that vegetable soups made without meat stock are infinitely more intriguing. The results are often so delicate and unexpected that one is inspired to improvise constantly and find new and even more delicious combinations, for to my mind, success with vegetable soups is entirely a matter of inspiration, taste, and inventiveness.

I remember going through the refrigerator and the vegetable basket one winter day while living in France and coming up with a considerable array of bits and pieces, which I turned into a thoroughly good soup.

This continued with a series of variations for four days (hence the name of the soup), resulting in three hot soups and one cold. Each time I had a totally different and distinctive product. This recipe, then, is not to be slavishly followed, but to serve as a starting point for your own ideas.

1 large yellow onion, finely chopped
3 garlic cloves, finely chopped
2 cups finely chopped cooked cabbage
2 carrots, shredded
1 small turnip, peeled and finely diced
4 white button mushrooms, chopped
4 Swiss chard leaves, with stems, well rinsed, chopped
2 small zucchini, finely diced
1 tomato, peeled, seeded, and chopped
3 or 4 leaves fresh rosemary or 1 teaspoon dried
rosemary, crushed
Kosher salt and freshly ground black pepper

Put all of the ingredients in a deep saucepan with water to cover, seasoning with salt and pepper to taste—about 1 tablespoon salt and 1 teaspoon pepper. Bring to a boil gradually over low heat. Cover and simmer the soup gently for 1½ to 2 hours, or until all the flavors are well blended. Taste and correct the seasoning.

Four of us ate the soup that night. The next day, I added to the remainder another couple of peeled and chopped tomatoes, a few leaves of finely chopped spinach, another zucchini, and a few leftover cooked chickpeas. I added a bit of grated lemon zest and a touch of onion about 10 minutes before serving.

For lunch on the following day I had the soup cold with a dollop of crème fraîche.

Finally, on the fourth day, I added 2 or 3 peeled and diced beets, another cup of cabbage, 3 or 4 more mushrooms, and a little vegetable broth from vegetables I had cooked for lunch.

Of course, if you have some chicken or vegetable stock you can add it to your soup. The secret is to have variations of color and texture and flavor.

AVGOLEMONO
(EGG-LEMON SOUP)

 MAKES 6 SERVINGS

Editor: The eggs give this famous Greek soup a luscious creaminess, and the lemon is bracingly tart, making it a perfect light first course. To make it more substantial, add chopped cooked chicken and shredded leaf spinach.

---

2 quarts Chicken Stock (page 349)

½ cup long-grain white rice

Kosher salt to taste

2 whole eggs plus 2 large yolks

½ cup freshly squeezed lemon juice

Bring the stock to a boil in a large pot and add the rice. Simmer until the rice is tender, 15 to 20 minutes. Taste and add salt, if needed; this will depend on how seasoned the stock is.

Whisk the eggs and egg yolks together in a bowl until light and frothy. Slowly whisk in the lemon juice.

Add a cup of the hot broth to the mixture, little by little, whisking it in until well blended, then slowly add the mixture to the pan, stirring constantly. Heat through, stirring, but do not allow to overheat or come to a simmer or the eggs will curdle. The soup should be lightly and delicately thickened, of a thin custard-like consistency.

GARBURE BASQUAISE

 MAKES 8–10 SERVINGS

A hearty soup-stew from the Basque country, which combines beans, other vegetables, and ham. It can be varied in all kinds of ways by adding leftover meat or poultry. Serve it with crusty French bread.

1 pound dried white navy beans

½ pound split green or yellow peas

1 ham bone, with meat

1 medium yellow onion, stuck with
    2 whole cloves

3 bay leaves

3 quarts water

Kosher salt

6 red-skinned potatoes, scrubbed and cut into
    small pieces

4 white turnips, peeled and cut into small pieces

4 carrots, sliced

4 leeks, white and pale green part only, well washed
    and sliced

6 garlic cloves, finely chopped

1 teaspoon dried thyme

12 links sweet Italian sausage

1 small cabbage, cored and shredded

Grated Gruyère cheese, for serving

Put the beans and split peas in a pot, cover with water, and bring to a boil. Boil 2 minutes, then remove from the heat and let stand 1 hour. Drain. Put in a large, deep pot with the ham bone, onion, bay leaves, and 3 quarts water, and cook until the beans are just tender, but not mushy, 1 to 1½ hours, adding salt, if needed (if the ham is salty, it may not be necessary). Strain the beans over a bowl, reserving the liquid, and remove meat from the ham bone; discard the bone, onion, and bay leaves. Return the bean liquid to the pot with the potatoes, turnips, carrots, leeks, garlic, and thyme, and cook until tender, about 25 minutes.

Prick the sausages with a fork and cook in a skillet with water to cover for 10 minutes to draw out the fat. Add the cabbage, beans, ham, and drained sausages to the soup. Cook until the cabbage is just done and the soup thick enough to almost hold a spoon upright, about 20 minutes. Serve in bowls or deep soup plates, sprinkled with the cheese.

GARLIC SOUP

⤫ MAKES 6 TO 8 SERVINGS

Don't be alarmed by the quantity of garlic called for here. After garlic had been cooked slowly for a certain length of time it loses its harshness and becomes quite delicate. The beautiful flavor of this soup is something that could never be achieved with garlic powder. So don't even think about it.

3 tablespoons unsalted butter, or, preferably,
    rendered chicken, goose, or pork fat
30 peeled garlic cloves, more or less, to taste
6 to 8 cups Chicken Stock (page 349)
Kosher salt and freshly ground black pepper
Pinch of freshly grated nutmeg
4 or 5 large egg yolks
3 to 4 tablespoons olive oil
Crisp toast

Melt the butter in a large heavy-bottomed saucepan over low heat. Add the garlic and cook gently, shaking the pan often, so that it softens in the fat without browning. (Browning will make the flavor bitter.) Add the stock and season to taste with salt, pepper, and nutmeg. Simmer for 15 to 20 minutes, then drain the garlic—reserving the broth—and purée the garlic in a food processor. Return the garlic and broth to the saucepan and reheat. Beat the egg yolks in a medium bowl and stir the olive oil into them. Blend a little of the soup into the yolk mixture to temper the eggs, then stir it all very gently back into the soup. Heat thoroughly but do not allow to boil, or the yolks will curdle. Place a piece of toast in each soup plate and ladle the soup over it.

GRUYÈRE SOUP

MAKES 6 SERVINGS

This is very close to the more usual Cheddar soup, but the flavor and texture are entirely different. Be sure to use Gruyère cheese from Switzerland, or your soup will not be a success.

4 tablespoons (½ stick) unsalted butter, melted

4 tablespoons all-purpose flour

2 cups whole milk

1 teaspoon or more Dijon mustard

2 cups Chicken Stock (page 349)

2½ cups (10 ounces) shredded Swiss
    Gruyère cheese

Tabasco

Croutons, for garnish

Finely chopped fresh flat-leaf parsley,
    for garnish

Whisk the melted butter and flour in a medium saucepan and cook over very low heat for several minutes. Add in the milk and continue whisking until simmering and slightly thickened. Whisk the mustard into the stock in a medium bowl. Stir into the milk mixture and heat through. Gradually stir in the cheese and season with a dash or two of Tabasco, stirring until the cheese is just melted. Correct the seasoning, adding a little salt, if necessary. Serve in heated cups or soup plates, adding a few croutons to each and a bit of finely chopped parsley.

ONION SOUP AU GRATIN

MAKES 4 SERVINGS

Editor: Beard loved everything about French cooking, and his book with Alexander Watt, Paris Cuisine, *was an early exploration by an American on the subject. Here is his rendition of that famous restorative, onion soup.*

2 medium-large onions, peeled and coarsely chopped

6 tablespoons (¾ stick) unsalted butter

1 tablespoon all-purpose flour

1 cup dry white wine

2 cups Beef Stock (page 349)

Kosher salt and freshly ground black pepper

Pinch of freshly grated nutmeg

½ cup plus 2 tablespoons shredded Gruyère cheese

8 to 12 small slices of French bread or small squares
    of bread

Sauté the onions in 3 tablespoons of the butter in a large heavy-bottomed saucepan over medium heat until they are limp and golden brown, shaking the pan well as they cook so they don't stick or burn, about 10 minutes. Stir in the flour, then mix in the wine and the stock. Season with salt and pepper to taste, and add the nutmeg. Cover and simmer over very low heat for 1 hour, then add 2 tablespoons of the cheese.

While the soup simmers, melt the remaining 3 tablespoons butter in a skillet and sauté the bread over medium-high heat until crisply brown on both sides.

Ladle the soup into ovenproof bowls; arrange 2 or 3 of the fried bread croutons on top of each and sprinkle each with about 2 tablespoons of the remaining cheese. Put in a 450°F oven or under a hot broiler until the cheese melts and forms a thick browned crust.

LENTIL SOUP WITH CHARD AND LEMON

〰 **MAKES 6 SERVINGS**

A rather different, Syrian version of lentil soup, tartened by lemon juice, that is also delicious served cold. Serve with crusty French or Italian bread.

  1½ cups lentils

  2½ pounds Swiss chard or spinach

  ½ cup olive oil

  3 to 4 garlic cloves

  Kosher salt

  ¾ cup chopped yellow onion

  1 celery rib, chopped

  ¾ cup freshly squeezed lemon juice

  1 teaspoon all-purpose flour

Put the lentils in a large saucepan, cover with cold water, and simmer, covered, until tender—between 30 and 45 minutes, depending upon processing; taste to see when done. Wash and chop the chard or spinach, and add to the lentils with 1 cup water. Cook until the chard is wilted.

Meanwhile, heat the oil in a skillet. Crush the garlic with ½ teaspoon salt. Sauté the onion, celery, and garlic until soft, then add to the lentils. Mix the lemon juice and flour and stir into the soup. Simmer, stirring, until the soup thickens

slightly. Taste and correct seasoning. Serve in soup bowls, with crusty French or Italian bread.

VARIATION

LENTIL SOUP WITH COTECHINO: Poach a cotechino with the lentils during the first cooking. Remove, slice, and add to the finished soup.

Editor: Cotechino is a not-too-spicy Italian sausage, somewhat similar to salami, but raw. It must be cooked before serving. Look for it at Italian specialty butchers or online.

SORREL SOUP

〰 **MAKES 4 TO 6 SERVINGS**

Editor: Sorrel makes its annual appearance in spring. Soup, either piping hot (but not boiling) or icy cold, is one of the most popular ways to use this tart green. Note that Beard uses oil, and not butter, as the fat here, because butter hardens into a gritty consistency in a chilled soup.

---

  1 pound sorrel

  6 tablespoons peanut oil

  3 cups Chicken Stock (page 349)

  1 cup heavy cream

  3 large egg yolks

  Kosher salt and freshly ground black pepper

Wash the sorrel well, remove the stems, and cut the leaves into thin strips. Heat the oil in a medium heavy-bottomed saucepan over medium heat, add the sorrel, and cook for 5 to 6 minutes, or until it is wilted. Add the stock and simmer for 5 to 6 minutes over medium heat. Remove the pan from the stove and allow the soup to cool slightly. Purée the sorrel in a blender with the lid ajar or a food processor. Return to the saucepan. Beat together the heavy cream and egg yolks in a bowl. Gradually whisk this into the soup, and season with salt and pepper. Return the saucepan to the stovetop and cook the soup over medium heat until it thickens slightly—being sure not to let it boil. Serve hot, or chill the soup and serve cold.

VARIATIONS

SORREL SOUP WITH CRÈME FRAÎCHE:
Add ½ cup crème fraîche to the soup after thickening with egg yolks and cream.

SORREL-YOGURT SOUP: Do not add the cream and egg thickening. After chilling the soup, stir in plain yogurt to taste. Serve cold.

TURKISH CUCUMBER AND YOGURT SOUP

∽ MAKES 4 TO 6 SERVINGS

Editor: For a light soup, use low-fat, but not nonfat, yogurt. Whole milk yogurt is not low in fat or calories, but it makes a superior end product. If you find the elongated, thin-skinned Persian cucumbers at a farmers' market, just scrub and seed them without peeling.

1 large or 2 small cucumbers

Kosher salt

2 to 3 garlic cloves, peeled

3 cups yogurt, preferably whole milk

3 tablespoons finely chopped fresh mint or
    1 tablespoon dried mint, crushed

Freshly ground black pepper

Peel the cucumber and either shred or dice finely. If diced, sprinkle lightly with salt and put in a colander over a bowl to drain for 30 minutes (shredding will remove most of the water from the cucumber), then taste. If salty, rinse with cold water, then drain again.

Crush the garlic cloves with ¼ teaspoon salt to a paste with a mortar and pestle. Mix in 3 tablespoons of the yogurt, then mix the garlic paste into the remaining yogurt. Beat the yogurt with an electric hand mixer (or whirl it briefly in the blender), which will liquidize it slightly. Mix in the cucumber and mint. Taste and add more salt, if needed, and 1 teaspoon pepper. If the soup seems rather thick, thin with a little cold water to the desired consistency, but do not make it too liquid. Serve in chilled soup cups.

VARIATION

IRANIAN CUCUMBER AND YOGURT SOUP:
Omit the mint and add ½ cup seedless raisins, 1 tablespoon finely chopped fresh dill, and just before serving, 2 chopped hard-boiled eggs.

SQUASH AND CORN SOUP

This interesting combination of squash and corn is typical of Latin America, but the touch of ginger makes it a little different.

Editor: The soup is usually served with sliced corn on the cob, but it is just as good with the corn kernels cut from the cob. In that case, add the cob to the pot when making the vegetable broth.

---

5 to 6 cups Vegetable Broth (page 351)

1 or 2 small yellow crookneck or other summer squash, cut into ½-inch slices

1 leek, white and pale green part only, cut into ½-inch rounds, well washed

1 green bell pepper, seeds and ribs removed, cut into thin strips

1 large garlic clove, crushed

2 or 3 slices peeled fresh ginger

¼ teaspoon dried thyme

1 ear corn, shucked, split lengthwise, and cut into thin slices

Kosher salt

Freshly grated Parmesan or Romano cheese, for serving

Put the vegetable broth, squash, leek, bell pepper, garlic, ginger, and thyme in a large saucepan. Bring to a boil over high heat. Reduce the heat to medium-low and simmer for 1 hour. Add the corn. Taste and adjust the seasoning. Serve sprinkled with the grated cheese.

UDON NOODLE SOUP

The Japanese make a specialty of hearty soups full of thick, slippery udon noodles. Buy them in an Asian grocery. And be sure that the broth is dense with good things to eat.

6 cups cold water

1½ pounds chicken necks, wings, and backs

2 leeks, white part plus 2 inches of the green, split lengthwise and washed well to remove grit

6 slices fresh ginger

1½ teaspoons kosher salt

½ teaspoon freshly ground black pepper

2 large egg whites, beaten

4 ounces udon noodles

1 bunch radishes, thinly sliced

1 bunch scallions, white part plus 2 inches of the green, thinly sliced on the diagonal

2 packed cups thinly sliced napa cabbage

Combine the water and chicken parts in a large saucepan. Add the leeks, ginger, salt, and pepper. Bring the water to a boil over high heat, skim off the froth that rises to the top, and simmer 30 to 45 minutes, partially covered.

Line a colander with several layers of rinsed cheesecloth and pour the hot broth through it into a bowl. Discard the solids in the colander, wash out the saucepan, and return the soup to the pot. Bring to a boil and swirl in the beaten egg whites. When the broth returns to the boil, remove from the heat, and strain it again through a colander lined with rinsed cheesecloth.

Cook the noodles in boiling water according

to the package instructions. Drain and rinse well. Place the noodles, radishes, scallions, and napa cabbage in individual soup bowls. Ladle the hot broth over the vegetables and serve at once.

VICHYSSOISE

∽ **MAKES 6 SERVINGS**

Louis Diat, who created this famous soup while he was chef at the Ritz in New York, allowed me and my partner, the late William Rhode, to sell it in our shop Hors d'Oeuvre Inc. It was a great hit with New Yorkers in our vicinity, who would order it to take away on weekends.

Editor: In the early 1940s, Beard was co-owner, with Bill Rhode and his sister Irma, of Hors d'Oeuvre Inc., a catering business that put him on the culinary map. Note that Beard always insisted that Hors d'Oeuvre be spelled without a final "s," as this is correct French, meaning "outside or apart from the main work" (i.e., the main course).

---

6 leeks

4 cups Chicken Stock (page 349)

3 baking potatoes, peeled and finely diced

1 cup sour cream or heavy cream (preferably sour cream)

Kosher salt

Freshly grated nutmeg

Finely chopped chives, for garnish

Trim and wash the leeks well. Cut off green tops, leaving only the white part. Slice this rather fine. Put the leeks in a large saucepan with the broth and potatoes. Bring to a boil and then simmer, covered, for 30 minutes, or until the potatoes are well cooked. Strain the potato mixture into a bowl, reserving the broth. Purée the vegetables in a blender with the lid ajar or in a food processor. Combine the broth and purée and chill for 24 hours. A few minutes before serving, stir in the sour cream. Add salt to taste and a dash of nutmeg, and chill again for a few minutes. Serve in chilled cups with finely chopped chives on top.

SALADS

SALADS

AVOCADO, ONION, AND GRAPEFRUIT SALAD

MAKES 4 SERVINGS

Editor: This recipe, featuring two very Californian ingredients, surely shows the influence of Beard's great friend, Helen Evans Brown, author of The West Coast Cookbook. *Beard and Brown also collaborated on* The Complete Book of Outdoor Cookery. *You can use your favorite lettuce, but crisp romaine would make a nice contrast with the smooth avocado.*

1 large ripe avocado

1 large grapefruit

1 small red Italian onion

1 head lettuce, washed, dried and crisped

½ cup Basic Vinaigrette Sauce (page 359)

Halve the avocado lengthwise; remove the pit; peel and cut into crescent-shaped strips, about ½ inch wide. Remove the peel and pith from the grapefruit by cutting it off in a long spiral around the fruit, with a sharp knife, holding the grapefruit over a bowl to catch the juice. Then remove the segments, one by one, by cutting downward on either side of the membrane surrounding them. Peel the onion and slice thinly. Arrange the lettuce leaves on a platter, or in a bowl, then put alternating slices of avocado, grapefruit, and onion on top of them. Dress with the vinaigrette sauce.

CAESAR SALAD

MAKES 6 SERVINGS

The famous salad is often served but seldom made correctly.

Editor: Beard loved anchovies and used them whenever he could in his recipes. However, it should be noted that the original recipe for Caesar Salad used Worcestershire sauce, which is made from anchovies, and not anchovy fillets. And the salad's creator, Caesar Cardini, used whole romaine lettuce leaves. You can tear or chop the leaves for easier eating, if you wish.

For the Croutons

4 slices firm white sandwich bread, cut into
    ½-inch cubes

4 tablespoons (½ stick) unsalted butter

2 tablespoons olive oil

3 garlic cloves, crushed under a knife and peeled

For the Salad

1 large egg

1 garlic clove, crushed under a knife and peeled

1 or 2 heads romaine, washed, chilled, and dried

½ cup olive oil

24 or more anchovy fillets in oil, drained and diced

Freshly squeezed juice of 1 lemon, or to taste

Kosher salt and freshly ground black pepper

Freshly grated Parmesan cheese

To make the croutons: Heat the butter and oil in a large skillet over medium-high heat. Add the garlic. Add the bread and sauté until golden, about 3 minutes. Transfer to paper towels to drain and cool.

To coddle the egg: Bring a small saucepan of water to a boil over high heat. Reduce to a simmer. Using a slotted spoon, gently add the egg to the water and cook for 1 minute. Remove the egg with the slotted spoon. Let cool slightly before cracking into a small bowl.

Rub a glass or china salad bowl with the garlic and add the romaine. Pour over the olive oil and toss well.

To make the salad: Add the croutons, anchovies, and lemon juice. Toss lightly and taste for salt. Add freshly ground black pepper to taste, the coddled egg, and a handful of the Parmesan cheese. Toss well and add additional cheese, if desired. Serve at once.

GREEN SALAD, VINTNER'S STYLE

⁂ **MAKES 8 SERVINGS**

This should be made with walnut oil, if available. It is mainly a good, crisp green salad interestingly flavored with blanched fresh walnut halves and a dressing made partly with red wine. Sometimes shredded Gruyère cheese is added to it.

For the Salad

6 heads Bibb lettuce

1 head romaine lettuce

1 bunch watercress, thick stems removed

1 cup walnut halves

1 cup shredded Gruyère (optional)

For the Dressing

¼ cup dry red wine

2 tablespoons red wine vinegar

1 teaspoon kosher salt

1 teaspoon freshly ground pepper

1 cup walnut or olive oil

To prepare the salad: Wash and dry the greens. Tear the larger lettuce leaves into smaller pieces. Arrange in a bowl, and add the watercress, walnut halves, and Gruyère, if using.

To make the dressing: Whisk the wine, vinegar, salt, and pepper in a medium bowl. Gradually whisk in the oil. Pour the dressing over the salad at the last minute (watercress wilts easily) and toss.

ONION AND ROMAINE SALAD

⁂ **MAKES 4 SERVINGS**

Editor: A soak in vinaigrette tames the onion's burly flavor. You may find yourself using this trick with other salad recipes, as well.

1 head romaine lettuce

1 large yellow onion

Basic Vinaigrette Sauce (page 359)

Chopped fresh flat-leaf parsley

Wash, dry, and tear the romaine and place in the refrigerator until ready to use. Slice the onion very thinly, blend with vinaigrette sauce in a salad bowl, and allow to stand for 1 hour. When ready to serve, add the romaine and toss. Sprinkle with the chopped parsley.

BEET AND MUSHROOM SALAD

〰️ MAKES 4 SERVINGS

This unusually good mixed salad goes well with hot or cold lamb, pork, or veal.

    ½ pound very firm white mushrooms, wiped clean
    3 tablespoons olive oil, or more as needed
    2 teaspoons red or white wine vinegar, or more
        as needed
    1 teaspoon finely chopped fresh tarragon or
        ½ teaspoon dried
    ½ teaspoon kosher salt
    ¾ cup fresh-cooked or canned beets, sliced
    ½ cup freshly squeezed orange juice (about half
        an orange)
    5 to 6 cups mixed greens of your choice, torn into
        bite-size pieces
    2 tablespoons finely chopped flat-leaf parsley

Slice the mushrooms into a bowl, and add the 3 tablespoons of oil, 2 teaspoons of vinegar, tarragon, and salt. Gently toss, then cover and let stand for an hour. In another bowl, mix the beets, chopped onion, and orange juice, and also let stand for an hour. Place the torn lettuce leaves in a salad bowl, add the mushrooms and beets, with their dressings, and toss well. Add additional oil and vinegar to taste, if needed. Sprinkle with the parsley.

WILTED CELERY SALAD

〰️ MAKES 4 SERVINGS

Make this salad 3 to 8 hours before you plan to serve, as it needs lengthy marinating. It goes very well with all kinds of meat.

    1 head celery, separated into ribs and
        well washed
    2 tablespoons red or white wine vinegar
    2 tablespoons Dijon mustard
    ½ teaspoon kosher salt
    ½ teaspoon freshly ground black pepper
    ½ cup olive oil
    1 tablespoon chopped fresh tarragon or
        1 teaspoon dried tarragon
    Crisp salad greens
    2 tablespoons chopped parsley or chopped
        hard-boiled egg, for garnish

Remove the tough strings from the outer ribs of the celery, then slice the ribs rather finely. Put the celery in a bowl. Mix the vinegar, mustard, salt, and pepper in a small bowl. Whisk in the oil. Add the tarragon and pour over the celery. Toss extremely well, then cover with plastic wrap and leave at room temperature until ready to serve, shaking the bowl every now and then so the vinaigrette and celery mix well. Line a salad bowl with the salad greens, add the marinated celery to the bowl, and sprinkle with chopped parsley or egg.

CELERY ROOT RÉMOULADE

 MAKES 4 SERVINGS

Celery root (celeriac) is a knobby root vegetable that is most generally used for a purée (page 229), or sliced in fine julienne and combine with a spicy mayonnaise. There are two schools of thought about the preparation of celery root. Some blanch the celery root for a minute or two in boiling water before slicing it. Personally, I prefer to peel it and slice it raw, using a mandoline slicer, a rotary grater, or the coarse shredding attachment of a food processor. If you have none of these aids, slice thin and then cut into fine julienne with a sharp knife. Celery root rémoulade is usually served as a first course, either on lettuce leaves or as part of the hors d'oeuvre selection. It also makes a good accompaniment to thinly sliced, dry (ready-to-eat) sausages like salami and cervelat.

> 1 pound celery root, peeled and cut into fine
>   julienne strips
> 1 cup Mayonnaise (page 355)
> 1 tablespoon Dijon mustard
> 1 tablespoon German-style mustard or
>   1½ teaspoons English mustard
> Kosher salt

Put the celery root strips in a mixing bowl. Blend the mayonnaise and mustards (for a spicier sauce, use English mustard), mix with the celery root, and let it mellow for 1 hour. Taste for seasoning and add salt, if necessary.

Editor: Dijon, German, and English mustard are all made differently and have different spice levels.

English mustard is the hottest of the three, so use it with caution.

BILLY'S COLESLAW

 MAKES 6 TO 8 SERVINGS

This is a slaw on which I was brought up. Billy was a Chinese chef, a pal of my mother's chef, Let, and his coleslaw was superb. He often mixed it with tiny shrimp, crabmeat, or bits of lobster, which made it entirely different but equally delicious.

> ½ cup olive oil
> 2 tablespoons all-purpose flour
> ½ cup red or white wine vinegar
> ¼ cup plus 2 tablespoons sugar
> 2 teaspoons dry mustard
> ½ teaspoon kosher salt
> Dash of Tabasco
> 1 cup heavy cream
> 2 large egg yolks
> One 2-pound green cabbage, quartered
>   and cored

Heat the oil in a heavy skillet over medium heat, add the flour, and whisk well. Whisk in the vinegar, sugar, mustard, salt, and Tabasco and cook just until thickened. Whisk together the heavy cream and yolks in a medium bowl. Whisk in some of the hot oil mixture with the egg-cream mixture, and then pour into the oil mixture. Stir over low heat just until it thickens. Do not boil. Shred the cabbage very thinly and combine with the hot dressing. Cool and chill several hours. If the dressing is too thick, mix with a little more heavy cream or a touch of mayonnaise.

MY FAVORITE COLESLAW

✎ MAKES 6 TO 8 SERVINGS

Coleslaw must be one of the oldest and certainly one of the most popular American dishes. There are innumerable ways of making it, some with a boiled dressing, others with a very spicy vinaigrette, but to my mind it is best when simply tossed with homemade mayonnaise and sour cream.

  One 2-pound green cabbage
  1 cup Mayonnaise (page 355)
  1 cup sour cream
  1 teaspoon kosher salt
  ½ teaspoon freshly ground black pepper

Wash and dry the cabbage, then trim it, cutting off the stalk end and removing discolored or limp outer leaves. Cut into quarters, lengthwise; cut out the hard core at the bottom with a small sharp knife; then put the cabbage on a board and cut the quarters into thin shreds with a large sharp knife, cutting down through the rounded side. Put the shreds into cold water and leave for 1 hour to crisp. Drain well and combine with the mayonnaise, sour cream, salt, and pepper. Toss well and refrigerate for 30 minutes.

SPICY COLESLAW

✎ MAKES 4 SERVINGS

This version is made with shredded cabbage, which should be soaked in salted water to crisp it, and a vinaigrette sauce.

  ½ head green cabbage, quartered and cored
  ⅔ cup Basic Vinaigrette Sauce (page 359)
  1 teaspoon celery seed
  1 teaspoon mustard seed

Cut the cabbage into fine shreds with a large knife. Soak in a bowl of salted water for 1 hour, then drain well. Combine the vinaigrette and celery and mustard seeds in a large bowl, add the cabbage, and toss well. Refrigerate for 1 hour to allow the flavors to blend and mellow.

SPICY SZECHUAN SALAD

✎ MAKES 6 TO 8 SERVINGS

This could make an interesting first course or a main course for lunch.

Editor: Fresh cilantro was a rarity when this recipe was developed, and Beard probably substituted dried basil out of necessity. If you wish, substitute 3 or 4 tablespoons chopped fresh cilantro leaves.

For the Salad
  1 small napa cabbage, cored and sliced crosswise into long, thin strips

1 small head red cabbage, cored and sliced crosswise
into long thin strips

2 cups fresh bean sprouts

2 cups fresh alfalfa sprouts

1 or 2 carrots, cut into julienne strips

8 radishes, thinly sliced

For the Dressing

2 teaspoons dried basil, pounded in a mortar
and pestle

1 garlic clove, finely chopped

1/2 teaspoon kosher salt

1/4 teaspoon freshly ground black pepper

1/3 cup red wine vinegar

1/3 cup soy sauce

1/3 cup Asian sesame oil

1 tablespoon hot chili-flavored sesame oil
(available at Asian grocers and most
supermarkets)

To prepare the salad: Combine the napa and red cabbages, bean sprouts, alfalfa sprouts, carrots, and radishes in a large bowl.

To make the dressing: Combine the basil, garlic, salt, and pepper in a small bowl. Add vinegar and soy sauce and mix the ingredients well. Slowly whisk in the sesame and hot sesame oils. Taste for seasoning and add more hot sesame oil, if desired. Pour the dressing over the vegetables and toss well.

SCANDINAVIAN CUCUMBER SALAD

✑ MAKES 4 SERVINGS

The cucumber is about as universal a vegetable as there is, and is found in salads around the world. The Scandinavians use it as we do coleslaw, as the accompaniment to many different dishes.

2 medium cucumbers or 1 hothouse (seedless)
cucumber

Kosher salt

1/2 cup cider or white wine vinegar

3 tablespoons sugar

2 tablespoons water

1/8 teaspoon freshly ground black pepper

3 to 4 tablespoons finely chopped fresh dill, or use
half dill and half fresh flat-leaf parsley

If they are big, waxy, coarse cucumbers, peel them, cut lengthwise in two, and scrape out the seeds. If using a hothouse cucumber, leave unpeeled and unseeded. In either case, slice very thinly, put in a colander, and sprinkle with 1/2 teaspoon salt. Allow to drain for an hour or so, then rinse briefly under cold water and pat dry. Transfer the cucumbers to a bowl. Whisk the vinegar, sugar, water, pepper, and dill together and pour the dressing over the cucumbers, cover with plastic wrap, and let stand for at least 3 hours before serving, by which time the cucumbers will have wilted. Season with more salt, if needed.

FRESH MUSHROOM SALAD

∽ MAKES 6 TO 8 SERVINGS

Salads of vegetables, cooked, canned, or raw, served with a vinaigrette sauce, are more commonly known as vegetables vinaigrette. They can be served alone as a salad or first course, or as part of an hors d'oeuvre selection, along with other vegetables vinaigrette, canned, fresh, and cured fish and shellfish, pâtés, ham, and sliced sausages such as salami and mortadella. Some vegetables benefit from being marinated first for an hour or two.

  2 pounds very firm mushrooms, wiped clean
  ½ cup Basic Vinaigrette Sauce (page 359)
  1½ tablespoons chopped fresh tarragon or dill
  2 tablespoons finely chopped flat-leaf parsley

Break off the mushroom stems and reserve them for some other use (they can be chopped and cooked down in butter until all the liquid evaporates, then used for an omelet filling or swirled into scrambled eggs).

Slice large mushroom caps lengthwise about ¼ inch thick. Small mushrooms may be left whole, or halved. Put the mushrooms into a mixing bowl, add the vinaigrette sauce and tarragon, and toss well. Let the salad stand for 1 or 2 hours. To serve, put into a serving bowl or dish, add additional oil and vinegar, if needed, and sprinkle with the chopped parsley.

OLD-FASHIONED OREGON POTATO SALAD

∽ MAKES 6 SERVINGS

This salad, which was very popular when I was growing up, is one I like to serve with very simple foods, such as ham, cold chicken, and other cold meats. The nasturtium leaves, a particularly Western addition, were picked from the garden and tossed into the salad bowl to add a peppery zest. If you don't grow nasturtiums, you might add a little garden cress, arugula, or watercress.

  2½ pounds small new potatoes, unpeeled
  1 large yellow onion, finely chopped
  2 celery ribs, finely diced
  1 or 2 carrots, shredded
  ½ cup chopped fresh flat-leaf parsley, plus more
    for garnish
  ⅓ cup cider vinegar
  4 or 5 unsprayed nasturtium leaves, cut into
    shreds (optional)
  ¾ cup Mayonnaise (page 355), as needed
  Kosher salt and freshly ground black pepper
  Mixed salad greens, for serving
  3 hard-boiled eggs, quartered or sliced,
    for serving
  12 stuffed green olives, sliced, for serving
  Chopped fresh chives, for garnish

Boil the potatoes in their skins in a large saucepan of salted water to cover until they can just be pierced with a fork, about 15 minutes. Drain. Peel and slice into a large bowl while still warm and combine with the onion, celery, carrot, and parsley. Add the vinegar, and the nasturtium leaves, if using, and toss to mix well. Let the salad stand at room temperature for 15 minutes. Blend with enough mayonnaise to coat the vegetables well, and season with salt and pepper. Refrigerate for 2 to 3 hours.

Line a deep platter with greens and unmold the chilled salad onto it. Top with the hard-cooked eggs and olives. Sprinkle with more chopped parsley and the chopped chives.

The minute the rice is drained, put it into a bowl; add the oil, and toss well with two forks until the grains are completely coated. Cool the rice at room temperature.

Mix in the chopped scallions, cucumber, bell pepper, tomato, parsley, and basil. Add vinaigrette to taste, according to how moist you like your rice salad—it should be well coated but not soggy. Toss lightly with two forks. Season with salt and pepper.

RICE SALAD WITH SUMMER VEGETABLES

MAKES 6 SERVINGS

The secret of a good rice salad is to use freshly cooked rice and toss it with oil while it is hot. This coats the cooling grains and keeps them separate and fluffy. Line the salad bowl with salad greens, if you like. This is a good summer accompaniment to broiled or grilled meat and poultry.

4½ cups freshly cooked long-grain white rice (page 255)

3 tablespoons olive oil

¾ cup finely chopped scallions (white and green parts) or red onion

½ cup peeled, seeded, and diced cucumber

½ cup seeded and diced green or red bell pepper

½ cup peeled, seeded, and chopped tomato

¼ cup finely chopped fresh flat-leaf parsley

2 tablespoons chopped fresh basil

½ to ¾ cup Basic Vinaigrette Sauce (page 359)

Kosher salt and freshly ground black pepper

WHITE BEAN AND TUNA SALAD

MAKES 6 SERVINGS

A delicious summer salad for a buffet or a luncheon main dish that may be made either with cooked white beans or canned Italian cannellini beans, which can be found in any supermarket.

For the Dressing

¼ cup red wine vinegar

2 tablespoons chopped fresh basil or 2 teaspoons dried basil

1 teaspoon kosher salt

½ teaspoon freshly ground black pepper

¾ cup olive oil

For the Salad

Three 20-ounce cans cannellini beans (about 6 cups)

1 cup finely chopped yellow onion

Two 6-ounce cans solid white albacore tuna, drained and flaked

1 tablespoon chopped fresh basil

¼ cup finely chopped fresh flat-leaf parsley

Additional oil and vinegar, if necessary

To prepare the dressing: In a small bowl whisk together the vinegar, basil, and salt and pepper. Then whisk in the olive oil.

To assemble the salad: Drain the beans through a colander and rinse them well under cold running water to get rid of the thick, gummy liquid that clings to them. Shake well to free of excess water, then put the beans into a serving bowl or dish. Pour the dressing over the beans, letting it run through to coat them, then toss very lightly to distribute the dressing—don't toss too much or the beans will break up. Put the onion and tuna on top of the beans. Sprinkle with the basil and parsley. Just before serving, add a little more oil and vinegar, if the salad seems to need it, and toss lightly to combine ingredients.

VARIATIONS

- Add ½ cup small black olives and 6 chopped anchovy fillets with the onion and tuna.

- Use canned salmon, or boneless skinless canned sardines instead of tuna.

- Omit the tuna. Serve the bean salad in tomato shells, as a first course. To prepare the shells, slice off about ½ inch of the top, scoop out the seeds and pulp, and turn the hollow shells upside down to drain.

GREASED PIG SALAD

 MAKES 1 SALAD

This is really a BLT sandwich without the benefit of bread. It was discovered at a small soul food restaurant in Montmartre run by Americans and had become a popular hors d'oeuvre with the French.

Crisp leaves of Boston, romaine, or Bibb lettuce

Slices of really ripe tomatoes

A slice of red onion (optional)

3 or 4 slices of cooked crisp bacon

Mayonnaise (page 355)

Arrange a few crisp leaves of lettuce on a plate. Top with the tomato slices and maybe a slice of red onion. At the last minute add the hot bacon. Serve with mayonnaise.

HEARTY BEEF SALAD

MAKES 6 SERVINGS

This beef salad is served as a first course in France, but I find it very satisfactory as a buffet, luncheon, or supper dish.

For the Salad:

Mixed salad greens, for the serving platter

3 cups lean boiled or pot-roasted beef, sliced and then cut into 1-inch squares

2 cups boiled and sliced new potatoes (see instructions in Old-Fashioned Potato Salad, page 59)

1 cup finely chopped scallions, green and white parts

2 cups coarsely chopped celery, with leaves

1 cup cherry tomatoes or 4 peeled tomatoes cut into
sixths

1 cucumber, peeled, seeded, and diced

½ cup roasted and peeled green bell pepper strips

12 cornichons (French tiny sour gherkins)

¼ cup drained bottled nonpareil capers

For the Dressing

6 hard-boiled eggs

1 tablespoon Dijon mustard

1 garlic clove

1½ teaspoons kosher salt

⅓ cup wine vinegar

1 teaspoon freshly ground black pepper

Dash of Tabasco

1 cup olive oil

To assemble the salad: Line a serving platter with the greens. Arrange the beef, potatoes, scallions, celery, cherry tomatoes, cucumber, bell pepper strips, cornichons, and capers on top.

To make the dressing: Shell the eggs, separating the whites and yolks. Chop and reserve the whites. Mash the yolks in a medium bowl with a fork and work in the mustard. Mash and smear the garlic with the salt on a chopping board into a paste. Stir into the egg yolk mixture along with the vinegar, pepper, and Tabasco, then gradually whisk in the oil. Pour the dressing over the salad. Garnish with the reserved egg whites.

Editor: True enough, this salad is usually made with leftover braised beef. However, it is equally tasty with sliced roast beef, either homemade or straight from the delicatessen counter.

HUSSAR SALAD

〰 MAKES 6 TO 8 SERVINGS

A very different kind of beef salad that came to me by way of my column, from a reader of Dutch ancestry, Max Dekking. This Dutch national dish is called Huzarensla (Hussar Salad) because it was the favorite meal of the Hussars when they invaded the Netherlands many centuries ago. This is the kind of salad that should be prepared well in advance and left to mellow in a bowl in the refrigerator. Unmolded on a bed of greens it is a most attractive dish for a buffet.

3 cups finely chopped rare roast beef, cold

2 large yellow onions, very finely chopped

2 cups boiled, peeled, and very finely chopped new
potatoes (see instructions in Old-Fashioned
Potato Salad, page 59), cold

1 cup very finely chopped cooked or canned
beets, cold

½ cup very finely chopped apple

½ cup very finely chopped celery

1 finely chopped shallot or garlic clove

1 large kosher sour dill pickle, very finely chopped

1 cup Mustard Vinaigrette Sauce (page 300),
as needed

2 tablespoons Mayonnaise (page 355),
as needed

Mixed salad greens for serving

2 hard-boiled eggs, sliced, for garnish

Chopped fresh flat-leaf parsley, for garnish

Combine the roast beef, onions, potatoes, beets, apple, celery, shallot, and pickle (and for this salad they must be *very* finely chopped) in a large bowl. Mix in just enough vinaigrette sauce, plus a spoonful or two of mayonnaise, to bind. The salad must not be sloppy, but firm enough to unmold. Mix everything together well, pack into a 2½- to 3-quart mold or bowl, and leave in the refrigerator for 3 hours. When ready to serve, unmold onto a bed of greens on a platter and garnish with the sliced eggs and chopped parsley.

SALADE NIÇOISE

╭⁄○ MAKES 4 TO 6 MAIN-COURSE SERVINGS

This Provençal salad is one of the best of all luncheon dishes. You can vary it to taste, adding other vegetable of your choice. The only constants are the tuna, anchovies, hard-boiled eggs, tomatoes, and tiny black olives. You can also serve small helpings of the salad as a first course, as they do in Provence. Certain other cooked vegetables may also be added to the salad, such as tiny, boiled new potatoes or sliced boiled potatoes, green beans cooked until just bitey-crisp, or cooked artichoke hearts rather than canned. Little croutons of bread, sautéed until golden brown in oil with a garlic clove, are another good addition. Serve with French bread.

  1 head Boston or romaine lettuce
  Two 6-ounce cans solid white albacore tuna, drained
  20 to 30 anchovy fillets in oil, drained
  4 to 6 ripe tomatoes, cored and quartered, or 12 to 18 cherry tomatoes
  4 to 6 hard-boiled eggs, quartered
  ½ cup small Mediterranean black olives, preferably Niçoise olives, pitted
  ½ cup finely chopped yellow onion or 1 small red onion, sliced into thin rings (optional)
  ¼ cup pimiento strips (optional)
  1 green bell pepper, sliced into thin rings (optional)
  ½ cup drained canned artichoke hearts (optional)
  1 tablespoon chopped fresh basil or 1 teaspoon dried basil
  1 cup Basic Vinaigrette Sauce (page 359)

Cover a large platter or line a larger salad bowl with the lettuce leaves. Place the tuna in the center and surround it with the anchovy fillets. Arrange the tomatoes and eggs around the edge of the platter or bowl and sprinkle the olives on top. Add any of the optional ingredients, if using—onion is good in a salade Niçoise, and so are green bell pepper rings. Sprinkle the salad with the basil. When you are ready to serve, pour the vinaigrette sauce over the salad at the table and toss lightly.

BASIC CHICKEN SALAD

╭⁄○ MAKES 4 SERVINGS

Of all the main-dish salads in our culinary lexicon, chicken salad is far and away the most popular—and yet it is all too often as badly prepared as many other simple foods. The first necessity is that the salad be made with freshly poached chicken, preferably a plump roasting chicken well endowed with fat. The second is that it should be cooled at room temperature so the meat remains juicy and delicious. Use dark as well as white meat, to add more flavor, and cut it into fairly generous bite-size pieces. (It's amusing to note that in the old days, when chicken was expensive, many restaurants used cold veal or pork instead. You can too, if you want to be extravagant.)

Garnishing options include halved or quartered hard-boiled eggs and chopped parsley; toasted salted walnut halves and watercress; or toasted salted almonds, thin strips of green pepper, and finely chopped fresh chervil or flat-leaf parsley

3 cups cooled Poached Chicken (page 130), or roast or poached turkey breast, skinned, boned, and cut in bite-size pieces

1 cup (or to taste) Mayonnaise (page 355), or use ½ cup each mayonnaise and sour cream or plain yogurt

Salad greens, such as watercress, Boston or Bibb lettuce, or chicory

Mix the chicken and mayonnaise together in a bowl. Arrange on a bed of the greens. Garnish as desired.

CHICKEN SALAD WITH CELERY: Add 1 cup finely chopped crisp celery to the chicken. Garnish with sliced hard-boiled eggs, capers, and black olives.

CHICKEN SALAD WITH CELERY AND GRAPES: Add ¾ cup peeled white grapes to the chicken and celery. Garnish with sliced toasted almonds and a few more peeled grapes.

BEEF
AND
VEAL

BEEF AND VEAL

BOEUF À LA FICELLE
(BEEF ON A STRING)

This most unusual way of cooking beef is quite different from boiled beef. Although it is simmered in stock, the end result is rare and deliciously tender. The *ficelle* of the name refers to the string by which the meat is suspended. Serve the same kinds of vegetables you should have with boiled beef—boiled potatoes, carrots, leeks, turnips—and a horseradish and sour cream sauce.

One 2½-pound boneless beef roast (eye-of-the-rib, strip top sirloin, or fillet)

3 pounds beef marrowbones

2 tablespoons kosher salt

2 garlic cloves, crushed under a knife and peeled

1 tablespoon dried thyme

1 tablespoon freshly ground black pepper

1 bay leaf

Tie the beef securely with kitchen twine, crosswise and lengthwise, leaving at each end a piece long enough to suspend the meat in the pot. Pour enough cold water into a deep pot to almost cover the meat; add the marrowbones and the salt, garlic, thyme, pepper, and bay leaf. This is for a broth in which the beef will cook. The meat should not be added until later. Bring the liquid to a boil, skim off the scum that rises to the surface, reduce the heat, cover, and simmer for 1 hour. Then remove the bones and skim the fat off the top of the broth.

Suspend the meat in the broth (it should not touch the bottom of the pot) by tying the ends of the string to the handles of the pot. Bring the broth to a full boil (the shock of heat seals the surface of the meat and keeps the juices in), then reduce the heat to a simmer, cover the pot tightly with aluminum foil and the lid so no steam escapes, and simmer the meat for approximately 15 minutes a pound, about 35 minutes in all, testing the internal temperature by inserting a meat thermometer after 25 minutes. The temperature should register 125° to 135°F depending on how rare you like your beef. Transfer the beef to a carving board, let it rest for 5 minutes, then remove the strings and carve crosswise with a very sharp knife into fairly thick slices, about ½ inch thick. Save the stock, strain, and use for bouillon or as the base for vegetable soups.

BOILED CORNED BEEF AND CABBAGE

This might qualify as a New England boiled dinner. It's a good, hearty, basic dish that will serve 6, with some meat left over for cold corned beef sandwiches or 4 to 6 servings of corned beef hash.

When we talk about "boiled beef" or a "boiled dinner" we don't really mean boiled; we mean simmered. Naturally, to create a simmer you first have to bring liquid to a boil and you do have to let the liquid boil for a little at the start of the cooking, to draw off certain elements in the beef that would cloud the broth. These form a grayish-brown scum on the surface and should be skimmed off with a skimmer or spoon.

Corned beef is beef that has been cured in a pickling solution, which used to be the way beef, pork, and sometimes lamb were preserved for the winter. It's very traditional and one of the most delicious American beef dishes. There are different kinds of corned beef. There's a very spicy kosher corned beef, the plain corned beef, and some simulated corned beef that is not nearly as good as the old-fashioned, pure kind we are so used to. Corned beef brisket is the choicest cut because it has some fat and good marbling and makes a flavorful, tender finished product that slices well and looks good on the plate.

To cook the corned beef, you will need a good, big pot, an 8- to 10-quart size, which can be aluminum, Magnalite or anything of that sort. The size is more important than the material.

For the Corned Beef

One 6-pound corned beef brisket

1 medium yellow onion, peeled and stuck with 3 whole cloves

10 large garlic cloves, crushed under a knife and peeled

1 tablespoon freshly ground black pepper

For the Vegetables

6 medium yellow onions, peeled

6 medium carrots, peeled

6 to 10 medium potatoes, scrubbed

6 turnips, peeled

1 medium cabbage

Mustards, prepared horseradish, and pickles, for serving

To prepare the corned beef: Wipe the corned beef well with a damp cloth. Put it in the pot and cover with cold water. Bring to a boil over rather high heat, and boil for 5 to 6 minutes, skimming off the gray foam scum that rises to the surface with a wire skimmer or large spoon. This will give you a clearer, purer broth. It's very important, with a boiled meat, to skim off the scum drawn from the meat. [*Editor: The scum is only the gelatins and collagens from the meat, and while they aren't harmful, they are unattractive and will give the broth an off flavor and texture.*]

Add the onion stuck with cloves, the garlic cloves, and the pepper and boil for another 10 minutes, skimming as needed. Then reduce the heat to a simmer, cover the pot, and let it simmer at a faint, gentle ebullition for 2 hours. At this point, test the meat for tenderness with a large fork. As this is not a very tender piece of meat, it will offer some resistance, but it should just yield to the fork. You must be careful not to overcook corned beef or the meat will become dry and stringy. It's very important to maintain some moisture in the meat. If you are not sure about tenderness, remove the meat, transfer to a plate, and cut off a tiny piece from the edge to taste. If you have a meat thermometer, check the internal temperature, which should register 145° to 150°F.

If the meat seems tender, turn off the heat and let it rest in the liquid. If it does not test tender, either continue cooking or, if you have started it in the morning and are ahead of serving time, leave it in the liquid and finish the cooking later.

Traditionally, all the vegetables for a corned beef dinner are cooked in the pot with the meat. I have long since decided that the vegetables look and taste better if they are cooked separately in plain salted water, instead of the briny fatty broth. If you have sufficient pots and burners,

I recommend that you follow this procedure—each vegetable will then retain its own character and flavor. However, it is perfectly acceptable to cook the potatoes with the beef, provided you scrub them and leave them in their skins so they don't absorb the fat, and to use only one extra pot, first putting in the longest cooking vegetables: first, the onions, followed by the carrots, then the turnips, and finally the cabbage. Or, if you have a large pot and a steamer, put the onions and carrots in the water and steam the turnips over them. Cook the cabbage separately.

One hour before serving, cook the vegetables.

TIMETABLE FOR COOKING THE VEGETABLES

ONIONS: Put in a pot with water to cover, seasoned with 1 tablespoon salt. Bring to a boil. Cover, and simmer 1 hour, or until crisply tender when tested with the point of a knife.

CARROTS: Follow the same procedure, seasoning the water with 2 teaspoons salt and ½ teaspoon dried marjoram. Simmer 30 minutes, or until tender when tested.

POTATOES: Scrub but do not peel. Follow the same procedure, seasoning the water with 1 tablespoon salt, or simmer with the corned beef for 30 minutes, or until tender. If you are planning to make corned beef hash, cook the 4 extra potatoes, otherwise allow 1 per person.

TURNIPS: Leave whole if small, halve or quarter if large. Follow the same procedure, seasoning the water with 2 teaspoons salt. Simmer for 20 minutes, or until tender when tested.

CABBAGE: Remove the coarse or discolored outer leaves and cut into sixths. Put in a pot with water to cover, seasoned with 2 teaspoons salt. Bring to a boil and boil rapidly, covered, for 10 to 12 minutes, or until just tender but not overcooked or soggy.

When you are ready to serve, remove the beef from the broth (discard the broth; it cannot be saved for any other use) and let stand on a hot platter in a warm place for 10 minutes, to firm and settle the meat. This makes it easier to carve. Surround it with the drained vegetables, the potatoes still in their jackets. Do not add butter—the vegetables are better plain. Slice only as much meat as you need, keeping the rest in one piece for future use. Serve with the vegetables, with a variety of mustards, horseradish, and, if you have any, good homemade pickles.

POT ROAST

MAKES 10 SERVINGS

The braised beef dish we know as pot roast, one of the most popular foods in this country, is far too often served overcooked and dry. This is mainly the result of using the wrong cuts of beef or from a lack of fat—either in the beef or in the cooking. The best choice for a pot roast is a piece of well-marbled beef rump or chuck. You may, if you wish, further lubricate it with Cognac-soaked lardons, small strips of fatback inserted with a larding needle. While not strictly necessary for well-marbled beef, this does add a very pleasant flavor and looks attractive when sliced.

Surround the sliced pot roast with cooked noodles sprinkled with grated Parmesan cheese, and have a salad or braised celery as the vegetable.

One 5-pound beef rump or chuck roast

¼ pound fresh fatback, cut into 6 to 8 strips

¼ cup Cognac

Salt and freshly ground black pepper

2 teaspoons dried basil

4 tablespoons (½ stick) unsalted butter (optional)

¼ cup vegetable oil (optional)

1½ cups Beef Stock (page 349)

1 cup drained and coarsely chopped canned Italian plum tomatoes

2 leeks, white and pale green parts only, trimmed, coarsely chopped, and well washed to remove grit

2 carrots, coarsely chopped

1 large yellow onion, stuck with 2 whole cloves

4 to 6 garlic cloves, crushed under a knife and peeled

1 bay leaf

3 tablespoons tomato paste

1 tablespoon freshly squeezed lemon juice

The strips of fatback, known as lardons, should be rather longer than the depth of the piece of beef and just wide enough to fit into the groove of a long larding needle. Soak these lardons in the Cognac for 3 to 4 hours before larding the beef. Following the meat's grain, push the grooved blade of the needle through the roast, turning it to make a hole, withdraw, and insert a strip of fatback into the groove of the needle. Then insert the blade into the hole, pushing the top of the lardon with your thumb so it stays inside the meat. Withdraw the needle, leaving the fat behind. Repeat this with all the lardons, and trim off any overhanging ends level with the meat. [*Editor: Lacking a larding needle, use a metal knife sharpening steel to poke long holes through the meat, and force the fatback into the holes. Note that Beard says in the headnote that larding is not necessary for well-marbled meat.*] Rub the meat well with salt, pepper, and 1 teaspoon of the basil.

You can either brown the meat in the butter and oil in a skillet or pan on top of the stove or put it on the rack of the broiler pan under the broiler, 7 or 8 inches from the heat, turning to brown all sides.

Transfer the browned beef to a deep Dutch oven and pour over it the fat in which it browned, or the drippings from the broiler pan. Add the beef stock, leeks, carrots, onion, garlic, remaining basil, and the bay leaf. Bring to a boil over high heat, cover the meat with a piece of oiled waxed paper, oiled-side down, cover the pan, and reduce the heat. Simmer over low heat on top of the stove or in a 325°F oven for 1 hour. Add the tomatoes. Continue cooking until the meat is just tender when tested with the point of a knife, 1½ to 2 hours. Do not make the common mistake of cooking the beef until it is grainy and coarse. The difference is slight but important.

Remove the meat and keep warm on a hot platter. Skim the excess fat from the sauce and strain through a wire sieve into a large saucepan, pushing through any vegetables to make the sauce thicker. Add the tomato paste and lemon juice, taste, and correct the seasonings. Bring the sauce to a boil and simmer 3 to 4 minutes to blend the flavors. Serve the sauce separately.

VARIATIONS

ANCHOVIED POT ROAST: Stud the beef with garlic slivers and anchovy fillets (do not lard). Brown the beef and put it in a Dutch oven with 1½ cups canned Italian plum tomatoes, 3 carrots, and 1 celery rib, both chopped, 1 tablespoon dried basil, and 1 bay leaf; season with freshly ground black pepper. Cover and simmer until tender, about 2½ hours, turning once and adding a little water or tomato juice if the cooking liquid reduces too much. During the last 15 minutes of cooking, add 1 cup pitted black Mediterranean olives, such as Kalamata. Serve the meat sliced, with the sauce, buttered macaroni, and a green salad.

FLEMISH POT ROAST: Sauté 6 large yellow onions, sliced, in 5 tablespoons (½ stick plus 1 tablespoon) unsalted butter in a large skillet until limp and golden, about 6 minutes. Season with salt and pepper. Put in a deep Dutch oven with the browned beef, 1 teaspoon dried thyme, 1 bay leaf, and 1 pint lager beer. Cover and simmer until tender, about 2½ hours. Remove the meat and slice. Adjust the seasoning in the sauce, and serve over the sliced beef. Serve with parslied potatoes.

MEXICAN POT ROAST: Stud the beef with slivers of garlic (do not lard). Sauté 4 sliced yellow onions in ½ cup rendered beef suet or beef fat in a Dutch oven over medium heat until tender, about 4 minutes. Add the browned beef, 1 cup beef broth, ½ cup tomato purée, 2 tablespoons chili powder, 1 teaspoon dried oregano, ½ teaspoon coarsely crushed cumin seed, ½ teaspoon ground coriander, and ¼ teaspoon Tabasco; season with salt. Cover and simmer until tender, about 2½ hours, turning the meat several times in the sauce. If the sauce becomes too reduced, add more broth or tomato purée. Serve the meat sliced, with the sauce skimmed of all fat. Garnish with chopped fresh cilantro or flat-leaf parsley, and serve with pinto beans and tortillas.

RIB ROAST OF BEEF

MAKES 6 SERVINGS

Choose preferably a **4- or 5-rib roast** cut from the first ribs, to serve 6 people, with some leftovers; if you are having a large dinner party you may need a 7- or 8-rib roast. Have the roast "cut short"— with the short ribs removed, sometimes referred to as a 7-inch cut. The chine bone should be removed by the butcher, the ribs left intact, and the roast well trimmed of any connective tissue and gristle, and the excess of fat. A properly prepared rib roast should be well balanced—even in size and compact. Rub the meat well with ½ **teaspoon freshly ground black pepper** and ½ **teaspoon of dried thyme** if you wish. For added zest, you can also rub the fat and bone with **a crushed garlic clove,** but this is a matter of taste.

Place the roast on a rack in a shallow roasting pan and roast bone side down in a preheated 500°F oven for 35 to 40 minutes, basting twice with **2 to 3 tablespoons melted butter or rendered beef fat.** Reduce the heat to 325°F and continue to roast the beef for 30 minutes longer. Test the internal temperature by thrusting the meat thermometer into the thickest part of the eye of the rib, being careful not to touch the bone at any point. Remove the thermometer and continue roasting, basting every 20 minutes with the pan juices or butter. You may salt the roast after any of the bastings. Test again for temperature after 30 min-utes and make a final test within 20 minutes after that. Estimate about 12 to 14 minutes of cooking time per pound of roast. When the roast reaches 120° to 125°F for medium-rare, transfer it to a hot platter or carving board and let it rest in a warm place for at least 20 minutes. If you are making Yorkshire pudding, turn up the oven to 450°F and bake the pudding while the beef is resting. Pour off and measure ½ cup of the beef drippings (melted beef fat); add vegetable oil, if needed.

To carve, turn the roast on the side that gives it the best balance for carving and hold it in place with the back of a heavy fork while carving with a good sharp knife. Serve it with the pan juices and Yorkshire pudding, or with a **Quick Brown** or **Béarnaise Sauce** (pages 352 and 355). If you like roast potatoes with your roast beef, place peeled, parboiled pieces of potatoes in the pan juices after the searing period and cook them with the meat, turning once during the cooking time and basting along with the beef. Salt and pepper them and arrange them around the carved roast, or serve them in a separate dish with a sprinkling of chopped fresh parsley.

Yorkshire Pudding for Roast Beef

Makes 6 servings

2 large eggs

1 cup whole milk

1 cup sifted all-purpose flour

½ teaspoon salt

½ teaspoon freshly ground black pepper

½ cup beef drippings (melted beef fat), heated

Position the rack in the center of the oven and preheat the oven to 450°F. Whisk the eggs in a medium bowl until very pale and quite light in texture, then gradually whisk in the milk and flour. (Or, put the eggs, milk, and flour in an electric blender and blend just until the batter is smooth.) Season with the salt and pepper. Put a metal baking pan measuring about 11 by 14 by 2½ inches in the oven and let it get very hot. Remove and pour in the hot drippings and then the batter. Bake for 10 minutes, then reduce the heat to 375°F and continue to bake for 15 to 20 minutes, or until the pudding has risen and is puffed and brown. Do not open the oven door during the first 20 minutes of baking. Cut into squares and serve immediately with roast beef.

ROAST FILLET OF BEEF

⟳ MAKES 8 TO 10 SERVINGS

To my thinking, a beef fillet, an expensive but meltingly tender boneless piece of meat that should always be served very rare, is best roasted quickly at a high temperature with several bastings. Now that so many ranges are equipped with self-cleaning ovens, high-temperature roasting, an inevitably messy business, presents few problems and seems to be increasingly popular.

When you buy the fillet, have the filet mignon (the thin tapering piece at one side of the fillet) removed, as it is too thin for roasting. [*Editor: Some butchers call this the chain of the roast.*] Use it for another recipe—beef scallops or brochette of beef. Ask the butcher to bard the fillet, that is, to wrap it with two sheets of pork fat or flattened beef suet and tie it well. [*Editor: Lacking a top-notch butcher, use blanched bacon: Simmer bacon strips in water for 5 minutes, drain, cool, and lay over the tenderloin.*]

Serve it with a Béarnaise Sauce (page 355). Potatoes Anna (page 240) and a purée of broccoli go well with this. Drink a fine red Burgundy.

> 4- to 5-pound fillet of beef (beef tenderloin),
>   well trimmed with all fat and tendon
>   removed, then tied and barded with fat
> 6 tablespoons (¾ stick) unsalted butter,
>   melted, or use 3 tablespoons unsalted
>   butter, melted and mixed with 3 tablespoons
>   olive oil
> Kosher salt and freshly ground black pepper

Place the barded fillet on a rack in a shallow roasting pan. Roast in a preheated 500°F oven for 25 minutes, basting it well every 8 minutes with the melted butter. Remove the barding fat after the fillet has roasted for 20 minutes to allow the surface to brown, and season the fillet with salt and pepper. After 25 minutes, test the internal temperature by inserting a meat thermometer in the center of the beef—for rare fillet, it should register 120°F. When the meat reaches that temperature, transfer it to a hot platter or a carving board and let it rest for at least 5 minutes before carving. Unlike other beef roasts, I always carve a delicate rare fillet into slices ½ inch thick.

ELIZABETH DAVID'S STUFFED FILLET OF BEEF

✑ MAKES 10 TO 12 SERVINGS

This stuffed fillet needs slightly longer cooking at a lower temperature to allow the meat to become permeated with the flavors of the stuffing. Serve with Quick Brown Sauce (page 352) and tiny buttered new potatoes.

> 4 to 5 medium yellow onions, thinly sliced
> 3 tablespoons unsalted butter
> 3 tablespoons olive oil
> ¼ pound thinly sliced ham, preferably Smithfield,
>   cut into julienne strips
> 10 anchovy fillets in oil, drained and coarsely
>   chopped
> 1 garlic clove, finely chopped
> 16 to 18 Mediterranean black olives, pitted and
>   coarsely chopped
> 1 teaspoon dried thyme
> ½ teaspoon dried rosemary
> ¼ cup finely chopped fresh flat-leaf parsley
> 2 large eggs
> Kosher salt and freshly ground black pepper
> 5- to 6-pound fillet of beef (beef tenderloin), well
>   trimmed with all fat and tendon removed
> 2 to 3 tablespoons unsalted butter, melted,
>   for brushing the fillet

Cook the onions in the 3 tablespoons butter and oil in a large skillet over medium-high heat until just limp, about 5 minutes. Add the ham, anchovies, garlic, olives, thyme, rosemary, and parsley and mix well. Remove from heat, quickly stir in the eggs, return to low heat, and stir until mixture thickens, about 3 minutes. Season with very little salt, as the anchovies and ham are salty, and 1 teaspoon pepper.

Cut the fillet crosswise into 1-inch slices, cutting about two-thirds of the way down. Spoon the stuffing between the slices. Reshape and tie securely with kitchen twine. Brush well with melted butter. Place on a rack in a roasting pan, and roast in a preheated 350°F oven for 40 to 50 minutes, or until a meat thermometer inserted in the center of the roast registers 125°F for medium rare. Let stand for 10 minutes before serving.

Editor: Elizabeth David is generally acknowledged to be the doyenne of modern British cookery, and her reign as such in England roughly coincided with Beard's tenure as the dean of American cooking.

LONDON BROIL
(BROILED FLANK STEAK)

∽ MAKES 4 SERVINGS

Although this thin fibrous steak, the triangular piece on the underside, below the loin, is not a tender cut, it is delicious if broiled very fast and sliced very thinly. If you can, get a prime flank steak, which will be a tenderer, better quality. If not, buy the choice grade. Serve with Sauce Diable (page 353) and sliced French bread. Flank steak also makes great sandwiches.

Rub the steak well on both sides with **kosher salt, freshly ground black pepper,** and a little **Tabasco.**

Preheat the broiler. Rub the broiling rack with **vegetable oil**; arrange the flank steak on the rack and put the boiler pan and rack on the top oven shelf, so that the surface of the steak is 1½ to 2 inches from the heat. Broil for 3 to 4 minutes on each side for rare meat—which this has to be.

Carve into very thin slices on the diagonal, slicing across the fibers, which will give you tender, edible pieces of meat.

VARIATION

TERIYAKI FLANK STEAK: Do not season the meat. Make a teriyaki marinade by mixing **½ cup Japanese soy sauce, ½ cup olive oil, ¼ cup dry sherry, 2 chopped garlic cloves, 2 tablespoons grated fresh ginger,** and the finely **grated zest of 1 tangerine or orange** in a bowl. Put the steak in a dish or deep platter in which it can lay flat and pour the marinade over it. Marinate for 2 to 3 hours, turning the steak occasionally. Broil as before, 1½ to 2 inches from the heat, for 3 to 4 minutes a side. When you turn the meat, brush the upturned side with the marinade.

BEEF SHASHLIK

MAKES 4 TO 6 SERVINGS

Serve the shashlik with steamed rice, Bulghur Pilaf (page 260), or Potatoes Anna (page 240).

3 pounds lean beef sirloin, cut into 2-inch cubes

For the Red Wine Marinade

⅔ cup dry red wine

½ cup olive oil

2 tablespoons freshly squeezed lemon juice

3 garlic cloves, finely chopped

1 tablespoon chopped fresh dill or 1 teaspoon dried dill

1 teaspoon kosher salt

1 teaspoon freshly ground black pepper

Whole cherry or plum tomatoes (optional)

Mushroom caps (optional)

Squares of green bell pepper (optional)

2 tablespoons olive oil

To make the marinade: Whisk the ingredients together in a glass or pottery bowl. Add the beef cubes, cover with plastic wrap, and refrigerate from 4 to 48 hours, turning frequently.

When ready to cook, thread the beef on metal grilling skewers, as for shish kebab, alternating the cubes, if you wish, with the optional vegeta-bles. Arrange the skewers on the broiler pan and brush with oil, lubricating the vegetables well.

Preheat the broiler. Broil the shashlik 3 inches from the heat, turning and brushing with the marinade during the first 5 minutes, until the meat is crusty on the outside and rare within, about 8 to 9 minutes for rare and 9 to 10 minutes for medium-rare. Test by making a small cut with a knife in one of the cubes.

BOEUF BOURGUIGNON
(BEEF IN RED BURGUNDY)

MAKES 10 SERVINGS

Boeuf bourguignon, or beef in red Burgundy, is probably one of the most universally favored of all braised beef dishes, but it is also one that is often ruined by poor cooking and overseasoning. The usual method is to cut the beef into cubes, and they invariably become boiled-tasting and stringy. A much more successful way is to cook the meat like a pot roast, in one piece so that you can lard it, thus providing natural basting of fat as it cooks. Serve with boiled potatoes.

One 5-pound bottom round of beef roast

6 to 8 lardons (½-inch-thick strips of pork fatback, cut as long as the roast), soaked for 1 hour in Cognac

All-purpose flour

10 tablespoons (1¼ sticks) unsalted butter, plus 4 tablespoons (½ stick) unsalted butter, at room temperature (optional)

12 mushrooms caps, trimmed

2 leeks, white and green parts only, coarsely
    chopped, and washed well to remove grit

3 garlic cloves, coarsely chopped

Kosher salt and freshly ground black pepper

3 cups good red Burgundy wine [*Editor: California or*
    Oregon Pinot Noir will do]

2 cups Beef Stock (page 349)

1 teaspoon dried thyme or a sprig of fresh thyme

3 or 4 sprigs fresh flat-leaf parsley

1 bay leaf

24 small white boiling onions, peeled
    (see page 237)

1 teaspoon sugar

Four ½-inch-thick slices salt pork, rind removed,
    cut into ½-inch dice

Chopped fresh flat-leaf parsley, for garnish

Lard the beef as for pot roast (see page 70). Brown the larded beef on all sides under the broiler. Sprinkle the browned roast lightly with flour, and turn so the flour browns lightly.

Melt 6 tablespoons of the butter over medium-high heat in a Dutch oven. Add the mushrooms, leeks, and garlic and sauté until the mushrooms are lightly browned, about 5 minutes. Remove and reserve the mushrooms. Add the beef to the Dutch oven, salt and pepper well, then add the wine, stock, thyme, parsley, and bay leaf. Bring to a boil, reduce the heat to medium-low, put a piece of buttered waxed paper on top of the meat, cover the Dutch oven, and simmer for 1 hour.

Meanwhile, brown the onions in a skillet in 2 tablespoons of the butter over medium heat, about 3 minutes. Sprinkle with the sugar, and shake until lightly glazed. Set aside. Melt the remaining 2 tablespoons butter in the skillet over medium

heat, add the salt pork, and cook until browned and slightly crisp, about 5 minutes. Set aside.

Test the beef for tenderness. If it seems fairly tender, add the onions and cook until just tender, 50 to 60 minutes. Remove from the heat, uncover, and let stand 15 minutes to allow the fat to rise to the top of the cooking liquid. Skim off the excess fat, add the mushrooms and salt pork to the pot and simmer for 10 minutes. Transfer the beef to a hot platter and arrange the onions, mushrooms, and salt pork around it. If desired, thicken the sauce with beurre manié: mash the softened butter with ¼ cup flour in a medium bowl with a rubber spatula until smooth. Whisk in about 2 cups of the cooking liquid. Now whisk this mixture back into the Dutch oven, bring to a simmer, and cook, stirring often, until thickened and no raw flour taste remains in the sauce, about 5 minutes. Taste and correct the seasoning. Spoon some of the sauce onto the platter with the vegetables and sprinkle with the chopped parsley. Carve the meat and serve.

NOTE: The beef is much better if made in advance, skimmed of all fat, and reheated the next day. In this case, prepare the mushrooms, onions, and salt pork, and add to the beef when reheated.

BEEF BOURGUIGNON SAUTÉ

✐ MAKES 6 SERVINGS

This quick version of the classic Beef Bourguignon is to my mind infinitely better, as the beef does not get dry from long cooking and it remains rare in the center. For this you must have a very tender beef fillet or sirloin. [*Editor: The original title was "Instant Beef Bourguignon," but today's cooks would call this a sauté.*]

2½ cups Quick Brown Sauce (page 352) *[350 handwritten]*

1½ cups red wine, preferably Burgundy or California or Oregon Pinot Noir

½ teaspoon dried thyme

1 slice of lemon

One 1-inch strip orange zest, removed from the orange with a vegetable peeler

1 bay leaf

Kosher salt and freshly ground black pepper

14 tablespoons (1¾ sticks) unsalted butter

12 to 18 small white boiling onions, peeled

2 teaspoons sugar

¼ cup Beef Stock (page 349)

12 to 18 firm white mushroom caps

Four ½-inch thick slices salt pork, rind removed, cut into ½-inch dice

2½ pounds beef tenderloin or sirloin, cut into 1¼-inch cubes

Chopped fresh flat-leaf parsley for garnish

To make the Sauce Bourguignon: Have your brown sauce in one pan. In another saucepan, bring the wine, thyme, lemon slice, orange zest, bay leaf, and 1 teaspoon salt and 1 teaspoon pepper to a boil, then reduce the heat and simmer until reduced to 1 cup. Strain into the brown sauce, bring to a boil, and simmer gently for 30 to 45 minutes. This is our Sauce Bourguignon. Taste, and correct the seasoning, then cover the surface of the sauce with buttered waxed paper and set aside until ready to complete the dish.

While the sauce simmers, heat 4 tablespoons of the butter in a skillet, add the onions, and sauté over medium-high heat, sprinkling with the white sugar so they glaze and brown. Add the stock, cover, and steam until just crisply tender, about 10 minutes. In another skillet, melt 3 tablespoons of the butter, add the mushrooms, and sauté over medium-high heat until lightly colored, about 5 minutes. Remove the mushrooms, add 2 tablespoons of the butter to the skillet, and sauté the salt pork until crisply browned. Remove, drain, combine with onions and mushrooms, and set aside, covered with aluminum foil.

About 10 minutes before you are ready to serve, heat the remaining 5 tablespoons butter in a heavy skillet. Add the beef cubes, a few at a time, and sauté over high heat until well seared and browned on all sides, about 3 minutes. Transfer to a plate. Return all of the beef to the skillet. Add the Sauce Bourguignon, let it just come to a boil. Add the onions, mushrooms, and salt pork, and cook until just heated through—not long enough to overcook the beef. This has to be a very fast operation. Garnish with chopped parsley and serve.

JEANNE OWEN'S CHILI CON CARNE

♒ **MAKES 6 SERVINGS**

This recipe for southwestern chili con carne, while not for purists, is rather different and utterly delicious. It improves with aging, so make it the day before you wish to serve it, and reheat. Toasted French bread, tortillas, or corn bread go well with this, and a crisp green salad.

Editor: Jeanne Owen worked for the International Food & Wine Society, a New York–based gourmet club consisting of well-heeled Manhattanites. It is interesting that the Francophile Ms. Owen shares a recipe for chili.

⅓ cup olive oil

3 pounds lean round steak, cut into 1-inch cubes

2 medium yellow onions, finely chopped

3 garlic cloves, finely chopped

Kosher salt

2 to 4 tablespoons chili powder, or to taste

2 teaspoons sesame seeds

1 teaspoon caraway seeds

½ teaspoon dried oregano

4 cups boiling water

1 cup pitted green olives

Two 15- to 19-ounce cans kidney beans, drained
    and well rinsed

Heat the oil in a Dutch oven over medium-high heat. Working in batches, add the beef, and sauté, turning to brown on all sides, for about 3 minutes. Transfer to a plate. Add the chopped onions and sauté over medium heat for 2 or 3 minutes, then add the garlic. Return the beef to the pot. Season with salt. Stir in the chili powder, sesame seeds, caraway seeds, and oregano and cook for 1 minute. Stir in the boiling water. Reduce the heat to medium-low, cover, and simmer for 1 hour.

Add the olives and continue cooking until the beef is tender, about 1 hour more. Taste, and correct the seasoning, then mix in the beans and heat through.

DAUBE PROVENÇAL

 MAKES 8 TO 10 SERVINGS

Editor: Daube is the Provençal version of beef stew. Marinate it one day before cooking. It is even better if you refrigerate the cooled stew overnight and reheat it before serving.

One 750-ml bottle dry red wine

4 pounds beef shin or 3 pounds beef rump roast

2 pig's feet, split lengthwise

Four ½-inch slices salt pork, rind removed

1 teaspoon dried rosemary

Several sprigs of fresh flat-leaf parsley

8 garlic cloves, chopped

1 whole clove

2 bay leaves

One 2-inch strip of orange zest, removed from the
    orange with a vegetable peeler

1 tablespoon kosher salt

2 teaspoons freshly ground black pepper

1 pound macaroni, cooked and drained, for serving

Combine all of the ingredients (except the macaroni) in a large stainless steel, glass, or crockery bowl and mix well. Cover with plastic wrap and refrigerate for 24 hours.

Transfer the marinated ingredients to a large Dutch oven (not uncoated cast-iron). Bake in a preheated 225°F oven until the meat is very tender, about 6 hours. Remove from the oven and let stand for 20 to 25 minutes. Skim off the excess fat. Transfer the meats (you may discard the pig's feet) to a hot deep platter. Strain the sauce. Mix about 2 cups of the sauce with the macaroni.

(This is called *macaronnade*.) Pour the remaining sauce over the meats.

To serve cold, strain the sauce. Let it cool, and remove the excess fat. Slice the meat, arrange in a serving dish, and cover with the sauce. Chill, then serve in its own sauce, which will have gelatinized.

ESTOUFFAT DE NOËL

✐ MAKES 8 TO 10 SERVINGS

One of the most famous dishes of Gascony, in France, is the *estouffat*, or *estouffade*, a dish of braised beef cooked in a covered earthenware casserole, always with Armagnac, the brandy of the region. This *estouffat de Noël* is a traditional Christmas Eve dish, to which the Armagnac and the gelatin content of the pork rind give a special rich, luscious body and taste. If you can't get pork rind (sold by pork stores and butchers) substitute a pig's foot, split. Serve the *estouffat* with either boiled potatoes or macaroni to soak up the lovely sauce. Drink the same kind of red wine you used for cooking.

1 pound pork rind or 1 pig's foot, split lengthwise

3 or 4 medium onions, peeled and quartered

8 shallots, peeled and quartered

1 medium carrot, cut into 3 by ½-inch strips

1 garlic clove, chopped

1 teaspoon dried thyme

A few gratings of nutmeg

One 6-pound piece top round of beef roast, tied

Kosher salt and freshly ground black pepper

1½ cups Armagnac

2 cups full-bodied red wine, such as a Rhône or a California Syrah

Preheat the oven to 350°F. Put the pork rind or pig's foot on the bottom of a very large (8-quart) Dutch oven (not uncoated cast iron). On this, make a bed of the onions, shallots, and carrot, add the garlic, thyme, and nutmeg. Salt the beef lightly. Make an indentation in the center of the vegetables and in it place the beef. Add the Armagnac and red wine. Cover the pot with a piece of aluminum foil and then the lid.

Bake for 35 minutes. Reduce the heat to 300°F and bake for 1 hour. Then reduce the heat to 250°F and bake for at least 2 hours (and preferably 3 hours, as long, slow cooking is essential to the success of this dish). Or you may simmer the *estouffat* on top of the stove for 1½ hours, then finish the cooking in a 250°F oven.

Remove the casserole or pot from the oven, and let stand for about an hour to let the fat rise to the top of the sauce. Skim off the fat and reheat the beef in the sauce. Or you can make the *estouffat* the day before and refrigerate it overnight, then remove the fat before serving and reheat the meat—to my mind the dish tastes better when made ahead and allowed to cool completely. Before serving, taste the sauce and correct the seasoning. Cut up the pork rind (or the meat from the pig's foot) and serve it with the beef.

VIENNESE GOULASH

The principal flavoring for a Hungarian goulash is paprika, which should also be Hungarian and of the best quality. Hungarian paprika has much more flavor than the standard type and is well worth buying for any dish requiring paprika. You'll find it in specialty shops that sell spices and herbs. [Editor: Hungarian paprika is now available in supermarkets, usually in red cans.] The difference in this recipe, which is a Viennese variation, is the paste of caraway seeds, garlic, and lemon zest stirred in for the final cooking time, which gives a fresh and spicy flavor.

- 4 tablespoons (½ stick) unsalted butter
- 2 tablespoons vegetable oil
- 6 medium yellow onions, thinly sliced
- ¼ cup sweet Hungarian paprika
- ¼ cup dry white wine or cider vinegar
- 3 pounds beef rump or chuck roast, cut into 2-inch cubes
- Kosher salt and freshly ground black pepper
- 1 teaspoon dried thyme
- ½ cup tomato purée
- ¼ cup all-purpose flour
- 2 cups Beef Stock (page 349) or canned beef broth
- 1 tablespoon caraway seeds
- Grated zest of 1 lemon
- 2 garlic cloves, chopped
- Cooked egg noodles, for serving

Heat the butter and oil in a Dutch oven (not uncoated cast iron). Add the onions and sauté until golden over medium heat, stirring them so they do not stick to the pan or brown, about 6 minutes. Mix in the paprika and wine. Cook for 4 minutes. (Spices such as paprika and curry powder should always be cooked a little in fat, to bring out the flavor and prevent the raw taste that occurs when they are not cooked first.)

Push the onions to the side of the pan, add the beef cubes, a few at a time, and sear them on all sides. Don't overcrowd the cubes or they will reduce the heat too much and not brown properly. Transfer them to a plate as they brown.

When all the beef is browned, return it to the pan, season to taste with salt and pepper, add the thyme and tomato purée, and simmer over medium-low heat until the liquid is reduced to a glaze, about 5 minutes. Sprinkle the beef with the flour, and toss with a wooden spatula until the flour is well colored. Add the beef stock (there should be just enough to cover the meat) and simmer, covered, until the beef is tender when pierced with the point of a knife—about 2 hours.

Meanwhile, grind the caraway seeds, lemon zest, and garlic to a paste with a mortar and pestle. When the beef is cooked, stir this paste into the goulash and cook a further 10 minutes to blend the flavors. Serve with the noodles.

DEVILED BEEF BONES

When you carve a standing rib roast, leave some meat on the rib bones and you can turn them into crunchy deviled beef bones. If you freeze the bones from 2 or 3 roasts, you should have enough for a meal—3 or 4 ribs a serving. When you are ready to cook them, thaw them until they have reached room temperature, then cut the ribs apart, leaving some meat between them.

    8 to 10 beef ribs from rib roasts

    8 tablespoons (1 stick) unsalted butter, melted

    2 tablespoons tarragon vinegar

    2 to 2½ cups very fine fresh bread crumbs

    Sauce Diable (page 353)

Have the ribs at room temperature. Preheat the broiler. Combine the butter and vinegar in a deep soup bowl and put the crumbs in a pie plate. First dip the ribs in the butter mixture, and then roll them in the crumbs, pressing into the bones so the crumbs adhere. Arrange them in a broiler pan, leaving space between them. Broil 6 or 7 inches from the heat so they cook very slowly and the crumbs don't burn. Keep turning the ribs with tongs until you get a good crisp brown coating on all sides. The cooking time will be 15 to 20 minutes. Serve hot, with the sauce.

Editor: You don't have to wait until you have left-over ribs from beef roasts, as uncooked beef ribs are sold at supermarkets and wholesale clubs, especially during the summer grilling and winter holiday seasons. Season the ribs with kosher salt and freshly ground black pepper and bake in a preheated 400°F oven until browned, about 20 minutes. Let cool completely, then follow the recipe as directed.

BROILED STEAK

Steaks should be bought by thickness, not by weight. Because of the variance in size and shape between different cuts, it is very difficult to gauge how much a steak is going to weigh. It's my feeling that a 1- to 1½-inch steak is the minimum thickness for broiling; anything thinner is better sautéed. Then, of course, there are times when you splurge and get a very thick steak of 2½ to 3 inches. However, for now, let us take a 1½-inch steak as our example.

When you buy a steak, you must consider the grade. The better the grade, the tenderer the cut. Prime is the top grade, but most of this goes to restaurants. Choice is the grade you are likely to find in your meat market and it is the best buy. When picking out steak, look for meat that is deep red in color and well marbled with cream-colored fat. If you can, have the steaks specially cut for you rather than picking up a ready-packaged steak in the supermarket. The butcher will weigh the steak after cutting it to the thickness you want.

Allow roughly 6 to 8 ounces of boneless meat per serving. If you are not buying a boneless cut like the eye of the rib or eye of the sirloin, but rather a larger bone-in steak such as a sirloin or porterhouse, estimate ¾ to 1 pound of meat per serving to compensate for the weight and waste of the bone.

You don't have to buy individual steaks for everyone. A large bone-in sirloin steak of 4 pounds will feed 4 people nicely if you carve it at table, first cutting around the bone and then slicing it diagonally into ½-inch strips. If you're just cooking steak for yourself, however, you are better off with a small club steak, a rib or eye of the rib, or a strip steak from the loin. If it is rather more than you want to eat, don't worry. Cold steak makes great sandwiches.

Broiling Method for Any 1½-Inch Steak

Preheat the broiler. Trim excess fat from the steak, leaving a rim about ½ inch thick. Slash the rim to keep it from curling.

Brush the broiler rack with oil or rub it with some of the fat trimmed from the steak. Salt and pepper one side of the meat and arrange it, seasoned side up, on the rack of the broiler pan. Before putting the steak under the broiler, press it with your finger. It will feel very soft. Remember this later when you test the cooked steak.

Put the broiler pan under the broiler with the surface of the steak 3 inches from the heat, or as close to 3 inches as possible.

For a very rare steak, broil for 8 to 12 minutes, 4 to 6 minutes a side. For a rare steak, broil for 10 to 14 minutes, 5 to 7 minutes a side. When I'm broiling a steak, I sometimes give it an extra half minute on the first side, because it doesn't really begin to sear until it has been in the oven for a half minute. Halfway through the cooking time, turn the steak with metal tongs, not with a fork, which would pierce the flesh and let the juices escape, and season the second side before broiling it.

There are two schools of thought about how often to turn a steak during cooking. Some people like to sear one side, turn and sear the second side, turn it back again and cook on each side for the rest of the cooking time. Frankly, I don't think it does anything for a steak to keep turning it back and forth. Once is enough.

About 2 minutes before the end of the cooking time, test the steak to see if it is done to your liking. There are three ways you can determine this. One is to remove the pan from the broiler and insert a meat thermometer horizontally through the side (not in the top) of the steak to the center, but not touching the bone, if there is one. The internal temperature for a very rare steak is 120° to 125°F and for a rare steak 130° to 135°F. (Medium, if you must, would be 140° to 145°F.)

The second way is to make a little cut in the meat near the bone or the rim of fat with a small sharp knife and check the inside of the meat. If it is done the way you like it, that's fine. If not, return the pan to the broiler and continue to cook the steak for a minute or so longer.

The third test, which is one professionals use and you will gradually learn to rely on, is to press the center of the steak lightly with your finger (it won't burn you), remembering how it felt when raw. A rare steak will feel firm on the surface but soft within. Were it to be medium, the steak would feel slightly resistant, and a well-done one, perish the thought, would be quite firm. Practice touching steak broiled to the state you prefer and you'll soon become accustomed to testing this way.

When your steaks are broiled, put them on hot plates or a hot platter, or if you are going to carve a large steak at table, on a carving board. I like to put a pat of butter on a steak the minute it comes out of the oven, either plain unsalted butter or butter mixed with an herb such as crushed rosemary or thyme (use a ratio of about ½ teaspoon dried herbs to 2 tablespoons butter, see Compound Butters, page 17.) The butter melts and runs over the meat, mingling with the juices when you cut into or carve the meat and making a little sauce. If you are carving the steak into slices, spoon some of the luscious mingled juices and butter over each serving.

A good steak needs little or no embellishment. You can sit down and eat it just as it is, or you can have broiled tomatoes or broiled mushrooms with it or a green salad, or you can shoot the works and have potatoes or French fries, a green vegetable, and a salad. That's up to you. If you wish to be really elegant, you might have a Béarnaise Sauce (page 355), sautéed potatoes, and a vegetable or salad.

Timings for Steaks of Other Thicknesses

- **FOR A STEAK 1 INCH THICK:** Broil 2 inches from the heat, 3 minutes a side for very rare; 4 to 5 minutes a side for rare.

- **FOR A STEAK 2 INCHES THICK:** Allow the longer broiling time given for a 1½-inch steak, broiling 3 inches from the heat.

- **FOR A STEAK 2½ TO 3 INCHES THICK:** Broil with the surface of the steak 5 to 6 inches from the heat and allow 20 to 35 minutes total broiling time for very rare; 30 to 40 minutes for rare.

With an extremely thick steak you must allow time for the heat to penetrate and warm the interior, even though it does not actually cook it. You'll have a fairly charred surface and a rare interior. The lowering of the rack compensates for the longer broiling time.

STEAK AU POIVRE

MAKES 2 SERVINGS

One of the simplest of all sautés is a *steak au poivre*, which is now popular throughout the world, although I can remember the time when you found it only in France. Gradually, people became so enamored of this delicious combination of pepper-flavored beef and Cognac, with sometimes a little cream, that you find it served from New York to Seattle. Sautéed potatoes, a green salad, and a good red wine are all you'll need with this delicious steak.

The best cut for individual steaks au poivre is the loin strip, otherwise known as a shell steak, a *faux filet*, a sirloin strip steak, or a New York cut, according to what part of the country you live in. This is the loin steak without the smaller part, the fillet, and usually with the bone trimmed away, although sometimes a little bit of the bone is left on. The steak should be 1½ inches thick.

To cook the steaks you will need a heavy-duty skillet or sauté pan, 12 inches in diameter—it must be large enough to accommodate the two steaks, side by side, with some room left over. They must not be squeezed together.

> 2 loin strip steaks, about 1½ inches thick
> 1½ tablespoons whole black peppercorns
> 1 teaspoon or more kosher salt
> 3 tablespoons unsalted butter
> 3 tablespoons vegetable oil
> ⅓ cup Cognac or bourbon

About 2 hours before you plan to cook the steaks, remove them from the refrigerator and leave them at room temperature. Before cooking, trim any excess fat from the side of the steak with a small, sharp paring knife, leaving just a thin strip for lubrication—a good piece of sirloin will be well marbled with fat and that will also lubricate the meat as it cooks. Fat is the flavor-giver for meat, and if you cut off all the fat you will take away some of the flavor of the meat, the part that has settled in the fat.

Now crush or grind the peppercorns very, very coarsely. If your peppermill doesn't grind coarsely enough, it is advisable to crush them in a mortar and pestle, or to wrap them in a towel and beat them with a mallet, or you may use a blender or food processor, which does the job fast and isn't so arduous.

Sprinkle the top of each steak with 1 to 1½ teaspoons of the coarsely ground peppercorns, and with the heel of your hand (which has the most strength in it), press the pepper into the meat. Turn the steaks and repeat on the other side. Let the steaks rest for 15 minutes before sautéing. Just about 2 minutes before you put the steaks on to cook, sprinkle one side with salt, using about ½ teaspoon for each steak. Many people tell you that this will draw out the juices but I maintain that when meat sears as fast as this does, the salt is absorbed and the surface immediately sealed.

Heat the butter and oil in the skillet over medium-high heat. As oil can be heated to a higher temperature than butter without burning, the oil prevents the butter from burning at the rather high heat one uses to sauté steak. For this reason, you should also use unsalted rather than salted butter, which is more inclined to burn. If you prefer, you may omit the butter and use all

oil, or you can substitute beef drippings, if you have any, or chop up the fat you trimmed from the steak, throw that into the skillet and let it melt and render into fat.

When the fat is sizzling but not smoking (if it smokes, it is too hot, and you will have to throw it out and start again), place the steaks, salted side down, in the hot fat. The steak will sizzle as it hits the fat and you don't want it to stick, so shake the skillet very gently to move the steaks around. Cook for about 3 minutes on that side, shaking the skillet back and forth very gently, then salt the uncooked side, turn the steaks with tongs, and cook 3 minutes on that side. Now reduce the heat to medium, turn the steaks again, and cook for 3 minutes more on each side—that's 3 minutes a side for searing plus 3 minutes a side for cooking at the lower temperature, for a total of 12 minutes.

To make sure the steak is done to your taste, remove the skillet from the heat and with a very sharp paring knife and a fork make a small incision in the thickest part of the steak (or, if there is bone, next to the bone) and push the meat apart to see if it is cooked as you like it. If not, you may give the steaks a minute or two more. For this thickness, 6 minutes a side should give you a really rare steak. Eight minutes a side will give you medium-rare steak.

Transfer the steaks to a hot platter and keep warm. Shake the skillet well, remove it from the heat, and pour the Cognac into the skillet. Strike a long match and very carefully place it at the side of the skillet—the fumes of alcohol from the heated Cognac will immediately ignite and burn with a great flame, so keep your head and hands well out of range as you do this. Hold the skillet by the handle and shake it gently until the flames die down—they will have burned off all the excess fat and lifted the brown glaze from the bottom of the skillet, making a little sauce for the steak. Should a tiny bit of flame linger, tightly cover the pan. Pour the sauce over the steak and serve it at once.

Contrary to what some people think, the pepper should on no account be scraped off the steak before you eat it, but eaten and enjoyed. It's really like a condiment, and it is that lovely charred peppery taste and crunchy crustiness on the outside that makes steak au poivre the great dish it is. You may serve the steaks as they come, or cut them into thin diagonal slices.

STEAK TARTARE

∞ MAKES 6 SERVINGS

Probably the most famous of all raw meat dishes, steak tartare requires beef that is very tender and absolutely fresh. Serve as a light main course for luncheon with toast fingers on the side, or as a snack.

Editor: Because of the risk of food-borne illness associated with raw and undercooked meat, the USDA recommends cooking ground beef to an internal temperature of 160°F. And raw eggs have been known to carry the potentially harmful salmonella bacterium, and should not be served to people with compromised immune systems, the very young, or the elderly.

---

2 pounds beef fillet, sirloin, or top round, trimmed very well, with no fat

2 medium yellow onions, finely chopped

½ cup drained and rinsed nonpareil capers

⅓ cup Cognac

¼ cup finely chopped fresh flat-leaf parsley

2 teaspoons Dijon mustard

2 large egg yolks

2 teaspoons kosher salt

1 teaspoon freshly ground black pepper

Tabasco

6 anchovy fillets in oil, drained (optional)

1 tablespoon finely chopped fresh flat-leaf parsley, plus more for garnish

6 large egg yolks, for serving (optional)

The best steak tartare is made of chopped (not ground) fillet. Using a heavy chef's knife, cut the meat into finger strips and then chop it very finely. [*Editor: It helps if the meat is very well chilled, even partially frozen, for this step.*] Combine the meat with the onions, capers, Cognac, parsley, mustard, yolks, salt, and pepper, and season with Tabasco. You may, if you wish, add finely chopped anchovy fillets (in which case, reduce the salt, as anchovies are very salty), or serve the whole anchovy fillets on the side. Mix everything together very well and taste for seasoning.

If you have a food processor, cut the meat into cubes and put into the processor with the onions, roughly cut up, and the other ingredients, omitting the egg yolks (which will give the machine-chopped mixture an undesirable texture) and following the above advice about the anchovies. Process until the meat is finely ground and well mixed with the other ingredients.

Transfer the steak tartare to a bowl and gently mix in the parsley. For individual servings, form the tartare into 6 mounds on serving plates. Make a hollow in the top of each mound, drop a raw egg into each hollow, and garnish with more chopped parsley. The egg is to be mixed into the beef by each person.

VARIATION

COCKTAIL STEAK TARTARE: For cocktail food, form the mixture into balls about ¼ inch in diameter, roll them in chopped fresh parsley or chopped hazelnuts, and pile them in a mound, to be speared with toothpicks.

SWISS STEAK

MAKES 4 SERVINGS

Swiss steak is a dependable, economical, easily prepared braised beef dish that has been an American favorite for a long time. How, I wonder, did it ever get that name? It's not Swiss, and it's not really steak, in our accepted usage of that word. Be that as it may, it's delicious, simple, and enables you to make a good meal from an inexpensive and less tender cut of meat that needs long, slow cooking to make it tender. The best cuts for this are a piece of chuck steak from the shoulder or a bottom round of beef. If you are shopping in the supermarket, where meats are precut and packaged, look at the chuck steak carefully. If it has part of the blade bone in it and a lot of fat, don't buy it. You are better off paying a little more and buying a piece of bottom round, which is all meat, rather than a piece of chuck with a lot of waste. The meat should be cut like a steak, from 2 to 2½ inches thick, weighing about 2 to 2½ pounds, which will serve 4 persons of good appetite. If you find a chuck steak without too much fat and just a tiny bit of bone, buy it. You can cut around the bone. Meat that has the least bone is the best buy, even though you may pay more for it.

To cook the Swiss steak you'll need a very heavy skillet or sauté pan with a tight-fitting cover, about 2 to 3 inches deep, made of iron, stainless steel, or enameled cast iron. You'll also need kitchen tongs and an old dinner plate or a cleaver or a meat pounder, to pound the flour into the steak. Plain boiled potatoes or boiled buttered noodles go well with this, and a salad. Drink the same kind of red wine you used in cooking and follow with cheese and fruit.

One 2- to 2½-pound chuck or bottom round steak, cut 2 to 2½ inches thick

½ cup or more of all-purpose flour

1 teaspoon freshly ground black pepper

4 tablespoons (½ stick) unsalted butter, butter and oil, bacon fat, or beef drippings

2 medium yellow onions, sliced

2 garlic cloves, coarsely chopped

1½ teaspoons kosher salt

1 to 1½ cups dry red wine

½ cup water or Beef Stock (page 349)

Chopped fresh flat-leaf parsley, for garnish

Put the meat on a cutting board and sprinkle the top quite heavily with flour—at least 2 or 3 tablespoons. Then grind ½ teaspoon pepper over it. Using the edge of the dinner plate, the back of a cleaver, or a meat pounder, pound the flour into the meat until a good deal of the flour is absorbed, working first along the width of the meat and then the length. Keep pounding so that the plate makes pressure marks in the meat and the flour holds in there. When you have done one side, dust off the excess flour and repeat the flour-and-pepper process on the other side. The steak should absorb 4 to 5 tablespoons of flour, which will give body to the sauce as it cooks and thickens it—this is the technique that makes it Swiss steak.

After the flour is pounded in, let the meat rest for 10 minutes. Melt the fat in the skillet over medium-high heat until is it bubbling and sizzling, but not smoking. Dip the meat in the remaining flour and place it in the hot fat. Let it bubble and sizzle over medium-high heat for 4 to 5 minutes, until deliciously brown on the underside, being careful not to let the flour burn. Just as you are about to turn the steak, add the onions and garlic to the pan. Turn the steak, brown it on the other side, and let the onions and garlic take on color. Sprinkle with the salt, remove the pan from the heat, and add the red wine and water. The wine will give the sauce a good color and richness, and when blended with the broth and water the flavor is not too intense. You should add just enough liquid to come halfway up the steak—you don't want to inundate it, as you will get some liquid from the onions as they cook down.

Return the skillet to the heat, reduce to a simmer, cover tightly, and simmer for 1½ hours. Test for doneness with a fork or the point of a sharp knife and turn the steak. If it is tender enough (the fork or knife should penetrate the meat easily), taste the sauce to see if it needs more salt and pepper or more garlic. If it still needs cooking, cover again and continue simmering until tender. You don't want the meat to be so tender that it loses all its texture, but it should be tender enough to cut easily.

When done, transfer the steak to a hot platter and, using a slotted spoon to drain off the liquid, spoon the onions over it. Then see if there is a lot of fat on the top of the sauce—there shouldn't be, unless your beef was too fatty. To remove excess fat, let the sauce boil up for a minute, then remove the skillet from the heat and skim off the fat on the surface.

Pour the sauce over the steak, putting any surplus in a small bowl or gravy boat to be served separately, and sprinkle with some chopped parsley.

ZRAZYS NELSON

MAKES 6 SERVINGS

This Polish recipe involves three difference sautés—potatoes, cucumbers with mushrooms, and thick slices of tender fillet of beef.

[Editor: Zrazys are usually stuffed meat rolls, but this version is somewhat deconstructed from the classic. If you use the canned French-fried onions, heat them in a 350°F oven on a baking sheet until crisp, about 10 minutes.]

---

8 to 10 medium-small potatoes, scrubbed but unpeeled

12 tablespoons (1½ sticks) unsalted butter, or more as needed

Kosher salt and freshly ground black pepper

4 cucumbers, peeled and thinly sliced

18 firm white mushrooms, thinly sliced

¼ cup all-purpose flour

2 cups heavy cream

1 tablespoon tomato purée

Twelve ½-inch-thick slices of beef tenderloin

French Fried Onion Rings (page 238) or use canned
    French-fried onion rings

Put the potatoes in a large pot of lightly salted water. Bring to a boil and reduce the heat to medium. Cook until almost, but not quite, tender, when pierced with a sharp knife. Drain and rinse under cold running water. Peel the potatoes and slice about ¼ inch thick. Heat 4 tablespoons of the butter in a heavy skillet over medium-high heat. Sauté the potatoes in batches until nicely browned and crisp at the edges, about 10 minutes. Add more butter as needed. As they are cooked, sprinkle lightly with salt and pepper and transfer them to a large heatproof serving platter, making a bed for the beef. Keep warm in a 250°F oven.

Wipe out the skillet with paper towels, add 4 tablespoons of the butter and heat until bubbling over medium-high heat. Add the cucumbers and mushrooms and sauté, tossing and turning, until the cucumbers are soft and the mushrooms lightly browned, about 8 minutes. Mix in the flour. Gradually add the cream and cook over medium heat, stirring constantly, until thickened, about 3 minutes. Mix in the tomato purée and season with salt and pepper. Keep warm while sautéing the beef.

Melt 4 tablespoons of the butter in another heavy skillet and heat until the foam subsides. Working in batches, sauté the beef slices on both sides, for 2 to 3 minutes a side, or until nicely browned on the outside but still rare inside. Do not overcook. As they are cooked, sprinkle them

lightly with salt and arrange them on the bed of potatoes. Cover with the cucumber-mushroom sauce and serve topped with French-fried onion rings.

SAUTÉED HAMBURGERS

MAKES 4 SERVINGS

The hamburger, as we know it, along with the hot dog and the ice cream cone, supposedly came into being at the St. Louis Fair in 1904. Certainly by the time I was growing up, in the early part of the twentieth century, we often took chopped meat patties, well seasoned and sometimes mixed with onion, to the beach and either broiled them or cooked them in an iron skillet on a rack over the coals. We served them on the kind of round bun a hamburger goes on, and sometimes we had onion on them. I suppose some of our friends might have had ketchup, too, though our family wasn't too keen on ketchup, nor am I now.

A good hamburger is one of the most basic meat dishes you can make, but even here there are one or two tricks you should know. In my opinion, hamburgers are best pan-fried or sautéed in a heavy skillet in oil, a combination of butter and oil, or clarified butter, all of which can be heated to a higher temperature without burning than plain butter. I think this gives a juicier, crustier hamburger than broiling, and it is easier to control the degree of doneness. You will need a heavy cast-iron skillet, or whatever you normally use for sautéing (with a nonstick skillet, you won't need much fat, just about 1 tablespoon for flavor), and a large spatula for turning the hamburgers.

2 pounds chopped beef, preferably top round
 or chuck

Kosher salt

Freshly ground black pepper

2 tablespoons peanut oil, or equal amounts of oil and
 butter or clarified butter

Divide the meat into 4 equal portions, seasoning it to taste with salt and pepper, and form it gently and lightly into patties with your hands, almost tossing it back and forth. Be careful not to press or overhandle the meat. Too much handling makes for heavy, solid patties, and that is not what you want at all. The meat should just hold together. You can make your patties round or oval, thick or fairly flat, according to how you like them. For rare hamburgers, make them thick. For medium, make them thinner. They won't be perfectly shaped. They'll be sort of free-form, but that's all right. Taste is more important than appearance.

Heat the oil, or whatever you are using, in a heavy skillet. There should be just a film of fat on the surface. When it is hot, but not smoking, put the patties in the pan and cook briskly on one side for 4 minutes over fairly high heat until good and brown. Turn them carefully with a large spatula and cook 4 minutes on the other side. Press the browned surface gently with your finger. See how much firmer it is than uncooked meat. Then press the sides. These will be less firm because the center meat has not cooked as much.

At this point you can almost gauge how near to done the hamburgers are. Reduce the heat slightly and, if you like them rare, give them 2 more minutes on each side. Press them again and you'll find they are slightly resistant to the touch. Transfer them to hot plates and serve at once. When you cut into the hamburger and find it done to your liking, remember the way the patty felt when pressed. This is a very simple test, but it will give you confidence in the message your fingers can send to your brain.

OLD-FASHIONED MEAT LOAF

MAKES 6 TO 8 SERVINGS

To my mind the most delicious meat loaves are made with a combination of ground beef, veal, and pork. The veal adds a gelatinous quality, and the pork richness and fat, which keep the meat loaf juicy. (If you have a food processor, you can grind the meats yourself.) This simple recipe can be varied to taste by using different seasonings and combinations of ingredients. It should not be baked in a loaf pan, incidentally. A meat loaf, if molded and baked free-form on a bed of bacon or salt pork, sheds excess fat and makes a more firmly textured loaf, whereas, if baked in a loaf pan, it becomes much too moist and is sometimes not easily sliced. Hot meat loaf may be served with rice or puréed potatoes and a good homemade tomato sauce, brown sauce with mushrooms, or onion sauce. Cold meat loaf is good with a potato or rice salad, some pickles and relishes, or just a sharp horseradish sauce.

3/4 cup fresh bread crumbs, made in a food processor
 or blender from day-old bread

1/2 cup heavy cream

2 pounds ground beef round or chuck, preferably
  ground twice

1 pound pork shoulder, ground twice

1 pound veal shoulder, ground twice

1 large yellow onion, grated

2 carrots, finely shredded

4 to 6 garlic cloves, finely chopped

2 teaspoons kosher salt

2 teaspoons Dijon mustard

1 teaspoon crushed dried rosemary

1 teaspoon freshly ground black pepper

½ teaspoon Tabasco

¼ teaspoon freshly grated nutmeg

3 large eggs, slightly beaten

12 strips bacon or rindless salt pork

Soak the bread crumbs in the heavy cream in a small bowl for 5 minutes. Combine the beef, pork, veal, onion, carrot, garlic, salt, mustard, rosemary, pepper, Tabasco, and nutmeg in a large bowl. Mix in the eggs and soaked crumbs, combining thoroughly. Make a bed of bacon or salt pork strips in a shallow baking pan, reserving 4 or 5 for the top of the loaf. Form the meat mixture into a firm loaf with your hands and place it on the bed of bacon or salt pork. Put the remaining strips across the top.

Bake in a preheated 350°F oven for 1½ to 2 hours, depending on how thick you have made the loaf, and baste several times with the pan juices. If you want to serve the meat loaf cold, wrap it tightly in aluminum foil and weight it as it cools, until firm. It will taste rather like a French country pâté.

Editor: Unless you are purchasing your meat from an old-school artisan butcher, it is difficult to get *twice-ground meat. If you wish, buy standard ground meat, freeze until firm, then pulse in batches in the food processor fitted with the chopped blade until it is a bit finer. To check for doneness, a meat thermometer inserted in the center of the loaf should register 165°F.*

ROAST BREAST OF VEAL

MAKES 6 SERVINGS

Most people stuff and braise breast of veal (see the following recipe), but I've found that it is absolutely delicious roasted until crisp and carved like a flank steak, with the little bones reserved for munching. If you want to flavor it with an herb, tarragon would be my choice, but frankly I think good veal needs no seasoning other than a little garlic.

One 5- to 6-pound breast of veal

2 to 3 tablespoons olive oil

2 garlic cloves, finely chopped

2 teaspoons finely chopped fresh tarragon
  (optional)

Kosher salt and freshly ground black pepper

Rub the veal with the oil, then with the garlic and the tarragon, if using. Place the veal on the rack of a broiler pan, and broil approximately 4 inches from the heat until the veal is nicely browned—about 20 minutes. Drape aluminum foil over the pan and roast in a 400°F oven for about 30 minutes. Season with salt and pepper. Carve the meat from the bones across the grain on the diagonal in medium-thick slices, removing only the top meat. Cut the bones apart and serve with the sliced meat.

STUFFED BREAST OF VEAL

✑ MAKES 6 SERVINGS

Hot or cold, a stuffed breast of veal is both spectacular and as simple as any dish can be. This is the least expensive cut of veal and the braising process makes it very tender and flavorful. A good butcher who has been trained to bone meat properly will be able to bone the breasts and cut a pocket in it for the stuffing, so that when stuffed it may be formed into a good shape that will slice easily.

If this is not possible, buy the breast unboned and merely have the pocket cut in it—you can remove the little rib bones after the meat is cooked by breaking them away from the joints and pulling them free from the flesh. In either case, you will need some bones for the braising—either those removed from the breast or a veal knuckle or some veal neck bones. Side dishes could be tiny new potatoes browned in butter and a purée of green beans. Drink a Beaujolais.

One 6-pound breast of veal with bones

For the Stuffing
3 tablespoons unsalted butter
8 tablespoons olive oil
3 large onions, peeled and finely chopped
¾ pound bulk pork sausage
½ pound smoked ham, finely chopped
1 cup fresh bread crumbs, made in a food processor or blender from day-old bread
1 truffle, finely chopped, canning liquid reserved (optional)
1 teaspoon dried thyme
Kosher salt and freshly ground black pepper
¼ teaspoon ground cloves
¼ teaspoon freshly grated nutmeg
2 eggs, slightly beaten

For the Braising Mixture and Sauce
Softened butter, for the roasting pan
Bones from veal breast or 1 pound veal knuckle, veal bones, or veal neck with bone
1 medium yellow onion, finely chopped
1 carrot, finely chopped
2 garlic cloves, chopped
1 bay leaf
1½ cups Veal Stock (see variation, page 350), Chicken Stock (page 349), or dry white wine
1½ cups peeled, seeded, and finely chopped tomatoes
1 cup pitted black Mediterranean olives, such as Kalamata
½ cup pine nuts
¼ cup chopped fresh flat-leaf parsley

Using a thin bladed knife, cut the bones from the breast meat in a single slab; set the bones aside. Starting at the thick end of the breast meat, cut a deep, wide pocket into the meat.

To make the stuffing: Heat the butter and 3 tablespoons of the oil in a large skillet. Add the onions, and sauté over medium heat until just limp, about 3 minutes. Transfer to a large bowl. Add the sausage, ham, bread crumbs, truffle and

1 tablespoon of its canning liquid, if using, thyme, 1½ teaspoons salt, 1 teaspoon pepper, and the cloves and nutmeg. Blend the stuffing well and mix in the eggs. Stuff the pocket in the breast, molding with your hands so that it is fairly even in shape.

Secure the stuffing by sewing up the pocket with a trussing needle and fine string or by closing the opening with small metal or bamboo skewers. Heat the remaining 5 tablespoons oil in a heavy skillet and brown the stuffed breast on both sides over medium-high heat. Butter the bottom of a roasting pan large enough to accommodate the breast. Arrange the veal bones, onion, carrot, garlic, and bay leaf in a bed in the bottom of the pan.

Lay the breast on this bed and add the stock and tomatoes. Cover the pan with its lid (or a double thickness of aluminum foil) and braise the meat in a preheated 325°F oven for about 2½ hours, or until a meat thermometer inserted into the veal registers 170°F. If the liquid reduces too much (it should be just sufficient to cover the vegetables), add more stock or wine.

Transfer the cooked meat to a hot platter. Skim the fat from the pan juices. Purée the pan juices and vegetables in a food processor fitted with the metal chopping blade or in a blender with the lid ajar. Reheat the purée in a saucepan with the olives, pine nuts, and parsley, bringing the sauce to a boil and then simmering it for 5 minutes. Carve the veal crosswise into slices about ¾ inch thick and serve with the sauce.

Editor: Beard also recommends serving the breast of veal cold: "Slice it, and serve with a spinach salad dressed with olive oil, lemon juice, and a touch of soy sauce, with finely chopped onion, a little chopped garlic, and a handful of pine nuts added just before it is tossed. Or you might vary this and have the cold meat with a dish of hot macaroni and the reheated sauce from the veal, plus a salad of Bibb lettuce and raw mushrooms."

ROAST LOIN OR SHOULDER OF VEAL

〰 MAKES 8 TO 10 SERVINGS

Editor: Elegant and simple, roast veal can be served with nothing more complicated than buttered asparagus and oven-roasted potatoes. The loin roast is considerably more expensive than the shoulder, and it is a very tender cut fit for very special guests, while veal shoulder makes a fine casual supper.

One 4- to 5-pound veal loin roast, or boned and
    rolled shoulder
1 garlic clove, chopped
1 tablespoon chopped fresh tarragon or 2 teaspoons
    dried tarragon
Kosher salt and freshly ground black pepper
3 strips bacon
⅓ cup dry white wine

Rub the veal well with garlic, tarragon, salt, and pepper, and place on a rack in a shallow roasting pan. Place the strips of bacon over it. Roast in a preheated 325°F oven for approximately 22 minutes per pound, or until a meat thermometer registers 150° for the loin or 165° for the shoulder. Baste occasionally with the wine, then the pan juices.

During the last half hour, remove the bacon so the veal roast can brown. Let stand for 10 minutes before carving. Spoon off all fat from the pan juices and serve the juices with the carved veal.

VITELLO TONNATO
(VEAL WITH TUNA SAUCE)

∽ MAKES 6 TO 8 SERVINGS

There are many ways of preparing this famous Italian specialty, one of the best hot-weather dishes I know. It bears a lively piquant quality that arouses the appetite and pleases the nose. Some people slice cold roast veal and serve it with tuna mayonnaise, but I think it tastes better if the veal is braised and the sauce made with the pan juices. More time-consuming, but worth the extra trouble. Serve with a rice salad or sliced tomatoes.

For the Veal

3 pounds boneless veal loin roast, tied

3 garlic cloves, cut into thin slivers

6 anchovy fillets in oil, drained

1 teaspoon dried basil

5 to 6 tablespoons olive oil

3 medium onions, peeled and thinly sliced

1 carrot, scraped

1 leek, trimmed and washed clean

2 or 3 sprigs fresh flat-leaf parsley

2 pig's feet or 1 veal knuckle, split

1½ cups dry white wine

1 cup water or Chicken Stock (page 349)

1 teaspoon freshly ground black pepper

½ teaspoon salt

For the Tuna Sauce

1½ cups jellied cooking liquid

One-and-a-half (5-ounce) cans tuna packed in olive oil, drained

4 anchovy fillets in oil, drained

2 garlic cloves, peeled

Nonpareil capers, chopped fresh flat-leaf parsley, and chopped fresh basil, for garnish

To prepare the veal: The day before serving, make incisions in the veal with the point of a sharp paring knife. Stuff the garlic slivers into the holes, then insert the anchovy fillets, pushing them in very deeply with the garlic. Rub the meat with the basil and brown it on all sides in the oil in a deep 8-quart Dutch oven. Add the onions, carrot, leek, and parsley, and cook the vegetables a little in the oil. Then add the pig's feet, wine, water, pepper, and salt.

Bring the liquid to a boil, reduce the heat, cover, and simmer the meat on top of the stove or in a preheated 300°F oven for 1½ hours, or until tender when tested with a fork, but not soft and mushy. Remove the meat from the pan to a platter, cover with aluminum foil, and refrigerate overnight. Strain the cooking liquid into a bowl, discarding the solids. Cool the liquid until tepid, cover with plastic wrap, and reserve in the refrigerator overnight.

To make the sauce: Skim the fat from the cold cooking liquid (it should have jellied). Combine 1½ cups jellied juices, the tuna and its oil, the anchovies, and garlic in a food processor or blender. Whirl until well blended and thick.

Remove the veal from the refrigerator and

slice thinly. Arrange on a platter and spoon the tuna sauce over it. Return to the refrigerator until ready to serve, so the veal absorbs the flavor of the sauce. To serve, garnish with capers, chopped parsley, and chopped basil.

VARIATION

VEAL WITH TUNA SAUCE, YOGURT, AND MAYONNAISE: Combine the tuna-anchovy purée with 1 cup each mayonnaise and plain low-fat yogurt. Add additional capers and finely cut scallions. Spoon the sauce over the veal and chill.

OSSI BUCHI

〜 MAKES 4 SERVINGS

Editor: Beard believed that osso buco, *which is Italian for the singular "bone with a hole" and the way this dish is described on many menus, is incorrect. After all, it is cooked with multiple bones, not just one. Ossi buchi are traditionally served with Risotto (page 257). To simplify the side dish, you could substitute Saffron Rice (page 256) for the risotto. The gremolata is a very important element in ossi buchi, as it adds bright, fresh notes to the rich stew.*

For the Veal Shanks

8 veal shanks with marrow, cut about 2 inches thick

6 tablespoons (¾ stick) unsalted butter

1½ cups dry white wine

1½ cups chopped canned Italian plum or chopped fresh plum tomatoes

1½ cups Chicken Stock (page 349)

Kosher salt and freshly ground black pepper

For the Gremolata

2 to 4 garlic cloves, coarsely chopped

⅔ cup coarsely chopped fresh flat-leaf parsley

Freshly grated zest of 1 lemon

To prepare the veal shanks: Tie each veal shank with kitchen twine, in both directions (like the ribbon on a gift box), so as to keep the marrow intact. Melt the butter in a large Dutch oven over medium-high heat. Working in batches, sauté the shanks, turning once, until lightly browned, about 5 minutes. Transfer to a plate. Return them to the Dutch oven, standing them upright. Add the white wine and cook over medium heat until reduced by half, about 10 minutes. Add the tomatoes and stock and season with salt and pepper. Bring to a boil over high heat, then reduce the heat to medium-low. Cover and simmer for 1½ to 2 hours, or until tender.

To make the gremolata: Chop the garlic and parsley together well. Transfer to a small bowl and mix in the lemon zest. Place the veal shanks on a deep serving platter, and remove the strings. Spoon the sauce over them and sprinkle with the gremolata. Serve hot.

VEAL RAGOUT

A simple veal ragout of stew is a great delicacy unless subjected to overcooking, a common habit of many stew makers. Somehow the idea took root that if long cooking is good, longer cooking must be better. This is not the case with a delicate meat like veal. Even the less tender sections are not tough enough to warrant very lengthy cooking. Noodles or rice go well with veal stew.

2½ to 3 pounds veal leg or shoulder cut into
   1½-inch cubes (or riblets cut from the breast)

4 tablespoons (½ stick) unsalted butter

2 tablespoons olive or vegetable oil

1½ tablespoons kosher salt

½ teaspoon freshly ground black pepper

2 medium yellow onions, thinly sliced

2 medium green bell peppers, broiled to blacken the
   skins, peeled, seeded, and cut into strips

1 to 1½ cups drained canned Italian plum tomatoes

¾ cup dry white wine

2 tablespoons chopped fresh basil or ½ teaspoon
   dried basil

2 garlic cloves, finely chopped

¾ cup pitted Mediterranean black olives, preferably
   Italian or Kalamata

Finely chopped fresh flat-leaf parsley, for garnish

Working in batches, brown the veal in a Dutch oven in the butter and oil over medium-high heat. Transfer to a platter. Season with salt and pepper and return to the Dutch oven. Add the onions, bell peppers, tomatoes, wine, basil, and garlic. Bring to a boil, then reduce the heat to medium-low. Simmer, covered, for about 1½ hours, or un-til tender. Add the olives and let the sauce reduce slightly over high heat, uncovered, for 3 to 4 minutes. Transfer the veal to a deep platter with a slotted spoon. Continue boiling the sauce for 4 to 5 minutes more. Correct the seasoning. Pour over the veal and sprinkle with the chopped parsley.

VEAL CHOPS NIÇOISE

Veal chops are extraordinarily good when braised with the proper seasonings. Thickly cut loin chops of the choicest veal are the best to buy. Accompany with a brisk white wine from Provence, well chilled.

For the Tomato Sauce

2½ cups canned Italian plum tomatoes,
   coarsely crushed, juices reserved

1 small onion, finely chopped

3 garlic cloves, finely chopped

3 tablespoons unsalted butter

1 teaspoon kosher salt

½ teaspoon freshly ground black pepper

1 or 2 leaves fresh basil, torn into small bits, or
   ½ teaspoon dried basil

2 tablespoons tomato paste

For the Veal Chops

6 veal loin chops, cut 2 inches thick

¼ cup all-purpose flour

6 tablespoons olive oil

Kosher salt and freshly ground black pepper

3 garlic cloves, peeled and finely chopped

36 black French olives, such as Niçoise or Nyons, pitted

2 tablespoons thinly sliced fresh basil leaves or

   1 teaspoon dried basil

Saffron Rice (page 256)

1 tablespoon finely chopped fresh flat-leaf parsley,

   for garnish (optional)

To make the tomato sauce: Put the tomatoes, onions, garlic, butter, salt, pepper, and basil in a medium saucepan and cook down over medium heat until the mixture is reduced by one-third, about 20 minutes. Add the tomato paste and cook for 5 minutes, or until the sauce is reduced to about 1½ cups. Taste, and correct the seasoning.

To cook the veal chops: Sprinkle both sides of the chops lightly with flour, shaking off any excess. Heat the oil in a large skillet over medium-high heat. Sear the veal chops quickly on both sides, salting and peppering them as they cook, until delicately browned, about 5 minutes. Add the tomato sauce and garlic, cover, and simmer for about 20 to 40 minutes (depending on the age of the veal) or until tender but not overcooked; the point of a knife should penetrate easily. Add the pitted olives and basil and heat through. Taste and correct the seasoning.

Arrange the chops and sauce on a mound of saffron rice and garnish, if desired, with finely chopped parsley.

VEAL SCALLOPS WITH LEMON

∽ MAKES 4 SERVINGS

I find that many people—just because flour in cooking is so out of fashion today—object to flouring veal scallops before cooking. I consider the flour as optional, though it does enable the meat to brown better. You'll find it more convenient to use two skillets for sautéing the scallops, as that way you can serve them all at once, hot from the pan.

8 large or 12 medium-size veal scallops, pounded

   until thin

½ to ¾ cup all-purpose flour

6 tablespoons (¾ stick) unsalted butter, preferably

   clarified

3 tablespoons olive oil

Kosher salt and freshly ground black pepper

¼ cup freshly squeezed lemon juice

8 or 12 thin slices of lemon

2 tablespoons finely chopped fresh flat-leaf parsley

Lightly flour the scallops, shaking off any excess flour. Heat the butter and oil in 2 large heavy skillets over medium-high heat until the foaming stops. Add the scallops, a few at a time (do not crowd the pan). Sauté them quickly, about 1 minute per side, until lightly browned, seasoning with salt and pepper. Divide the lemon juice, lemon slices, and parsley among the pans. Transfer the scallops to a warm platter and pour the pan juices over them.

SAUTÉED CALF'S LIVER WITH BACON

~ MAKES 4 SERVINGS

Editor: Beard's basic recipe is simplicity itself, but he also offers some interesting variations. You can substitute lamb, baby beef, or pork liver for the common calves' liver. He liked to serve liver with boiled new potatoes.

8 to 12 slices bacon

1½ to 2 pounds calf's liver, sliced ½ inch thick (about 3 slices per serving)

½ cup all-purpose flour

3 tablespoons unsalted butter

3 tablespoons vegetable oil

Kosher salt and freshly ground black pepper

Be sure that the butcher has removed the membrane covering the liver. If not, peel it off.

Working in batches, cook the bacon in a large skillet over medium heat, turning once, until browned and crisp, about 10 minutes. Transfer to paper towels to drain. Pour out the bacon fat. Wipe the skillet clean.

Lightly flour the liver slices and shake off any excess flour. Melt the butter and oil together in the skillet over medium-high heat until it is very hot and the butter foam subsides. Add the liver and brown quickly on both sides, 4 to 5 minutes. Never overcook liver; it should be pink inside. Season with salt and pepper. Serve with the bacon.

VARIATIONS

SAUTÉED LIVER WITH ONION: Before cooking the liver, sauté 2 yellow onions, sliced, in 4 tablespoons (½ stick) unsalted butter in a large skillet over medium heat, stirring frequently, until lightly colored and soft, about 10 minutes. Add 1½ tablespoons red wine vinegar and mix well. Season with salt and pepper. Serve on top of the sautéed liver, with or without the bacon.

SAUTÉED LIVER WITH SHALLOTS AND MADEIRA: Sauté ¼ cup finely chopped shallots in the butter and oil until limp. Add the floured liver and sauté. Season; add ¼ cup Madeira and ¼ cup finely chopped fresh flat-leaf parsley. Turn the liver once in the sauce. Transfer the liver to a platter and pour the sauce over it. You may choose to omit the bacon.

SAUTÉED LIVER WITH MUSTARD SAUCE: After removing the liver, deglaze the skillet with ¼ cup dry white wine. Blend in 2 tablespoons Dijon mustard. Remove from the heat and add ½ cup plain low-fat or whole-milk yogurt, stirring until warmed throughout, but do not boil. Pour the sauce over the liver. Omit the bacon.

SWEETBREADS PANNÉ

One of the simplest and best ways to prepare sweetbreads is to pannè them—which means they are coated with flour, egg, and bread crumbs, then sautéed. [*Editor: Panné is derived from* pain, *the French word for bread.*]

2 pairs sweetbreads

½ cup all-purpose flour

2 large eggs

1½ cups fresh bread crumbs, made in a food
     processor or blender from day-old bread

4 tablespoons (½ stick) unsalted butter

2 tablespoons vegetable oil

Kosher salt and freshly ground pepper

Finely chopped fresh flat-leaf parsley and lemon
     wedges, for garnish

Put the sweetbreads in a large skillet and add cold water to cover. Bring just to a boil over high heat. Carefully drain and rinse the sweetbreads under cold running water. Transfer the sweetbreads to a bowl of ice water and chill for 10 minutes or so. Drain and pat dry with paper towels. Peel the membrane from the sweetbreads, and trim any veins, gristle, or hard parts.

Line a rimmed baking sheet with a clean kitchen towel. Place the sweetbreads in a single layer on the towel and cover with waxed paper, put a board on top, and weigh down with cans. Refrigerate for at least 2 and up to 24 hours. (This flattens the sweetbreads for even cooking.) Cut into serving-size pieces just before cooking.

Put the flour on a plate, beat the eggs in a shallow bowl, and put the bread crumbs on another plate. Coat the pieces lightly with flour, then dip in the egg, and then roll in the bread crumbs. Heat the butter and oil in a heavy skillet over medium-high heat. Add the sweetbreads, and sauté until nicely browned on both sides, about 6 minutes. Season with salt and pepper as they sauté. Remove to a hot platter. Sprinkle with the chopped parsley and serve with the lemon wedges.

PORK

PORK

GLAZED HAM

∞ **A WHOLE HAM MAKES 16 TO 20 SERVINGS;**
   A HALF HAM 8 TO 10 SERVINGS

The smoked hams sold in supermarkets are usually labeled "cook before eating," "fully cooked," or "ready-to-eat"—the last two mean the same thing. According to USDA inspection regulations, hams must be heated to a certain internal temperature during the smoking process. The "ready-to-eat" have been heated to a higher temperature (around 160°F) than the "cook before eating" and are perfectly safe to eat cold, but I find that in order to be really palatable they need a certain amount of cooking and flavoring and are much tastier if basted with sherry, Madeira, dry (hard) cider, wine, or ginger ale during baking. Ready-to-eat or fully cooked hams need only to be baked until they reach an internal temperature of 130°F, just sufficient to heat them through, but a cook-before-eating ham should be boiled or baked to an internal temperature of 160° to 165°F.

A whole ham can weigh from 10 to 20 pounds, but if that is just too much meat for you, you can buy half of a ham, either the meatier butt end or the less expensive but equally tasty shank end. Allow about ½ pound of ham per person, or ¾ to 1 pound for a shank end with a lot of bone. If you want an even smaller ham, buy the smoked butt or smoked picnic shoulder—these come from the foreleg and are fattier but less expensive than hams from the hind legs.

With hot ham, serve Spinach with Cream and Nutmeg (page 246), and Mustard Hollandaise (page 353), or Cumberland Sauce (see Box, page 103). [*Editor: Beard recommends potato and semolina gnocchi as a side dish, too, but that is not included in this collection. Cornmeal Gnocchi on page 220 would be just fine.*]

With cold ham, serve a salad of white beans and tiny bits of chopped tomato, cucumber, and green bell pepper, tossed with well-flavored vinaigrette sauce and garnished with thinly sliced red onions. A hot corn or spinach soufflé (Philip Brown's Romaine Soufflé, page 236, would also be good) is a nice accompaniment to a cold ham, with a selection of French or German mustards. Champagne or a very fruity Alsatian white wine or rosé wine goes well with either hot or cold ham.

One 10- to 12-pound ready-to-eat (fully cooked)
   ham , or a 6- to 8-pound half ham
2 cups dry sherry, Madeira, or dry white wine
1 to 1½ cups dried bread crumbs
1 tablespoon dry mustard
½ cup packed light or dark brown sugar
2 tablespoons Dijon mustard

Put the ham, skin and fat side down, in a large deep roasting pan with the wine. Bake in a preheated 350°F oven approximately 12 minutes per pound for a whole ham, or about 16 minutes per pound for a half ham, basting from time to time with the liquid. When tested with a meat thermometer, inserted in the thickest part but not touching a bone, the internal temperature should register 130°F.

Remove the ham from the oven and trim off the skin or rind and all but about ¼ inch of the fat. Mix together the bread crumbs and dry mustard, and rub the mixture into the fat with your hand. Press the brown sugar into the crumbs and dot all over with Dijon mustard. To glaze the ham (that is, to melt the sugar and give the fat a glossy brown finish), put the ham under the broiler, if it is deep enough, about 10 inches from the heat, and watch carefully to see that the mixture does not scorch—the sugar should melt into the crumbs and leave a nice glaze. Otherwise, turn up the heat to 450°F and bake the ham 15 to 20 minutes more, until nicely glazed. Let rest for 20 minutes before carving.

MARBLEIZED FRESH HAM

〰 **MAKES 16 TO 20 SERVINGS**

The fresh ham or leg of pork is a most satisfactory roast for a large number of people, and equally good hot or cold. I find that my Italian pork store in New York always handles fresh hams, and is well acquainted with boning and stuffing them with herbed and other mixtures that make them particularly succulent. The English and sometimes the Italians leave the scored skin on and roast it to a crisp, chewy perfection. I find this delicious, but most people prefer to have the skin removed. This rather elaborate dish is best served cold. Roast it early in the morning and let it cool until evening, without refrigerating, if possible. This is a good choice for a buffet party.

Serve the ham with Cumberland Sauce (see Box, page 103) or Rémoulade Sauce (page 356), and white beans vinaigrette sprinkled with chopped fresh basil and parsley and garnished with tomato sections. Crisp Italian bread goes well with this meal, as does a fine sparkling wine—a good American version or French Champagne of a pleasant vintage. The famous mostarda di Cremona, or mustard fruits, (available in specialty food shops) are admirable with this ham.

¼ cup golden raisins

½ cup dry sherry

8 garlic cloves

½ cup packed fresh flat-leaf parsley leaves

1 cup coarsely chopped pistachios

One 12- to 15-pound fresh ham, skin removed,
    meat boned, rolled, and well tied

1 teaspoon crushed dried sage

Kosher salt

Freshly ground black pepper

6 tablespoons (¾ stick) unsalted butter

⅓ cup apple jelly

1 teaspoon crushed aniseed (optional)

Soak the raisins in sherry to cover until puffed, about 1 hour. Strain and reserve the raisins and sherry.

Chop 5 of the garlic cloves and the parsley together rather coarsely. Make deep incisions in the ham with a long, thin knife. [*Editor: Beard originally used a larding needle, which is not a common kitchen tool, but a knife works just as well.*] Combine the raisins, chopped parsley mixture, and pistachios and stuff the mixture into the cavities with your fingers, packing it in as tightly as possible—a wooden chopstick is a good aid. Push in any stray pistachios here and there.

Mince the remaining 3 garlic cloves and blend with the sage. Rub the outside fat with the mixture, then sprinkle with salt and pepper. Put the ham on a rack in a roasting pan and roast in a preheated 325°F oven for 25 to 30 minutes per pound. Combine the sherry drained from the raisins, the butter, and the apple jelly in a small saucepan and heat gently in a saucepan until butter and jelly are melted. If you like the flavor of anise, add the crushed aniseed to the mixture—this will result in a more highly perfumed ham. Baste the ham every half hour with the mixture as it roasts. Reheat the basting mixture as needed while using it.

When the ham reaches an internal temperature of 165°F degrees (insert a meat thermometer in the thickest part), in about 6 to 7 hours, remove the pork from the oven and let it cool. [*Editor: Large fresh ham is best when cooked to well done, as this temperature melts the tough connective tissues that help keep the cooked meat moist.*] If you are going to chill the ham, brush it well with the pan juices, wrap it in plastic wrap, and refrigerate until ready to serve. If you must refrigerate it, take it out of the refrigerator and let sit at room temperature for at least several hours before serving.

Cumberland Sauce

Makes about 1 cup

Editor: This easy Port-and-currant jelly sauce is traditional British fare for ham, pork, or game.

Remove the zest from **1 orange** with a vegetable peeler and chop the zest very finely. Put in a pan with **1 cup of Port wine or Madeira** and cook over medium-high heat until the liquid is reduced to ⅓ cup. Add the **1 cup red currant jelly, the juice of the orange, 1 tablespoon freshly squeezed lemon juice,** and **a pinch of cayenne pepper or ground ginger.** Stir until the jelly has melted, then serve the sauce warm.

Carve the ham into thin slices. They will be beautifully marbled with the mixture of raisins, nuts, and herbs.

CROWN ROAST OF PORK

MAKES 8 GENEROUS SERVINGS

A spectacular and festive roast for the holidays or a dinner party. The crown is made with 2 rib ends of the loin, tied together, or with the center cuts or the entire loin, tied together, according to how many people you wish to serve. Two chops from the crown roast are an ample serving. A salad of Bibb lettuce or endive with julienne strips of beet is good with this and, if the stuffing is not a starchy one, boiled parslied potatoes or a purée of potatoes, or potatoes and celery root.

Editor: Beard suggests garnishing the roast with garlic sausages, poached in water until hot, and then sliced. This may be gilding the lily, but try it for another layer of flavor and texture.

One 9-pound crown roast of pork
2 teaspoons kosher salt
3 garlic cloves, minced
2 teaspoons dried sage
2 teaspoons dried thyme
½ cup dry white wine
4 tablespoons (½ stick) unsalted butter, melted
Double Recipe Braised Sauerkraut (page 245)

When the butcher ties the loin, he will scrape the ends of the bones (keep the scraps; they can be used for stock). Cover the exposed rib ends with aluminum foil to prevent them from charring.

Rub the meat well with a combination of the salt, garlic, sage, and thyme. Fill the center of the roast with crumpled aluminum foil. Roast on a rack in a large roasting pan in a preheated 325°F oven, allowing about 20 minutes per pound, until the internal temperature registers 145°F (test by inserting a meat thermometer in the thickest part of the meat, not touching the bone), about 3 hours. Baste frequently with the pan juices and the wine and butter.

When the meat is cooked, replace the foil on the bone ends with paper frills, if you wish. Remove the foil from the center and fill with the sauerkraut.

Carve the roast into chops and serve 1 or 2 to a person, with some of the stuffing from the center.

Stuffings for Crown Roast of Pork

Fill the center of the crown roast with any of the following combinations:

Buttered homemade noodles, mixed with sliced, sautéed mushrooms.

Rice mixed with peas and parsley.

Braised Brussels sprouts with or without chestnuts.

Sautéed lentils with onion, crisp pieces of bacon, and chopped parsley.

Sautéed mushroom caps.

Sautéed apple slices.

Chestnut purée with melted butter, seasoned with ground ginger and nutmeg.

RED-COOKED PORK SHOULDER

MAKES 10 SERVINGS

Editor: Beard learned much about cooking from the Chinese kitchen staff at his mother's boarding house in Oregon, as this recipe shows. Serve it with stir-fried Asian vegetables and lots of white rice. To smash rock sugar (available at Asian grocers), wrap it in a sturdy kitchen towel, then hit it with a flat meat pounder or hammer to pulverize it into coarse crystals. It won't be as fine as granulated sugar.

One 5- to 6-pound pork shoulder, bone in, skin on
¼ cup dry sherry
6 quarter-size slices of fresh ginger
1¼ cups soy sauce
⅓ cup smashed rock sugar or granulated sugar

Rinse the pork and make a few slashes with a knife on the skin side of the meat to allow the sauce to penetrate more easily during cooking. Place the pork in a heavy, medium pot, and add enough water to cover. Cover the pot and bring the water to a boil over high heat. Skim off any scum that forms. Add the sherry and ginger. Cover again, reduce the heat to low, and simmer

1 hour. Drain off one-third of the liquid, and add the soy sauce to the pot. Simmer over low heat for another 1½ hours, occasionally turning the pork. Add the sugar (rock sugar will give the skin a more glazed appearance), and cook for a further 30 minutes, basting the skin very often with the hot sauce. To test for tenderness, pierce the meat with a fork or chopstick. If it penetrates easily, the meat is done. If not, cook a little longer. Place the whole shoulder and sauce in a deep dish. Slice the meat thinly, and serve with the sauce.

ROAST PORK LOIN

MAKES 6 SERVINGS

Probably the most commonly used cut of pork is the loin. In United States parlance the loin is the stretch from the shoulder to the leg that takes in the ribs and the loin chops with the tenderloin. It is usually sold divided into the rib end, the center cut, which includes a small portion of the loin, and the loin end. Or you can buy the entire loin. The roast may be bought boned and tied, or left with the bones intact. In the latter case, the chine bone that runs the length of the loin should be removed or cut through to facilitate carving, and the roast should be trimmed of excess fat and securely tied.

Editor: Beard originally cooked this pork roast to 165°F, which is much too high for today's leaner pork; an internal temperature of 145°F ensures juicy meat. As the meat stands before carving, the temperature will rise 5° to 10°F.

One 5-pound pork loin, trimmed and tied

2 to 3 garlic cloves, peeled and cut into thin slivers

1 teaspoon dried thyme or summer savory

Kosher salt and freshly ground black pepper

12 small new potatoes, peeled

3 large carrots, quartered

12 small white onions, peeled (see page 237)

Watercress, for garnish

About 1 hour before roasting the pork, pierce it all over with the point of a small sharp knife and insert slivers of garlic into the holes. Rub the loin lightly with thyme and then with salt and pepper to taste.

Put the loin, fat side up, on a rack in a shallow roasting pan and roast in a preheated 325°F oven for 20 to 25 minutes per pound, 2¼ to 2½ hours.

Parboil the potatoes, carrots, and onions for 5 minutes in salted water to cover (this softens them slightly, so they cook faster) and arrange them around the meat in the roasting pan for the last hour of roasting time. When you add the vegetables, baste them with the pan juices and sprinkle with a little salt and pepper. Continue to roast the meat until the internal temperature registers 145°F. Check 30 to 40 minutes after adding the vegetables to find how near the meat is to that mark, inserting the thermometer at the thickest part, but not touching the bone.

When the meat is done, transfer it to a hot platter and let it rest in a warm place for 10 to 15 minutes before carving. Keep the vegetables warm in the turned-off oven. Arrange the roasted vegetables around the pork and garnish with watercress.

Carve the roast downward, cutting between the bones. If the meat has been boned, cut into slices about ⅜ inch thick. Skim the fat from the pan juices and serve them with the pork. A dish of sautéed, glazed apple rings is a perfect accompaniment. Wine for such a dish might be a chilled Riesling.

ROAST SMOKED LOIN OF PORK

⟡ MAKE 6 SERVINGS

Editor: Here's what Beard has to say about smoked pork roast: "Smoked pork loin is a great delicacy. When buying, ask how much cooking it needs. Some types require 30 minutes a pound in a 300°F oven, while others which are hot smoked and more fully cooked, require little more than reheating, 12 to 15 minutes a pound at most. Baste a smoked loin of pork during roasting with dry white wine or sherry, and serve it with buttered new potatoes and sauerkraut." This tasty cut, a roast with hamlike flavor on succulent bones, can be found at Eastern European butchers. Take a moderate approach with modern smoked pork, and bake it just until hot enough to serve at about 12 minutes per pound.

One 3-pound smoked pork loin with bones

½ cup dry white wine or sherry

Place the pork, bone side down, in a roasting pan. Pour the wine over the pork into the pan. Bake in a preheated 300°F oven, basting occasionally with the wine in the pan, until the pork registers 130°F

on a meat thermometer, about 1 hour. Let stand for 10 minutes at room temperature. Carve and serve with the skimmed pan juices.

COLD BARBECUED LOIN OF PORK

⟡ MAKES 6 TO 8 SERVINGS

Editor: Beard's glazed pork dish was developed before every backyard sported an outdoor grill, so it isn't truly barbecued. But it is delicious, with faintly Asian flavors. He suggests garnishing the platter with sliced tomatoes, thinly sliced onions, and sliced cucumbers.

For the Horseradish Applesauce

2 cups prepared applesauce

6 tablespoons peeled and freshly grated horseradish or ¼ cup drained bottled horseradish

For the Pork Loin

One 4-pound boneless, center-cut pork loin roast, tied

1 teaspoon dry mustard

1 teaspoon dried thyme

½ cup plus 2 tablespoons dry sherry

½ cup plus 1 tablespoon Japanese soy sauce

3 garlic cloves, finely chopped

2 tablespoons peeled and grated fresh ginger, or 6 pieces candied stem ginger cut into slivers

⅔ cup apple or currant jelly

To make the horseradish applesauce: Mix the applesauce and horseradish together in a medium bowl. Cover and refrigerate until ready to serve. Vary the amount of horseradish to make the sauce hotter or milder.

To prepare the pork loin: Rub the roast with the dry mustard and thyme. Make a marinade with ½ cup of sherry, ½ cup of soy sauce, and the garlic and the ginger, and pour it over the roast. Let the pork marinate at room temperature for no more than 2 hours, turning it several times as it soaks. You may let it stand all night in the refrigerator and roast it early in the morning, if you wish.

To cook, remove the roast from the marinade. Bake in a preheated 325°F oven, allowing about 20 minutes per pound, for 1 hour, 20 minutes, or until a meat thermometer reads 145°F. Let the roast cool to room temperature. Do not refrigerate unless the day is exceptionally hot.

Melt the jelly in a heavy pan over medium heat and when it is bubbly, add the remaining sherry and soy sauce. Remove from the heat and let it cool down for a minute or two, stirring constantly. Spoon over the pork which has been placed on a rack and refrigerate briefly to set the glaze. Slice and serve with horseradish applesauce.

CASSOULET

〰 MAKES 10 TO 12 SERVINGS

There are many versions of cassoulet, all monumentally substantial. This version, one of the best I've ever eaten, was originated by a fine cook of an independent turn of mind, a Frenchwoman who had lived for many years in this country and adapted the recipes of her native land to the local ingredients. You can vary this recipe by adding roast or preserved goose or crisp roast duck, or you can make it with just roast lamb and sausages, omitting the pork, or leave out the tomato paste and add more garlic. Serve the cassoulet with crusty bread and a hearty red wine.

2 pounds dry white beans, such as Great Northern

1 medium yellow onion, stuck with 2 whole cloves

1 pig's foot, split lengthwise

8 to 10 garlic cloves

1 bay leaf

Kosher salt

Freshly ground black pepper

One 3½-pound leg of lamb, with the bone

3 pounds pork loin (from the rib end) or shoulder roast, on the bone

2 cups hearty red wine

1 *saucisson à l'ail* (garlic sausage), cotechino, or kielbasa)

1½ teaspoons dried thyme

2 tablespoons tomato paste

6 thin slices salt pork

1 cup fresh bread crumbs, made from day-old bread

Soak the beans overnight in a large bowl with water to cover by at least 2 inches. The next day, drain well. Put in a pot with the onion, the pig foot, 4 garlic cloves, and the bay leaf. Bring to a boil over high heat. Reduce the heat to medium-low and simmer until the beans are tender, about 1½ hours, adding 1 tablespoon salt halfway through the cooking. Set the beans aside.

While the beans are cooking, salt and pepper the lamb and pork and roast in a large roasting pan in a preheated 325°F oven for 1½ hours, basting from time to time with 1½ cups of the red wine. Let the meats cool, then chill in the roasting pan until the fat congeals on the pan juices and can be skimmed off. Reserve the juices. Cut the meats into 2-inch cubes and reserve.

Poach the sausage in water to cover for 35 to 40 minutes. Drain and slice ½ inch thick. Finely chop the remaining garlic cloves and mix with the thyme and 1 teaspoon pepper.

When the beans are cooked, strain them, reserving the liquid. Remove the bay leaf, onion, and pig's foot. Cut the skin and meat from the pig's foot and reserve. Discard the onion and bay leaf. Put a layer of the beans in a large earthenware or enameled cast-iron casserole and sprinkle with some of the garlic mixture, cubed meats, meat from the pig's foot, and sliced sausage. Continue making layers until all these ingredients are used, ending with beans. Combine the reserved pan juices with the bean liquid, ½ cup red wine, and the tomato paste. Pour enough of this liquid over the cassoulet to reach almost to the top layer of the beans, reserve any remaining liquid. Top the casserole with salt pork slices and cover tightly with aluminum foil. Bake in a preheated 350°F oven for 1 hour. Remove the foil and sprinkle the bread crumbs on top. Bake for 1 hour more, or until the liquid is absorbed, the top is glazed, and the crumbs are browned. If too much liquid is absorbed during the first hour of cooking, add more.

CHOUCROUTE GARNIE

MAKES 8 TO 12 SERVINGS

This dish happens to be one of my all-time favorites, and I've found that it is a great stimulus to the appetite. The sight of the glistening mound of sauerkraut surrounded by delicate pink pieces of smoked pork loin and sausage is calculated to nudge the most jaded palate. If you are serving choucroute, make it for a large group of people so you can have an interesting selection of meats.

Wash **4 pounds of sauerkraut** well and drain thoroughly. Wash a **2-pound piece of rather lean salt pork.** Cut several fairly thick slices (about ½ pound) of the pork, and parboil them for 10 minutes in simmering water. Drain, and arrange in the bottom of a heavy 8-quart pot or flameproof casserole. Cover with the sauerkraut, and bury the remaining salt pork in the center. Add **3 to 4 cups Chicken Stock (page 349) or Beef Stock (page 349),** or enough to cover the sauerkraut, bring to a boil over brisk heat, and boil for 5 minutes. Add **2 finely chopped garlic cloves** and **½ teaspoon freshly ground black pepper,** and simmer, covered, for 1½ hours. Add **1 or 2 *saucisson à l'ail*,** and simmer for another 40 minutes. Add **10 to 12 juicy knackwurst** and **1 or 2 rings of Polish sausage or ring bologna,** and simmer for 20 minutes more.

Meanwhile, bake a **3- to 4-pound smoked loin of pork** in a preheated 350°F oven for about 1 hour, until browned. Most smoked pork loin is already cooked and merely needs heating through. It can be kept separate after browning or added to the sauerkraut mixture for the last few moments of cooking.

Boil **16 small red-skinned potatoes**, peeled and trimmed to fairly equal size, in salted water to cover for about 20 minutes, or until they are tender. Drain, return to the pan, and set over low heat to dry for 1 or 2 minutes.

Gently heat **8 fairly thin slices of cooked ham** in white wine barely to cover, but do not let them simmer.

To serve the choucroute garnie: Mound the sauerkraut on a large platter. Slice the smoked pork loin, the cotechino, and the Polish sausage or ring bologna, and place them around the sauerkraut, along with the whole knackwurst. Put some slices of the salt pork at one end of the sauerkraut. Roll the ham slices, and place them at the other end.

Serve with the boiled potatoes, lightly dusted with **chopped parsley, mustards of all types**, and **rye or French bread**. Drink an Alsatian Riesling or a California Johannesburg Riesling. This makes a truly gargantuan feast. The meats can be varied still further to include boiled beef, fresh pork, spareribs, pig's feet, duck, or goose.

BAKED SPARERIBS WITH SAUERKRAUT, APPLES, AND POTATOES

MAKES 4 TO 6 SERVINGS

While spareribs have a lot of bone (count on at least 1 pound per serving), they go further if cooked or served with other ingredients. For this dish, buy the country spareribs, which have more meat on them than the regular kind. [*Editor: Sauerkraut is highly salted, so you probably won't need to salt the ribs. You can always add it at the table during serving, if need be.*]

4 pounds country spareribs

3 to 4 pounds fresh sauerkraut, well rinsed, drained, and squeezed to remove excess water

2 tart apples, peeled, cored, and sliced

3 medium red-skinned potatoes, peeled and thinly sliced

1 to 2 teaspoons caraway seeds

1 teaspoon freshly ground black pepper

Place half of the ribs in a lightly buttered baking pan, fat side down. Layer the sauerkraut, apples, and potatoes on top, sprinkling the layers with caraway seeds. Season with the pepper. Top with the remaining ribs and press down onto the sauerkraut mixture. Cover the pan with aluminum foil. Bake in a preheated 350°F oven for 1 hour, then remove foil and bake 1 hour more, or until the top ribs are browned and tender.

SALT AND PEPPER SPARERIBS

✐ MAKES 4 SERVINGS

Editor: Beard's original recipe called for one hour of roasting, but that is not enough for today's larger pigs. Let the final tenderness of the meat be your guide, and allow at least 1½ hours.

---

4 pounds spareribs

1 tablespoon kosher salt

2 teaspoons freshly grated black pepper

Cut the spareribs into manageable slabs. Sprinkle liberally with the salt and pepper. Place on the rack of a broiling pan. Roast 30 minutes in a preheated 350°F oven. Turn the ribs and roast 30 minutes longer. Turn again and continue roasting until browned and very tender, about 30 minutes longer. Let stand for 10 minutes, then cut between the bones into individual ribs.

ROAST SUCKLING PIG WITH PISTACHIO-RICE STUFFING

✐ MAKES 12 TO 14 SERVINGS

A spectacular roast for a holiday party. Suckling pigs may be bought most easily around Christmas, but if you order far enough ahead you can get them during the summer months and spit-roast them over charcoal.

Try to get the smallest pig possible, about 12 to 14 pounds. Take out your tape measure and see whether it will fit into the oven—this is vital. If you can't get a pig of a size to fit in your oven, forget it! For oven roasting, the pig should rest on a rack in a fairly shallow pan. It is nice to stuff the pig, but since the meat is so rich, the stuffing must not be too rich.

I've been battling a long time about the way roast suckling pig is usually served. I'm against the rather pagan way people have of decorating them. I feel that a roast suckling pig can be a beautiful sight without the silly embellishments. There is nothing wrong with simply garnishing it with masses of parsley or watercress or with roasted apples and onions. One really needn't make a caricature of the poor beast. [*Editor: For the roast apples and onions, peel and quarter tart apples and yellow onions, and core the apple wedges. During the last 30 minutes or so of roasting time, add to the roasting pan with the pig and stir to coat with the pan juices. Roast with the pig until the pig is done. Keep the apples and onions warm in the turned-off oven while the pig is resting before carving.*]

One 12- to 14-pound suckling pig, heart, liver, and kidneys reserved

For the Stuffing

8 tablespoons (1 stick) unsalted butter

1 cup chopped shallots

6 cups cooked white rice (page 255)

½ cup coarsely chopped pistachios

½ cup finely chopped fresh flat-leaf parsley

Kosher salt and freshly ground black pepper

Olive oil

For the Sauce

2½ cups Chicken Stock (page XXX)

¼ cup finely chopped shallots

4 tablespoons (½ stick) unsalted butter

3 tablespoons all-purpose flour

1 cup heavy cream

Kosher salt and freshly ground black pepper

To make the stuffing: Melt the butter in a large heavy skillet over medium heat and sauté the shallots until they are limp, about 3 minutes. Add the rice, pistachios, and parsley. Toss well to mix. Season with the salt and pepper. Taste the stuffing and correct the seasoning, if necessary.

Stuff the pig rather loosely and sew the cavity up or skewer it securely. Arrange the pig on a rack in a large roasting pan and rub well with olive oil. Roast in a preheated 350°F oven, basting or brushing occasionally with olive oil, for about 3½ to 4 hours, or until an internal temperature of 150°F is reached (insert the meat thermometer into the thickest part of leg, not touching the bone). [*Editor: While 145°F is the accepted median temperature for roast pork, the leg does not get tender until it is a bit more well done.*]

To make the sauce: While the pig is roasting, cook the liver, heart, and kidneys in a saucepan with broth to cover over medium heat until just tender, about 30 minutes. Strain, reserving the broth, and finely chop the pork innards. Sauté the shallots in the butter in a large skillet until limp, about 5 minutes. Sprinkle in the flour and stir well. Gradually stir in the reserved stock and simmer over low heat for 10 minutes. Add the cream and chopped innards, and season with salt and pepper. Simmer over very low heat until lightly thickened, about 10 minutes more.

Transfer the pig to a carving board and garnish as you wish. Let stand for 15 to 20 minutes before carving. To carve, first remove and slice the small hams, then cut down the backbone and remove the head. Carve the rib and loin sections into chops. Serve some of each kind of meat with the stuffing and sauce.

VARATION

ROAST SUCKLING PIG WITH AIOLI: In Spain, especially in Barcelona, roast suckling pig is served with Aioli (page XXX), which, of course, gives it an entirely new dimension, and I find I like it very much.

LAMB

LAMB

BROILED BUTTERFLIED LEG OF LAMB

⤳ MAKES 6 TO 8 SERVINGS

This unusual way of cooking leg of lamb gives you absolutely delicious, juicy meat. Ask your butcher to trim the fell and most of the fat from the leg and to bone and butterfly it—cut it open and spread it flat—so that the meat is approximately the same thickness all across, about 2½ to 3 inches. It will resemble a thick steak with some fat on one side. Serve with a Hollandaise Sauce (page 353) into which you have mixed finely chopped fresh mint or finely chopped anchovies to taste. Sautéed potatoes and a purée of green beans are good with this.

One 6- to 7-pound leg of lamb, trimmed, boned,
and butterflied (about 5 pounds of
boneless meat)
2 to 4 garlic cloves, cut into small slivers
Kosher and freshly ground black pepper
½ teaspoon dried rosemary or summer savory
(optional)
2 tablespoons unsalted butter, melted

Spread out the lamb, fat side down. Make tiny incisions in the meat with the point of a small sharp knife and insert the slivers of garlic. Season the meat well with salt and pepper and, if you wish, rub it with the rosemary or savory, crushed in a mortar and pestle or in the palm of your hand with your thumb.

Preheat the broiler. Lay the lamb on the oiled rack of the broiler pan with the fleshy side up, fat side down. Broil 6 inches from the heat for 15 to 18 minutes; depending on thickness (if some parts of the lamb are thicker than others, determine the cooking time by the thicker portions). Brush the surface with melted butter, turn the lamb with tongs, and broil, fat side up, for 16 minutes for rare or 20 minutes for medium-rare meat. Test about 5 minutes before the end of the cooking time by removing the lamb from the broiler and inserting a meat thermometer in the thickest part—it should register 135°F for rare, 140°F for medium-rare. [*Editor: Over the years, these temperatures have adjusted to 130°F for rare, and 135°F for medium-rare.*]

Continue cooking until the meat reaches the desired temperature, then transfer it to a hot platter or carving board, fat side down, and allow to stand for 5 minutes before carving. Carve crosswise on the diagonal, into slices ¼ to ½ inch thick.

ROAST LEG OF LAMB

⤳ MAKES 8 TO 12 SERVINGS

At one time, lamb was very unpopular in this country—all because it was usually overcooked. I don't blame anyone turning against lamb that has been roasted until it is gray—brown, stringy, and unpalatable. Fortunately I grew up in a home where lamb was treated properly.

Lamb is perfect when it is from rare to pink. The French like it very rare. Most Americans prefer it pink. I'm on the side of the very rare, but I will settle for pink. I suggest you try it pink first and see how juicy and delicious it can be when it is not overcooked, and then gradually you may find you want it rare. I can assure you that once you have had properly cooked lamb, you'll never again roast it to death.

A leg of lamb is covered with a tight, papery tissue called the fell, which should be removed before cooking. If the butcher has not already removed it, take a very sharp, pointed paring knife and loosen the fell from the fat and flesh, then cut or tear it off in chunks. It usually comes off easily. At the same time, remove a good deal of the fat from the lamb—this will improve the flavor considerably. Now you are ready to prepare the lamb for roasting.

One 5-to 8-pound leg of lamb, with the bones, fell
    and most fat removed
6 to 8 garlic cloves
2 to 3 tablespoons olive oil
1 teaspoon dried rosemary
Kosher salt and freshly ground black pepper

Make 10 to 12 small incisions all over the top of the lamb with a small sharp paring knife, pushing the point in about 1 inch deep. Lightly crush the garlic cloves with the side of a heavy knife or cleaver, or with a meat pounder, to break the skins so they peel easily. Peel the garlic and cut the cloves into thin slivers. With your fingers, push the slivers of garlic into the incisions in the lamb. Then rub the roast all over with a little of the oil, massaging it in with your hands.

Crush the rosemary in the palm of one hand, pressing it down with your other thumb to break up the spiky little leaves. (Rosemary is an easy herb to grow in the garden or in a pot, and you'll save money by drying your own.) Rub the crushed rosemary onto the lamb and then sprinkle it with freshly ground black pepper.

I find a broiling pan is perfect for roasting a leg of lamb. It allows the heat to circulate all around the meat so that it cooks more evenly and doesn't need basting. Oil the rack of the pan lightly and put the roast on it. Just before you put the roast in the oven, sprinkle it with salt. Many people will tell you that this will draw out the juices, but it is my feeling that when meat is salted just before roasting, the seasoning penetrates better and aids the flavor, while the oven heat helps to seal the surface.

Put the roast in a preheated 350°F oven and forget about it for 1 hour. After an hour, test the internal temperature with a meat thermometer to see how it is progressing. Insert the thermometer into the meatiest part of the leg, being careful not to let it touch the bone. The desirable finished temperature for the lamb, rare, is 135°F. [*Editor: Today's cooks would consider this medium-rare to*

Mint Sauce for Lamb

Makes about ¼ cup

Wash, dry, and finely chop enough **fresh mint leaves** to make ¼ cup. Dissolve **2 teaspoons superfine sugar** in **2 tablespoons boiling water** and add to the mint leaves with ¼ **teaspoon kosher salt** and **3 tablespoons cider vinegar or white wine vinegar**. Taste, and add more sugar or vinegar as needed. The sauce should be thick. Let stand for 30 minutes before serving for the flavors to mellow.

medium. For rare meat, roast to 125°F.] At the end of the first hour, the temperature should be between 90° and 100°F, depending on the thickness of the meat.

When the thermometer registers around 100°F, you know that you have perhaps 25 to 30 minutes to go. If it is only 90°F, you may need 35 to 40 minutes more. Return the roast to the oven, let it cook 15 to 20 minutes, then retest. When it has reached 135°F transfer the lamb to a carving board or a hot platter and let it rest for 10 to 15 minutes in a warm place before carving. Lamb fat congeals at a low temperature, so always be sure to serve the lamb on hot plates and a hot platter.

SPOON LEG OF LAMB

∽∞ **MAKES 6 SERVINGS**

One of the most famous of the lamb dishes in the French repertoire is *gigot de sept heures*, or boned leg of lamb slowly cooked for seven hours until it is so soft and tender it can almost be served with a spoon—from which comes its Anglicized name, Spoon Leg of Lamb. This is one case where leg of lamb is not served rare—far from it.

One 5- to 6-pound leg of lamb, boned and tied,
    (ask for the bones and have them sawed into
    1- to 2-inch pieces)
Kosher salt and freshly ground black pepper
3 medium yellow onions, each stuck with
    2 whole cloves
3 carrots, split lengthwise

6 or 7 garlic cloves
½ cup olive oil
4 or 5 ripe tomatoes, peeled, seeded, and coarsely
    chopped
1 teaspoon dried thyme
1 bay leaf
1 sprig fresh flat-leaf parsley
1 cup dry red wine
Chopped fresh flat-leaf parsley, for garnish

Rub the leg with salt and pepper and arrange on a rack in a roasting pan. Surround with the bones, onions, carrots, and 4 or 5 garlic cloves. Pour the oil over the bones and vegetables and roast the lamb in a preheated 400°F oven for 30 minutes, then reduce the heat to 350°F, and roast 30 minutes more. Reduce the oven temperature to 200°F.

Transfer the lamb to a Dutch oven and add the tomatoes, the remaining 2 garlic cloves, 1 teaspoon each of salt and pepper, the thyme, bay leaf, parsley, and the bones and vegetables from the roasting pan. Deglaze the roasting pan with the wine; pour over the lamb. Cover the pot tightly and cook in a 200°F oven for 6 hours, by which time the meat should be meltingly tender. Transfer it to a hot platter, remove the strings, and tent with aluminum foil to keep it warm.

Discard the bones and bay leaf, and skim the excess fat from the pan juices. Remove the cloves from the onions. Strain the vegetables, reserving the pan juices. Purée the vegetables in a blender or food processor. Combine the purée with the pan juices. Slice the lamb and arrange on the platter. Spoon some of the sauce over the lamb and sprinkle with chopped parsley.

BRAISED SHOULDER OF LAMB WITH RATATOUILLE

≈ MAKES 6 SERVINGS

Serve with crisp hot French bread, and drink a light red wine, such as a Macon.

Editor: These days, most lamb shoulder is cut into chops. Special-order a boneless lamb shoulder from an Italian or halal butcher. Ask the butcher to trim the surface fat from the meat to a very thin layer before rolling and tying the roast. You could also substitute 4 pounds of lamb neck, cut into 1½- to 2-inch chunks, for the shoulder roast. Roast them in the oven for about 20 minutes, or until browned, and simmer with the ratatouille until tender, about 1½ hours.

One 3-pound boned and tied lamb shoulder roast

6 garlic cloves, peeled and cut into slivers

2 or 3 anchovy fillets in oil, drained and coarsely chopped

Kosher salt and freshly ground black pepper

7 tablespoons olive oil

2 medium yellow onions, thinly sliced

4 small zucchini, trimmed and cut into ½-inch slices

1 green bell pepper, seeds and ribs removed, cut into ½-inch strips

1 globe eggplant, peeled and cut into ½-inch dice

2 tablespoons chopped fresh basil or 1 teaspoon dried basil

2½ cups canned Italian plum tomatoes

¾ cup pitted black Mediterranean olives

¼ cup plus 2 tablespoons finely chopped fresh flat-leaf parsley

Make small incisions in the meat with the point of a small sharp knife and insert half the slivered garlic (reserve the rest for later) and the anchovy pieces in the incisions. Rub the meat well with salt, pepper, and 2 tablespoons of olive oil. Put it on a rack in a roasting pan. Roast for 30 minutes in a preheated 400°F oven, or until lightly browned.

Meanwhile, heat 5 tablespoons olive oil in a large Dutch oven over medium heat. Add the onions and sauté until just wilted and pale gold, about 5 minutes. Add the reserved garlic, with the zucchini and bell pepper. Sauté over medium-high heat for 5 minutes, then add the eggplant. Mix the vegetables well with a wooden spatula; season them with 2 teaspoons salt, 1 teaspoon pepper, and the basil.

Remove the lamb from the oven and place in the middle of the vegetable mixture in the Dutch oven. Add the tomatoes and bring the mixture to a boil on top of the stove. Reduce the oven temperature to 325°F and braise the lamb in the oven, covered, for 1½ to 1¾ hours, or until the lamb is tender and the ratatouille cooked down and well blended. Add the olives and ¼ cup of the chopped parsley and cook 10 minutes move. [*Editor: This roast needs to be cooked until well done.*]

Transfer the lamb to a hot platter and remove the strings. If the ratatouille is too liquid (it should be thick, without visible liquid), reduce it over rather high heat for a few minutes, stirring it well so it doesn't stick. Taste and correct the seasoning. Slice the meat, discarding the string, and serve with the ratatouille spooned over and around it. Sprinkle the dish with the remaining 2 tablespoons chopped parsley.

SHISH KEBAB

MAKES 4 TO 6 SERVINGS

Shish kebab has become a popular addition to American outdoor cookery. For my own taste, I feel this dish is usually overseasoned or overly marinated. Most people, I know, think that the longer the bits of lamb soak in a mixture of herbs, spices, wines, juices, etc., the better they taste. I disagree. I believe that the true essence of the meat is by far the most important flavor, and therefore I prefer to enhance it very simply.

Editor: To grill the shish kebabs outside, cook them over medium-hot, not searingly hot, fire. For a gas grill, preheat the grill, then adjust the temperature to 450°F. For a charcoal grill, let the coals burn down until they are covered with white ash and you can hold your hand just above the cooking grate for 2 to 3 seconds.

---

3 pounds lean lamb, either leg or shoulder, with most of the fat removed, cut into 1½- to 2-inch cubes

For the Marinade

1 cup olive oil

⅓ cup freshly squeezed lemon juice

2 garlic cloves, crushed under a knife and peeled

1 teaspoon kosher salt

1 teaspoon freshly ground black pepper

Whole cherry or plum tomatoes

Green bell pepper, seeded, cut into 1½-inch cubes

Mushroom caps

Eggplant, unpeeled, cut into 1½-inch cubes

Small white onions, peeled (see page 237), then parboiled for 5 to 10 minutes, according to size

¼ cup olive oil or unsalted butter, melted

There should be practically no fat on the meat. Trim off as much as possible. Combine the marinade ingredients in a glass or pottery bowl, add the meat, and marinate for 2 hours, turning frequently.

Remove the meat cubes from the marinade (there is no need to dry them) and string them on steel or iron skewers, about 14 inches long, leaving about 2 inches of space at the handle and tip of the skewers. Push the pieces close together. This gives a juicier, rarer result than spacing out the meat, as it protects the inner surfaces from the heat. If you like to cook vegetables on the same skewer as the meat, alternate the meat cubes. Or place the vegetables on separate skewers and cook them alone.

To cook the kebabs: Preheat the broiler. Remove the rack from the broiler pan. Arrange the skewers across the pan, handles resting on one side, tips on the other (you should be able to get about 6 skewers on the pan). Or use aluminum foil broiling pans to support the skewers. Brush kebabs and vegetables with oil. Broil with the surface of the meat approximately 3 inches from the heat, turning the skewers often and brushing with the marinade, for about 9 minutes for rare, 12 minutes for medium rare. Test by making a small cut in one of the cubes to see if it is done to your taste. Do not overcook.

If you are broiling the vegetables separately,

after putting them on the skewers brush them liberally with olive oil or melted butter and sprinkle lightly with salt and pepper. Keep brushing them with oil or butter as you turn the skewers—mushrooms are especially likely to dry out if not well lubricated.

PERSIAN LAMB WITH RHUBARB

✎ MAKES 4 SERVINGS

Some years ago, a friend cooked a wonderfully spicy and aromatic dish for me that one might almost term a Middle Eastern version of sweet and sour, using lamb instead of pork. I obtained the recipe, of course, and make the dish when spring rhubarb first comes into the markets. If you want to try it, get cherry red rhubarb (rather than green) if you can. It has an excellent flavor.

Put **2½ cups of sliced fresh rhubarb** in a bowl with **¾ cup of sugar** and **¾ cup of water,** and let stand for 30 minutes. Peel and chop **1 large yellow onion.** In a large, heavy skillet, melt **4 tablespoons (½ stick) of unsalted butter.** Sauté the onion until transparent, then transfer it to a heavy Dutch oven. In the same skillet, sauté **1 pound of lean leg of lamb, cut into 1-inch cubes,** until brown on all sides. Season with **1 teaspoon of kosher salt,** ½ **teaspoon of freshly ground black pepper,** ½ **teaspoon of ground cinnamon,** and ½ **teaspoon of freshly grated nutmeg.** Stir in **1 cup of finely chopped fresh flat-leaf parsley,** and continue cooking for another 2 minutes. Add the syrup from the rhubarb.

Transfer the meat mixture to the casserole. Cover with a circle of waxed paper cut to the same diameter as the casserole. Put on the lid and simmer very gently for 30 minutes. Stir in the drained rhubarb, and continue simmering for another 20 to 30 minutes, or until the meat is very tender. Taste for seasoning. Combine **1 tablespoon of cornstarch with 1 tablespoon of cold water,** and stir into the meat mixture. Cook gently for another 2 or 3 minutes, or until the sauce thickens, by which time the rhubarb and onions will have melted down. Serve **over hot cooked rice.**

LAMB COUSCOUS WITH SAUCE PIQUANTE

✎ MAKES 8 SERVINGS

Couscous, the national dish of Morocco, Algeria, and Tunisia, is great party food. Arranged on a big platter, it looks inviting, feeds a lot of people economically, and is fun to eat. There isn't much meat in the dish, which is usually only part of a North African meal, so I like to serve it with chicken cooked in the Moroccan style, with Pickled Lemons (page 140) and olives .

The traditional cooker for couscous is a couscousière, a piece of equipment with a deep bottom and perforated top in which the couscous, a tiny semolina pasta, steams over spicy, aromatic broth. (You can substitute an 8-quart cooking pot over which a colander will fit.)

Couscous is sold in Middle Eastern and specialty food shops. Be careful not to buy the instant variety; you need the traditional, long-cooking type.

For the Sauce Piquante (Red Pepper Sauce)

2 or 3 fresh hot red chile peppers, seeds
   and ribs removed, and coarsely
   chopped

¼ cup finely ground walnuts

3 tablespoons olive oil

1 teaspoon Tabasco

1 garlic clove, crushed

For the Couscous

2 pounds boneless shoulder of lamb
   (or 3 pounds lamb neck with bones),
   cut into 1½-inch cubes

2 large yellow onions, thinly sliced

¾ cup vegetable oil

8 tablespoons (1 stick) unsalted butter

1 teaspoon ground ginger

1 teaspoon ground turmeric

2 teaspoons freshly ground black pepper

Pinch of saffron threads

1½ pounds (4 cups) long-cooking couscous

6 carrots, scraped and quartered

4 turnips, peeled and quartered

4 red-skinned potatoes, peeled and quartered

1 tablespoon kosher salt

3 zucchini, cut into thick slices

One 19-ounce can chickpeas, drained and rinsed
   (about 2 cups)

¼ cup dark seedless raisins

To make the sauce: Combine all the ingredients in a blender or food processor and blend to a paste. Transfer to a bowl, cover with plastic wrap, and let stand while making the couscous.

To make the couscous: Start the couscous about 2 hours before serving time. Put the lamb, onions, ½ cup of the oil, 4 tablespoons (½ stick) of the butter, the ginger, turmeric, pepper, and saffron in the bottom of a couscousière or a large saucepan. Add enough water to come 2 inches above the ingredients. Bring to a rapid boil.

Line the steamer top of the couscousière or a metal colander with a triple thickness of rinsed cheesecloth (this prevents the tiny beads from falling through). Add the couscous and place over the boiling mixture. Cover with the lid of the couscousière or wrap aluminum foil tightly over the colander and the edges of the pot to keep the steam from escaping. Steam for 1 hour, then remove the steamer section or colander and run cold water over the puffed-up couscous for 2 or 3 minutes, breaking up the lumps with your fingers. Set aside to cool and drain.

Add the carrots, turnips, and potatoes to the lamb mixture. Cover and cook 20 minutes. Meanwhile, turn the cooled couscous into a big bowl and mix in the remaining ¼ cup oil and the salt with your fingers. Return the couscous to the cheesecloth-lined steamer or colander. Add the zucchini, chickpeas, and raisins to the lamb mixture, replace the steamer or colander on top, cover again, and steam for another 15 to 20 minutes. Then transfer the hot couscous to a bowl and mix in the remaining 4 tablespoons (½ stick) butter.

To serve, mound the couscous on a very large platter. Make a well in the center. Strain the lamb stew, reserving the liquid. Put about 2 cups of the drained lamb and vegetables into it. Serve the rest of the stew in another dish, the reserved liquid in a large bowl, and the sauce piquante in a small bowl.

LAMB SHANKS WITH BEANS

⌒ MAKES 6 SERVINGS

A part of the lamb that is often overlooked, the ends of the legs are wonderfully flavorful and take well to long, slow cooking. Combined with white beans they are excellent and economical eating. A salad of crisp greens tossed with grated carrot and chopped onion would go well with this substantial dish.

For the Beans

2 cups dried Great Northern or white navy beans

1 large yellow onion, stuck with 2 whole cloves

1 tablespoon kosher salt

7 garlic cloves

1 bay leaf

For the Lamb Shanks

Six 1- to 1¼-pound meaty lamb shanks

5 garlic cloves, 2 cut into slivers, and 3 finely chopped

2 teaspoons dried rosemary, crushed with a mortar and pestle

Kosher salt

5 tablespoons unsalted butter (½ stick plus 1 tablespoon)

6 tablespoons olive or vegetable oil

Freshly ground black pepper

1 cup dry red wine

1½ cups water or Beef Stock (page 349)

2 large onions, thinly sliced

6 slices thick-sliced bacon

½ cup fresh bread crumbs (made in a blender or food processor from day-old bread)

To prepare the beans: Put the beans in a large saucepan with water to cover by 2 inches. Bring to a boil, boil 5 minutes, then remove the saucepan from the heat. Let the beans cool, covered, in the cooking water for 1 hour only—no longer or they will be too soft. Add more water to cover, if needed, plus the clove-studded onion, salt, garlic, and bay leaf. Bring to a boil, reduce the heat to medium-low, cover, and simmer until just tender to the bite—do not overcook or the resulting dish will be mushy. [*Editor: This will take about 45 minutes, depending on the age and dryness of the beans.*]

While the beans are cooking, prepare the lamb shanks: Make incisions in the lamb shanks and stuff the garlic slivers into them. Rub the shanks with 1½ teaspoons rosemary and 1 teaspoon salt. Heat 3 tablespoons of the butter and 3 tablespoons of the oil in a very large, deep, heavy skillet (not uncoated cast iron). Brown the lamb shanks on all sides, turning with tongs and sprinkling with pepper as they cook. Add the wine and water with the remaining rosemary. Bring to a boil over high heat. Reduce the heat to medium-low, cover, and simmer for 1 hour.

Sauté the sliced onions in the remaining 3 tablespoons oil until lightly browned. Cover and cook over low heat until soft but not browned, about 6 minutes.

Drain the beans, reserving the liquid. Put a layer of half the beans in a very large enameled Dutch oven top with a layer of the onions and the 3 finely chopped garlic cloves. Put the lamb shanks on top, and add the remaining beans and the broth from the pan in which the shanks cooked. If there is not enough liquid (there should be enough to cover the shanks), add some of the reserved bean liquid. Lay the bacon slices on top and cook in a preheated 350°F oven for 1 hour, adding more of the bean liquid if the mixture cooks down too much and the beans seem dry. Melt the remaining 2 tablespoons butter in a large skillet. Add the bread crumbs and stir well. Sprinkle them into the Dutch oven. Bake 20 minutes longer, or until the crumbs are golden. Serve from the Dutch oven.

ROAST RACK OF LAMB

⤜ **MAKES 2 TO 3 SERVINGS**

The rack of lamb has come into increasing favor in restaurants, and now people are beginning to appreciate its utter simplicity of preparation in their own homes. The rack consists of one side of the ribs. In young lamb, or baby lamb, when the ribs have been well trimmed, all excess fat removed, the rack will consist of 6 to 7 delicate small chops, a perfect piece of meat for two people.

Ask the butcher to cut through the chine bone so that you can carve right through the chops without having to struggle with the bones. If you want to put little paper frills on the rib ends after the rack is cooked, protect the bone ends by twisting pieces of aluminum foil around each one before roasting. A rack of lamb should always be roasted at a high temperature and served rare.

1 rack of lamb, 6 to 7 chops, trimmed of all but about
⅓ inch of fat, with the bones frenched

1 garlic clove, crushed under a knife and peeled
1 teaspoon dried rosemary or thyme, crushed with
a mortar and pestle
Kosher salt and freshly ground black pepper

Rub the rack of lamb well with the garlic and rosemary. Twist pieces of aluminum foil around the bone ends.

Put the roast, fat side down, on a rack in a roasting pan. Roast in a preheated 450°F oven for 15 minutes, then turn it over so the bone side is down. Reduce the heat to 400°F and roast 5 minutes more. Test the meat by pressing it lightly with your fingers, protecting them with paper towels. The meat should feel firmly springy to the touch. If it seems to need more cooking time, return it to the oven for a further 5 to 7 minutes. It should take 20 to 27 minutes for rare lamb. The internal temperature, tested with a meat thermometer, should register 125° to 130°F.

Transfer the cooked meat to a carving board, substitute paper frills for the foil (if you like to gnaw the little bones, this prevents your fingers from getting greasy). Let it stand 3 minutes, then carve.

There are two ways to carve rack of lamb. The more usual is to separate the chops by cutting between the bones and serving 2 to 3 chops to each person, according to appetite. The other way is to carve the meat in long, thin slices parallel to the bone. If you serve the rack that way, serve each person 1 or 2 of the tiny bones to gnaw on.

BROILED LAMB CHOPS

Thick loin or rib chops are the best for broiling. As they have a good deal of fat and most people like their lamb chops broiled rare or pink (medium rare), you should move the chops nearer to the heat, about 2 inches away, 2 minutes before the end of the broiling time in order to char the fat. Thin chops (1 inch thick) are best broiled fast and close to the heat, or the meat will be overcooked before the fat is brown.

Ideally, lamb chops should be at least 1½ to 2 inches thick. Even 2½ or 3 inches is not too much, if your chops are to be deliciously rare. As the single lamb chops sold in markets are usually cut 1 inch thick and the double lamb chops 2 inches thick, you will have to ask your butcher to cut them specially if you want other than the standard size. Allow 1 large or thick, or 2 small or thinner lamb chops per serving.

Broiling time depends not only on the thickness of the chops but also on the intensity of heat put out by your broiler. The following chart gives approximate times and distances for chops of different thicknesses. The time given is total broiling time. Allow half the time per side.

Timings for Lamb Chops According to Thickness

- **FOR A CHOP 1 INCH THICK.**
  Broil 2 inches from the heat; 5 to 6 minutes for rare.

- **FOR A CHOP 1½ INCHES THICK.**
  Broil 4 inches from the heat; 6 to 8 minutes for medium rare.

- **FOR A CHOP 2 INCHES THICK.**
  Broil 4 inches from the heat; 12 to 14 minutes for medium rare.

- **FOR A CHOP 3 INCHES THICK.**
  First give them 3 minutes a side at 4 inches from the heat, then lower to 5 inches from the heat and continue to broil for a further 9 to 12 minutes for rare, 12 to 15 minutes for medium rare.

Preheat the broiler. Rub the rack of the broiler pan with oil. (If you are broiling 1-inch chops, broil them in a disposable aluminum foil broiling pan, which can be put nearer the heat. Be sure to put the pan on a cookie or baking sheet first.)

Season the chops on one side with salt and pepper and arrange on the broiler rack or in the foil pan. Broil according to the chart, turning the chops with tongs midway through the broiling time and seasoning the second side with salt and pepper when turned.

If necessary, raise the chops to within 2 inches of the heat for the last 2 minutes of broiling to brown the fat.

To check for doneness, make a tiny slit in the meat, near the bone. Or, if the chops are very thick, insert a meat thermometer horizontally into the thickest part of the meat, not touching the bone. The internal temperature should register 130°F for rare, 135°F for medium rare.

Serve the broiled lamb chops on very hot plates, as the fat congeals quickly. Crisp fried potatoes or broiled tomatoes and watercress are good accompaniments.

IRISH STEW

✐ MAKES 6 SERVINGS

Probably the most basic braised lamb dish, which manages to be both simple and elegant, is Irish stew. Recipes for Irish stew can be found in Escoffier, Montagné, and practically every good lexicon of good cooking—and they differ a great deal. Good Irish stew is not a thin soup with meat and vegetables floating in it, but a hearty dish of meat, potatoes, and onions cooked slowly until rather thick in texture. In the purest version, it contains neither carrots nor turnips.

3 pounds lamb rib or shoulder chops

Softened butter for the Dutch oven

1 tablespoon finely chopped flat-leaf parsley,
   plus more for garnish

1½ teaspoons dried thyme

5 to 6 medium red-skinned potatoes, peeled and
   cut into ½-inch rounds

3 large yellow onions, sliced

Kosher salt and freshly ground black pepper

2 cups water

2 to 3 tablespoons chopped fresh flat-leaf parsley

Trim the fat from the chops, leaving the meat on the bones. Butter a large shallow baking dish.

Mix the parsley and the thyme together in a small bowl. Spread one-third of the potatoes in the bottom of the casserole and cover with a layer of chops topped with a third of the parsley-thyme mixture. Add a layer of half the onions, then a third more of potatoes, the remaining chops, herbs, remaining onions, and finally, the remaining potatoes and parsley mixture. Season well with salt and pepper and add the water. Cover tightly with aluminum foil. Bake in a preheated 300°F for 2 to 2½ hours, or until the meat is tender and the potatoes and onions are soft. Serve in soup plates with a sprinkling of chopped parsley on top.

Irish stew always benefits from being cooked the day before and allowed to cool thoroughly. Skim off any fat and reheat the stew.

POULTRY
AND
GAME
BIRDS

POULTRY AND GAME BIRDS

PERFECT ROAST CHICKEN

〰 MAKES 4 SERVINGS

A simple dish, but one of the best when it is properly cooked. Allow one-quarter chicken for each serving, but you may want to cook an extra chicken to accommodate white-meat or dark-meat eaters. Leftover chicken is never a problem.

One 4- to 4½-pound chicken

Half of 1 lemon

1 tablespoon finely chopped fresh tarragon or
    1 teaspoon dried

Kosher salt and freshly ground black pepper

2 bacon strips

2 tablespoons unsalted butter, melted

Rinse the chicken under cold running water and pat dry with paper towels. Freshen the cavity by rubbing it with the half lemon. Place the tarragon in the cavity. Rub the outside of the chicken with a seasoning of salt and pepper. Place the chicken on its side on a rack in a shallow roasting pan. Drape the bacon strips over it. Roast in a preheated 400°F oven for 25 minutes. Remove the bacon, turn the chicken on its other side, and cover with the same strips of bacon. Roast for another 25 minutes, basting once during that time. Turn the chicken breast side up, remove the bacon, and brush the chicken with melted butter. Roast for another 30 to 35 minutes, or until the skin is crisp and the legs can be moved easily. Do not overcook. [See Editor's Note.]

Remove the chicken from the oven and allow the juices to settle for 5 to 10 minutes or so before carving the chicken into quarters. Skim off the grease from the pan juices, and spoon the juices over the chicken.

Editor: When Beard wrote these poultry recipes, few people used a meat thermometer to judge the doneness of their roast chicken. The usual method was to pierce the cooked bird with the tines of a meat fork to release the juices onto a white saucer, and check the color of the juices. If the juices were clear or yellowish, the bird was done; if they had any hint of pink, the bird was considered undercooked, and returned to the oven for more roasting.

Today, an instant-read thermometer is a common gauge for checking temperatures of meat and poultry. For roast chicken, insert the thermometer in the thickest part of the thigh, not touching a bone. The temperature should register 165°F to 170°F, keeping in mind that it will rise from carry-over cooking, as the bird's temperature will continue to climb for a few degrees, even though it is out of the oven. We have retained the original suggestions for checking for doneness, but the thermometer is more reliable.

POACHED CHICKEN

To poach a chicken sounds deceptively simple—and that may be the reason so many birds are cooked too long or at too high heat until the flesh is dry, grainy, stringy, and flavorless. For moist, succulent poached chicken, the liquid should be kept at the gentlest simmer and the bird removed when the breast is firm to the touch and the legs barely wiggle when moved. On no account should it be cooked until the skin shrinks and breaks and the flesh starts to fall from the bone.

Good accompaniments are boiled or puréed potatoes, steamed rice, or buttered noodles. If you want a creamy sauce, whisk 3 egg yolks with 1 cup heavy cream and add to 1 cup Sauce Velouté (page 352) made with some of the poaching liquid. Stir into the pot of cooking liquid and heat until slightly thickened, but do not allow to boil. Season to taste with chopped fresh tarragon. For a green vegetable, you might have tiny buttered green peas or green peas and little pearl onions. If you want to use the chicken for cold dishes, such as chicken salad, it will yield about 4 to 4½ cups meat.

Matzoh Stuffing for Chicken or Turkey

Makes about 4 cups

Editor: Unless the chicken is very large, you will have leftover stuffing. Stuff the chicken loosely with the matzoh mixture. Put the excess stuffing in a buttered shallow dish and bake in the oven with the bird for about 20 minutes, or until heated through. For a turkey, double the recipe.

Giblets, chopped

2 medium yellow onions, finely chopped

3 tablespoons butter, or rendered fat from the bird

Kosher salt and freshly ground black pepper

5 to 8 matzohs

4 large egg yolks, beaten

1 tablespoon peeled and grated fresh ginger

¼ teaspoon dried thyme

¼ teaspoon dried marjoram

Pinch of freshly grated nutmeg

In a skillet, sauté the chopped giblets and onions in the butter or rendered fat from the bird. Season with salt and pepper. Transfer the giblets and onions to a bowl.

Soak matzohs in water to cover in a bowl until they are soft. Drain, squeeze dry, and add to the fat in the skillet in which you sautéed the giblets. Stir well over a very low heat and to firm them slightly, and add to the giblets. Add the egg yolks, ginger, thyme, marjoram, and nutmeg. Blend well and correct the seasoning.

One 4- to 5-pound chicken

1 medium yellow onion, stuck with 1 whole clove

1 bay leaf

1 to 2 sprigs fresh flat-leaf parsley

2 to 3 garlic cloves

1 thin sliver lemon zest

½ teaspoon freshly ground black pepper

About 1½ quarts Chicken Stock (page 349), canned
    chicken broth, or water, as needed

1 tablespoon kosher salt

Put the chicken in a deep pot with the onion, bay leaf, parsley, garlic, lemon zest, and pepper. Add stock barely to cover. Bring to a boil over high heat. Skim off the scum that rises to the surface and reduce the heat to medium-low. Add the salt, cover the pot, and cook at the gentlest simmer (the water should not bubble, but merely move) for 50 minutes to 1¼ hours, or until the breast is firm but still moist and the legs can be wiggled. Transfer the chicken to a hot platter and strain the broth. Cut the chicken into serving pieces. [ED: *For a sauce suggestion, see the headnote on page 130.*]

VARIATIONS

POACHED CHICKEN WITH VEGETABLES: Add thinly sliced carrots and tiny white onions to the pot during the last 30 minutes of cooking time. Serve with the chicken, some of the broth, and separately boiled potatoes.

POACHED CHICKEN WITH GARLIC: Simmer 15 to 20 unpeeled large garlic cloves with the chicken. Serve these with the chicken, to be squeezed from the husks and spread on thin slices of French bread.

POACHED CHICKEN WITH LIGHT DUMPLINGS

MAKES 4 TO 6 SERVINGS

Editor: Here is another dish that James must have learned at his mother's side when she was running her hotel business.

For the Poached Chicken

One 5- to 6-pound chicken

Half of 1 lemon

Several sprigs of fresh flat-leaf parsley

2 quarts cold water, as needed

1 medium yellow onion, peeled and stuck with
    2 or 3 whole cloves

8 whole black peppercorns

Dash of freshly grated nutmeg

1 bay leaf

Kosher salt

For the Light Dumplings

2 cups all-purpose flour

1 tablespoon plus 1½ teaspoons baking powder

¼ teaspoon kosher salt

1 cup whole milk

Finely chopped fresh flat-leaf parsley, for garnish

To poach the chicken: Rub the chicken, inside and out, with the lemon half. Put the parsley sprigs in the cavity of the chicken and truss with kitchen twine. Put in a deep pot and cover with cold water. Add the onion, peppercorns, nutmeg, and bay leaf, and season lightly with salt. Bring to a boil over medium-high heat. Remove the scum that rises to the surface of the cooking liquid, reduce the heat to medium-low, and cover tightly. Simmer until tender and the meat shows no sign of pink when pierced with the tip of a small sharp knife at the thighbone, about 1¼ hours. Do not overcook or you will have a stringy mess. Transfer the chicken to a hot platter and cover with aluminum foil to keep it warm. Strain the broth, return to the pot, and boil over high heat until reduced to about 1 quart and nicely flavored, about 20 minutes.

To make the dumplings: Sift together the flour, baking powder, and salt into a medium bowl. Add the milk and toss together lightly with a fork to make a sticky dough. Reduce the heat under the broth to medium-low. Drop the dough by heaping dessertspoons into the gently boiling broth. Cover the pot tightly and allow to cook until the dumplings have risen, 13 minutes to the dot. Transfer the dumplings to a serving bowl with a slotted spoon and cover with aluminum foil to keep them warm.

To serve: First ladle the soup into bowls, sprinkle with chopped parsley, and serve as a soup course. For the main course, carve the chicken, sprinkle it and the dumplings with more chopped parsley, and serve.

VARIATION

POACHED CHICKEN WITH NELLIE COX'S DUMPLINGS: Mix **2 cups all-purpose flour, 2 tablespoons softened unsalted butter,** and ½ **teaspoon salt.** Add enough **water** to make a stiff dough. Turn the dough out onto a floured work surface and pat or roll out to thickness of ⅛ inch. Cut into 1- by 3-inch pieces. Drop into the gently boiling broth

and cook for 20 minutes, uncovered, stirring frequently to keep them from sticking together. Transfer to a serving bowl with a slotted spoon.

BRAISED LEMON CHICKEN

MAKES 4 SERVINGS

Editor: This dish is inspired by the cuisine of the Middle East and should be served on fragrant basmati rice.

One 4-pound chicken

2½ lemons

2 tablespoons olive oil

1 large yellow onion, finely chopped

2 teaspoons ground turmeric

2 cups Chicken Stock (page 349) or water

Two 15- to 19-ounce cans chickpeas (garbanzo beans), drained and rinsed

4 garlic cloves, crushed under a knife and peeled

Kosher salt and freshly ground black pepper

Rub the chicken inside and out with a lemon half. Heat the oil in a deep Dutch oven over medium heat. Sauté the onion in the oil until soft and golden, about 4 minutes. Sprinkle with 1 teaspoon of the turmeric and mix well. Rub the chicken with the remaining teaspoon of turmeric.

Move the onion to one side of the Dutch oven. Add the whole chicken and cook, turning to sear and color it to deep yellow on all sides, about 5 minutes. Add the stock, chickpeas, the juice of the 2 remaining lemons, and the garlic, and season with salt and pepper. Bring to a boil over high heat, then reduce the heat to medium-low and cover. Simmer for 1 hour or longer, or just until the chicken shows no sign of pink when pierced with the tip of a sharp knife at the thighbone. Remove the chicken from the sauce, cut into serving pieces, and serve with the chickpeas and the sauce.

CHICKEN IN THE POT

∾ **MAKES 4 SERVINGS**

This is a version of the French dish known to the world as *poule au pot*. Carrots and onions may be added to the broth while it is cooking and then may be served with the soup. You may also flavor the broth with parsley, thyme, and rosemary. Serve the broth first, then follow with the carved chicken and stuffing, accompanied by Mustard Mayonnaise (page 356) and a green salad.

For the Chicken

One 5-pound chicken, gizzard and liver reserved for the stuffing

Half of 1 lemon

1 pound veal shoulder, preferably on the bone, cut into 2-inch chunks

1 pound beef shin, cut into 2 or 3 rounds

4 ounces salt pork or slab bacon, rind removed, in one piece

For the Stuffing

8 ounces sausage meat

2 medium onions, finely chopped

1 garlic clove, chopped

1½ cups fresh bread crumbs (made in a food processor from day-old bread)

Reserved chicken liver and gizzard

1 tablespoon chopped fresh flat-leaf parsley

Pinch of dried thyme

Kosher salt and freshly ground black pepper

6 large egg yolks, beaten

1 slice of day-old bread (preferably the end slice or "heel" of the loaf)

Rub the interior of the chicken with the lemon half. Trim the gizzard of the tough membrane and remove any green spots from the liver. Finely chop the gizzard and liver. Refrigerate the chicken and chopped giblets.

Put the veal shoulder and beef shank in a large pot and add enough cold water to cover. Bring to a boil over high heat, skimming off any scum that rises to the surface. Reduce the heat to very low and simmer for 1½ hours.

To make the stuffing: Fry the sausage meat in a large skillet until it is browned and rendered of its fat, about 10 minutes. Pour off most of the fat. Add the onions and garlic to the skillet and cook for a few minutes, until the onions are translucent, about 5 minutes. Stir in the bread crumbs, chopped liver and gizzard, parsley, and thyme; season with salt and pepper. Transfer to a bowl and let cool slightly. Add the egg yolks and mix thoroughly.

Stuff the body cavity of the chicken with the

stuffing, but not too tightly. Place the crusty bread slice over the stuffing and sew up the opening securely with kitchen twine. Pin the neck skin to the back skin with a skewer or a wooden toothpick. Truss the bird with kitchen twine.

After the veal and beef have simmered for 1½ hours, add the chicken and salt pork to the pot. Add hot water, if needed, to cover the chicken. Simmer until the chicken shows no sign of pink when pierced at the thighbone with the tip of a small sharp knife, about 1¼ hours. Transfer the chicken, veal, beef, and salt pork to a platter and cover with aluminum foil to keep warm.

Meanwhile, skim any fat from the surface of the broth. Increase the heat to high and reduce by one-third until you have a rich, strong broth, about 15 minutes. Season with salt and pepper. Slice the meat into serving pieces and moisten with a ladleful of the broth. Cover again with aluminum foil to keep warm.

First, serve the hot broth in bowls. When ready to serve the main course, remove the twine from the chicken. Carve the chicken and serve with the stuffing and meats.

CHICKEN SAUTÉ WITH TOMATO

〰 MAKES 4 SERVINGS

Editor: Substitute fresh basil for the parsley, if you wish.

One 3½-pound chicken, quartered
6 tablespoons (¾ stick) butter
Kosher salt and freshly ground black pepper
3 tablespoons finely chopped onion
1 small garlic clove, finely chopped
½ cup dry white wine
3 medium tomatoes, peeled, seeded, chopped
1 tablespoon finely chopped fresh flat-leaf parsley

Melt the butter in a very large heavy skillet (not uncoated cast-iron) over medium-high heat. Working in batches, if necessary, add the chicken to the skillet, skin side down, and brown quickly, about 3 minutes. Season with salt and pepper. Turn the chicken over and add the onion and garlic. Cover the skillet and reduce the heat to medium-low. Cook until the onion softens, about 5 minutes. Add the wine, cover, and cook for 10 minutes more. Add the tomatoes, cover, and cook, turning the chicken occasionally, until the chicken shows no sign of pink when pierced with the tip of a sharp knife at the thighbone, about 25 minutes more. Arrange on a hot platter. Add the parsley to the tomato mixture, increase the heat to high, and cook until slightly reduced, about 2 minutes. Pour over the chicken and serve hot.

COQ AU VIN

Editor: Coq au vin is a perfect dish for entertaining, as it can be made well ahead and warmed up just before serving. Beard's recipe calls for salt pork, but pancetta, which was not readily available in the U.S. when he wrote this, would also be a better substitute for the cured pork that a French cook would use. Serve it on egg noodles or mashed potatoes.

6 tablespoons (¾ stick) unsalted butter

One 3½-pound chicken, quartered

1 teaspoon kosher salt

½ teaspoon freshly ground black pepper

¼ cup Cognac

One 750-ml hearty red wine, as needed

Bouquet garni (1 sprig fresh thyme, 1 sprig fresh flat-
    leaf parsley, 6 whole peppercorns, and 1 bay leaf,
    tied in rinsed cheesecloth)

12 small white onions, peeled (see page 237)

Three ½-inch-thick slices salt pork, rind trimmed,
    or unrolled pancetta, cut in sticks about
    2 inches long

12 mushroom caps, quartered

For the Beurre Manié
3 tablespoons all-purpose flour
3 tablespoons unsalted butter

Melt 3 tablespoons of the butter in a large, heavy skillet (not uncoated cast iron) over medium-high heat. Working in batches, add the chicken and cook, turning occasionally, until browned on all sides, about 10 minutes. Season with salt and pepper and transfer to a platter. Pour the butter out of the skillet. Return the chicken to the skillet and pour in the Cognac. Let burn for 30 seconds; if the Cognac doesn't extinguish by itself, cover with the skillet lid. Add enough wine to just cover the chicken, then add the bouquet garni. Cover the pan and simmer until the meat shows no sign of pink when pierced with the tip of a sharp knife, about 30 minutes. The white meat will be done first, so transfer to a warm platter while the dark meat continues to cook.

Meanwhile, melt the remaining 3 tablespoons butter in another skillet over medium heat. Add the white onions and salt pork and cook, turning occasionally, until lightly browned, about 5 minutes. Reduce the heat to low, cover, and cook until the onions are tender, about 20 minutes. Add the mushrooms, cover, and cook until they are softened, about 4 minutes. Remove from the heat and cover the skillet to keep warm.

When the chicken is cooked, and removed from the skillet, discard the bouquet garni, and skim off any fat from the surface of the red wine cooking liquid. Bring the liquid to a boil over high heat.

To make the beurre manié: Mash together the flour and softened butter in a small bowl with a rubber spatula until smooth. Gradually whisk bits of the beurre manié into the cooking liquid and cook until the sauce is smooth and thickened, about 3 minutes. Correct the seasoning with salt and pepper. Spoon the onion and mushroom mixture over the chicken on the platter, then pour the sauce over all.

JEANNE OWEN'S SAUTÉ WITH TARRAGON

~ MAKES 4 SERVINGS

Editor: Jeanne Owen was unusual for the early 1940s—a true gourmand who was also a woman. She was one of James's early mentors as he navigated the food professional world in New York after newly arriving from Oregon. Also, the original recipe called for two broiler chickens, weighing 2 pounds each, so this recipe has been adjusted to use a single, large bird.

6 tablespoons (¾ stick) unsalted butter

One 3½-pound chicken, quartered

½ cup dry Alsatian Riesling

Kosher salt and freshly ground black pepper

2 tablespoons finely chopped fresh tarragon

Melt the butter in a very large heavy skillet (not uncoated cast iron) over medium-high heat. Working in batches, if necessary, add the chicken to the skillet, skin side down, and brown quickly, about 3 minutes. Turn the chicken skin side up, add the Riesling, and reduce the heat to medium-low. Season with salt and pepper to taste. Cover and cook, turning the chicken occasionally, for 30 minutes. Sprinkle with the tarragon. Continue cooking, turning the chicken occasionally, until the chicken shows no sign of pink when pierced with the tip of a sharp knife at the thighbone, about 5 minutes more. Arrange on a hot platter. Bring the pan juices to a boil over high heat, scraping up the browned bits in the skillet, and cook until slightly reduced, about 2 minutes. Pour over the chicken and serve hot.

OLD-FASHIONED CHICKEN FRICASSEE WITH WAGON WHEELS

~ MAKES 6 SERVINGS

A wonderfully soothing dish, a great old favorite. If your family likes only the white or only the dark meat, you can buy your chicken in parts instead of whole and no one will feel disappointed. Wide noodles are traditional, but I served a fricassee with wagon wheels recently, and it made an amusing change.

4 tablespoons (½ stick) unsalted butter

One 4-pound chicken, cut into 8 serving pieces

¾ cup sliced celery

½ cup finely chopped yellow onion

2 tablespoons minced shallots

2 tablespoons all-purpose flour

1½ cups Chicken Stock (page 349)

1 cup heavy cream

1 teaspoon kosher salt

¼ teaspoon freshly ground black pepper

⅛ teaspoon freshly grated nutmeg

Pinch of cayenne pepper

2 large egg yolks

2 teaspoons freshly squeezed lemon juice

1 pound wagon wheel pasta or egg noodles

Melt 2 tablespoons of the butter in a large skillet over medium-high heat. Working in batches, add the chicken to the pan and sear for 1 minute, until it becomes firm on the outside but has not yet browned. Turn and sear the other side, then remove the chicken from the pan and transfer to a plate.

Melt the remaining 2 tablespoons butter in the

skillet. Reduce the heat to medium-low. Stir in the celery, onions, and shallots. When they are nicely coated with butter, sprinkle with the flour and cook, stirring, for about 30 seconds without browning the flour. Gradually whisk in the chicken stock.

Return the chicken to the skillet with ½ cup of the cream, the salt, black pepper, nutmeg and cayenne. Shake the pan to blend the spices. Bring the sauce to a low simmer, cover, and reduce the heat to medium-low. Simmer until the meat shows no sign of pink when pierced at the thighbone with the tip of a sharp knife, about 40 minutes.

Meanwhile, bring a large pot of lightly salted water to a boil over high heat. About 10 minutes before the sauce is done, add the pasta to the water and cook according to the package directions.

Meanwhile, transfer the chicken to a rimmed baking sheet and keep warm in a preheated 250°F oven. Tip the skillet and, using a flat spoon, skim off the surface fat from the sauce. Whisk the remaining ½ cup heavy cream and the egg yolks together in a small bowl. Gradually whisk about 1 cup of the hot sauce into the egg mixture, then whisk back into the skillet. Whisk over low heat until the sauce thickens to a light creamy consistency that just coats the spoon. It must not overheat or begin to simmer, or it will curdle. Season with the salt.

Drain the pasta and return to the cooking pot. Toss about half of the sauce with the pasta. Spread on a deep platter, top with the chicken, and pour the remaining sauce on top.

COUNTRY CAPTAIN

 MAKES 4 SERVINGS

Based on an East Indian curry, this dish owes its name to the term for a native Indian captain in the pay of his English colonizers. If you wish, after the initial sautéing of the chicken and vegetables, the dish can be baked in a 325°F oven until done.

Editor: The version given here comes from Cecily Brownstone, the food editor for Associated Press food columnist, and who was Beard's friend for decades.

¼ cup all-purpose flour

1 teaspoon kosher salt

¼ teaspoon freshly ground black pepper

One 3½-pound chicken, cut into 8 serving pieces

4 tablespoons (½ stick) unsalted butter

⅓ cup finely diced yellow onion

⅓ cup finely diced green bell pepper

1 garlic clove, crushed under a knife

1½ teaspoons curry powder

½ teaspoon dried thyme, crumbled

One 15-ounce can stewed tomatoes

3 tablespoons dried currants, rinsed and dried

½ cup blanched slivered almonds, toasted

Mix the flour, salt, and pepper together on a plate. Dredge the chicken in the flour mixture, shaking off any excess flour. Melt the butter in a large skillet over medium-high heat. Add the chicken and cook, turning occasionally, until browned on all sides, about 10 minutes. Transfer the chicken to a warm platter. Add the onion, bell pepper, garlic, curry powder, and thyme to the skillet. Cook over low heat, scraping up the browned residue in the pan with a wooden spatula. Add the stewed tomatoes with their liquid. Return the chicken to the skillet, skin side up. Cover and cook slowly over medium-low heat until the meat shows no sign of pink when pierced at the thighbone, about 30 minutes. Stir in the currants. Top with the toasted almonds and serve hot.

CREOLE FRIED CHICKEN

〰 MAKES 4 SERVINGS

Editor: Coated with cracker crumbs, this is just the kind of fried chicken that you night find in Louisiana's Bayou country. Make the effort to find small chickens, available at natural food stores. If the bird is too big, the outside crust will burn before the meat is cooked.

One 3- to 3½-pound chicken, cut into
　　8 serving pieces
1 lemon, halved
2 large eggs
½ cup whole milk
½ cup all-purpose flour
½ cup cracker meal
Lard or vegetable oil, for deep-frying
Kosher salt and freshly ground black pepper

Rub the chicken well with the lemon halves. Beat the eggs with the milk in a medium bowl. Add the chicken and refrigerate for 1 to 1½ hours. Combine the flour and cracker meal. Remove

each piece of chicken from the egg mixture and roll in the crumb mixture to coat. Let stand 15 minutes. Add enough lard or oil to come halfway up the sides of a large, deep saucepan. Heat over high heat to 350°F on a deep-frying thermometer. Carefully add the chicken to the oil and cook, turning occasionally, until the chicken is tender and well browned, about 18 minutes. Transfer to paper towels to drain briefly. Season with salt and pepper and serve hot.

CURRIED CHICKEN

〰 MAKES 4 SERVINGS

Editor: Eggplant lends its flavor and body to this curry's sauce. Serve it with boiled basmati rice, and a full contingency of condiments, such as mango chutney, chopped unsalted peanuts or slivered almonds, grated coconut, chopped hard-boiled egg, and raisins soaked in Cognac.

One 4-pound chicken, cut into 2 wings, 2 breast
　　halves, 2 thighs, 2 drumsticks, and 1 back, with
　　neck, heart, and gizzard reserved
2½ cups water
1 eggplant, peeled and cut into 1-inch cubes
3 tablespoons olive oil
½ cup water
6 tablespoons (¾ stick) unsalted butter
2 apples, washed but unpeeled, cored and cut
　　into ½-inch dice
2 medium onions, chopped
2 tablespoons curry powder

Pinch of cayenne pepper

1 teaspoon chopped garlic

½ teaspoon ground ginger

2 tablespoons Major Grey's chutney

2 tablespoons tomato purée or 1 tablespoon
    tomato paste diluted with 1 tablespoon water

Kosher salt

Chop the chicken back with a heavy chef's knife into 3-inch pieces. Put the back, neck, heart, and gizzard in a medium saucepan, and add enough cold water to cover the chicken pieces by 1 inch. Bring to a boil over high heat. Reduce the heat to low and simmer, skimming off any foam that rises to the surface, until full-flavored, about 2 hours. Strain and reserve the broth. You should have about 2½ cups broth.

Heat the oil in a large skillet over medium-high heat until shimmering. Add the eggplant and cook, stirring occasionally, until browned, about 5 minutes. Add the water and simmer until the eggplant is soft, about 5 minutes more. In another skillet heat 4 tablespoons of the butter. Add the apples and onions and cook, stirring often, until softened. Add the curry powder, cayenne, garlic, ginger, and 1 cup of the reserved broth. Cover and simmer for 30 minutes. Then add the chutney, tomato purée, softened eggplant, and a second cup of broth, and simmer for another 30 minutes.

Heat the remaining 2 tablespoons butter in a large skillet over medium heat. Working in batches, add the chicken and cook, turning occasionally, until nicely browned on all sides, about 10 minutes. Sprinkle with salt. Taste the curry sauce for seasoning, and dilute with a little water or broth if it is too thick. Add the chicken to the skillet with the sauce and cover. Simmer for about 25 minutes, or until cooked through and well flavored with the sauce.

DJAJ M'KALLI

MAKES 6 TO 8 SERVINGS

This is an interesting poached chicken dish from North Africa. Serve with steamed rice cooked with a large pinch of saffron. [*Editor: The Pickled Lemons need to age for at least a week before serving.*]

Two 3½-pound chickens, each cut into 8 serving
    pieces

2 tablespoons kosher salt

6 garlic cloves, finely chopped

1 cup vegetable oil

2 teaspoons ground ginger

1 teaspoon ground turmeric

1 teaspoon freshly ground black pepper

Good pinch of saffron threads

3 large yellow onions, grated

4 tablespoons (½ stick) unsalted butter

2 cups Chicken Stock (page 349)

2 cups water

1 cup Mediterranean black or green olives, pitted

A few slices of Pickled Lemon (see Box page 140)

Start this chicken dish the day before serving. Wash and drain the chicken pieces and remove all fat. Mix the salt with 3 of the garlic cloves and rub all over the chicken pieces. Let stand 1 hour; wipe off. Rub with a paste of 2 tablespoons of oil, ginger, turmeric, black pepper, and saffron. Put the rubbed chicken in a large bowl with the remaining oil, cover with plastic wrap, and refrigerate overnight.

The next day drain the chicken from the oil. Put the chicken with its spice coating in a very large Dutch oven with the onions, butter, and the remaining garlic. Add the stock and water. Bring to a boil, reduce the heat, cover, and simmer until the chicken is tender, 40 to 45 minutes. Transfer the chicken to a platter. Rapidly boil the broth down to a thick, rich sauce, stirring often—this should take about 15 minutes. Correct the seasoning. Add the olives and a few slices of pickled lemon. Reduce the heat to medium-low. Return the chicken to the simmering sauce to reheat. Serve hot.

Pickled Lemons

Makes about 2 quarts

Editor: Preserved lemons are a staple of Moroccan cuisine. To use them, chop the lemon rind, and all. Both the lemon and the lemon-flavored oil are great in salad dressings, marinades, and fish dishes, as well as stews where a little acidity would brighten the flavor.

To sterilize jars: Place a canning rack in a large pot and put the jars in the rack. Add enough cold water to cover the jars. Bring to a boil, then boil for 10 minutes. Meanwhile, soak the rings and lids in a bowl of hot tap water. Using tongs, remove the jars from the rack, drain, and dry immediately with a clean kitchen towel. Fill the jar while it is still hot, then close with the lids and rings. Or, simply run the jars through the dishwasher and use immediately after the rinse cycle has finished.

8 large lemons

½ cup kosher salt

Olive oil, as needed

Slice the lemons ½ inch thick and place in a colander. Cover with salt and wrap the colander entirely with plastic wrap. Let stand at room temperature for 24 hours. Remove the wrap, and rinse and drain the lemons well in the colander. Arrange the lemons in the sterilized canning jars. Add enough oil to completely cover the slices. Cover and let stand in a cool, dark place for 1 to 2 weeks before using. Pickled lemons will keep indefinitely if kept covered with oil. If the lemons taste bland after they have ripened, add 1 tablespoon of salt to each jar.

POULET
AU VINAIGRE

Editor: An old French dish, chicken in vinegar sauce enjoyed a revival in the 1970s, and is still on many bistro menus. For the best results, use naturally fermented French vinegar.

6 tablespoons (¾ stick) unsalted butter

One 4-pound chicken, cut into 8 serving pieces

Kosher salt and freshly ground black pepper

¾ cup water

2 scallions, white and green parts, finely chopped

¼ cup plus 1 tablespoon finely chopped fresh
     flat-leaf parsley

¼ cup top-quality red wine vinegar

Melt the butter in a large heavy skillet over medium-high heat. Working in batches, if necessary, add the chicken and brown on all sides, about 8 minutes. Lower the heat, and season the chicken to taste with salt and pepper. Add ½ cup of water, reduce the heat to low, cover, and simmer for 15 minutes. Add the scallions and 1 tablespoon of chopped parsley. Move the pieces of white meat to the top so the dark meat, which takes longer to cook, can get more heat. Cover again and cook until the meat shows no sign of pink when pierced with the tip of a sharp knife at the thighbone, about 20 minutes.

Transfer the chicken to a platter. Add the vinegar to the skillet. Increase the heat to high, bring to a boil, and cook, scraping up the brown residue in the pan, until the vinegar has reduced to a thick glaze, about 3 minutes. Stir in the remaining ¼ cup of water and mix until smooth. Add ¼ cup of chopped parsley, pour the sauce over the chicken, and serve hot.

CHICKEN WITH FORTY
CLOVES OF GARLIC

∽ MAKES 4 SERVINGS

You will find that the garlic has been tamed in the cooking and acquired a delicious buttery quality. Serve with hot toast or thin slices of pumpernickel—to be spread with the garlic sauce.

8 chicken leg quarters

⅔ cup extra-virgin olive oil

4 celery ribs, thinly sliced

6 sprigs fresh flat-leaf parsley

1 tablespoon finely chopped fresh tarragon or
     1½ teaspoons dried tarragon

½ cup dry vermouth

2½ teaspoons salt

¼ teaspoon freshly ground black pepper

Pinch of freshly grated nutmeg

40 garlic cloves, crushed under a knife and peeled

Wash the chicken legs and thighs and thoroughly dry with paper towels. Put the oil in a shallow dish or a plate and turn the chicken in the oil to coat on all sides. Reserve the unused oil. Lay the sliced celery in the bottom of a heavy casserole or Dutch oven (not uncoated cast iron) with a tight-fitting lid. Add the parsley and tarragon, then lay the chicken pieces on top. Pour the vermouth over the chicken, and add 1 teaspoon salt, the pepper, and the nutmeg.

Pour the reserved oil into the casserole, then toss in all the garlic and sprinkle with the remaining salt. Put a piece of aluminum foil over the casserole and then cover to make a tight seal; or make a thick, heavy flour and water paste to seal the lid, and cover the lid and paste with another layer of foil. Bake in a preheated 375°F oven for 1½ hours without removing the lid. To serve remove the foil (or break and remove the flour paste seal) and serve hot, from the pot.

BAKED MUSTARD CHICKEN

⌒ MAKES 4 SERVINGS

Editor: You will want to serve this luscious chicken with rice to be sure that you get every last drop of the creamy mushroom and mustard sauce.

Four 7-ounce boneless, skinless chicken
    breast halves
⅓ cup all-purpose flour
3 tablespoons unsalted butter
1 tablespoon olive oil
2 tablespoons Dijon or herbed Dijon mustard
1 medium yellow onion, finely chopped
½ cup finely chopped white mushrooms
1 cup heavy cream
Kosher salt and freshly ground black pepper
2 teaspoons freshly squeezed lemon juice
2 tablespoons finely chopped flat-leaf parsley

Dredge the chicken breasts in the flour and shake off the excess flour. Heat 2 tablespoons of the butter and the oil in a large, heavy skillet over medium-high heat. Add the chicken and cook, turning once, until lightly browned and not cooked through, about 4 minutes. Transfer to a shallow baking dish, and spread each breast generously with mustard. Add the onion and the remaining 1 tablespoon butter to the skillet, and cook over medium heat until softened, 2 or 3 minutes. Add the mushrooms and cook until they soften, about 2 minutes more. Blend in the heavy cream and heat through. Season with salt and pepper—start with ¼ teaspoon of salt; go easy on the pepper. Pour the mixture over the chicken, and bake in a preheated 350°F oven for about 30 minutes, or until the chicken is tender to the fork. Transfer the chicken to a platter. Stir the lemon juice into the sauce and correct the seasoning. Pour over the chicken and sprinkle with the chopped parsley.

CHICKEN LEGS WITH PAPRIKA AND SOUR CREAM

ᗡᗡ MAKES 6 SERVINGS

Editor: Chicken legs braise beautifully, and don't dry out as quickly as chicken breasts. By another name, this would be called Chicken Paprikash.

---

3 tablespoons vegetable oil

3 tablespoons unsalted butter

6 chicken leg quarters

Kosher salt and freshly ground black pepper

1 large yellow onion, chopped (1½ cups)

1 tablespoon sweet paprika, preferably Hungarian

1 cup Chicken Stock (page 349)

1 cup sour cream

Grated zest of 1 lemon

Heat the oil and butter together in a very large skillet over medium-high heat. Working in batches, add the chicken and cook, turning occasionally, until browned, about 8 minutes. Transfer to a plate. Season with salt and pepper. Add the onions to the fat in the skillet, and sauté over medium heat until lightly colored, about 5 minutes. Stir in the paprika and cook another 1 or 2 minutes. Return the chicken to the skillet, add the broth, and simmer until the meat shows no sign of pink when pierced with the tip of a sharp knife at the thighbone, about 25 minutes. Transfer the chicken to a serving platter. Stir the sour cream into the pan juices. Gently reheat but do not allow to boil. Pour over the chicken, and sprinkle with the lemon zest.

OVEN-FRIED CHICKEN LEGS

ᗡᗡ MAKES 4 SERVINGS

The pan juices from this baked dish are delicious, but don't pour them over the chicken because you want to keep that crispness; pour them around it. Serve with a good salad and a bottle of wine. You may also serve the chicken on a bed of rice or buttered noodles if you like.

2 cups plain whole or low-fat yogurt

1 garlic clove, crushed

½ teaspoon ground ginger

Kosher salt and freshly ground black pepper

4 chicken drumsticks

4 chicken thighs

1 cup all-purpose flour, yellow cornmeal, or coarsely crushed cornflakes

Combine the yogurt, garlic, and ginger in a large flat dish. Season with salt and pepper. Lay the chicken in the yogurt mixture and marinate for at least 2 hours, turning the pieces once during that time.

Remove the chicken from the yogurt. Roll each in the flour and arrange in a lightly oiled large baking pan or the bottom of a broiler pan. Bake in a preheated 350°F oven for 1 hour, until the chicken shows no sign of pink when pierced with the tip of a sharp knife at the thighbone, and the coating crisp and delicately browned.

CHICKEN MARYLAND

◇◇ MAKES 4 SERVINGS

There are countless recipes for this dish, and which is the original I cannot tell you. Escoffier, in his book *Ma Cuisine*, calls for a chicken to be floured, coated with egg and bread crumbs, and cooked in clarified butter until golden brown. This is put on a serving plate with sweet corn fritters, potato croquettes, bacon and banana, and served with a béchamel sauce to which a little horseradish has been added. M. Escoffier also suggests serving this dish with a tomato sauce!

A more authentic source, a very old Maryland and Virginia cookbook, says the chicken should be dredged with flour and cooked in a skillet in boiling lard about 2½ inches deep and served with a gravy made with drippings from the chicken, flour, milk, and salt and pepper—this to be served with rice. The most delicious dish I have ever eaten under the name of Chicken Maryland had a crisp crust on it and was served with a smooth cream gravy and corn fritters. Here is a version that I have found successful.

Four 8-ounce chicken breast halves, bone-in,
  skin on
1 lemon, halved
1 cup whole milk

John Beard's Sautéed Chicken

My father, who came of stalwart pioneer stock—he crossed the continent to Oregon in a covered wagon when he was five—had many definite ideas about food and life. Not only did he have the ideas, but he worked at them with a vengeance. One of them, which became a tradition in our home, must have had its influence on me at an early age.

Father felt that he could sauté a chicken better than anyone else in the family, in fact better than anyone else he had ever known. He liked a young chicken sautéed for Sunday morning breakfast. So, early on Sunday—Father was never a late sleeper—he could be found in the kitchen complete with chicken, utensils, and an apron. No one dared set foot in the "domestic offices" until the chicken was in the pan and wafting its glorious aroma throughout the lower floor of the house. He never would keep doors closed.

Father cut the chickens, or chicken, in ten pieces and dredged them lightly with flour. He then cut several slices of bacon from "the side" (don't think for one minute that sliced bacon was ever allowed in his house) and cut it in thin strips. These were fried out over a slow fire so that they became crisp and left a good deal of delicious fat in the iron skillet. The strips were removed to a platter, which was heating, and the pieces of chicken were lovingly lowered into the hot bacon fat. These he seared quickly, turning them and arranging them in the pan so that each morsel received the same degree of brownness and crispness.

Then the pan was covered, the flame turned low, and the chicken simmered for about 15 minutes. The cover was then removed and the pieces allowed just a few more minutes to take on additional crispness before being transferred to a hot platter.

2 large eggs, beaten

Kosher salt and freshly ground black pepper

1½ cups dried bread crumbs

½ pound sliced bacon, cut into ½-inch pieces

2 tablespoons all-purpose flour

2 cups half-and-half or 1 cup each whole milk and
heavy cream

Rub the chicken well with the lemon halves. Whisk the milk, eggs, 1 teaspoon salt, and ¼ teaspoon pepper together in a medium bowl. Add the chicken, turn to coat on all sides, and refrigerate for 2 hours.

Dip the soaked chicken pieces in the bread crumbs. Let stand for 15 minutes. Cook the bacon in a large skillet over medium heat until crisp, about 10 minutes. Transfer the bacon to paper towels to drain; reserve the bacon. Add the chicken to the hot bacon fat, skin side down. Reduce the heat to medium-low and cook, turning occasionally, until golden brown and tender, about 12 minutes. Transfer the chicken to a wire rack set over a plate to drain.

Pour off all but 2 tablespoons of fat from the skillet. Return the skillet to low heat. Whisk in the flour and cook, without browning, for about 2 minutes. Add the half-and-half and whisk until thickened and smooth. Simmer for 2 minutes,

Next came another rite: a heaping tablespoon of flour was put in the pan, after all the excess grease had been poured off, and was blended thoroughly with the little bits of goodness left in the pan. When these bits had been scraped around and melted with the flour, 2 cups of rich milk were poured in, the careful stirring began, and the seasoning was added, to Father's taste. He loved freshly ground black pepper and seemed to have a magic touch with it, for no one else I know has ever made it blend and yet retain its individuality the way Father did. When the sauce had achieved the proper degree of thickness for him, it was transferred to a hot bowl and breakfast was announced.

Of course, I neglected to say that he admitted someone else to the kitchen in time to make a huge pan of crispy hot biscuits or an iron pan filled with magnificent popovers.

Need I add that friends of the family and of mine were always pleased to stay overnight at our house?

Editor: When Beard's father was cooking chicken in the first decades of the twentieth century, the birds were much smaller than they are now. The average chicken weighed about 2½ pounds. Today this size chicken is very difficult to find, but you may find chickens weighing around 3½ pounds at natural food stores. For the larger bird, increase the total cooking time to about 45 minutes, or until the cooked chicken meat shows no sign of pink when pierced at the thighbone with the tip of a sharp knife. For the gravy, pour off all but 2 tablespoons of the "excess grease," and then proceed with the recipe using 2 tablespoons of flour. Half-and-half is a good substitute for "rich milk."

or until no raw flour taste remains in the sauce. Season with salt and pepper.

Pour the sauce on a platter. Add the chicken and top with the bacon strips. Serve hot.

Editor: The original was made with small "fryer" chickens weighing about 2 pounds each, split lengthwise. You won't be able to find this size chicken unless they are special-ordered from a poultry farm. The recipe has been adjusted for today's kitchens with large chicken breasts, and it is just as tasty as the original that uses split fryers.

CHICKEN CRÊPES

〰 MAKES 12 TO 14 CRÊPES; 6 SERVINGS

Editor: Crêpes remain a reliable dinner and brunch dish. Save the cooking broth from the poached chicken to make the Sauce Suprême.

For the Basic Crêpes

¾ cup plus 2 tablespoons all-purpose flour

3 large eggs

4 to 5 tablespoons unsalted butter, melted

⅛ teaspoon kosher salt

1 to 1½ cups whole milk, or as needed

Melted butter, for cooking the crêpes

For the Chicken Filling

3 cups Poached Chicken (page 130), cut into
   ½-inch dice

2 cups Sauce Suprême (page 352), flavored with
   2 tablespoons Madeira

2 tablespoons finely chopped fresh flat-leaf parsley

Freshly grated Parmesan cheese

To make the crêpe batter: Whisk the flour, eggs, melted butter, and salt together in a bowl. Gradually whisk in the milk until the batter has the consistency of light cream. (Or process all of the ingredients together in a blender.) Cover and let the batter rest for 2 hours before using.

To cook the crêpes, butter a 6-inch nonstick skillet with rounded sides and heat over medium-high heat. When the butter sizzles, pour about ¼ cup of the batter into the skillet, tilting and rotating so the batter coats the bottom evenly. Pour any excess batter back into the bowl. Cook about 30 seconds, until lightly browned on the underside, then turn with your fingers and brown the other side. Remove from the pan and transfer to a plate. Repeat with the remaining batter, separating the crêpes with pieces of waxed paper.

To make the filling: Mix the chicken, two-thirds of the sauce, and the chopped parsley. Place a generous spoonful down the center of each crêpe, and roll. Arrange, seam side down, in a buttered 13- by 9-inch baking dish. Spoon the remaining sauce over the crêpes and sprinkle lightly with the Parmesan cheese. Bake in a 375°F oven until heated through and the cheese is lightly browned, about 20 minutes.

SUPERB CHICKEN HASH

1 large yellow onion, finely chopped

2 green bell peppers, seeded and diced

5 tablespoons (½ stick plus 1 tablespoon) unsalted butter

2 tablespoons vegetable oil

4 cups Poached Chicken (page 130), cut into ½-inch dice

¼ cup finely chopped fresh flat-leaf parsley

½ cup coarsely chopped blanched almonds or walnuts

1½ teaspoons dried tarragon

Kosher salt and freshly ground black pepper to taste

Tabasco

8 large eggs

¼ cup freshly grated Parmesan cheese

Preheat the broiler. Sauté the onion and bell peppers in the butter and oil in a large skillet until just wilted, about 3 minutes. Add the chicken and mix well. Add the parsley, almonds, and tarragon, and season with salt and pepper. Press the chicken down well in the skillet, cover, and cook over medium heat for 2 or 3 minutes. When the chicken is heated through, beat the eggs with the Parmesan cheese. Pour into the skillet and cook over low heat until set. Put the skillet under the broiler and broil for 2 or 3 minutes to brown the top.

PENNSYLVANIA DUTCH CHICKEN "POT PIE"

∽ MAKES 6 TO 8 SERVINGS

Not at all what you think it is. In Pennsylvania Dutch cooking, "pot pies" are noodle squares that are added to rich chicken or beef broth. You serve them in a bowl, with a lot of broth and some of the chicken. If you wish, cook the chicken in chicken stock instead of the water.

For the Filling

One 4- to 5-pound stewing fowl or standard chicken

1 leek, white and pale green part only, coarsely chopped and well washed to remove grit

1 medium yellow onion, peeled and stuck with 1 whole clove

1 carrot, scrubbed

1 garlic clove, smashed and peeled

1 bay leaf

2 sprigs fresh flat-leaf parsley

3 whole black peppercorns

2 quarts cold water, as needed

Kosher salt

For the Noodles

2½ cups all-purpose flour

2 large eggs, beaten

1 tablespoon or rendered chicken fat or unsalted butter, softened

½ teaspoon kosher salt

½ cup cold water, or as needed

Chopped fresh flat-leaf parsley, for garnish

To make the pot pie filling: Put the chicken, leek, onion, carrot, garlic, bay leaf, parsley, and peppercorns into a large pot. Barely cover with water. Bring the liquid slowly to a boil over medium heat. Reduce the heat to medium-low and skim off any scum that rises to the surface. Cover the pot and simmer very gently, so that the surface barely moves, until the chicken is tender, about 2½ hours for a stewing fowl and 1¼ hours for the young, standard chicken.

Transfer the chicken to a platter and, when it is cool enough to handle, discard the skin and bones, and cut the meat into large pieces; set the meat aside. (If not serving within 2 hours, cover and refrigerate the meat.) Strain the broth, correct the seasoning with salt, and put it back on the stove over very low heat while you make the noodles.

To make the noodles: Combine the flour, eggs, chicken fat, and salt in a medium bowl. Stir in enough water to make a stiff dough. Turn out on a lightly floured work surface and knead for a few minutes, until smooth. Cover with a clean kitchen towel and let rest for 30 minutes. Cut the dough into quarters. Using a rolling pin, and keeping the other pieces covered, roll out one-fourth of the dough on a lightly floured work surface until it is very thin. Using a knife or a pastry wheel, cut the dough into 2-inch squares. Use them immediately or dry them as you would any other noodles, on lightly floured kitchen towels.

When you are ready to serve, return the chicken pieces to the broth and simmer for a few minutes to heat through. Then carefully add the noodles to the simmering broth and cook them until risen and tender, about 15 minutes. Ladle the broth, chicken, and noodles into soup bowls, and sprinkle with lots of chopped parsley.

BAKED CHICKEN POT PIE

MAKES 8 SERVINGS

Editor: Unless you live in Pennsylvania (see page 147), this is what chicken pot pie means to most cooks—a creamy chicken and vegetable filling topped with pastry.

For the Chicken and Vegetables

One 3½-pound chicken

Half of 1 lemon

Kosher salt

1 medium yellow onion, stuck with 3 whole cloves

A few celery leaves

12 small white boiling onions, peeled (see Note, page 237)

6 carrots, scraped and quartered

16 potato balls (cut from peeled baking potatoes with a melon baller) or very small new potatoes, peeled

Freshly ground black pepper

2 teaspoons chopped fresh flat-leaf parsley

Pinch of dried marjoram

For the Sauce

3 tablespoons unsalted butter

3 tablespoons all-purpose flour

2 cups reserved broth from the chicken

Kosher salt and freshly ground black pepper

Rich Tart Pastry (*Pâte Brisée*) (page 334), without the sugar

To cook the chicken and vegetables: Rub the inside of the chicken with the lemon half. Place the chicken in a large, deep pot and add enough lightly salted cold water to cover the chicken. Add the onion and celery leaves. Bring to boil over high heat, skimming off any scum that rises to the surface. Reduce the heat to medium-low and simmer until tender, about 50 minutes. Let cool in the broth. Discarding the skin and bones, cut the meat into bite-size chunks; reserve the broth.

In a separate saucepan, combine the boiling onions, carrots, and potatoes and add enough lightly salted water to cover. Cover and simmer over medium-low heat until tender, about 10 minutes. Drain well. Arrange the chicken and vegetables in a large shallow baking dish or deep-dish pie pan. Season with salt and pepper, and sprinkle with the parsley and marjoram.

To make the béchamel sauce: Skim the fat from the reserved broth. Measure 2 cups and save the remaining broth for another use. Melt the butter in a medium saucepan over medium heat. Whisk in the flour and let bubble without browning for 1 minute. Whisk in the broth and bring to a simmer. Reduce the heat to low and simmer, whisking often, until lightly thickened and no taste of raw flour remains, about 3 minutes. Season with salt and pepper. Pour over the chicken and vegetables and let cool.

Preheat the oven to 450°F. Roll out the pastry on a floured work surface into an 1/8-inch-thick shape that is about 1/2 inch larger than the baking dish; trim as needed. Place the pastry over the baking dish and refrigerate for 15 minutes. Bake for 10 minutes. Reduce the oven temperature to 375°F and continue baking until the pastry is golden brown, about 30 minutes. Serve hot.

CLUB HOUSE SANDWICH

✎ MAKES 1 SANDWICH

It may seem superfluous to include this veteran, but it is so often badly or incorrectly made that is could stand reviewing. To serve at a large party have the toasters going, arrange plates of the other makings, and let everyone do his or her own construction work. Green olives and sweet pickles are the traditional accompaniments.

> 2 slices crisp, hot buttered toast
>
> Cooked sliced chicken, as much as you want
>
> 4 slices peeled ripe tomato
>
> Mayonnaise, homemade (page 355) or
>   store-bought
>
> 3 or 4 slices crisp, hot bacon
>
> Lettuce (optional)

Construct in this order: 1 slice of toast, chicken, tomato, mayonnaise, bacon, lettuce, and the second slice of toast. The mayonnaise then holds the bacon and prevents slipping and sliding.

CHICKEN TETRAZZINI

~∞~ MAKES 6 TO 8 SERVINGS

Despite its Italian name, this is an all-American dish, probably invented in San Francisco to honor a famous singer. Now we remember her because of the dish. The whole point is in the chicken broth; if you have good, rich broth, your sauce will be properly flavored. If it's good it's marvelous, if bad—a mess.

For the Sauce

6 tablespoons (¾ stick) unsalted butter

6 tablespoons all-purpose flour

2½ cups cooking liquid from Poached Chicken (page 130) or canned chicken broth

1 cup heavy cream

½ cup dry sherry

¼ teaspoon Tabasco

Kosher salt and freshly ground black pepper

About 4 cups Poached Chicken (page 130), cut into bite-size pieces

2 red bell peppers, broiled until the skins blacken, peeled, seeded, and diced

1 pound spaghetti

¾ cup fresh bread crumbs, made in a blender or food processor from day-old bread

½ cup freshly grated Parmesan cheese

2 tablespoons cold unsalted butter, plus softened butter for the baking dish

To make the sauce: Melt the butter in a heavy-bottomed saucepan over medium-low heat, then whisk in the flour. Let it bubble without browning for 1 minute. Gradually whisk in the chicken cooking liquid, and cook, whisking constantly, until the sauce is thickened. Add the cream and sherry and season with the salt, pepper, and Tabasco. Add the chicken and bell peppers to the sauce and keep the sauce warm over low heat.

Meanwhile, bring a large pot of lightly salted water to a boil over high heat. Stir in the spaghetti and cook, stirring occasionally, according to the package directions, until al dente. Drain well.

Butter a large shallow baking dish. Add the spaghetti to the dish, and spoon the chicken and sauce over the spaghetti. Cover the top with the bread crumbs and Parmesan cheese and dot with butter. Place in a preheated 475°F oven for a few minutes until the topping is glazed and the sauce is bubbling.

VARIATIONS

CURRIED TETRAZZINI: Add 1 tablespoon or more curry powder to the butter when you first make the sauce. Let it cook for a minute before you add the flour.

TRUFFLED TETRAZZINI: If you are feeling rich and elegant, add a finely chopped black truffle to the chicken. Instead of a mixture of crumbs and cheese, sprinkle ½ cup toasted sliced almonds over the top.

ROAST STUFFED CORNISH GAME HEN

Four 1- to 1¼-pound Cornish game hens
1 lemon, halved

For the Stuffing

1⅓ cups chopped yellow onions or shallots
8 tablespoons (1 stick) unsalted butter
2⅓ cups fresh bread crumbs (made in a food
    processor or blender from day-old bread)
2 teaspoons chopped fresh tarragon, rosemary,
    or thyme, or use 1 teaspoon dried
1 tablespoon Cognac or Madeira
Kosher salt and freshly ground black pepper

Rub each bird inside and out with the lemon halves. Melt the butter in a medium skillet over medium heat. Pour out and reserve half of the butter. Add the onions to the skillet and cook until softened, about 5 minutes. Add the bread crumbs and stir in enough of the reserved melted butter to moisten them. Stir in your choice of herb and the Cognac, and season with salt and pepper. Stuff each bird, and skewer the vents closed or cover with a piece of aluminum foil. Truss with kitchen twine. Roast on a rack in a roasting pan in a preheated 350°F oven until the juices run clear when pricked with the tip of a sharp knife at the thigh, about 1 hour.

Remove from the oven and place on a hot platter. Let rest 15 minutes before removing the twine and skewers.

BASIC ROAST TURKEY

∽ MAKES 14 TO 18 SERVINGS

Editor: To test with an instant-read thermometer, insert the thermometer in the thickest part of the thigh, but not touching a bone. It should register 175°F.

One 18- to 20-pound turkey, giblets removed and
    reserved for another use
Half of 1 lemon
Basic Turkey Stuffing (page 152)
12 tablespoons (1½ sticks) unsalted butter,
    softened
Kosher salt and freshly ground black pepper
Strips of fresh pork fatback, bacon rind from slab
    bacon, or thick-sliced bacon

To stuff the turkey: Rub the inside of the turkey with the lemon half and dry with paper towels.

Stuff both the vent and neck cavity of the birds, using approximately ½ to ¾ cup of stuffing per pound. Do not pack, but fill loosely. If you like, use one type of stuffing for the vent and another for the neck—for example, a bread stuffing and a sausage stuffing. Draw the neck skin over the stuffing and tie it well or secure with skewers. Sew up the vent or arrange a piece of folded aluminum foil over the stuffing and skewer the opening.

To truss the turkey: Turn the wing tips under the back of the turkey. Using a long piece of kitchen twine, tie the legs together, wrap around the tail, and then secure the legs and tail together, leaving two lengths of string. Cross these under the middle of the back, wrap around each wing, bring together over the breast and tie. To keep the legs closer to the body, insert a skewer in the joint between each leg and thigh. Tie a piece of string from one skewer to the other, running it under the back. Massage the skin well with 6 tablespoons of softened butter, then salt and pepper it.

Line a roasting rack with strips of fatback. Set the rack in a fairly shallow roasting pan and place the turkey, breast side down, on the rack. Roast in a preheated 350°F oven for 1 hour, then turn the turkey on its side (to turn the bird, I use wads of paper towels), and rub the exposed turkey with 2 tablespoons softened butter. Roast for another hour. Turn on its other side, and rub with 2 more tablespoons of butter. Roast for a third hour. Turn the turkey on its back and rub the breast with the final 2 tablespoons of butter. Return to the oven and continue roasting until the turkey tests done. The trick of roasting a turkey is to keep the white meat from becoming dry while cooking the dark meat sufficiently. There is no certain test to tell you when the turkey is done, and you must rely a good bit on your judgment. Here are two general rules to help you. First, see if the leg can be moved up and down somewhat flexibly. (To my mind, by the time the leg is really loose, the bird is over-done.) Second, prick the leg joint with a fork; if the juices run clear or faintly pink, the bird is done.

Remove from the oven and place on a hot platter. Allow the bird to rest for 15 minutes if being served hot. If being served tepid, let it cool gently at room temperature. Remove all the twine and skewers. Proceed to carve.

Basic Turkey Stuffing

Makes about 12 cups

One of the simplest and best stuffings is prepared in the following way. Gauge about ½ to ¾ cup of stuffing per pound of turkey.

2 large yellow onions, finely chopped
10 tablespoons (2¼ sticks) unsalted butter
9 cups stale bread crumbs or toasted crumbs
2½ cups finely cut celery
2½ tablespoons finely chopped flat-leaf parsley
1¼ teaspoons dried thyme
1¼ teaspoons dried marjoram
Kosher salt and freshly ground black pepper

Sauté the onions in 2½ tablespoons of butter in a large skillet until translucent. Add the remaining butter, and allow to melt. Pour into a large bowl, and mix with the crumbs, celery, parsley, thyme, and marjoram. Season with salt and pepper.

VARIATION

TURKEY WITH GARLIC AND BLACK PEPPER: Stuff the turkey with a 6-inch length of dry French bread that has been rubbed with garlic to saturate it, and then rolled in freshly ground black pepper. This makes a fairly heady seasoning, and is especially good for small turkeys roasted on the spit.

TRUFFLED TURKEY: Use either the white Italian truffles or the black French variety. The night before roasting the turkey, cut the truffles in slices ⅛ inch thick. Loosen the breast skin with your fingers and arrange the truffle slices underneath. Also place several slices in the cavity of the bird if you are not stuffing it. Secure the neck and skin and vent, and truss. Rub well with a mixture of salt, freshly ground black pepper, butter, and a little thyme. Follow the basic roasting directions above.

BRAISED TURKEY WINGS

〰 MAKES 4 SERVINGS

Braising is excellent for turkey wings, which are not the tenderest or most toothsome parts of the bird. Be sure to remove the cover toward the end of the cooking time so they brown nicely. Serve with puréed potatoes and a cucumber and watercress salad.

    3 tablespoons unsalted butter

    1 large yellow onion, sliced

    2 carrots, cut in julienne strips

    2 celery stalks, cut in julienne strips

    2 or 3 sprigs fresh flat-leaf parsley

    6 garlic cloves, smashed under a knife and peeled

    1 cup dry white wine

    4 turkey wings

    Kosher salt and freshly ground black pepper

Heat the butter in a braising pan or flameproof casserole or Dutch oven over medium heat, add the onion, carrot, celery, and parsley and let them wilt down in the fat for 5 minutes. Toss in the garlic, add the wine, arrange the turkey wings on top, and season them well with salt and pepper. Cover and braise in a preheated 350°F oven for about 1½ hours, or until tender, removing the cover for the last 20 minutes.

VARIATION

TURKEY WINGS PROVENÇAL: Add 4 or 5 additional garlic cloves, 1 teaspoon dried rosemary, and a cup or more tomato sauce—homemade, naturally!—see Light Tomato Sauce (page 204) and proceed as above. Serve with polenta.

TURKEY WINGS PIQUANT: Proceed as in basic recipe, but add one 4-ounce can chopped green chilies and 1 tablespoon (or more to taste) chili powder.

TURKEY CHILI

〰 MAKES 8 TO 10 SERVINGS

Serve the chili with rice, polenta, or tortillas.

    5 to 6 pounds turkey parts on the bone:
        breast halves, drumsticks, and thighs

    1 medium yellow onion stuck with 2 or 3 whole cloves

    2 celery stalks

    2 sprigs fresh flat-leaf parsley

    2 small dried hot chile peppers

    Kosher salt

    1 cup ground sliced natural almonds

    ½ cup ground peanuts

    One 4-ounce can chopped green chilies

    2 tablespoons chili powder

1 large yellow onion, finely chopped

2 green bell peppers, seeded and finely chopped

3 garlic cloves, finely chopped

¼ cup extra-virgin olive oil

1 cup small pitted green olives

½ cup blanched almonds

Cover the turkey parts with salted water in a deep pot, and add the clove-studded onion, celery, parsley, and hot chilies. Bring to a boil over high heat and skim off any scum that rises to the surface. Reduce the heat and cover the pot. Simmer until the turkey is tender but not falling off the bones, about 1 hour. Remove the turkey from the broth, and when it is cool enough to handle, strip the meat from the bones in good size chunks. Discard the skin and bones.

Strain the broth into a bowl and discard the vegetables. Degrease the broth and return it to the pot. Boil over high heat until reduced to 4 cups (this should take at least 15 minutes). Add the ground almonds, ground peanuts, green chilies, and chili powder. Simmer until nicely thickened. Meanwhile, sauté the chopped onions, bell peppers, and garlic in a large skillet with the olive oil until limp, about 5 minutes. Add to the sauce and cook for 5 minutes. Add the turkey meat, and heat though. Finally add the olives and blanched almonds, and cook for another 2 or 3 minutes. Serve hot.

TURKEY MOLE

MAKES 8 SERVINGS

Editor: Turkey mole is traditionally made with a whole turkey, but Beard's version, with turkey parts, is much more practical. The turkey wing will add extra flavor to the mole, much more than using the breast half by itself. Serve on top of polenta or rice, or with warm corn or flour tortillas.

One 2½-pound turkey breast half, bone in, skin on

One 1-pound turkey wing, cut apart at the joints

Kosher salt

2 medium yellow onions, chopped

2 tablespoons rendered bacon fat or vegetable oil

1 cup ground almonds, walnuts, peanuts, or cashews

2 ounces unsweetened chocolate, finely chopped

2 tablespoons chili powder

2 garlic cloves

1 small dried hot chile pepper

1 cup drained ripe, pitted California black olives

Place the turkey breast and wing in a deep pot, add water to cover, and bring to a boil. Add 1½ teaspoons salt and simmer for 30 minutes, skimming off any foam that rises to the surface.

Meanwhile, brown the onions in bacon fat in a medium skillet over medium heat, about 5 minutes. Add to the pot along with the almonds, chocolate, chili powder, garlic, and dried chile. Cover the pot and simmer over medium-low heat until the sauce is thickened and the turkey is tender, about 30 minutes more. Ten minutes before serving, add the olives and heat through. Season with salt and more chili powder, if desired. Transfer the turkey breast and wing to a carving board. Cut the meat into bite-size pieces, discarding the skin and bones, and return the meat to the pot. Serve hot.

DUCK GLAZED WITH CURRY AND HONEY

MAKES 6 TO 8 SERVINGS

These timings and temperatures should give you ducks that are medium-rare—that is, still a bit pink at the joints. If you like your duck well-done, cook longer.

Two 4- to 5-pound ducks

2½ tablespoons curry powder

2 garlic cloves, finely chopped

1 teaspoon ground turmeric

½ teaspoon Tabasco

Kosher salt

½ cup honey

¼ cup freshly squeezed orange juice

¼ cup freshly squeezed lemon juice

Rub the ducks inside and out with 1 tablespoon of the curry powder mixed with the garlic, turmeric, and Tabasco. Season with salt. Stir the honey, orange juice, and lemon juice together in a small bowl.

If you are using a spit, truss, spit, and balance the ducks. Roast over medium coals for about 1½ hours. During the last half of the roasting, baste with a mixture of the honey, orange juice, lemon, juice, and the remaining curry powder. Prick the skin from time to time with the tines of a meat fork to release the fat.

If you are using the oven, roast the ducks on a large rack on a roasting pan in a preheated 350°F oven for 1½ hours. Baste frequently with the honey-curry mixture. Be sure to prick the skin occasionally with the meat fork. During the last 20 minutes of roasting time, increase the oven temperature to 475°F to crisp the skin. The ducks are done when the skin is crisp and the juices run pink when the ducks are pierced with a meat fork.

Let the ducks stand for 10 minutes. Using poultry shears, cut into quarters and serve hot.

ROAST DUCK WITH ORANGES

MAKES 2 SERVINGS

Editor: This is a much simplified version of the French standard canard à l'orange.

4 navel oranges

1 garlic clove

One 4- to 5-pound duck

Kosher salt and freshly ground black pepper

1 cup freshly squeezed orange juice

Grated zest of 1 orange

¼ cup Grand Marnier or other orange-flavored liqueur

1½ teaspoons unsalted butter

Grate the zest from 1 orange; set the zest aside. Using your hands, peel another orange and separate it into sections; set the sections aside.

Insert the garlic and orange sections in the duck cavity. Rub the skin with salt and pepper. Place on a rack in a roasting pan. Roast in a pre-heated 350°F oven, occasionally brushing the duck with ½ cup orange juice and pricking the skin with the tines of a meat fork, for 1 hour, 10 minutes. Increase the oven temperature to 475°F and continue roasting until the skin is crisp and the juices run pink when the duck is pierced with a meat fork, about 20 minutes more. Transfer the duck to a warm platter.

Skim the excess fat from the roasting pan. Add the remaining ½ cup of orange juice, zest, and the orange liqueur. Cook the orange juice mixture over high heat, scraping up the browned residue in the pan with a wooden spatula, until it has reduced by half. Remove from the heat and whisk in the butter. Season with salt and pepper. Using poultry shears, cut the duck into quarters and serve with the orange sections and sauce.

ROAST DUCKLING AU POIVRE

⌒ **MAKES 2 SERVINGS**

Duck takes nicely to this peppery treatment, based on the same idea as steak au poivre.

One 4- to 5-pound duck
Kosher salt
Dried thyme or rosemary
1 small yellow onion, stuck with 2 whole cloves
1 tablespoon crushed black peppercorns

Rub the duck skin with salt and the herb of your choice. Put the onion in the cavity. Place the duck on a rack in a shallow roasting pan. Roast in a preheated oven at 350°F for 30 minutes. Prick the skin with a meat fork all over to release the fat. Roast for 30 minutes longer. Remove the duck from the oven and press the peppercorns into the skin. Return it to the oven and roast for 15 minutes. Increase the oven heat to 500°F and continue roasting until the duck juices run pink when pierced at the thigh joint with the meat fork, about 15 minutes longer. (For well-done duck, roast for 15 to 30 minutes longer, or until the juices run clear when the thigh is pricked.) Let the duck stand for 10 minutes. To serve, cut into halves or quarters with poultry shears.

ROASTED STUFFED WILD DUCK

⌒ **MAKES 2 SERVINGS**

Serve fresh corn bread, a puree of fresh turnips, and an orange and onion salad with a rosemary-hinted vinaigrette with this duck.

For the Stuffing
8 tablespoons (1 stick) unsalted butter
½ cup thinly cut celery
1 medium yellow onion, finely chopped
1 teaspoon finely chopped fresh thyme
¼ cup chopped fresh flat-leaf parsley
2 cups fresh bread crumbs (made in the blender or food processor from day-old bread)
1 teaspoon kosher salt

½ teaspoon freshly ground black pepper

4 tablespoons (½ stick) butter, melted

1 large egg, slightly beaten

For the Ducks

Two 2½- to 3-pound wild ducks, liver and heart
reserved

4 tablespoons (½ stick) unsalted butter, at room
temperature

Kosher salt and freshly ground black pepper

⅓ cup unsalted butter, melted

⅓ cup red wine, Port, Marsala, or Madeira

The duck giblets

To make the stuffing: Melt the butter in a large skillet over medium heat. Pour out half of the butter and set aside. Sauté the celery and onion in the remaining butter in the skillet until they are beginning to soften, about 3 minutes. Mix the onion, parsley, thyme, and bread crumbs, with the reserved melted butter. Season with salt and pepper then mix in the egg.

To prepare the ducks: Stuff the ducks with the bread mixture, tie and truss them, and place on a rack in a shallow roasting pan. Rub the ducks with 2 tablespoons of butter and sprinkle them with salt and pepper. Mix the melted butter and red wine together in a medium bowl. Roast the ducks in a preheated 350°F oven, basting every 10 minutes with the red wine mixture, for 45 minutes to 1 hour, depending on how well-done you like your ducks. When pierced with the tip of a sharp knife, pink juices indicate medium-rare duck and clear juices indicate well-done duck.

While the ducks are roasting, sauté the liver and heart in a small skillet with the remaining 2 tablespoons butter until cooked through, about 5 minutes. Finely chop the liver and heart and season with salt and pepper.

Remove the ducks from the oven and transfer to a hot platter. Let stand for 10 minutes. Blend the pan juices with the giblets, and reheat until hot. To serve, split the ducks in half lengthwise with poultry shears and serve with the pan juices as a sauce.

VARIATION

SOUTHERN-FRENCH-STYLE WILD DUCK: Sauté **1 thinly sliced yellow onion, ¾ cup finely cut celery, ¼ cup finely chopped fresh flat-leaf parsley, 10 to 20 pitted Mediterranean black olives (such as Kalamata), and 1 minced garlic clove** in **4 tablespoons (½ stick) butter.** Stir in **1 cup fresh bread crumbs, ⅛ cup Armagnac, 1 teaspoon freshly ground black pepper,** and **¾ teaspoon salt.** Stuff 2 ducks with this mixture, truss, and rub with butter. Roast as above, basting every few minutes with a mixture of **½ cup dry red wine** and **½ cup hot Chicken Stock (page 349).** Split the ducks lengthwise and serve with a purée of broccoli.

ROAST HOLIDAY GOOSE WITH APPLE AND PRUNE STUFFING

∽ MAKES 8 SERVINGS

If you cannot find a fresh goose, there are excellent frozen ones on the market. A frozen goose should be thoroughly thawed before roasting, preferably in the refrigerator, in its original wrap, which will take 1½ to 2 days. There is a great deal of fat on a goose. Therefore it should be roasted slowly and on a rack so the bird crisps while the fat drips down into the roasting pan. Reserve the fat for future cooking; it can be used for many dishes.

For the Goose Stock

One 8- to 10-pound goose, neck and giblets
    reserved for stock, liver reserved for another use
1 small yellow onion, coarsely chopped
1 small carrot, coarsely chopped
Pinch of dried thyme
½ bay leaf
A few black peppercorns
2 tablespoons cornstarch

For the Stuffing

½ cup finely chopped yellow onion
6 tablespoons (¾ stick) unsalted butter
5 to 6 cups fresh bread crumbs (made in a food pro-
    cessor from day-old bread)
2 cups peeled, cored, and chopped tart apples
1 cup pitted and chopped dried plums (prunes),
    steeped in hot water or Madeira until puffed
1 cup cooked peeled chestnuts or canned chestnuts
1 teaspoon dried thyme
½ teaspoon freshly grated nutmeg
Kosher salt

To prepare the goose stock: Remove any excess fat from the cavity of the goose. Using a heavy knife or cleaver, chop the neck into 2- to 3-inch chunks. Using poultry shears, trim off the wings tips, and snip them into 2-inch pieces.

Heat the fat slowly in a medium saucepan over medium-high heat until it begins to render. Add the neck and wing tip pieces, the heart, and gizzard and cook, stirring occasionally, until they are nicely browned, about 10 minutes. Add the onion and carrot and cook, stirring occasionally, until softened, about 5 minutes. Pour in enough cold water to cover the ingredients by 1 inch. Bring to a boil over high heat, skimming off the scum that rises to the surface. Reduce the heat to low and add the thyme, bay leaf, and peppercorns. Simmer until richly flavored, about 2 hours. Strain into a heatproof bowl. Let stand and cool to room temperature. Skim off the fat that rises to the surface of the stock and transfer the fat to a large jar with a lid. Measure and reserve 3 cups of the stock. (Any extra stock can be used like chicken stock in any recipe.)

To prepare the stuffing: Sauté the onion in the melted butter in a large skillet over medium heat until tender, about 5 minutes. Add the bread crumbs and toss to moisten throughout. Add the apples, dried plums (prunes), chestnuts, thyme, and nutmeg, season with salt, and blend well. Stuff the goose with this mixture, and truss (see page 151); or just skewer the cavity closed and tie the legs together. Place the goose, breast side up, on a rack in a roasting pan. Roast for 1 hour in a preheated 400°F oven, then prick the skin all over with the tines of a meat fork to release the fat. Reduce the oven temperature to 350°F and roast for another hour, without basting. As the fat is rendered, remove it from the roasting pan with a bulb baster and add to the other rendered fat from the stock. After the second hour, test the bird to see if it is done. It should be well browned, the leg meat should be soft when pressed, and the juices should run clear, with the faintest blush of pink when the thigh is pricked. If more cooking is required, reduce the heat to 325°F and continue roasting. The total cooking time will be from 2 to 2½ hours. Remove the goose from the oven and allow to stand for 15 minutes before carving.

Degrease the pan juices, removing as much fat as possible, and add the fat to the jar with the fat from the stock. (Refrigerate the fat for another use; it is excellent for sautéing potatoes.) Add the stock to the roasting pan and bring to a boil over high heat. Reduce to about 2½ cups. Dissolve 2 teaspoons of cornstarch in ¼ cup of water, whisk into the boiling goose stock mixture, and let the sauce thicken lightly. Strain into a sauceboat. Carve the goose and serve with the sauce.

SAUTÉ OF QUAIL WITH WHITE GRAPES

∅ MAKES 3 SERVINGS

Editor: White grapes are the same thing as green grapes.

6 slices stale bread about 2 inches thick

6 quail, cleaned

6 tablespoons (¾ stick) unsalted butter, at room temperature, plus more for buttering the croustades

Kosher salt and freshly ground black pepper

½ cup Chicken Stock (page 349) or canned chicken broth

6 tablespoons Cognac

1 cup seedless white (green) grapes

Trim each slice of bread into an oval croustade a little larger than the quail. Hollow out a shallow cavity into which the quail will fit and toast the croustades gently in a 300°F oven for about 15 minutes. Butter the cavity into which you will place the bird.

Melt the butter in a very large skillet over medium-high heat. Add the quail and cook, turning occasionally, until browned on all sides, about 5 minutes. Season with salt and pepper and add the broth. Cover, reduce the heat to medium-low, and simmer for 10 minutes. Pour the Cognac over the birds and remove from the heat. Ignite the Cognac with a long match. If the fire doesn't burn out on its own after 30 seconds, cover the skillet with its lid. Return the skillet to medium heat, add the grapes, and shake the pan to coat the grapes with the juices. Serve the quail and grapes in the croustades, and pass the pan juices separately.

SAUTÉED PHEASANT WITH CALVADOS AND APPLES

~ MAKES 4 SERVINGS

For this dish, it is preferable to use only the pheasant breasts, although you may, if you wish, cook the dark meat in another skillet as a second helping for guests with hearty appetites. Serve with steamed buttered rice garnished with pistachio nuts.

Breasts of 2 young pheasants
12 tablespoons (1½ sticks) unsalted butter
⅓ cup Calvados or applejack
Kosher salt and freshly ground black pepper
½ cup dry white wine
6 apples, peeled, cored, and thinly sliced
2 teaspoons sugar
1 cup heavy cream
3 large egg yolks

Cut the breasts in half lengthwise; discard the breastbone. Sauté the breasts in a large nonreactive skillet over medium heat in 6 tablespoons of the butter until they are a rich ivory color—do not brown, as this is a blond sauce. Pour in ¼ cup of Calvados and remove from the heat. Ignite the Calvados with a long match. If the fire doesn't burn out on its own after 30 seconds, cover the skillet with its lid. Season the breasts with salt and pepper. Return to medium-low heat, add the white wine, and cover. Simmer for 8 to 10 minutes, or until the pheasant meat looks barely cooked through when pierced in the thickest part with the tip of a sharp knife. Do not overcook. Transfer to a hot platter and tent with aluminum foil to keep warm.

In the same skillet, melt the remaining 6 tablespoons butter over medium-high heat. Add the apples, sprinkle with the sugar, and cook, turning occasionally, until they are glazed, about 3 minutes. Add the apples to the platter with the pheasant and cover with aluminum foil.

Add remaining Calvados to the skillet and reduce the heat to low. Whisk the cream and egg yolks together lightly in a small bowl. Whisk a little of the hot skillet juices into the bowl, then whisk back into the skillet, and cook, whisking constantly, until smooth and lightly thickened. Do not allow to boil. Serve in a sauceboat.

FISH AND SHELLFISH

FISH AND SHELLFISH

Whole Broiled Fish

Whole fish, either small ones or those of fairly good size, are delicious broiled. Have the fish scaled and gutted and the head and tail left on (unless this would make it too large for your broiling facilities).

Rub the skin with **oil** on both sides and then with **kosher salt** and **freshly ground black pepper**. Slash the skin in two or three places on each side with a sharp knife, to prevent its splitting when broiled. You can also salt and pepper the inside of the fish and put a **slice or two of lemon** inside, or, if you wish, stuff a few sprigs of fresh herbs or a sprinkling of **dried herbs** inside. Crushed or chopped herbs may be rubbed on the skin with the seasonings. **Thyme, rosemary,** and **summer savory** are good herbs for fish.

Measure the fish at the thickest point to estimate the cooking time—the rule for any type of fish cookery is to allow 10 minutes per inch of measured thickness. Place a strip of aluminum foil on the broiler rack or in the broiler pan; brush it with oil, and arrange the fish on it to allow for easy turning. Or, if the fish is not too large, arrange in a disposable aluminum foil broiler pan with a corrugated surface.

Broil the fish approximately 4 inches from the preheated broiler, according to size (large fish 4 to 6 inches from the heat; smaller fish 2 to 4 inches away), allowing 10 minutes per measured inch of thickness for total cooking time. Halfway through the cooking turn the fish with a large spatula, using the foil to help. Be careful not to overcook or let the skin char too much. If the heat seems too intense, lower the pan an inch or two. Test the flesh with a toothpick or a fork 3 or 4 minutes before the end of the estimated time. If it flakes, it is done.

When done, transfer to a heated platter and serve at once with an appropriate sauce, such as Mustard Sauce (page 352), Hollandaise Sauce (page 353), Béarnaise Sauce (page 355), or Caper Sauce (page 352).

You may also split the whole fish and broil it, removing the head but leaving the backbone in (which seems to keep the juiciness and flavor). Lay the split fish, skin side down, on the oiled aluminum foil, brush the flesh well with melted butter, and broil 3 inches from the heat, allowing 10 minutes per measured inch. Do not turn the fish but baste it several times during the cooking with melted butter. Season with salt and pepper.

Estimate about ½ pound whole or split fish per serving, to allow for the inedible parts.

BROILED MARINATED HALIBUT STEAKS

✒ MAKES 2 TO 4 SERVINGS

Thick steaks of firm-fleshed fish such as halibut or swordfish can be marinated before cooking, which gives them flavor and prevents them from drying out.

For the Marinade

6 tablespoons olive oil

1 tablespoon freshly squeezed lemon or lime juice

2 small garlic cloves, finely chopped

1 teaspoon dried basil

1½ teaspoons kosher salt

1 teaspoon freshly ground black pepper

For the Fish

2 halibut steaks, 1 inch thick

Chopped fresh flat-leaf parsley, for garnish

To make the marinade: Combine the ingredients in a glass or pottery dish large enough to hold the halibut in one layer. Add the halibut and marinate for 2 hours, turning them two or three times in the marinade.

To cook the fish: Line a broiler pan or rack with aluminum foil; oil or butter the foil; put the steaks on the foil and broil 4 inches from the heat for 5 minutes a side, brushing with the marinade. Transfer to hot plates and sprinkle with the parsley.

COLD POACHED SALMON IN RED WINE ASPIC

✒ MAKES 12 SERVINGS

A whole poached salmon in aspic is a glorious sight on a buffet table. You should use fish bones and heads to provide a strong, concentrated, flavorful stock with natural gelatin, and clarify it for your aspic. This recipe is rather unusual in that red wine is used in the poaching court bouillon, rather than the usual white.

Editor: Poached salmon remains one of the most elegant dishes to serve at a summer buffet. It is best to make it over a two-day period. On the first day, poach, cool, peel, and refrigerate the salmon. Also, make and reduce the stock, but refrigerate it overnight so the fat rises to the top of the stock and can be easily removed; the stock must be absolutely fat-free for the clarification to work. The next day, make the aspic and decorate the salmon. You can purchase reasonably priced fish poachers online—the stainless steel ones work just as well as the copper models. If your salmon doesn't fit into the poacher, cut off the fish head.

For the Court Bouillon

2 to 3 pounds fish bones and heads

[*Editor: Use a white-fleshed, nonoily fish, and not salmon or other dark-fleshed fish.*]

2 quarts water

4 to 5 cups dry red wine

½ cup red wine vinegar

1 medium yellow onion, peeled and stuck with
2 whole cloves

1 carrot, scraped

1 lemon, thinly sliced

1½ tablespoons kosher salt

1 tablespoon fresh thyme leaves

2 bay leaves

¼ teaspoon whole black peppercorns

For the Salmon

6- to 7-pound cleaned and scaled salmon

2 large egg whites, lightly beaten, and 2 crushed
eggshells

3 envelopes unflavored gelatin

¼ cup cold water

Thin slices of lemon, thin cucumber slices, tarragon
leaves, sprigs of fresh dill, for decoration

To make the court bouillon: Combine the fish bones and heads and water in a large pot. Bring to a boil, reduce the heat to medium-low, and simmer until the fish practically falls apart, 1 hour or more.

Strain the fish stock into a bowl and transfer it to a fish poacher with a rack, or a roasting pan with a rack large enough to hold the salmon. Add the wine, vinegar, onion, carrot, lemon, salt, thyme, bay leaves, and peppercorns, bring to a boil, reduce the heat, and simmer for 10 minutes.

To prepare the salmon: Measure the salmon at its thickest point to determine the cooking time (10 minutes per measured inch). Put it on the rack of the fish poacher or on a large piece of heavy-duty aluminum foil; lower it into the simmering liquid and poach at a simmer for the necessary time. Test for doneness with a fork, or toothpick. If the flesh flakes easily, it is done.

Transfer the salmon to a platter and cool completely. When cool, carefully peel off and discard all the skin, and scrape off the gray fat under the skin; put the fish on a board or serving platter, cover with plastic wrap, and chill while making the aspic.

Boil the poaching liquid rapidly until reduced to about 7 cups. Strain it through a large wire sieve lined with several thicknesses of rinsed cheesecloth into a deep saucepan. Put the saucepan in a large bowl of ice water to cool the stock. Skim off all fat from the surface of the stock. Beat the egg whites until frothy, and stir the whites and egg shells into the stock. Heat over medium heat, whisking often, until the stock comes to a boil and the egg whites rise to the surface. Remove the pan from the heat and let stand 5 minutes, to settle. Then, without agitating the stock, strain it through a large sieve lined with several fresh thicknesses of rinsed cheesecloth. Strain the clarified stock through a sieve lined with a linen towel or several thicknesses of cheesecloth into another saucepan. Reheat the stock until steaming.

Sprinkle the gelatin on the cold water in a small bowl and let stand 5 minutes, until softened. Stir it into the hot, clarified liquid until dissolved. Let the aspic mixture cool until tepid. Place the saucepan in a bowl of ice water and stir often until it starts to chill and get syrupy.

Remove the salmon from the refrigerator, take off the wrap, and coat the flesh on the best-looking side of the salmon with a thin coat of the syrupy aspic, pouring it over with a large spoon. Chill the fish until the aspic sets, then give it another coat and again chill until set. You may find when working with aspic that it gets too cold and sets. In this case, you have to melt it over very low heat and chill again until it starts to get syrupy. Decorate the fish with thin "scales" of lemon and cucumber and with sprays of tarragon leaves or sprigs of dill. Dip the decorations in aspic first so they will adhere to the coating. Then, very carefully, apply a final coat of aspic over the decorations and chill until set. Remove any aspic that ran onto the board or platter. Garnish with the tarragon leaves and dill sprigs. Leftover aspic can be chilled in a thin layer in a baking dish, chopped, and scattered around the fish. You might also serve a cucumber salad if you didn't use cucumbers for decoration.

SARDINES WITH MINT

〰 **MAKES 4 SERVINGS**

I discovered this at Le Bistrôt in Mougins, a lovely old hill town above Cannes, and asked for the recipe because it is such an unusual and delicious way to treat small fish like sardines or smelts. You could use the same stuffing in a baked whole fish, between fish steaks, or in rolled fish fillets.

> 12 fresh sardines or smelts
> 1½ pounds fresh leaf spinach, tough stems removed, well washed to remove grit
> ½ cup fresh bread crumbs (made in a food processor or blender from day-old bread)
> ¼ cup finely chopped fresh mint or 2 tablespoons crumbled dried mint
> ¼ cup finely chopped fresh flat-leaf parsley
> 2 shallots, finely chopped
> 2 garlic cloves, finely chopped
> Kosher salt and freshly ground black pepper
> Olive oil

Clean the fish, split and remove backbones; this is easy to do by pulling off the head—the whole bone will come with it. Cook the spinach in a large pot of boiling water for 1 minute; drain well, pressing out all the water, and chop finely. Mix the spinach with the bread crumbs, mint, parsley, shallots, and garlic, and season to taste with salt and pepper. Mix well. Spread the fish flat, flesh side up, and put a little bit of the stuffing on the widest end. Roll up toward the tail and pack the rolled fish tightly together in a baking dish so they can't unroll. Brush well with the oil and bake in a preheated 425°F oven for 10 minutes, basting once or twice with oil, until the edges of the fish look opaque. Serve hot.

SAUTÉED TROUT

〰 **MAKES 4 SERVINGS**

Select 4 whole trout of the same size and measure the fish from belly to backbone at the thickest point to estimate the cooking time—the rule for any kind of fish cookery is to allow 10 minutes per inch of measured thickness. A white wine such as a Muscadet or a Chardonnay is good with sautéed trout.

> 4 whole trout
> All-purpose flour
> 7 tablespoons (½ stick plus 3 tablespoons) unsalted butter
> ¼ cup peanut or vegetable oil
> Kosher salt and freshly ground black pepper
> 1 tablespoon finely chopped fresh flat-leaf parsley
> Lemon wedges, for serving

Put the flour on a sheet of waxed paper, add the fish and coat lightly with flour on both sides, shaking off excess. Heat 4 tablespoons of the butter and the oil in a very large, heavy skillet over medium-high heat. When the butter mixture is hot but not smoking, add the fish and cook them for half the estimated cooking time over medium-high heat, then turn and cook for the remainder of time on the other side. Salt and pepper to taste as they cook. Test the fish for doneness with a fork or toothpick—if they flake easily, they are done—and transfer to a hot platter. Add the rest of the butter to the pan, swirl it around until it melts, add the parsley, and pour the sauce over the fish. Serve at once with lemon wedges.

VARIATIONS

SAUTÉED TROUT WITH HERB BUTTER: Vary the flavoring by substituting chopped fresh dill, chives, or tarragon for the parsley.

SAUTÉED TROUT AMANDINE: Sauté ½ to ¾ cup thinly sliced almonds in 4 tablespoons of butter in the pan in which the fish were cooked until delicately golden, shaking the pan several times and lightly salting the nuts as they cook. Spoon over the trout and serve immediately.

Editor: You might have to cook the trout in two batches, and keep the first two fish warm in a 200°F oven while sautéing the second batch. Or double the butter and oil and cook the four trout at the same time in two skillets.

GOUJONETTES OF SOLE

 MAKES 4 SERVINGS

These delectable little bits of fried fish make a good first course or cocktail hors d'oeuvre, or a light luncheon entrée. The name comes from *goujons*, tiny fish fried whole, of which these are a sort of mock version.

4 to 5 fillets of sole or flounder

½ to ¾ cup all-purpose flour

3 large eggs

¼ cup half-and-half

3 cups fine fresh bread crumbs (made in a food
   processor or blender from day-old bread)

Vegetable oil for deep-frying

Fresh flat-leaf parsley, for garnish

Tartar Sauce (page 356) or Rémoulade Sauce
   (page 356), for serving

Cut the fillets into diagonal strips about ½ inch wide. Spread the flour in a shallow dish. Beat the eggs and half-and-half together in a second dish. Spread the bread crumbs in a third dish. Coat the strips with flour, shaking off the excess, then dip them in the egg-cream mixture and roll them in the bread crumbs, coating on all sides. Place on a waxed paper–lined baking sheet and let stand for a few minutes to set the coating.

Pour enough oil to come halfway up the sides of a large, heavy-bottomed saucepan and heat the oil to 370°F on a deep-frying thermometer. In batches (use a deep-frying basket, if you wish), add the fish and deep-fry just until lightly browned, about 2 minutes. Using a wire skimmer (or the basket) remove the strips, transfer to a baking sheet lined with paper towels, and keep warm in a 200°F oven. Just before serving, garnish with the parsley and serve with tartar or rémoulade sauce.

VARIATION

GOUJONETTES IN BEER BATTER: Omit the egg and cream mixture and the bread crumbs. Make Beer Batter on page 175. Dip the fish strips in the flour, then in the beer batter, and fry a delicate brown.

SOLE POACHED IN VERMOUTH

MAKES 4 SERVINGS

In certain French recipes, instead of being poached in court bouillon or wine and water, fish fillets are poached in undiluted wine, dry vermouth, or sometimes spirits. The aromatic cooking liquid becomes the basis for a rich and flavorful sauce.

4 large fillets of sole, folded in half, point-to-point

1¼ cups dry vermouth

4 large egg yolks

8 tablespoons (1 stick) cold unsalted butter, cut into ½-inch cubes

3 tablespoons heavy cream

Kosher salt

Measure the thickness of the folded fillets, then arrange them in large skillet in one layer. Add the vermouth, which should just cover them, bring to the boiling point, reduce the heat, and poach, allowing 10 minutes per measured inch, until just cooked through. Transfer the fillets with a spatula to a large flameproof baking dish and keep warm in a 200°F oven. Increase the heat to high and reduce the cooking liquid until it is reduced to 3 tablespoons and practically a glaze.

Put the egg yolks and pieces of butter in the top of a double boiler over barely simmering water. Beat with a wire whisk or electric hand beater until smooth and thickened, then beat in the cream, reduced cooking liquid, and salt to taste. Don't let the water boil at any time or the eggs will curdle. Pour the sauce over the fillets and brown the top quickly under a hot broiler.

WALNUT-BREADED SOLE

MAKES 6 SERVINGS

The walnuts, especially if you can get black walnuts, lend a satisfying crunchiness and flavor to the fish. Serve the fillets with boiled or steamed potatoes and perhaps a cucumber salad.

6 large fillets of sole, flounder, or other white fish

All-purpose flour

2 large eggs

3 tablespoons heavy cream

1 cup fresh bread crumbs

1½ cups coarsely chopped walnuts, preferably black walnuts

6 tablespoons Clarified Butter (see box, page 358), or 3 tablespoons unsalted butter and 3 tablespoons oil

Kosher salt and freshly ground black pepper

Lemon wedges, for serving

Flour the fillets lightly. Lightly beat the eggs in a wide shallow bowl and mix in the cream. Put the crumbs in another wide shallow bowl, and the walnuts in a third bowl. Dip the fillets in the egg-cream mixture, then into the crumbs, and then the nuts. Arrange on cookie sheets lined with waxed paper and let stand for a few minutes to set the coating.

Heat the clarified butter, or butter and oil, until hot but not smoking, add the fillets, 2 or 3 at a time (do not crowd the pan), and sauté until lightly browned on one side, then turn, using a broad-bladed spatula, and sauté the second side. Keep warm in a 200°F oven while cooking the remaining fish. Sprinkle with salt and pepper to taste and serve at once, with the lemon wedges.

Editor: Black walnuts are readily available online from such purveyors as Hammons Product Company, online at www.black-walnuts.com, *or phone (1-888-429-6887).*

SAUTÉED FISH STEAKS

Swordfish, salmon, and halibut steaks are excellent candidates for sautéing. Have the steaks cut 1 to 1½ inches thick from the best, center part of the fish (if the fish is very large, divide the steaks in half before or after cooking) and allow one steak or half a steak, according to size, for each serving. Measure the fish at the thickest point and allow 10 minutes cooking time per inch.

For **2 large or 4 medium swordfish, salmon or halibut steaks**, heat **4 tablespoons (½ stick) unsalted butter** and **¼ cup olive oil** in a large, heavy skillet until the fat is hot but not smoking. [*Editor: Reduce the butter and oil to 2 tablespoons each, if you wish.*]

Add the steaks and cook over medium-high heat for the allotted time, turning them once halfway during the cooking, until lightly browned on the outside. Serve with additional **melted butter** and **chopped parsley, lemon wedges**, and **boiled or sautéed potatoes**. If you prefer a sauce with the steaks, skip the melted butter and have a **Hollandaise or Béarnaise Sauce** (pages 353 and 355).

SHAD ROE POACHED IN BUTTER

MAKES 6 SERVINGS

Editor: Shad roe, which is only available for a couple of weeks, signals the arrival of spring. It is important to cook the roe in a covered pan, as it splatters quite a bit.

---

3 good-size pairs shad roe

12 tablespoons (1½ sticks) unsalted butter

3 tablespoons finely chopped fresh flat-leaf parsley

Kosher salt and freshly ground black pepper

Lemon wedges, for serving

Toast, for serving

Using scissors, carefully cut the pair of roe sacs in half lengthwise by snipping through the membrane separating the sacs. Use a heavy skillet with a cover. Melt the butter over medium heat, and bathe each roe in the butter. Cover the skillet and cook, turning once, until the roe are golden on both sides, 12 to 15 minutes total. Transfer to a hot platter. Add the chopped parsley to the butter and season with salt and pepper. Spoon over the roe. Serve with the lemon wedges and toast.

SOLIANKA
(RUSSIAN—PACIFIC NORTHWEST FISH STEW)

❧ MAKES 4 SERVINGS

This fish stew, introduced to the Pacific Northwest by Russian immigrants, became very popular in Oregon and Washington, where it is made with salmon from the Columbia River.

- 2 pounds fish bones and heads, or 2-pound bony
    fish with head (not salmon)
- 1½ quarts water
- Kosher salt and freshly ground black pepper
- 3 large ripe tomatoes, peeled, seeded, and chopped
- 7 tablespoons (½ stick plus 3 tablespoons) unsalted
    butter
- 1½ pounds salmon, cut in strips
- 2 medium yellow onions, finely chopped
- 4 dill pickles, finely chopped
- 1 tablespoon pitted and chopped black
    Mediterranean olives
- 1 tablespoon pitted and chopped green
    Mediterranean olives
- 2 teaspoons drained nonpareil capers
- 1 bay leaf
- Additional chopped green or black olives, finely
    chopped flat-leaf parsley, and lemon slices,
    for serving

Simmer the fish bones and heads in the water, well seasoned with salt and pepper, for 1½ hours. Strain the broth and reserve. Simmer the tomatoes in 3 tablespoons of the butter in a medium skillet over medium heat for 15 minutes. Season to taste.

Arrange the salmon strips in a deep pot with the tomatoes, onions, pickles, olives, and capers. Cover with the fish broth, add the bay leaf, and simmer 12 to 15 minutes. Add the remaining 4 tablespoons butter. Discard the bay leaf and serve in bowls, garnished with the chopped olives, chopped parsley, and lemon slices.

MUSSELS MARINIÈRE

❧ MAKES 4 SERVINGS

This is far and away the most popular of all the mussel dishes served in French restaurants in this country, yet surprisingly few people make it at home, considering how easy it is. Maybe they are daunted by the thought of having to scrub and debeard the mussels. But the result is well worth the time and effort. All you need with this is plenty of hot crusty French bread to sop up all the goodness.

Editor: Farm-raised mussels, such as the Prince Edward Island variety do not have beards, so you will not have to go through the chore of removing them.

- 2 quarts mussels
- 1 to 1½ cups dry white wine
- 1 large onion, finely chopped
- ⅓ cup finely chopped fresh flat-leaf parsley

8 tablespoons (1 stick) unsalted butter

⅛ teaspoon dried thyme

Freshly ground black pepper

Scrub the mussels well with a kitchen brush or scouring pad and scrape off any encrustations on the shells. Wash them thoroughly in several changes of water and pull or snip off the beards—the stringy black thread attached to the shells.

Put the mussels in a deep, heavy pot with the wine, onion, ¼ cup of the chopped parsley, 4 tablespoons of the butter, the thyme, and a couple of grinds of pepper—no salt; the mussel liquid will be salty enough. Cover and cook over medium-low heat, shaking the pot often, just until the shells open, 8 or 10 minutes. Transfer the opened mussels, in their shells, to a big tureen, add the remaining 4 tablespoons butter and tablespoon chopped parsley to the pan to heat, and taste for salt as you do so. Pour the liquid over the mussels. To serve, ladle the mussels and their broth into deep soup plates.

VARIATION

MUSSELS MARINIÈRE WITH GARLIC. Instead of onion, use 4 or 5 finely chopped garlic cloves.

Boiled Lobsters

Once an East Coast delicacy, lobsters are now shipped all over the country. Most lobsters sold in markets weigh a pound to a pound and a half, but it is definitely worth buying larger lobsters if you can find them. Always look for lobsters that are active and lively, for these give the best eating. If your fish market can pick out the females, they are preferable for they have the coral, or roe. Ask to have the claws tied, if that has not been done already, so you will have no trouble with the beast. Count on one lobster per person.

You will need a large pot—an 8-quart size, or larger if you are cooking more than a couple of lobsters. Fill it about half full of water, season with **3 tablespoons salt**, and bring to a boil. Grasp the lobsters firmly behind the head and sink them into the boiling water. This assures a sudden death. After the water returns to a boil, boil the lobsters for 4 minutes for the first pound and 3 minutes more for each additional pound.

Don't cool the lobsters in the water or they will be overcooked. Remove them immediately and serve hot or, if you are serving cold lobster, let cool.

If you are serving them hot, cut off a little piece of the shell at the head and drain the liquid from inside. Then split the lobsters in half lengthwise with a heavy chef's knife, remove the dark intestinal vein that runs down the center of the body, and crack the claws with lobster or nut crackers. Leave the tomalley (the greenish liver) and any coral (the bright red roe) in the shell.

Serve the lobsters with **melted butter**, **wedges of lemon**, **good bread**, and **chilled white wine**. Provide lobster crackers and picks for winkling the meat from the claws.

If you are serving them cold, split and crack the lobsters and serve with **Mayonnaise** (page 355).

FRIED OYSTERS

MAKES 4 SERVINGS

Unsalted butter or butter and vegetable oil

3 large eggs

3 tablespoons heavy cream

3 to 4 cups freshly rolled cracker crumbs

1 quart freshly opened oysters of medium size (about
  24 oysters)

Kosher and freshly ground black pepper

Lemon wedges or Tartar Sauce (page 356), for serving

Heat enough butter or mixed butter and oil in a heavy 12-inch skillet, preferably cast iron, to a depth of half an inch. Lightly beat the eggs in a medium bowl and mix in the cream. Put the cracker crumbs in another bowl. Dip the oysters in the egg-cream mixture, then roll them in the cracker crumbs. Arrange on cookie sheets lined with waxed paper. Let them stand several minutes for the coating to set. Drop them into the hot fat, a few at a time so as not to crowd the skillet, and fry just long enough to brown the coating and heat them through, no more than a minute or two. Remove, sprinkle with salt and pepper, and serve on plates with lemon wedges or tartar sauce. Allow 6 or more oysters, according to appetite.

VARIATION

OYSTER LOAVES. For each serving, use an oblong roll, either crusty French or Italian or soft white. Cut off the top crust about 1 inch down from the top and remove nearly all the crumb from the bottom half. Butter both pieces well. Place on a baking sheet and toast in a preheated 350°F oven for about 10 minutes. Fill the bottom of each loaf with fried oysters and replace the top. Serve with lemon wedges and tartar sauce.

Beard on . . . Clams

Mother thought clamming was a great sport and would arise at five in the morning when there was a good low tide, don her best alpaca bathing suit, and be off to the beach, equipped with a shovel and basket. She would meet a number of friends there, mostly men, for few women would bother to go clamming. I often went with her in later years, but my special joy at first was crabbing. The Dungeness used to hide in deep pools accessible at low tide, and if you wandered through with a rake you could trap a fair quantity. You had to be alert, though, and early, for everyone else wanted them, too.

Thus, we often went home with five dozen clams and six or eight crabs. If she was in the mood, Mother would clean a dozen or so clams and remove the diggers [*Editor: the tough part of the razor clam—the variety found in coastal Oregon—that it uses to dig a hole in the sand*], which she brushed with flour and sautéed quickly in butter. Most people cooked the whole clam. Mother was independent enough to think that only the diggers were fit to eat in this manner. The rest of the clam could be used for other dishes. Nowadays, alas, you are lucky if you can get the clams to sauté in their entirety. I am certain that if the razor clam existed in France, the recipes for them would be classic.

SCALLOPS SAUTÉ PROVENÇAL

∽ MAKES 6 SERVINGS

Editor: When you want a light supper in a hurry, this dish will fill the bill nicely.

2 pounds bay scallops

½ cup all-purpose flour

¼ cup olive oil

Kosher salt and freshly ground black pepper

3 to 4 garlic cloves, finely chopped

⅓ cup chopped fresh flat-leaf parsley

Flour the scallops lightly just before cooking. Heat the oil in a skillet, preferably nonstick, over high heat. (You may have to use 2 skillets for this amount.) When the oil is quite hot, add the scallops. Cook for just a minute or so until the scallops lose their translucent look. Season with salt and pepper, add the garlic and parsley, and toss with the scallops. Cook for a moment longer. Serve at once.

SHELLFISH À LA NAGE

∽ MAKES 4 TO 6 SERVINGS

One of the best ways I know to cook shellfish is *à la nage*, the French term for a style of preparation in which shellfish are both cooked and served "swimming" in a white wine court bouillon and eaten hot, tepid, or cold. If you live in a part of the country where you can get freshwater crayfish, try this recipe with them; otherwise use large raw shrimp, or small lobsters (use the timing for Boiled Lobsters on page 171).

For the Court Bouillon

2 or 3 carrots

4 cups dry white wine

1 or 2 cups water

2 medium yellow onions, very thinly sliced

½ cup packed fresh flat-leaf parsley sprigs

1 teaspoon fresh thyme leaves

1 bay leaf

1 tablespoon kosher salt

4 whole black peppercorns

For the Shellfish

4 dozen crayfish or large shrimp, or 4 to 6 small lobsters

Melted butter, for serving

Lemon wedges, for serving

To make the court bouillon: With the tines of a fork or a channel knife, the little gadget that cuts thin strips from lemon rind, score the outside of the carrot and then slice it very thinly—the idea is that the slices will look like flowers and be more attractive in the plate than plain old carrot rounds. Put all the remaining court bouillon ingredients in a deep pot with the carrots and bring to a rolling boil over high heat.

To cook the shellfish: Drop the crayfish in the court bouillon, reduce the heat, and cook for 10 minutes just at the boiling point—not a rolling boil. (If using shrimp, cook for 3 minutes. For lobster, see page 171 for timing.) Using a slotted spoon or a wire skimmer, remove the shellfish at once and arrange in deep serving bowls or soup plates and ladle some of the aromatic court bouillon around them, with little bits of the carrots and onions. Sip the bouillon as you eat the shellfish. It's a good idea to have some melted butter and lemon wedges to enhance the delicate flesh of the shellfish, which are shelled at the table by the diners.

Editor: Be sure to provide hot, moist napkins or hand towels to the guests for cleaning up after eating.

FRIED SHRIMP

 MAKES 4 SERVINGS

Deep-fried shrimp are one of the most popular dishes in this country. They can be sheer delight—crisp, tender, greaseless, and flavorful—or they can be a soggy mess. The secret of these fried shrimp is the lightness and crispness of the beer batter that encases them—the yeast in the beer has a leavening effect on the batter. Make the batter ahead of the time you plan to fry the shrimp and let it rest, anywhere from 1 to 2 hours. This allows the ingredients to expand and amalgamate after the vigorous beating, and the batter will be crisper for it. Serve at once with either tartar sauce or Béarnaise Sauce, or merely with mayonnaise and wedges of lemon. These may be served as a first course, as a cocktail tidbit, or as a main course. For a main course, you could have coleslaw with them.

Steamed Clams

Clams are found in great variety along our shores. The two East Coast species are the **soft-shelled or long-necked clams**, usually steamed, and the hard-shelled, known in New England as **quahogs**, that come in three sizes: the largest used for chowder, the smaller littlenecks and cherrystones eaten raw on the half shell, broiled, baked, or added to seafood stews and similar dishes. On the West Coast one finds both **hard-shelled clams** and the **soft-shelled razor clams** of Oregon and Washington. The long, meaty razor clams are sautéed, deep-fried, scalloped, or made into chowder and fritters. All clams need to be scrubbed well and soaked in cold water to remove the sand outside and inside the shells. Raw clams—one of my dislikes—are best served very cold, on the half shell like oysters, with nothing but **lemon juice** and **freshly ground pepper**. Red cocktail sauce ruins the flavor. Steam clams in a large pot with a **half inch of water** or **dry white wine**, covered, over high heat, from 5 to 10 minutes, shaking the pot occasionally, until the shells open. Discard any in the pot whose shells remain closed. The resulting broth may be strained and sipped with the clams or used as the liquid for a seafood sauce. If you live near the shore, gather your own clams if possible—a sport I loved to indulge in as a child. Clams can be minced and used for fritters, quiches, or clam sauce for pasta. Canned minced clams are extremely good and may be substituted for fresh.

For the Shrimp

1½ pounds large shrimp, unpeeled

Tartar Sauce (page 356), Béarnaise Sauce (page 355),
or Mayonnaise (page 355) and lemon wedges,
for serving

For the Beer Batter

¾ cup all-purpose flour

¾ cup lager beer, at room temperature

2 large eggs, separated

2 tablespoons vegetable oil

1½ teaspoons kosher salt

Freshly ground black pepper

Vegetable oil, for deep-frying

Wash the shrimp very carefully and dry on paper towels. Take a pair of sharp scissors and cut along the curved back of the shell toward the tail, then break off the body shell with your finger, leaving the tail shell on. If visible, use the tip of the scissors to remove the dark vein running along the back of each shrimp. Cover the cleaned and shelled shrimp with plastic wrap until ready to deep-fry.

To make the batter: Put the flour in a bowl and add the beer, egg yolks, oil, salt, and a grind or two of pepper. Starting in the center, stir clockwise with a wire whisk until well mixed and free of lumps. Cover the bowl with plastic wrap and let stand at room temperature for at least 1 to 2 hours. Then stir the batter. In a separate bowl beat the 2 egg whites with a wire whisk until stiff but not dry and very gently fold them into the batter.

To cook the shrimp: Preheat the oven to 250°F. Line a baking sheet with paper towels and put it near the stove. Pour enough oil to come halfway

up the sides of a large, heavy-bottomed saucepan. Heat over high heat to 375°F on a deep-frying thermometer.

Put the shrimp, one at a time, on a small ladle or large spoon and dip them into the batter so that they become completely coated, then lower them into the hot fat. Cook about 4 or 5, not more than 6, at a time—the batter expands in the fat and besides you don't want to lower the temperature too much. It will take about 3 to 4 minutes for the shrimp to brown and cook through.

As the shrimp are fried, lift them out in the basket or with a flat mesh skimmer (which can also be used to skim any stray pieces of batter from the fat) and let them drain and keep warm on the baking sheet in the oven. Serve at once.

CHUCK'S BAKED SHRIMP

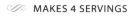 MAKES 4 SERVINGS

My friend Chuck Williams is a master at turning out a good dinner in next to no time. His baked shrimp are easy and quick and can be prepared well in advance, except for the final anointment of oil. Serve them with rice and a green salad. [*Editor: Williams is the founder of the granddaddy of kitchenware shops, Williams-Sonoma.*]

2 pounds large shrimp, unpeeled

2 tablespoons chopped fresh tarragon, or
1½ teaspoons dried tarragon soaked in
1 tablespoon dry white wine

Kosher salt and freshly ground black pepper

⅓ cup melted butter or olive oil

Split the shrimp down the back with scissors so they can almost be spread flat, butterfly fashion. Peel off the body shell, but leave the tail shell on. Remove the dark vein running down the back, if visible. Arrange the shrimp, tails up, in a lightly buttered round oven-to-table baking dish, and sprinkle with the tarragon, salt and pepper to taste, and enough butter or oil to moisten them. Bake in a preheated 350°F oven for 10 minutes, or until just cooked through.

CIOPPINO

〰️ **MAKES 6 SERVINGS**

This marvelous fish soup-stew originated among the Italian and Portuguese fishermen of the California coast. Serve it in deep soup plates or bowls with forks and spoons and lots of French or Italian bread.

- 1 quart cherrystone or littleneck clams, scrubbed under cold running water
- 3 cups hearty red wine, such as Pinot Noir or Zinfandel (you can use 1 cup dry white wine for steaming the clams, if you wish)
- ½ cup olive oil
- 1 large yellow onion, chopped
- 2 garlic cloves, chopped
- 1 green bell pepper, seeded and chopped
- ¼ pound dried mushrooms, such as porcini, soaked in hot water for 10 minutes, and drained
- 4 ripe tomatoes, peeled, seeded, and chopped
- ¼ cup tomato paste
- 2 teaspoons kosher salt
- 1 teaspoon freshly ground black pepper
- 2 tablespoons finely chopped fresh basil or 1 teaspoon dried basil
- 1 sea bass or striped bass, about 3 pounds, cleaned, scaled, and cut crosswise into serving pieces, or 3 pounds thick skinless fish fillets, cut into serving pieces
- 1 pound crabmeat, picked over for cartilage and shells
- 1 pound large raw shrimp, peeled and deveined
- 3 tablespoons finely chopped fresh flat-leaf parsley

Steam the clams in 1 cup of the red wine until they open—discard any that do not open. Strain the broth through two thicknesses of rinsed cheese-cloth and reserve.

Heat the olive oil in a deep pot over medium-high heat and cook the onion, garlic, bell pepper, and mushrooms for 3 minutes. Add the tomatoes and cook 4 minutes. Add the strained clam broth, tomato paste, and remaining 2 cups red wine. Season with salt and pepper and simmer for about 20 minutes. Taste and correct seasoning. Add the basil and the fish, and just cook the fish through, 3 to 5 minutes. Finally, add the steamed clams, crabmeat, and shrimp. Heat for a minute or two, or just until the shrimp are cooked. Do not overcook. Sprinkle with the chopped parsley and serve hot in deep bowls.

VARIATIONS

CIOPPINO WITH MUSSELS: Substitute mussels for the clams.

CIOPPINO WITH OYSTERS: Substitute oysters for the clams.

CLAM HASH

I've been a clam lover ever since my childhood in Oregon, when we used to dig for clams at the beach and cook them in every way imaginable. This hash was a family favorite.

6 tablespoons (¾ stick) unsalted butter

½ cup finely chopped onion

1½ cups drained and minced steamed clams (see page 174), or drained canned clams, clam liquid reserved in either case

1½ cups finely diced cooked potatoes

1 tablespoon Worcestershire sauce

Kosher salt and freshly ground black pepper

3 large eggs

½ cup freshly grated Parmesan cheese

3 tablespoons finely chopped fresh flat-leaf parsley

Melt the butter in a heavy skillet, preferably cast iron, over medium heat. Add the onion and sauté until just transparent, about 4 minutes. Add the drained clams and potatoes and press down with a spatula. Stir in the Worcestershire sauce and season with salt and pepper. Cook about 10 minutes over

Le Grand Aïoli

Makes 8 servings

Editor: Aïoli, served with a variety of seafood and vegetables, is a fine dish for entertaining, as all of the work can be done ahead of serving. Beard suggests that salt cod, potatoes, hot fish, and hard-cooked eggs are the most essential parts of the feast, but crudités, cooked artichokes, and shrimp are also great additions.

3¼ cups Aïoli (page 355)

Accompaniments:

SALT COD. Two pounds filleted in one piece. Soak in water to cover overnight or for 8 to 10 hours. Change the water once during the soaking. Drain, and cover with cold water. Bring to a boil, and simmer for 10 minutes, or until the fish is tender. Serve hot.

BOILED POTATOES. Peel and boil 10 to 12 medium potatoes in salted water until just pierceable. Drain, return to the pot, and dry over low heat. Serve hot.

A COLD OR HOT FRESH FISH. Striped bass poached in court bouillon and cooled; or poached red snapper or halibut. Serve with a garnish of cucumbers.

HARD-BOILED EGGS. Figure on at least 1 hard-boiled egg per person (page 182). Peel them, and arrange on a serving dish.

medium heat, stirring occasionally with a fork or spatula and mixing in some of the crust from the bottom. Press down again. Beat the eggs with ¼ cup of the reserved clam liquid (this intensifies the clam flavor), combine with the cheese, and pour over the hash. Cover tightly and cook until the eggs are set, 6 to 8 minutes. Sprinkle with the parsley and serve hot.

CRAB SOUFFLÉ

⌒ **MAKES 4 SERVINGS**

The mixture for the soufflé may be prepared ahead of time and the soufflé mold buttered. All that remains is for the egg whites to be beaten and the soufflé popped in the oven. Serve with Hollandaise Sauce (page 353) if you wish.

Editor: If you make the soufflé base ahead, dot the surface with about 2 teaspoons of small butter cubes to prevent a skin from forming. Keep at room temperature for no longer than 1 hour. Reheat the base over low heat, stirring constantly, just until warm; do not bring to a simmer or the yolks will curdle.

---

1 small yellow onion, finely chopped
5 tablespoons (½ stick plus 1 tablespoon)
     unsalted butter
3 tablespoons all-purpose flour
3 tablespoons tomato paste
½ cup heavy cream
2 tablespoons Cognac
1 teaspoon kosher salt
½ teaspoon freshly ground black pepper
Dash of Tabasco
2 teaspoons chopped fresh tarragon or 1 teaspoon
     dried tarragon
4 large eggs, separated, plus 2 large egg whites,
     at room temperature
Softened butter, for the soufflé mold
1 pound crabmeat, picked over for cartilage
     and shells

Sauté the onion in a large saucepan over medium heat with the 5 tablespoons of butter until soft, about 4 minutes. Whisk in the flour, then whisk in the tomato paste and cream until smooth. Add the cognac, salt, pepper, Tabasco, and tarragon, and let cool slightly. Whisk in the egg yolks and mix well.

Whip the egg whites in a large bowl until firm but not dry. Fold into the yolk mixture. Butter a 1½-quart soufflé dish. Place half of the crabmeat on the bottom of the dish. Add one-half of the soufflé mixture, then the remaining crabmeat, and the remaining soufflé mixture. Bake in a preheated 375°F oven for approximately 30 minutes, or until puffed and golden brown. Serve immediately.

EGGS

EGGS

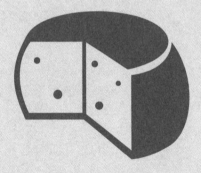

PERFECT SCRAMBLED EGGS

If you are adding chopped herbs, sliced sautéed mushrooms, chopped sautéed scallions, or grated cheese, lace them in as you scramble the eggs. For finely cut ham or smoked salmon, heat gently in the butter before adding and scrambling the eggs.

2 large eggs

Kosher salt and freshly ground black pepper

1 or 2 dashes of Tabasco

1 teaspoon water (optional)

2 tablespoons unsalted butter, plus softened butter, if desired

Break the eggs into a bowl, add salt, pepper, and Tabasco, and beat lightly with a fork. For lighter

Poached Eggs

The egg is a perfect object lesson in the techniques of boiling and poaching. To watch a poached egg form is to see a vivid example of the firming action of the cooking process. Eggs for poaching or soft-boiling should be the freshest possible. The fresher the egg, the firmer and more shapely the white of the poached egg will be.

There are many different theories about poaching eggs, but this is the method I have found works best.

Use a skillet or a flat-surfaced pan that is not too deep—this allows you to slip the eggs in easily. Add water to a depth of 2 to 3 inches, 1 teaspoon salt, and ½ teaspoon white distilled or cider vinegar, which helps the whites coagulate. Bring the water to a slow boil in which the bubbles just break the surface, not a fast, rolling boil which would whip the whites away before they could set, giving you a ragged-looking result. Have beside you paper towels or a linen cloth on which to drain the eggs, a slotted spoon or a flat, perforated skimmer for removing them from the water (I find the round, flat, well-perforated skimmer sold in Japanese stores that carry kitchen utensils ideal), and a large spoon for basting.

Break each egg into a tiny cup (such as a Japanese tea cup or a half-cup-size metal measuring cup with a handle), lower the cup into the water, and very quickly tip out the egg, holding the inverted cup there for a second or two to keep the whites from spreading. Don't try to do too many eggs at one time—two or three, according to the size of your skillet, are about as many as can be handled easily. As soon as all the eggs are in the water, remove the pan from the heat and let the eggs poach very gently in the hot water for 3 to 4 minutes, basting the tops with spoonfuls of hot water if necessary. When the whites are firm and set, and the yolks just filmed with white, remove the eggs with the perforated skimmer and place them on the towels to absorb the excess water.

If you aren't going to use the eggs right away, lower them gently into a dish of cold water to stop the cooking, then remove, dry on towels, and put on a plate, covered with plastic wrap, until required. If the white is at all ragged, you can trim it with scissors.

scrambled eggs, also beat in the water. If you like your scrambled eggs thick and eggy, don't use any water.

Melt the butter (a tablespoon for each egg) in a nonstick skillet over medium-high heat and when hot but not sizzling, pour in the eggs. As soon as the eggs begin to coagulate, start making pushing strokes with a rubber or wooden spatula so you get curds.

Lift the pan off the heat from side to side with a circular motion while you push. As the heat in the eggs increases, the curds will form faster and you will have to keep lifting the pan from the heat and pushing faster. When the curds are soft but not too runny, quickly transfer the eggs to a plate. You have to know exactly when to stop applying heat or the eggs will be overcooked, hard little lumps.

If you want very rich eggs, sometimes called "buttered eggs," as you push the curds in the pan add small pieces of softened butter, which will melt in and make the eggs taste even more luscious. [*Editor: About 1 tablespoon is sufficient.*]

OEUFS À LA TRIPE
(HARD-BOILED EGGS IN ONION SAUCE)

 MAKES 2 TO 3 SERVINGS

I have never been able to discover the origin of the name of this traditional and exquisitely simple French dish, which I like to serve for breakfast, brunch, a light lunch, or a late supper.

1 medium yellow onion, finely chopped
4 tablespoons (½ stick) unsalted butter
3 tablespoons all-purpose flour
1 teaspoon kosher salt
½ teaspoon freshly ground black pepper
A few gratings of fresh nutmeg
1¼ cups light cream or half-and-half
4 or 5 hard-boiled eggs, cut into ½-inch slices
Toast, for serving

Sauté the onion in butter in a large skillet over medium heat until soft and delicately golden,

Soft-boiled Eggs

Plunge large eggs into a pan of boiling water and let boil for 3 minutes after the water returns to the boil. Give very large eggs 30 seconds more. Then remove from the water and serve. If the eggs are very cold, take the precaution of pricking the large end of the shell with a needle before putting them in the water, which will prevent them from cracking. There's a little egg-pricking gadget on the market now, but the needle works just fine as well.

HARD-BOILED EGGS. Put the eggs in a pan of boiling water (if they are cold, prick them first with a needle as directed above) and boil for 3 minutes. Then leave them in the water, with the heat turned off, for 9 minutes. Remove and run cold water over them, or plunge them into cold water. Let them cool completely before refrigerating or shelling.

about 5 minutes. Stir in the flour and cook for 2 or 3 minutes to remove the raw taste of the flour. Add the salt, pepper, and nutmeg, then gradually stir in the light cream, stirring until the sauce simmers and thickens. Let it simmer gently for 3 or 4 minutes to get a good flavor. Taste for seasoning, then carefully fold in the sliced eggs. Heat through quickly and serve on toast.

A PERFECT OMELET

⮑ MAKES 1 INDIVIDUAL OMELET

Making an omelet requires deftness, speed, plenty of practice, and a pan 9 inches in diameter, with rounded sides and a heavy bottom that will hold the heat. If you use a cast-aluminum or cast-iron pan, it must be used only for omelets and never washed on the inside, merely wiped out with a damp cloth, or the omelet will stick. Should it stick, rub the pan with a sprinkling of kosher salt and a paper towel to remove the residue, then rub with a drop or two of oil and a clean paper towel.

However, after many years of omelet making I have come to the conclusion that the best pan to use is one with a nonstick coating, to which the egg will never stick, no matter how often you wash the pan or use it for other things.

My favorite omelet pan is made of nonstick-coated cast aluminum, 9 inches in diameter, sloping to a heavy bottom 6 inches across. Only the bottom is heavy, the pan itself is light enough to lift and shake with one hand. In this pan it is possible to make an omelet without using any kind of tool—all you need to do is shake the pan vigorously and the

eggs will move around and start to set of their own accord.

Don't worry if you can't make a perfect omelet at first. This is a technique you acquire by constant practice and by learning to judge the point when the omelet has set just enough and can be rolled and tipped out. The whole process takes only about 30 seconds, so you can make as many omelets as you need in practically no time. Always make your omelets individually. It's much more difficult, and not very satisfactory, to make a huge one in a big pan and divide it up.

> 2 extra-large eggs
> Scant ½ teaspoon kosher salt
> Pinch of freshly ground black pepper
> 1 tablespoon water
> 1 tablespoon unsalted butter

Break the eggs into a bowl, add the seasonings and water, and beat lightly with a fork—don't overbeat, only enough to blend yolks and whites.

Heat your omelet pan over high heat until a drop of water bounces when flicked onto the surface. Add the butter and swirl it around until it melts and foams, which will happen almost immediately if the pan is the right heat. If it browns or burns, the pan is too hot. Remove it from the heat, wipe out the butter with paper towels, swing the pan in the air a little to cool it, and start again.

When the butter stops foaming, quickly pour in the eggs and, shaking the pan with one hand so it moves over the heat, stir the eggs lightly with a fork as if you were making scrambled eggs. (If you use a nonstick pan, use a wooden spatula, not any sort of metal tool, or just shake the pan, which will move the eggs around enough.) When the eggs have set to the degree you like (I like mine French style, still creamy in the center, but you may prefer yours a little more set), start rolling the omelet with a fork or spatula, at the end of the pan near the handle. If you are adding a filling, do this before starting to roll. Tip the pan forward so the omelet rolls onto itself.

Now reverse your grip on the handle, holding it from underneath, hold a plate close to the pan with your other hand, and start to invert the pan, which will tip the omelet onto the plate in a neat roll, with the edges underneath and a lovely smooth surface on top. Serve immediately. Omelets can't wait.

If you are making more than one omelet, wipe the pan with paper towels after each one, reheat, and add fresh butter to the pan.

Omelet Fillings

Grated cheese (2 to 3 tablespoons) should be added just before the eggs are set, so it can melt.

Herbs, such as finely chopped chives, parsley, and chervil for an omelet fines herbes, or finely chopped watercress, should be mixed into the eggs before they are cooked. Use 1 tablespoon fresh herbs.

One-third cup any of the following, freshly cooked, or reheated, may be added to the omelet just before it is rolled, and any excess spooned over the top just before serving:

Sliced mushrooms, sautéed or creamed

Creamed chicken or chicken hash

Creamed dried beef

Buttered green vegetables, such as pieces of asparagus, broccoli, spinach

Creamed fish

Crumbled crisp bacon

Thin strips of ham, frizzled in butter

Ripe tomatoes, peeled, seeded, chopped, and sautéed

Sautéed lamb kidneys, cut into small pieces

Croutons of bread, fried in olive oil, with or without garlic

Sautéed sliced onions

PERUVIAN EGGS

A most unusual egg dish that makes a nice change from pasta as a first course or a light luncheon. Credit for this goes to a young Peruvian chef, Felipe Rojas-Lombardi, who at one point in his career helped me with my cooking classes.

Editor: Credited with bringing the concept of Spanish tapas to America at his restaurant-cabaret, The Ballroom, in New York, Felipe Rojas-Lombardi died at the untimely age of forty-six in 1991. Instead of the tomato sauce, Beard says that you can also sauté the egg strips in 2 tablespoons of unsalted butter.

---

12 large eggs

¼ cup freshly grated Parmesan cheese, plus more for serving

¼ cup whole milk

3 tablespoons crushed soda crackers or English water biscuits

½ teaspoon dried basil

2 teaspoons kosher salt

1 teaspoon freshly ground black pepper

Dash of Tabasco

1 tablespoon unsalted butter, as needed

1 cup Light Tomato Sauce with Garlic (page 205)

Whisk the eggs lightly in a medium bowl. Add the cheese, milk, crushed crackers, basil, salt, pepper, and Tabasco, and mix well. Melt the butter in a medium nonstick skillet over medium heat. Spoon 2 tablespoons of the egg mixture into the skillet, spread to about ¼ inch thickness, and cook until lightly browned on one side. Flip and brown the other side. Transfer to a plate. Continue with the remaining egg mixture and stack the small omelets on the plate. Roll each one up and cut crosswise into ½-inch-thick strips. Add the tomato sauce to the skillet and bring to a simmer. Heat the egg strips in the sauce for about 2 minutes. Serve with additional grated cheese.

CLASSIC QUICHE LORRAINE

The French quiche is one of the most popular of American culinary adoptions—and small wonder. While it is essentially a simple dish, it is infinitely accommodating, for the basis is nothing more than a savory custard tart to which different ingredients have been added. A quiche can be served as a cocktail appetizer, a first course, a luncheon dish, or with an entrée as a substitute for both the starch and the vegetable: a pea quiche with chicken; onion quiche with steak, roast beef, or pork; spinach quiche with roast lamb.

Rich Tart Pastry (page 334) without the sugar (Pâte Brisée)

1 tablespoon Dijon mustard

6 to 8 thick slices streaky (lean) bacon

4 large eggs

1½ cups light cream or 1 cup whole milk and ½ cup heavy cream

½ teaspoon kosher salt

¼ teaspoon freshly ground black pepper

Pinch of freshly grated nutmeg

Line a 9-inch pie pan with the pastry and crimp the edges. Line the pastry shell with aluminum foil, and fill with dried beans. Bake in a preheated 425°F oven for about 12 minutes, until the edges are slightly brown. Remove from the oven. Lift off the foil and beans. Brush the bottom of the pastry shell with the mustard. Return to the oven and bake 2 minutes, or until the mustard looks dry. Remove from the oven. Reduce the oven temperature to 375°F.

Meanwhile, cook the bacon in a skillet until it is cooked through but not crisp, about 7 minutes. Drain on paper towels. Cut the slices into small pieces. Spread evenly in the partially baked pastry shell. Beat the eggs lightly in a medium bowl and combine with cream, salt, pepper, and nutmeg. Pour the custard over the bacon. Bake in a 350°F oven for about 30 minutes, or until the custard is set, puffed, and lightly browned. Serve hot, cut into wedges.

NOTE. Buy bacon that is not flavored with artificial smoke and over-sugared, as most brands are today. Genuine bacon can still be found in many farmers' markets and good pork stores.

VARIATIONS

CREAM CHEESE OR COTTAGE CHEESE

QUICHE: Substitute 1 cup cream cheese or 1 cup cottage cheese for the milk. Beat the eggs with the remaining cream, combine with the cheese, and rub through a sieve or strainer before adding to the pastry shell. Add the custard and bake as directed.

HAM QUICHE: Substitute 1½ cups Virginia or country ham of good flavor, cut into small strips and distributed in the shell, for the bacon. Add the custard and bake as directed.

SWISS TARTE À L'OIGNON

MAKES ONE 9-INCH TART; 4 TO 6 SERVINGS

Editor: A quiche by any other name, this early incarnation from 1965 is still quiche.

Rich Tart Pastry (page 334), without the sugar (Pâte Brisée)

3 tablespoons unsalted butter

3 medium yellow onions, thinly sliced

½ teaspoon kosher salt

¼ teaspoon freshly ground black pepper

Pinch of freshly grated nutmeg

1 cup shredded Gruyère or Emmenthaler cheese

1 cup heavy cream

5 large egg yolks

Line a 9-inch pie pan with pastry. Place aluminum foil over the pastry, and fill with dried beans. Bake in a preheated 425°F oven for about 12 minutes, until the edges are slightly brown. Remove from the oven. Lift off and remove the foil with the beans. (The beans can be reserved for future use as pastry weights.) Reduce the oven temperature to 375°F.

Melt the butter in a large heavy-bottomed saucepan over medium heat. Add the onions, salt, pepper, and nutmeg. Cover and cook until the onions are just tender, about 10 minutes. Transfer to the pastry shell and mix gently with the Gruyère. Whisk together the cream and egg yolks and pour over the onion mixture. Bake for 25 to 35 minutes until the custard is set.

SHIRRED EGGS

∽ MAKES 6 SERVINGS

Achieving perfect shirred eggs, with a delicate white and a yolk that is still liquid, can be something of an art. They must be rushed from oven to table lest they continue to cook and become hard.

1 cup heavy cream, as needed
Kosher salt and freshly ground black pepper
6 large eggs

Pour a small amount of heavy cream in the bottoms of six ½- to ¾-cup ramekins. Carefully break 1 egg into each ramekin, add a little more heavy cream, and sprinkle with salt and pepper. Bake in a preheated 350°F oven for about 8 minutes, or until the eggs have barely set.

VARIATIONS

SHIRRED EGGS WITH GRUYÈRE CHEESE: After topping each egg with cream, sprinkle about 1 tablespoon shredded Gruyère cheese into each ramekin. Season and bake as above.

SHIRRED EGGS WITH DUCK LIVERS AND MADEIRA: Oil the ramekin dishes, omitting the heavy cream. Add 1 egg to each ramekin. Cut 1 or 2 trimmed duck livers into ½-inch cubes. Melt 1 tablespoon butter in a large skillet over medium heat. Add the duck livers and 1 tablespoon finely chopped shallot and cook, stirring occasionally, just to sear the duck livers, about 1½ minutes. Stir in 1 tablespoon Madeira—it will evaporate. Season with salt and pepper. Spoon equal amounts of the livers into the ramekins, and bake as above.

SHIRRED EGGS WITH PESTO: Oil the ramekin dishes, omitting the heavy cream. Add 1 egg to each ramekin. Place about 1 tablespoon peeled, seeded, and finely chopped tomato and ½ teaspoon pesto on each egg. Season and bake as above.

SHIRRED EGGS WITH HAM: Oil the ramekin dishes, omitting the heavy cream and the salt. Add 1 egg to each ramekin. Top each with about 1 tablespoon finely chopped baked ham or frizzled Virginia ham [*Editor: Sautéed in a little butter over high heat until browned*], and season and bake as above.

SHIRRED EGGS WITH SPINACH PURÉE: Oil the ramekin dishes, omitting the heavy cream. Add 1 egg to each ramekin. Place 1 tablespoon spinach purée [*Editor: Process thawed frozen chopped spinach in a food processor until puréed*] on top of each egg, and season and bake as above.

CHEESE SOUFFLÉ

✍ MAKES 4 SERVINGS

The most basic of all soufflés is the one with a bécha-mel sauce base, into which the yolks, seasonings, and flavoring ingredients are mixed and the beaten egg whites folded in. This is the type used for almost all savory soufflés and many dessert soufflés.

Softened butter, for the dish

4 large eggs, separated, plus 1 large egg white, at room temperature

3 tablespoons unsalted butter

3 tablespoons all-purpose flour

1 cup whole milk, heated

1 teaspoon kosher salt

¼ teaspoon freshly ground black pepper

Pinch of freshly grated nutmeg

¼ cup shredded sharp cheddar cheese

⅛ teaspoon cream of tartar (optional)

Grease the bottom and sides of a 1½-quart soufflé dish with butter. This will help the soufflé to rise and give it a nice shiny crust.

There are four steps in making a soufflé: sepa-rating the eggs, making the béchamel sauce base and adding the yolks and flavorings, beating the egg whites, and folding the egg whites into the soufflé base.

Start by separating the eggs, which should be at room temperature. Have beside you two small bowls and the large bowl in which you will beat the egg whites. Crack the center of the egg on the rim of one small bowl so the shell divides neatly into halves. Hold the egg over the bowl and tip it back and forth between the halves of the shell so the white slips into the bowl, leaving the yolk in the shell. When all the white is in the bowl, tip the egg yolk into the second small bowl and transfer the white to the bowl in which you will beat the whites. This is a precautionary measure. If by mischance a yolk should break and part of it mingles with the white, you only have to discard one egg white, not a whole batch. Continue this process until all the egg yolks are in one small bowl and all the egg whites have been transferred to the large beating bowl.

There is a safer way to separate eggs, and you should at least try it once to get the feel of the sep-arating. Break the eggshell and tip the whole egg into the palm of your hand. Let the egg white run between your slightly parted fingers into the small bowl. Your hand is softer than an eggshell and there is less chance of the yolk breaking.

You'll have one extra yolk in this recipe—don't throw it away after it has been separated from the extra egg white. Store it in the refrigerator in a small screw-topped jar and use it for mayonnaise or hollandaise.

With the eggs separated, turn your attention to the sauce. Melt the butter in saucepan over medium-low heat; stir in the flour; cook the roux until frothy and then mix in the hot milk. Stir and cook until it comes to the boiling point and thickens to a rather stiff sauce consistency. Season with the salt, pepper, and nutmeg and remove from the heat. Stir the egg yolks into the sauce with a whisk or spatula until thoroughly mixed, and then mix in the cheese with the spatula.

Preheat the oven to 375°F with the rack in the center of the oven; the soufflé needs room to rise.

If you are beating the egg whites by hand, use

the large balloon whip. Whisk with a vertical circular motion, at first fairly slowly and then, as the whites become foamy, more rapidly, so as to incorporate as much air as possible into the whites. If you are not using a copper bowl, add the cream of tartar when the whites are foamy. Continue to beat rapidly until the whites are thick and stiff enough to hold their shape when the beater is lifted—they should just droop over in soft peaks. Do not overbeat until they are dry and stand stiffly upright, as for a meringue. When a recipe directs you to beat egg whites until "stiff but not dry" or to the "soft-peak stage," this is what is meant. If you are using an electric mixer or electric hand beater, watch the whites carefully as it is very easy to overbeat them.

The beaten egg whites must be folded into the soufflé mixture immediately before they have a chance to subside. With the rubber spatula take up about one-fourth of the whites and mix into the cheese-sauce mixture in the pan, which lightens the rather heavy soufflé base.

Then tip the lightened cheese mixture into the bowl of egg whites and, with your rubber spatula, fold the egg whites lightly into it. Cut down through the center of the mixture with the edge of the spatula, then draw it toward the side of the bowl; pull it up and over and then cut down again. Continue to fold very rapidly and lightly for about a minute, turning the bowl as you do so, just until the cheese sauce has mixed with the egg whites. Don't overfold or the egg whites will deflate. There should still be little bits of unincorporated egg white visible. Immediately pour into the prepared soufflé dish and smooth the top with the rubber spatula. Put the dish in the center of the preheated oven and bake for 30 to 35 minutes, until the soufflé has risen about 2 inches above the rim of the dish and is browned on top. After 30 minutes the soufflé will be firm on the sides and still slightly creamy in the center. If you like a firmer center, bake the extra 5 minutes.

Serve the soufflé the minute you take it from the oven—soufflés can't wait. To serve, puncture the top of the soufflé with a serving spoon and fork, pull it gently apart, and spoon onto hot plates, giving each person some of the center and some of the crusty brown exterior. All you need with this is a green salad.

For a larger soufflé, to serve 6, use a 2-quart (8-cup) dish or mold. Increase the quantities to 4 tablespoons each of butter and flour, 1½ cups of milk, 6 egg yolks, 7 or 8 egg whites, and 1¼ cups of cheese or other ingredients. Also increase the seasoning to taste, and increase the cooking time to 35 to 45 minutes.

VARIATIONS

For a spicier cheese soufflé, add to the seasonings a dash or two of Tabasco and 1 tablespoon Dijon mustard or 1 teaspoon dry mustard (don't add mustard or Tabasco if using Roquefort, which has a very strong flavor).

Instead of cheese, use ¼ cup of any of the following: finely ground chicken; finely ground ham plus 1 teaspoon dry mustard; well-drained pureed, cooked spinach plus 2 teaspoons grated onion; pureed, cooked broccoli; canned tuna, drained and flaked, plus 1 teaspoon lemon juice; poached, flaked finnan haddie; well-drained canned minced clams.

Substitute 1 cup freshly grated Parmesan, ¾ cup shredded Emmenthaler or Gruyère, or ¾ cup crumbled Roquefort for the cheddar cheese.

SALMON AND SOUR CREAM ROLL

MAKES 4 TO 6 SERVINGS

A rolled soufflé makes a great light luncheon dish, and the fillings are only limited by your imagination.

Softened butter, for the jelly-roll pan

4 tablespoons (½ stick) unsalted butter

½ cup all-purpose flour

2 cups whole milk, heated

3 large eggs, separated, at room temperature

1 cup sour cream

1 tablespoon Cognac

1 teaspoon kosher salt

⅛ teaspoon cayenne pepper or Tabasco

4 to 6 finely chopped scallions, white and green parts

½ pound smoked salmon, cut into slivers

Preheat the oven to 325°F. Butter a 10 by 15 by 1-inch jelly-roll pan, line with waxed paper, and butter the waxed paper well.

Melt the butter in a large heavy saucepan over low heat. Whisk in the flour and cook until golden, about 2 minutes. Gradually whisk in the hot milk, whisking constantly to prevent the sauce from lumping. Cook, whisking often, until simmering and thickened. Remove from the heat. Whisk together the egg yolks, 2 tablespoons of the sour cream, the Cognac, salt, and pepper, stir in about half of the sauce, and stir back into the saucepan.

Beat the egg whites until they stand in soft peaks, as for a soufflé. Fold about one-third of the whites into the yolk mixture, incorporating them completely; pour the sauce mixture onto the whites in the bowl, then fold in the remaining whites. Spread in the prepared pan, evening the top with a rubber spatula. Bake for 40 minutes, or until golden and firm to the touch.

Remove the pan from the oven and invert onto large sheets of waxed paper. Loosen the paper from the roll, and carefully peel it off. Trim the edges of the roll with a large sharp knife. Spread the roll with the remaining sour cream and sprinkle with the scallions and smoked salmon. Use the long side of the waxed paper to roll it up like a jelly roll and slide it onto a board or heated platter.

ZUCCHINI FRITTATA

〰 MAKES 6 SERVINGS

1 cup thinly sliced onion

⅓ cup olive oil

3 very small zucchini, cut paper thin

Kosher salt and freshly ground black pepper

8 large eggs

5 tablespoons freshly grated Parmesan cheese

4 tablespoons (½ stick) unsalted butter

1 tablespoon finely chopped fresh flat-leaf parsley

1 or 2 fresh basil leaves, cut into thin strips

Cook the onion in olive oil in a medium skillet over medium heat until transparent, about 3 minutes. Add the zucchini and brown lightly, about 5 minutes. Reduce the heat and let the onion and zucchini cook down for 4 to 5 minutes, then season with the salt and pepper. Drain off the oil and excess liquid, and cool slightly.

Beat the eggs in a bowl with ½ teaspoon salt and ½ teaspoon pepper. Add the zucchini mixture and 4 tablespoons of the grated cheese. Heat the butter over medium-low heat in a heavy 10-inch skillet, preferably cast-iron, until it foams and begins to bubble. Pour the mixture into the skillet, and add the parsley and basil. Keeping the heat very low, cook only until the eggs have set, about 20 minutes. The top should still be a little runny. Sprinkle with the remaining tablespoon grated cheese, and put under a hot broiler for not less than 30 seconds nor more than a minute, until barely set on top, but not brown. Run a sharp knife or thin spatula around the edges of the frittata to loosen it from the pan, slide it out on a plate, and cool to room temperature. Cut into wedges and serve. This is equally good if it is chilled.

PASTA

PASTA

BASIC EGG PASTA

1½ cups all-purpose flour, plus more for kneading
by hand

½ teaspoon plain table or fine sea salt

2 large eggs, at room temperature

1 tablespoon olive oil, if mixing in an electric mixer
or food processor

To mix the dough by hand: Put the flour mixed with the salt on a wooden board or a countertop. Make a well in the center of the mound, and break the eggs into the well. Beat the eggs with a fork, slowly incorporating the flour from the sides of the well. As you beat the eggs with one hand, your other hand should be shoring up the sides of the mound.

After a while, the paste will begin to clog the tines of the fork. Clean it off and continue to mix the flour into the egg mixture with your fingertips, just as you would in making any paste. When the flour and egg are all mixed, press the dough into a ball. It will seem to be composed of flakes of dough. Set it aside to rest for a minute while you wash your hands, scrape and clean the board, and dust it with flour. If there are dry flakes that obstinately refuse to become part of the mass, get rid of them now.

Now begin to knead the dough. Push the heel of your hand down hard, stretching the dough firmly away from you. Fold the flap back toward you and give the lump of dough a quarter-turn. Press down on another section of the dough.

Hand-mixed dough isn't easy to work with. It is stiff-textured and requires a lot of hard pummeling. At first it may seem that the ball of dough won't hold together, but the act of kneading will distribute the moisture evenly through it, and, after a few minutes, it should begin to form a ball.

Knead for a full 10 minutes, pushing, folding, and turning until the dough is smooth. The thing to remember is that this is supposed to be harder than kneading bread, so don't despair. When you are done, pat the dough into a neat ball and cover it with a dish towel or a sheet of plastic wrap. Let it rest for at least 30 minutes. Two hours' rest is even better.

To make the dough with a heavy-duty stand mixer: Fit the paddle attachment into your electric mixer. Put the flour and salt into the bowl, and give it a quick whirl to mix them. Add the eggs and oil and turn on the beater. Let it go for half a minute, until you have coarse grains of dough in the bowl, something like the consistency of piecrust before it is gathered into a ball.

Replace the paddle with the dough hook and knead in the bowl for 5 minutes. Or take the dough from the bowl, dust a wooden surface with flour, pat the dough into a ball, and knead it for 10 minutes. You will find that this dough is much easier to work with than the hand-mixed dough. After 10 minutes, you should have a firm, smooth, pale yellow ball of dough. Put it to rest under a dish towel or in plastic wrap.

To mix the dough with a food processor: Put the metal blade into the food processor. Measure in the flour and salt, and process briefly to blend them. Drop the eggs and oil through the feeding tube, and let the machine run until the dough

Beard on . . . Pasta

I never get tired of pasta, any more than I can get tired of bread. I eat it when I'm exhausted and want a quick meal that will give me a lift. I eat it when I am in an ambitious mood, looking for something pleasant and different to compliment a guest.

When I want something spicy, I toss spaghetti with warm olive oil, garlic, and anchovies. When I want something voluptuous, I bake elbow macaroni in a cheese-rich béchamel sauce. And when I'm fed up with complicated foods, I fill a bowl with piping-hot green noodles and top them with icy tomatoes and scallions in a sharp vinaigrette.

Pasta is always the same, yet always different. It has a comforting familiarity, with its pale golden color and chewy, wheaten taste. And then there are all those amusing shapes, and the thousands of ways to sauce them: from avocado to zucchini, or from plain butter to cheese to purée of frog's legs. It's always different because we find pasta recipes in nearly every country in the world.

In my own life, pasta didn't begin as an Italian food at all. I must have been six or seven before I even ate spaghetti, but I was eating Chinese noodles long before that.

They were given to me by Let, the Chinese chef who worked for my mother. He used to make a soup that was a rather weak chicken stock absolutely full of noodles, ham, scallions, and thin strips of egg that he had beaten up, cooked in a thin pancake, and sliced into strips.

I didn't have Italian noodles until I was in school, when we started going to a pretty good Italian restaurant that served "family style" meals at great long tables. They'd bring you a little antipasto and then a dish of pasta. The menu never varied, and it was always fifty cents. They made a good tomato sauce, and one with butter and fresh herbs, and a version of carbonara. The sauces were nothing complicated, it was great fun, and I just loved it; and, after all, what can you do for fifty cents?

Oddly enough, when I began to cook pasta myself, it was in the German style. That was because my mother had close friends from a German family, and they used noodles in a lot of soups and with stews. They had one wonderful dish for which they took all the lesser parts of the pig—the backbone and tail and such—braised them, and served them with sauerkraut and noodles. That was fun.

The point of all these reminiscences is to show how, even in a small American city at the beginning of the [twentieth] century, there were several quite distinct traditions of cooking with pasta.

begins to form a ball; around 15 seconds should do it. Once you've become familiar with the method, you'll be able to correct the recipe at this point. If the dough seems too sticky, add a tablespoon or two more flour. If it's too dry, add a few drops of water or part of an egg. Process again briefly.

Turn out the dough onto a floured surface. You will notice that this method results in the yellowest and stickiest dough of all. That's because it's already half-kneaded. Dust your hands with flour and continue the kneading. Work for 3 to 5 minutes, adding more flour if necessary, until you have a smooth ball of dough. Set it to rest under a dish towel or in plastic wrap.

Let the dough rest: I cannot emphasize too strongly the importance of letting the dough rest between the kneading and rolling. During this period, which should last at least 30 minutes and can continue in the refrigerator for days, the gluten in the flour relaxes and the dough becomes soft, well blended, and easy to work. I've put many a worrisome dough to rest under a dish towel, only to retrieve it 2 hours later, in perfect condition for rolling.

To roll the dough by hand: There are two stages in rolling pasta by hand. In the first, the dough is worked just as it is when you are making piecrust, pressing down and out from the center of the disk. This usually presents no problems for the American cook. The second stage is harder to learn, because you have to be able to do two things at once. It's a little like learning to pat your head and rub your stomach at the same time: once you get it, it's easy; but the first few times you try to do it, it seems impossible.

To begin, place the ball of dough on a floured surface. Pat it into a flat disk, and start to roll it with your rolling pin. Move always from the center to the edges of the circle, giving the dough a quarter-turn after each roll to keep the circular shape. Keep checking to be sure that the dough isn't sticking to the board. If it is, loosen with a dough scraper and dust with flour. When the dough is about ¼ inch thick, the first stage is finished.

During the second stage, you will be pulling and stretching the dough instead of rolling it. Very often, I've seen experienced pasta rollers hang one end of the sheet over the edge of the table and lean their tummies against it as they roll. That way, they get a three-way action, pulling, rolling, and stretching!

Curl the far edge of the circle around the center of your rolling pin. Then roll the pin back toward you, wrapping some of the dough around it. Push and stretch it away from you as you unroll the dough. At the same time, slide your hands lightly out and in on the pin, stretching the sheet sideways. Don't press down. Pull out.

Turn the circle slightly after each stretch. You are trying to make a very thin sheet of dough, something like the thickness of good writing paper. It will be slightly transparent. You won't be able to read through it, but if you're rolling on a wooden surface, you should be able to see the grain of wood through the dough.

One way to be sure that you're rolling the dough evenly and that it isn't sticking to the board is to check its color. If the color is more intense at the center of the circle than at the edges, it means that the dough is thicker there. That often happens when it has stuck to the board. Roll it up onto a pin (a dough scraper will be helpful).

Dust the board with flour. Turn the dough facedown and flour its top side. Rub some flour onto the rolling pin.

If the business of stretching and pulling and sliding your hands in and out seems too much for you to master, you can roll out the dough as you might a very thin piecrust. It takes a lot of work, because you'll be fighting the gluten's elasticity, but it can definitely be done.

To roll the dough by machine: There are two kinds of wringer-style pasta machines—one that is turned by hand, and one that is operated by motor. Each has its advantages and its fans.

The hand-cranked model is considerably cheaper than the motorized machine. And it is my opinion that many people are intimidated by the speed with which the motor-driven machine processes the dough. They like the feeling of being in control that they get from turning the handle themselves.

Other people prefer the speed and efficiency of the motorized machine. They feel that there are never enough hands around to do everything that has to be done with a hand-cranked machine.

All of the machines work on the same principle. The dough is fed through a set of cylindrical rollers, which knead it, flatten it, and, when the rollers have been changed, cut it into noodles.

After the ball of dough has rested, cut it into four pieces. Put three of them back under the dish towel, and flatten the fourth with a rolling pin or with your palm. Set the machine so that the rollers are at the widest opening.

If you are using the electric model, turn on the machine (it will make an infernal racket); otherwise start cranking. Feed the flattened ball of dough through the rollers four or five times, folding it in half each time before it goes back through the rollers. This will further knead and smooth the dough.

It may come out with ragged edges or with holes torn in it. This often happened when the dough hasn't been kneaded enough. Don't worry. Patch the holes with bits torn from the end, and feed the dough back through the rollers. If the edges are ragged, fold the ribbon in half lengthwise. If the dough comes out in a distorted shape, just fold it up into a flat square and roll it through again. You'll know when it's rolled enough, because the dough will become smooth and satiny. The nice thing about pasta dough is that it isn't one of those delicate mixtures that shouldn't be overhandled. Go ahead and work it. It thrives on the human touch.

Now begin to narrow the opening between the rollers by turning the dial one mark each time the dough goes through. Keep going until you reach the thickness you want. Then make a note of the number on the dial, and you'll have something to aim for the next time you roll out pasta.

Lay the ribbon of pasta on a dish towel or a table lined with a clean tablecloth while you roll out the other three pieces of dough.

Let the dough rest again before cutting: Once the dough has been rolled out, it should lie on kitchen towels for around 5 minutes to give it a chance to dry. Machine-rolled dough dries faster than hand-rolled, so the first ribbons will probably be ready to cut by the time the last ones are rolled. Don't let it get too dry, however. The dough should be pliable, neither brittle nor moist and sticky. If it just doesn't dry, dust it with some more flour and no harm will be done.

To cut the pasta by hand: There are two ways to cut simple noodles by hand. The easier is to fold the dough and cut it into slices with a sharp knife. It's very important that the dough be well dried if you use this method, or it will stick to itself when it is folded.

Take one edge of the dough and fold it over loosely into a flat roll around 3 inches wide. Continue to fold until the whole strip or circle of dough is folded. Then take a sharp knife or cleaver and cut ¼- to ½-inch slices from the rolled dough. Don't saw. Press down evenly, trying to make the slices even in width. As soon as the whole roll has been cut, open up the noodles so they can dry further.

You can also cut noodles with a rolling pastry cutter. I have one that George Lang gave me that cuts four noodles at a time. Most pastry wheels are single, however, and the problem with using them is that you have to have a very steady hand and a good eye to make the noodles come out even in width. [*Editor: Born in Hungary and based in New York, Lang was one of the most influential food consultants and restaurateurs in the late twentieth century. The cutter Beard refers is generally used professionally to save time cutting out strips of croissant dough.*]

To cut the dough by machine: You can use the pasta machine to cut both the hand-rolled and the machine-rolled dough. If you have a circle of hand-rolled dough, just cut the circle into 4½-inch strips that will fit through the machine.

If you are using the electric model, remove the smooth rollers from the machine and fit one of the cutting attachments into place. For the hand-cranked model, insert the handle into one of the cutting slots. Turn on the motor or begin to turn the handle, and feed the ribbons into the right side of the machine. They will come out on the left side in nicely cut strands. If the machine doesn't cut them all the way through, your dough is probably too sticky, and you should set it aside to dry out a little longer.

To dry the dough: At this point you can simply drop the freshly cut noodles into boiling water. But it is probably more convenient to get the work of making pasta out of the way a little while before mealtime. And many Italians, I ought to mention, feel that drying is an essential step in the making of pasta; that omitting it changes the quality of the noodles. I can't say that I agree, but it is certainly more convenient to make your noodles early in the day and dry them out.

Take up strands of pasta and loop them loosely around your fingers, forming nests. Let them dry on a cloth towel or on a cookie rack. Or else dry the pasta on a rack. You can use anything—a broomstick, the back of a chair, a clothesline. I've been in Italian kitchens where the fettuccine hung like a curtain from a clothesline—strung across the corner of the kitchen. You might want to use one of those two- or three-tiered clothes racks that were designed to stand in the bathtub. I happen to have a marvelous pasta rack that was made for me by a friend. Unfortunately, it isn't available commercially. It's an upright pole with a disk on the top. Three wooden rods fit into holes on the disk. I drape the pasta over the rods. Then, when I want to cook it, I simply pull off one of the rods, carry it to the stove, and push the pasta into the boiling water.

Editor: You can now purchase pasta-drying racks similar to the one Beard describes online and at kitchenware stores.

Once the pasta is really dry, you can put it in a tin and store it in the pantry, just as though it were commercial spaghetti. Be careful when you handle it: it will be very brittle. Or you can put the rolled-up nests into plastic bags and stick them in the freezer. But, once you've gone to all the trouble of making it, you will probably just want to cook it.

To cook the pasta: The point to remember about homemade pasta is that it cooks in no time at all. Dried homemade pasta takes a little longer than the truly fresh made, but even so it will be done practically as soon as the water returns to the boil. Have your sauce ready before you put the noodles anywhere near the water. And don't pay attention to any recipe that tells you to cook noodles for 8 to 10 minutes. This is too long, even for most commercial brands.

(Although I have to say that cooking is the one inexplicable art in pasta making. I find that there is absolutely no way to figure it out when you use commercial pastas. You put it in the pot, and you taste it after 4 minutes, and then after 8 minutes, and finally in desperation after 12 minutes, and it still has the crunch in the middle. I remember cooking some commercial whole-wheat pasta and it seemed that it was never going to become soft.)

Have lots of water boiling furiously. I don't add any salt, because I think that your sauce and cheese will provide enough seasoning. But it's a good idea to add a splash of oil to keep the strands from sticking together.

Drop the homemade pasta into the boiling water. Start testing it as soon as it returns to the boil. I've heard all kinds of methods for testing pasta, but the best one is just to fish out a strand and bite into it. If the noodle is beautifully pliable, with no hard core to it, then your pasta is done. Pour the contents of the pot into a colander in the sink, and get ready to mix in your sauce.

Editor: For most uses, you will need to increase the yield of this basic recipe. For about 1 pound pasta, use 2¼ cups unbleached all-purpose flour, 3 large eggs at room temperature, ¾ teaspoon salt, and 1 tablespoon olive oil. Cut the dough into six portions before rolling it out.

Inexpensive hand-cranked metal pasta rolling machines can be purchased through many outlets—kitchenware shops, online, and even at many Italian delicatessens. While the electric pasta machine that Beard describes still exists, it is very expensive. (Don't confuse it with the extruder-style pasta machine that forces the dough through a die.) There are two wonderful alternatives to the electric machine. You can buy a separate motor that replaces the crank on the hand-operated machine. Also, there are pasta rolling and cutting attachments for some models of electric stand mixers. Both of these dramatically shorten the time needed to roll out the dough.

EGG WHITE NOODLES

Pasta is actually a low-fat main course, especially when it is served with a simple tomato sauce. But, for those who can't even take the cholesterol that is contributed by the egg yolks in the noodles, here is a noodle made with no yolks—ergo, no cholesterol— and with one tiny tablespoonful of olive oil.

- 4 cups all-purpose flour
- 1 teaspoon salt
- 1 tablespoon olive oil
- 7 to 8 large egg whites

Put the metal chopping blade in place in the bowl of the food processor. Add the flour, salt, and oil, and process for 8 to 10 seconds. Add the egg whites and process about 15 seconds, until the dough is pliable, but not damp or sticky. Knead by hand for a few minutes, then let rest and roll out by hand or in the pasta machine.

BARBARA KAFKA'S BUCKWHEAT NOODLES

MAKES 3 OR 4 SERVINGS

This recipe was given to me by Barbara Kafka, an imaginative and creative cook. The presence of beer and yeast makes the noodles very light.

- ½ cup lager beer, at room temperature, as needed
- 1 teaspoon active dry yeast
- ¼ cup buckwheat flour

- 1 cup all-purpose flour
- ¼ teaspoon kosher salt

In a small bowl, combine half the beer, the yeast, and 2 tablespoons of the buckwheat flour. Stir until combined, cover with plastic wrap and let the sponge rise in a warm place for 1 to 2 hours, or until very bubbly.

Transfer the sponge to a medium bowl. Stir in the remaining buckwheat flour, 2 tablespoons of beer, the all-purpose flour, and salt. If needed, stir in more beer to make a soft but firm dough. You will probably not use the whole ½ cup. Cover again, and let the dough rest for 30 minutes.

Divide it into quarters and roll it out thinly by hand or in the pasta machine. Don't hesitate to flour the dough if it seems sticky as you work it. Cut into medium-width noodles.

AVOCADO PASTA WITH CREAM

MAKES 6 TO 8 SERVINGS

Editor: Beard calls this "a suburb dish," but warns, "it is a bit tricky to handle because of the softness of the dough." It shows his never-ending curiosity and willingness to try new foods and bring them to his readers.

Avocado Pasta

- 3½ cups all-purpose flour, plus more for kneading
- ¼ teaspoon kosher salt
- 1 very ripe avocado, pitted, peeled, and cut up
- 3 large eggs, at room temperature

Sauce

2 cups heavy cream

2 very ripe avocados, pitted, peeled, and cubed

2 tablespoons unsalted butter

1 garlic clove, minced

½ teaspoon kosher salt

½ teaspoon freshly ground black pepper

3 tablespoons freshly grated Parmesan cheese,
    plus more for serving

Slivers of drained pimiento, for garnish

To make the pasta: Put the flour and salt in a large mixing bowl. In another bowl, mash the avocado. Stir in the eggs with a wooden spoon. Add the avocado mixture to the flour and blend thoroughly in the bowl or in the food processor.

Turn out the dough onto a floured board and knead it by hand for 5 minutes. The avocado will have made it very soft, so that you will have to sprinkle it frequently with more flour. Roll it into very thin sheets, using the machine as directed on page 198. Cut the sheets into 1½-inch squares. Lay them on a cookie sheet or a piece of foil and chill them in the freezer for about a half hour, until they are firm.

Bring a large pot of salted water to boil. When the dough squares are firm, take them out of the freezer, drop them into the boiling water, and cook for about 3 minutes, until they are properly done. Drain.

Return the noodles to the pot, and add the cream, avocados, butter, garlic, salt, and pepper. Sprinkle with Parmesan cheese and stir gently over medium heat so that everything is coated. Transfer to a serving dish, sprinkle with more cheese, and serve at once, garnished with slivers of red pimiento.

GREEN NOODLES BOLOGNESE

〜 MAKES 8 TO 10 SERVINGS

For the Green Noodles

5 or 6 cups all-purpose flour

6 large eggs

½ pound fresh leaf spinach, stems removed,
    well washed, and cooked according to the
    Editor's Note on page 211

For the Sauce

4 tablespoons (½ stick) unsalted butter

¾ pound ground beef round

¾ pound ground pork

1 medium yellow onion, finely chopped

1 carrot, finely chopped

1 celery rib, finely chopped

¼ cup chopped fresh flat-leaf parsley

1 garlic clove, finely chopped

Kosher salt and freshly ground black pepper

½ cup Beef Stock (page 349)

1 tablespoon tomato paste

¾ cup freshly grated Parmesan cheese, plus more
    for serving

1 or 2 tablespoons heavy cream

To make the noodles: On a work surface, make a ring of the flour, and place the eggs and spinach inside. Blend and knead very well by hand until smooth and supple, about 10 minutes. (Or combine and mix the ingredients in a heavy-duty stand electric mixer fitted with a dough hook.) Roll out several times in a pasta machine. Allow to dry 15 to 20 minutes. Using the pasta machine, cut into strips about ¼ inch wide. [*Editor: There are detailed instructions for this procedure on pages 195 to 200.*]

To make the sauce: Heat the butter in a large saucepan over medium-high heat. Add the ground beef and ground pork, onion, carrot, celery, parsley, and garlic and cook, stirring often, until nicely colored, about 10 minutes. Season with salt and pepper to taste, and add half the stock. Boil until the stock is cooked down. Stir in the remaining stock and the tomato paste. Cover, and simmer over medium-low heat for 1 hour longer.

Bring a large pot of lightly salted water to a boil over high heat. Add the noodles and cook until just tender, about 3 minutes. Drain the noodles well and return to their cooking pot. Add the sauce, grated cheese, and cream and toss well. Serve with more cheese passed on the side.

KREPLACH

◌ MAKES 6 SERVINGS

There are 10 dozen ways of doing kreplach, and 10 times that number of people telling you that theirs is the traditional way. This one is idiotically simple, but the sage and chives make a nice combination of flavors. Use plenty of chives. I grow them in my backyard, and they're usually the first thing up in the garden, so to me they taste like springtime. Here the kreplach are sautéed in butter (or chicken fat) until they are lightly browned to serve with pot roast or chicken. But you could also add the cooked kreplach to chicken soup.

½ pound ground beef chuck

3 tablespoons chopped fresh flat-leaf parsley

1 tablespoon chopped fresh sage, or ½ teaspoon dried sage

1 tablespoon minced fresh chives

½ teaspoon kosher salt

¼ teaspoon Tabasco

Basic Egg Pasta (page 195)

3 tablespoons unsalted butter or rendered chicken fat, as needed

Mix the ground beef, parsley, sage, chives, salt, and Tabasco. Roll out the dough thinly in the pasta machine. Then, using a pastry wheel, cut it into 2-inch squares. Place a scant teaspoonful of filling toward one corner of each square. Moisten the edges of the square, fold one corner over another to make a triangle, and seal tightly.

Let the kreplach sit at room temperature for 30 minutes before you cook them. Meanwhile, bring a large pot of lightly salted water to a boil over high heat. Drop the kreplach into the water, about 8 at a time. Cover the pot and cook each batch for about 15 minutes. Using a slotted spoon, transfer to an oiled baking sheet and add more kreplach to the pot.

Heat the butter in a large skillet over medium-high heat. In batches, add the kreplach and cook, stirring occasionally, until lightly browned, about 5 minutes, adding more butter as needed. (You may have to keep the batches warm in a 200°F oven until all of the kreplach are cooked.) Serve hot.

NOCKERLI

Nockerli are tiny dumplings made by pinching off bits of dough and rolling them into tiny balls. They are nice cooked in a rich beef broth, or mixed with a hearty vegetable, as in the Noodles with Cabbage on page 205.

For the Nockerli

3 cups all-purpose flour

2 large eggs

1 teaspoon coarse salt

1 tablespoon unsalted butter, melted

¾ cup water

2 quarts Beef Stock (page 349) or water

To make the nockerli: In a large bowl, mix the flour, eggs, and salt. Add the melted butter and water and beat with a wooden spoon for 4 minutes. Let sit for at least 20 minutes. Then, using your lightly floured hands, pinch off bits of dough and roll them gently between your palms to make tiny balls.

Bring the broth to a boil in a large saucepan over high heat. Add the nockerli and cook. They are done when they float to the top.

ANGEL HAIR WITH LIGHT TOMATO SAUCE

This recipe forms the basis for a nearly limitless number of variations. It also has the advantage of using canned tomatoes, so that you aren't dependent on the season or the quality of the fresh tomatoes in your market.

Editor: Fresh herbs are especially good here, so use 1 tablespoon chopped fresh basil or 2 teaspoons of the other recommended dried herb, if you wish.

For the Light Tomato Sauce

One 28-ounce can whole tomatoes in purée

2 small onions, sliced

1 teaspoon dried basil, oregano, rosemary, sage, marjoram, or thyme

Kosher salt and freshly ground black pepper

4 tablespoons (½ stick) unsalted butter

1 pound angel hair pasta

To make the tomato sauce: Cook the tomatoes, onions, and basil over medium-high heat for 20 minutes, stirring frequently, and seasoning with the salt and pepper. If you want a smooth sauce, strain it through a wire sieve or purée it in the food processor. I prefer to leave the sauce with lumps, just breaking up the tomatoes with a wooden spoon. Then add the butter and continue to cook until it melts. Keep the sauce warm.

Bring a large pot of lightly salted water to a boil over high heat. Add the pasta and cook according to the package directions until al dente. Drain and return to the cooking pot. Add the sauce, mix well, and serve.

VARIATION

LIGHT TOMATO SAUCE WITH GARLIC: Add 2 minced garlic cloves to the tomatoes and onions.

FETTUCCINE WITH ZUCCHINI

✺ MAKES 4 TO 6 SERVINGS

A very pretty dish when it is made with yellow egg noodles, green zucchini, and red pepper strips, like the Italian flag.

1 pound fettuccine

½ cup olive oil

2 medium yellow onions, chopped

1 pound small, firm zucchini, trimmed and cut into
    thin strips about 2 inches long

2 red bell peppers, broiled until the skins blacken,
    peeled, and seeded, and cut into thin strips about
    2 inches long

2 garlic cloves, minced

4 ripe plum tomatoes, peeled, seeded, and chopped,
    or one 16-ounce can whole tomatoes in purée

1 teaspoon kosher salt

⅛ teaspoon crushed hot red pepper flakes

Grated Parmesan cheese, for serving

Heat the olive oil in a skillet, and sauté the onions, zucchini, bell peppers, and garlic for 5 min-

utes, stirring occasionally. Add the tomatoes, salt, and hot pepper flakes, and cook over very low heat for another 5 to 10 minutes.

Meanwhile, bring a large pot of lightly salted water to a boil over high heat. Add the pasta to the water and cook according to the package directions until al dente. Drain the pasta in a colander. Return to its cooking pot, add the sauce, and toss well. Sprinkle with lots of grated cheese. Transfer to a warm serving bowl and serve hot.

NOODLES WITH CABBAGE

✺ MAKES 6 TO 8 SERVINGS

I made this up years ago, when I wanted something to serve with sausages and beer. Try it with wide egg noodles, noodle squares, or Nockerli (page 204).

One 2-to-3-pound green cabbage, cut into quarters,
    and hard core removed

5 tablespoons (½ stick plus 1 tablespoon) unsalted
    butter or bacon fat

3 tablespoons all-purpose flour

¾ cup light cream

Kosher salt and freshly ground black pepper

1 pound wide egg noodles

Put the cabbage through the slicing blade of the food processor. Melt the butter or fat in a large skillet and sauté the cabbage until it is lightly browned. Cover and cook until tender, about 10 minutes. Sprinkle on the flour and continue to cook, stirring, for a few minutes. Then add the cream, salt, and pepper, and cook, stirring constantly, until the sauce comes to a simmer and thickens. Keep the sauce warm.

Meanwhile, bring a large pot of lightly salted water to a boil over high heat. Add the noodles and cook according to the package directions until almost tender. Drain well. Return the noodles to their cooking pot. Add the sauce and let everything bubble together over medium heat for a few minutes to blend the flavors.

PASTA WITH PARSLEY PESTO, CHERRY TOMATOES, AND DILL

◠ MAKES 4 TO 6 SERVINGS

Editor: Beard doesn't specify what kind of pasta, but a delicate angel hair (capellini) or thin spaghetti would be appropriate with a light vegetarian sauce like this one. You won't need all of the pesto. It can be refrigerated in a covered container, with olive oil poured over the top to cover pesto surface, for about 1 month. Stir in the oil before using.

For the Parsley Pesto

4 to 5 bunches fresh flat-leaf parsley, stems removed

1 cup whole walnuts

1 cup extra-virgin olive oil

¾ cup freshly grated Parmesan cheese

3 large garlic cloves

1½ teaspoons kosher salt

1 pound pasta of your choice

4 tablespoons (½ stick) unsalted butter

¼ cup chopped fresh dill or 1 tablespoon dried dill

1 pound cherry tomatoes

2 tablespoons olive oil

To make the pesto: Combine the parsley, walnuts, olive oil, cheese, garlic, and salt in the bowl of a food processor fitted with the metal blade. Process the ingredients until well combined into a thick sauce. Transfer to a bowl and cover with plastic wrap until ready to serve.

Bring a large pot of lightly salted water to a boil over high heat. Add the pasta and cook according to the package directions until al dente, timing it so the pasta and tomatoes are done at the same time.

Meanwhile, melt the butter in the top of a double boiler over simmering water. Add the chopped dill and the tomatoes. Toss the tomatoes to coat with the dill butter and warm just long enough to heat through, about 3 minutes.

Drain the pasta, but only briefly, so the pasta remains moist. Return the pasta to its cooking pot. Toss with the oil. Divide the pasta among individual bowls. Top each with 2 to 3 tablespoons of the pesto, then equal amounts of the cherry tomatoes and dill butter. Serve at once.

PASTA PRIMAVERA

◠ MAKES 4 TO 6 SERVINGS

In Italian, *primavera* means "spring," and a primavera sauce should be made with the first, tiny vegetables that pop out in the spring. In the winter, of course, you would use the freshest vegetables you could get at that time, such as broccoli, red bell peppers, and zucchini, but I've suggested a springtime combination that would be just delicious. Just don't be formal about it. Use what you have in the garden or in the refrigerator. You can even cut up a couple of stalks of celery and add them for the bite.

1 pound angel hair, linguine, or even orzo

1/2 cup fresh peas

1/2 cup tiny, new green beans

1/2 cup (1/2-inch slices) stemmed thin asparagus

1/2 cup sliced mushrooms

4 tablespoons (1/2 stick) unsalted butter

1 cup light cream, warmed

Kosher salt and lots of freshly ground black pepper

Freshly grated Parmesan cheese

Bring a large pot of lightly salted water to a boil over high heat. Add the angel hair pasta and cook according to the package directions until the pasta is al dente, timing it so the sauce and pasta are done at the same time.

Lightly cook the peas, beans, asparagus, and mushrooms in the butter in a large, deep skillet over medium heat until everything is crisply tender, about 5 minutes. Add the cream and season with salt and pepper. Cook down briefly over high heat, about 2 minutes.

Drain the pasta in a colander. Return to its cooking pot, add the sauce, and toss well. Sprinkle with lots of grated cheese. Transfer to a warm serving bowl and serve hot.

PASTA CON QUATTRO FORMAGGI

MAKES 4 TO 6 SERVINGS

The only requirement for the four cheeses in this dish is that one of them be Parmesan. Evan Jones, in his book *World of Cheese*, makes it with Bel Paese, Fontina, Gorgonzola, and Parmesan. It's not traditional, but I like to use a goat cheese in this dish. It doesn't quite melt; it softens and becomes thick. But by all means go ahead and experiment: this is an excellent opportunity to use up all the leftover cheese in the refrigerator. [*Editor: Evan Jones was the husband of Beard's sometime editor, Judith Jones, and ultimately one of Beard's biographers.*]

8 tablespoons (1 stick) unsalted butter

1 pound penne or ziti

1/4 cup goat cheese, in chunks

1/2 cup freshly grated Parmesan cheese

1/2 cup freshly grated pecorino Romano cheese

1/4 cup shredded Gruyère cheese

Freshly ground black pepper

Melt the butter in a heavy-bottomed saucepan; set aside. Bring a large pot of lightly salted water to a boil over high heat. Add the penne and cook according to the package directions until al dente. Drain and add to the butter in the saucepan. Then mix in the cheeses, one at a time, turning the noodles thoroughly as you go. Serve very hot with lots of freshly ground black pepper.

SWORDFISH-OLIVE PASTA

I like to use twists, shells, or ridged ziti for this dish: something that will catch all the tangy bits of olive and capers. What you want is the rich, exciting olive taste, so use lots and lots of finely chopped Greek olives.

½ pound pasta (see suggestions above)
One 8-ounce swordfish steak, cut ½ inch thick
¾ cup pitted and finely chopped Greek olives, such as Kalamata
¼ cup olive oil
½ cup thinly sliced onion
3 large garlic cloves, finely chopped
1 teaspoon dried oregano
1 tablespoon drained nonpareil capers

Bring a pot of lightly salted water to a boil over high heat. Add the pasta and cook according to the package directions until al dente, timing it so the pasta and sauce are done at the same time.

Meanwhile, preheat the broiler and line the rack of a broiler pan with aluminum foil. Broil the swordfish 3 minutes on one side, turn, top with the olives, and broil 4 minutes longer. Pour the oil into a skillet and cook the onion and garlic over medium heat until softened, about 3 minutes. Add the oregano and capers.

When the swordfish is cooked, take it out of the broiler and cut it into thin strips, along with the olives. Discard the swordfish skin. Drain the pasta and put it into a warm serving bowl. Spoon the swordfish and olives, with the onion-caper mixture, over the freshly cooked pasta and toss gently.

PENNE WITH TOMATO—GROUND MEAT SAUCE

This is a good scheme to follow whenever you have some leftover meat in the refrigerator. It's delicious made with chicken, beef, pork, and veal, even brains. The seasoning will depend on whatever your meat was seasoned with when it was first cooked. If you have some meat juices left from underneath a roast or from a sauté pan, by all means add them to the sauce, too. And, if you don't, and have a delicate meat such as chicken or veal, add ¼ cup cream to the sauce at the end. A wonderful way to use leftovers—let imagination guide you!

1 pound penne or ziti
1 recipe Light Tomato Sauce (page 204)
1 cup cooked and ground meat or poultry
Pan juices, if available, or ¼ cup heavy cream (optional)
Kosher salt and freshly ground black pepper
Freshly grated Parmesan cheese, for serving

Bring a large pot of lightly salted water to a boil over high heat. Add the penne and cook according to the package directions until al dente, timing it so the sauce and pasta are done at the same time.

Bring the tomato sauce to a simmer in a medium saucepan. Add the ground cooked meat and the pan juices, if using. Season with salt and pepper, and simmer for 5 minutes.

Drain the pasta. Transfer to a warm serving bowl, add the sauce, and serve with the cheese passed on the side.

VARIATION

PENNE WITH TOMATO-SHRIMP SAUCE: Substitute ½ pound or more cooked shrimp for the meat, but do not grind the shrimp. Add a touch more black pepper and ½ cup finely chopped red or green bell peppers.

PENNE WITH TOMATO-CLAM SAUCE: Omit the ground cooked meat. Steam clams as described on page 174. Remove them from the shell and add the strained clam broth and shelled clams to the tomato sauce. Combine with pasta.

You may do the same with mussels as with clams.

CHÈVRE—TOMATO SAUCE SPAGHETTI

MAKES 4 TO 6 SERVINGS

This combination of tomato and goat cheese is just delicious. Chèvre softens in an especially creamy way: it seems to relax into the sauce. Make the sauce in a pan that's large enough so that you can pour the drained spaghetti into it and let it cook for about 2 minutes, long enough to soak up some of the flavor.

1 recipe Light Tomato Sauce (page 204)
2 ounces soft chèvre, cut into chunks
Tabasco
1 pound spaghetti

When the sauce is finished, add the chunks of cheese to it and let them soften. Season with Tabasco: it should be quite spicy. Remove from the heat and cover to keep warm.

Meanwhile, cook the spaghetti in a large pot of lightly salted water according to the package directions just until al dente. Drain the spaghetti, then add to the sauce. Simmer over low heat for a couple of minutes to blend the flavors.

VARIATION

BLUE CHEESE–TOMATO SAUCE SPAGHETTI: Instead of chèvre, use 2 ounces crumbled blue cheese (about ½ cup) and eliminate the Tabasco.

SPAGHETTI WITH CLAM SAUCE

∽ MAKES 4 TO 6 SERVINGS

I discovered this wonderfully light sauce, full of the essence of clams and garlic, during one of those periods when I was seriously trying to cut down on oil and salt. I don't think you will miss the oil at all.

1 pound spaghetti

2 quarts littleneck clams

Dry white wine

4 to 5 large garlic cloves, minced or crushed

¾ cup chopped fresh flat-leaf parsley

Bring a large pot of lightly salted water to a boil over high heat. Add the spaghetti and cook according to the package directions until al dente, timing it so the sauce and spaghetti are finished at the same time.

Scrub the clams well and wash them in cold water to remove the sand in the shells. Put them in a heavy-bottomed saucepan with ½ inch of white wine or water and the garlic. Cover the kettle tightly, and steam the clams until the shells open, 5 to 10 minutes.

Drain the pasta. Put the freshly cooked spaghetti in a warm bowl, pour the clams, still in their shells, and broth over it, and sprinkle the chopped parsley on the top.

VARIATION

SPAGHETTI WITH MUSSEL SAUCE: Instead of clams, you can use 2 quarts of mussels. Scrub the mussels well with a kitchen brush or scouring pad, scrape off the encrustations on the shells, and snip off the beards before you steam them. [*Editor: If you use farmed mussels, such as the Prince Edward Island variety, the mussels will be beardless.*]

SPAGHETTI WITH RAISIN AND PINE NUT SAUCE

∽ MAKES 4 SERVINGS

Editor: The intriguing mix of sweet raisins and buttery pine nuts identifies this dish as Sicilian.

1 pound spaghetti

4 garlic cloves, finely chopped

¾ cup olive oil

½ cup pine nuts

½ cup seedless raisins

Freshly ground black pepper

⅓ cup chopped fresh flat-leaf parsley

Bring a large pot of lightly salted water to a boil over high heat. Add the spaghetti and cook according to the package directions until al dente. Drain the pasta and return to its cooking pot.

Immediately, heat the garlic in the olive oil over low heat until the garlic begins to soften, about 2 minutes. Pour the oil over the pasta. Add the pine nuts and raisins and toss well. Season with the pepper and sprinkle with the chopped parsley.

RAISIN AND PINE NUT SAUCE WITH ANCHOVIES: Add 10 finely chopped anchovy fillets to the pasta and proceed as above.

RAISIN AND PINE NUT SAUCE WITH DRIED FIGS: Instead of anchovies add coarsely chopped dried figs to the pasta and proceed as above.

SPAGHETTINI WITH SPINACH-ANCHOVY SAUCE

❧ MAKES 4 TO 6 SERVINGS

Editor: This is a very rich dish, and may be best in small portions as a pasta course at an Italian-style meal rather than a main course.

One 28-ounce can whole tomatoes in purée

2 small onions, sliced

1 teaspoon dried basil, oregano, rosemary, sage, marjoram, or thyme

Kosher salt and freshly ground black pepper

2 tablespoons unsalted butter

2 garlic cloves, finely chopped

1 cup chopped cooked spinach (see Editor's Note)

4 anchovy fillets, coarsely chopped

3 tablespoons pine nuts, toasted in a skillet

1 pound spaghettini (thin spaghetti)

Bring the tomatoes, onions, and basil to a simmer in a medium saucepan over medium heat, breaking up the tomatoes with the side of a spoon. Reduce the heat to medium-low and simmer until lightly thickened, about 20 minutes

Melt the butter in a medium skillet over medium heat, add the garlic, and cook until it is golden brown, about 2 minutes. Stir in the spinach and anchovies, cook over medium heat for a few minutes, and then add to the tomato sauce.

Meanwhile, bring a large pot of lightly salted water to a boil over high heat. Add the spaghettini and cook according to the package directions until al dente. Drain and return to the cooking pot. Add the sauce, top with the pine nuts, toss well, and serve.

Editor: For the spinach, cook 1½ pounds fresh leaf spinach (stems removed and well washed), with the water clinging to the washed leaves in a large saucepan over medium heat until wilted and tender, about 5 minutes. Drain, rinse under cold water, and cool. Squeeze handfuls of the spinach to remove all excess moisture, and chop. Or substitute two 10-ounce packages chopped frozen spinach, thawed and squeezed to remove excess moisture.

TAGLIARINI VERDI ALLA PANCETTA

❧ MAKES 6 SERVINGS

Where I live, in Greenwich Village, there is no end to wonderful Italian markets, and I have no trouble buying pancetta, the Italian unsmoked bacon. If you can't locate pancetta, you can substitute prosciutto, unsmoked ham, or thick-sliced bacon that has been simmered in water for 10 minutes, drained, and rinsed with fresh cold water.

8 to 10 medium leeks

6 tablespoons (¾ stick) unsalted butter

2 tablespoons chopped fresh flat-leaf parsley

Kosher salt and freshly ground black pepper

Pinch of freshly grated nutmeg

½ pound sliced pancetta

1¼ pounds green tagliarini or other pasta

1 cup heavy cream

¼ cup freshly grated Parmesan cheese, plus more
   for serving

Trim off the root ends and most of the green parts of the leeks. Slit the tops and wash thoroughly under running water to remove the grit. Cut into julienne strips and pat dry with paper towels.

Melt 2 tablespoons of the butter in a skillet over medium heat. Add the leeks and parsley, and season with salt, pepper, and nutmeg. Sauté briskly until the leeks are golden, about 5 minutes, and remove them from the pan with a slotted spoon. Add the pancetta, increase the heat, and sauté until the pancetta is nearly crisp, about 3 minutes. Return the leeks to the pan, remove from the heat, and cover to keep warm.

Meanwhile, bring a large pot of lightly salted water to a boil over high heat. Add the tagliarini and cook according to the package directions until almost al dente. Drain well. Immediately melt the remaining 4 tablespoons butter in a large saucepan. Add the tagliarini and the leek mixture to the

butter in the saucepan. Blend in the cream and the cheese, and cook gently for 2 minutes more over very low heat. Season well with pepper. Serve with the rest of the cheese passed on the side.

BEEF AND SCALLOPS WITH CELLOPHANE NOODLES

MAKES 6 SERVINGS

This recipe is derived from one that I taught during a series of classes on "Taste" with Barbara Kafka. The beef and scallops make an interesting combination, and are delicate enough in flavor to work with cellophane noodles.

1 pound cellophane noodles (also called saifan,
   bean threads, or mung bean noodles)

Vegetable oil, for deep-frying

1 pound beef tenderloin, cut into 2 by ½-inch strips

¾ pound sea scallops

1 large garlic clove, minced

1½ cups diagonally sliced scallions, white and
   green parts

1 teaspoon kosher salt

Freshly ground black pepper

¼ teaspoon crushed hot red pepper flakes

Prepare the cellophane noodles a few hours before serving. Do not soak them—just break them apart. Working in batches, deep-fry the noodles in oil heated to 375°F for a few seconds until they puff up. Remove from the oil with a slotted spoon and drain on paper towels.

Heat 2 tablespoons of oil in a skillet. Add the beef, scallops, and garlic all at once and cook over high heat, stirring, for about 2 minutes. Add the scallions, salt, black pepper, and red pepper flakes. Cook for another 30 seconds, stirring furiously, and pour over a platter holding the fried cellophane noodles.

PEKING CURRY-TOMATO SAUCE ON NOODLES

〰 MAKES 6 TO 8 SERVINGS

This was a regular offering in Chinese restaurants when I was a boy in Oregon. I never see it on restaurant menus anymore, which is a shame: it has a strong tomato taste lightly flavored with curry. Use it on wheat Chinese noodles or Japanese udon. Cellophane noodles are too delicate to stand up to the sauce.

Editor: You can reduce the amount of butter by half, but it would be interesting to try the original as an example of retro cooking.

1 cup (2 sticks) unsalted butter

2 medium yellow onions, peeled and chopped

2 garlic cloves, finely chopped

1 tablespoon curry powder, or more to taste

Two 28-ounce cans whole plum tomatoes in purée

I pound ground beef round

Kosher salt

1 pound fresh or dried Chinese or Japanese noodles

Melt the butter in a large saucepan over medium heat. Add the onions and garlic and cook them,

stirring, until they are soft but not brown, about 3 minutes. Add the curry powder and cook for a minute to develop the flavor. Then add the canned tomatoes and break them up with a wooden spoon. Reduce the heat, cover loosely, and simmer the sauce until it is thick, around 1½ hours. Break up the chopped meat, drop it into the simmering sauce, and cook very gently, stirring often, for another half hour. Add salt to taste.

Bring a large pot of water to a boil over high heat. Add the noodles and cook according to the

Beard on . . . Chinese and Japanese Dried Noodles

In recent years, New York has become studded with hundreds of tiny produce stores run by Korean immigrants. In addition to selling broccoli and oranges, most of them stock a few Asian specialties, such as udon, buckwheat, rice, and mung bean noodles. I've found all brands to be quite reliable, although perhaps I don't bring to them the educated palate that I do to Western pastas. Just be sure to use them properly.

Rice noodles, made from ground rice, are more fragile than wheat noodles. They need a brief soaking before you cook them. Mung bean noodles are made from powdered mung beans. They too have to be soaked, after which they are gelatinous and springy. They don't actually need any cooking at all after their soaking, but can be briefly stir-fried, the way you do bean sprouts. Udon and soba buckwheat noodles act like American wheat noodles.

package directions until tender. Drain well. Transfer to a serving bowl, add the sauce, and serve.

HERBED NOODLE SALAD

✐ MAKES 4 TO 6 SERVINGS

When I made this salad on a Saturday afternoon, it tasted sharp and oily. It went into the refrigerator until the next day, when I served it at lunch. By then, the noodles had soaked up every bit of oil and vinegar, and the taste was wonderfully improved. Be sure to allow at least 12 hours to let this happen. You'll find that this is an unusually light and pleasant salad to serve as a first course, one that doesn't ruin the appetite.

8 ounces Japanese buckwheat noodles (soba)

¼ cup olive oil

3 tablespoons Asian sesame oil

2 tablespoons hot chili oil

3 tablespoons rice vinegar

⅔ cup finely chopped fresh chives

½ cup chopped fresh flat-leaf parsley

Bring a large pot of water to a boil over high heat. Add the buckwheat noodles and cook according to the package directions until tender. Drain well. Put the noodles into a bowl with the olive oil, so that they won't stick together as they cool. When cooled, add the sesame oil, chili oil, and rice vinegar. Toss well with the chives and parsley, and let stand for at least 12 hours.

BEACH PÂTÉ

✐ MAKES 8 SERVINGS

This is a meat loaf that has tiny pasta shells scattered through it. The shells make a pattern like the bits of tongue or pistachio nuts that are found in *pâté de campagne*. They're fun, but if you can't find them, try orzo, tubetti, funghini—any small, granular-shaped pasta. I've made this for years and years. It's a perfect dish to take on a picnic and slice on the spot. Hence the name.

4 ounces very small pasta shells

2 medium yellow onions, coarsely chopped

1 cup (1-inch) cut carrots

½ cup chopped fresh flat-leaf parsley

4 large garlic cloves

2 teaspoons dried thyme

2 teaspoons kosher salt

1 teaspoon freshly ground black pepper

2 pounds ground beef round or chuck

1 pound ground pork

1 cup fresh bread crumbs

2 large eggs, lightly beaten

6 strips bacon

Bring a medium saucepan of lightly salted water to a boil over high heat. Add the pasta and cook according to the package directions until al dente. Drain, rinse under cold water, and drain again.

Put the onions, carrots, parsley, garlic, thyme, salt, and pepper in the food processor fitted with the metal blade and process for 30 seconds until they are well minced and mixed. Turn this mixture into a large bowl, and add the beef, pork, bread crumbs, eggs, and the drained pasta shells.

Mix well. I like to use my hands for this job, but if you are squeamish, use wooden spoons. Form the meat mixture into a firm oval loaf.

Make a bed in a shallow baking pan with 3 bacon strips. Place the meat loaf on the bed of bacon, and put the remaining strips across the top. Bake in a preheated 350°F oven for 1½ hours, and serve hot or cold. You will find that if you make your meat loaf free-form instead of in a loaf pan, you'll get a firmer texture for slicing and plenty of flavorful outer crust.

CANNELLONI WITH TOMATO SAUCE

*◌ MAKES 8 SERVINGS

This is an Italian version of stuffed crêpes.

Editor: The recipe for crêpes on page 146 makes 12 to 14 crêpes. Make a double batch of batter, and cook up all of the crêpes, reserve 16 for this recipe, and freeze the remaining crêpes for another use.

For the Tomato Sauce

2 tablespoons olive oil

2 small yellow onions, finely chopped

2 garlic cloves, minced

One 28-ounce can whole Italian plum tomatoes with their juice

1 teaspoon dried basil

Kosher salt and freshly ground black pepper

1 cup tomato paste

2 tablespoons olive oil

For the Cannelloni:

16 sweet Italian sausages, pricked with a fork

16 Crêpes (page 146)

1 pound ricotta cheese

1½ cups freshly grated Parmesan cheese

2 tablespoons unsalted butter, cut into small pieces

To make the sauce: Heat the oil in a medium saucepan over medium heat. Add the onions and garlic and sauté for 3 minutes. Add the tomatoes and basil, and season with salt and pepper. Bring to a boil, reduce the heat, and simmer for 30 minutes, breaking up the tomatoes with the side of a spoon. Add the tomato paste, correct the seasoning, and cook for another 15 minutes, then increase the heat and let the sauce reduce a bit. [*Editor: Add water if the sauce seems too thick.*] Stir frequently so that the sauce does not scorch.

To make the cannelloni: Place the sausages in a saucepan of lightly salted water. Bring to a boil and reduce to simmer. Poach for 12 minutes. Remove from the water and, when cool enough to handle, remove from their casings and cut in long shreds.

Spread each crêpe with about 2 tablespoons of ricotta cheese, sprinkle with 1 tablespoon grated Parmesan, and give it a grind from the pepper-mill. Add the sausage bits, roll the crêpes, and place them in a shallow buttered baking dish so that they barely touch each other. Pour the tomato sauce over them, and sprinkle with additional grated Parmesan cheese. Bake in a preheated 375°F oven until bubbly, about 25 minutes.

NOTE: You may vary the filling by adding cooked chicken, veal, pork, or ham, highly seasoned.

MACARONI
AND CHEESE

This is a great American classic, one of our best dishes. It has to be gooey, made with a really rich béchamel and with a Cheddar that sings with flavor. I love it when the cheese on top gets burnt and chewy, and I love to scrape up the dried bits that stick to the pan.

    ½ pound elbow macaroni or cavatappi
    4 tablespoons (½ stick) unsalted butter
    ¼ cup all-purpose flour
    2 cups whole milk, heated
    Dash of freshly ground black pepper
    ½ teaspoon Tabasco
    ½ cup heavy cream or crème fraîche
    3 cups (12 ounces) shredded Cheddar cheese

Bring a large saucepan of lightly salted water to a boil over high heat. Add the macaroni and cook according to the package directions until just tender. Drain well, rinse under cold water, and drain again.

Meanwhile, melt the butter in another large saucepan over low heat. Whisk in the flour, and cook it for about 3 minutes, until the roux is frothy and the taste of raw flour is gone. Add the warm milk gradually to the roux, whisking all the while. Turn up the heat and cook, whisking, until the sauce is just at the boiling point. Turn down the heat and let it simmer for a few minutes. Now season with the pepper and Tabasco. Don't be afraid of the Tabasco: it will help to bring out the taste of the cheese. Stir in the cream and simmer a little longer, until the flavors are blended.

Mix about 2¼ cups of the Cheddar cheese into the simmering sauce. As soon as it melts, stir in the drained macaroni, and pour it into a baking dish. Sprinkle the top with the remaining ¾ cup of cheese. Bake in a preheated 350°F oven for 20 to 30 minutes.

LASAGNE

Often baked pasta dishes are a bore, but this one holds up, I think, because all the different sauces are first-rate and the final cooking is brief. It looks like a long recipe, but once you have prepared the different elements, you can put it together in a matter of minutes.

For the Meatballs
    ½ pound ground beef chuck
    ½ pound sweet Italian sausage, removed from
        its casings
    2 medium yellow onions, finely chopped
    ¼ cup chopped fresh flat-leaf parsley
    ¼ teaspoon crushed hot red pepper
        flakes
    1 large egg, beaten
    2 teaspoons Pesto (page 359)
    ½ teaspoon kosher salt
    ½ teaspoon freshly ground black pepper
    Pinch of freshly grated nutmeg

For the Sauce
    3 tablespoons unsalted butter
    ¼ cup all-purpose flour

2 cups Chicken Stock (page 349) or use canned
    chicken broth

1 teaspoon kosher salt

½ teaspoon freshly ground black pepper

⅛ teaspoon freshly grated nutmeg

1 cup heavy cream

For the Assembly

    4 ounces dried lasagne

    4 ounces dried whole-wheat lasagne

    2 tablespoons peanut or olive oil, plus more for the
        baking dish

    2 tablespoons unsalted butter

    Light Tomato Sauce (page 204)

    ¾ cup shredded Gruyère cheese

    ¾ cup freshly shredded Parmesan cheese

To make the meatballs: Put everything into a large bowl. Using your hands, blend the ingredients thoroughly and make small balls, around the size of large cherries. Refrigerate until needed.

To make the sauce: Melt the butter in a heavy-bottomed saucepan over medium heat. Whisk in the flour, and cook for 2 to 3 minutes, until the mixture is smooth and golden. Remove from the heat while you add the stock, whisking vigorously. Return the pan to the heat and whisk until the sauce is smooth and thick. Simmer for 3 to 4 minutes. Season with the salt, pepper, and nutmeg. Add the heavy cream, and keep the mixture just below the simmer for a few minutes to blend the flavors.

To assemble the lasagne: Bring a large pot of lightly salted water to a boil over high heat. Cook the lasagne strips, 3 or 4 at a time, according to the package directions, until they are just

done. Remove them with a slotted spoon, dip in cold water to stop the cooking, and lay on a clean kitchen towel. Continue until all the pasta is cooked.

Melt the 2 tablespoons of oil and of butter in a large heavy skillet. When the fats have blended and are hot, but not smoking, add the meatballs. Cook over medium-high heat, shaking the pan constantly to keep the meatballs in motion, until lightly browned all over. Be sure to keep them hopping in the pan so they do not flatten.

Spoon a thin layer of tomato sauce onto the bottom of an oiled 13 by 9-inch baking pan. Make a layer of plain lasagne over the sauce. Spread on more tomato sauce, and sprinkle with some meatballs. Spoon on half of the béchamel. Continue with a layer of whole-wheat pasta, tomato sauce, and meatballs and so forth until they are all used up, alternating the plain and whole-wheat lasagne and ending with the béchamel. Sprinkle with the grated cheeses and bake in a preheated 450°F oven for 15 minutes.

PASTA AND CHEESE ROLL IN TOMATO SAUCE

MAKES 5 SERVINGS

This is an amusing variation on a jelly roll. I love the tiny acini di pepe, which look like peppercorns, but you could use any other really small pasta. Try pastina, or orzo, or star-shaped stellini. They have to be light enough so that they don't drag down the soufflé mixture.

¾ cup acini di pepe

Softened butter, for the pan

6 large eggs, separated

6 tablespoons freshly grated Parmesan cheese

4 tablespoons (½ stick) unsalted butter, melted

1 teaspoon dried oregano

¼ teaspoon dried thyme

Kosher salt and freshly ground black pepper

1½ cups shredded mozzarella cheese

1½ cups Light Tomato Sauce (page204)

Bring a medium pot of lightly salted water to a boil over high heat. Add the pasta and cook according to the package directions until al dente. Drain in a wire sieve, rinse under cold water, and drain well.

Butter a 15 by 11-inch jelly-roll pan. Line the pan with parchment paper or aluminum foil, leaving an overhang of about 2 inches at each end. Butter the paper well to prevent the eggs from sticking.

Beat the egg yolks well with an electric mixer on high speed until they are light and lemon-colored, about 3 minutes. Gradually stir in the pasta, 2 tablespoons of the Parmesan cheese, the melted butter, oregano, thyme, salt, and pepper. In another bowl, using clean beaters, beat the egg whites until they hold soft, unwavering peaks. Fold the whites into the yolk mixture quite thoroughly. Spread the mixture in the prepared pan, smoothing it with a knife or a rubber spatula so that it is the same thickness overall. Sprinkle it evenly with the mozzarella cheese.

Bake in a preheated 375°F oven for 15 minutes, until it is firm and puffy. Take it out of the oven and turn the oven temperature down to 325°F.

With most soufflé-roll mixtures, you would now quickly invert the pan onto a towel and peel off the paper. But you want to keep the mozzarella on the inside of the roll; so, instead, you grasp the extended ends of the parchment paper, lift it out of the pan, and lay it on a large cooling rack. Let it cool for 10 minutes, and then use the paper to help roll it up, starting with one long side. As you roll, peel off the paper. You may have to use a small, sharp knife to help you along.

Slice the roll into 10 rounds. Arrange them in an overlapping row in a buttered baking dish. Cover them with the tomato sauce, sprinkle with the remaining ¼ cup Parmesan cheese, and bake for 20 minutes, until the cheese is melted.

PASTITSIO FOR A PARTY

✎ MAKES 12 SERVINGS

This is one of the best Greek dishes I know, a good oven dish that's very rich and full-flavored. It comes from Leon Lianides, the owner of the original Coach House [see Editor's Note, page 39].

For the Meat Sauce

3 tablespoons unsalted butter

1 cup finely chopped yellow onion

2 garlic cloves, minced

2 pounds lean ground lamb

1½ pounds ground beef sirloin

3 cups tomato sauce

1 cup dry red wine

½ cup finely chopped fresh flat-leaf parsley

1 teaspoon dried oregano

½ teaspoon ground cinnamon

½ teaspoon dried basil

1 bay leaf

Kosher salt and freshly ground black pepper

For the Cream Sauce

7 cups light cream

2 cups whole milk

1 cup (2 sticks) unsalted butter

1½ cups all-purpose flour

Kosher salt and freshly grated black pepper

Generous pinch of freshly grated nutmeg

10 large egg yolks

2 cups ricotta cheese, preferably fresh,
    available at cheese stores and some Italian
    delicatessens

Softened butter, for the baking dish

1½ pounds elbow macaroni or ziti

1½ cups freshly grated Pecorino Romano cheese

To make the meat sauce: In a large skillet, heat the butter over medium heat. Add the onion and cook until translucent, about 3 minutes. Add the garlic and cook for 2 minutes. Add the ground lamb and ground sirloin over high heat, add break the meat up with a wooden spoon until it is no longer red. Stir in the tomato sauce, wine, parsley, oregano, cinnamon, basil, bay leaf, ½ teaspoon salt, and ½ teaspoon pepper. Cook the sauce, stirring frequently, until most of the liquid has been absorbed. Remove the bay leaf. The meat sauce can be prepared in advance and kept in the refrigerator or freezer until you are ready to use it. I never think that far ahead about what I plan to eat, but it's a useful idea if you are making the pastitsio for a party.

To make the cream sauce: Bring 6 cups of the cream just to a boil with the milk. In another large saucepan, melt the butter. Whisk in the flour. When the roux is blended and smooth, pour in the hot cream mixture, whisking furiously with the whisk to keep it from lumping. Cook until the sauce is simmering, thick, and smooth, about 5 minutes. Season with salt, pepper, and nutmeg. Turn off the heat and let the sauce cool for 10 minutes.

In a bowl, beat the egg yolks with the unheated cup of cream. Gradually add about 2 cups of the warm cream sauce to this egg mixture, whisking all the while to make sure that the eggs don't curdle. Then pour the egg mixture into the cream sauce, continuing to stir until everything is blended. Finally, beat in the ricotta.

Bring a large pot of lightly salted water to a boil over high heat. Add the macaroni and cook according to the package directions until barely tender. Drain well.

Butter the inside of a large, deep baking dish. This recipe will need a dish at least 15 by 9 by 4 inches. Place half the macaroni in the dish and sprinkle with half of the Romano cheese. Spoon on half the cream sauce, smoothing it with the back of a large spoon. Spread on all of the meat sauce. Now add the rest of the macaroni, the rest of the cream sauce, and the rest of the Romano cheese, and place in a preheated 400°F oven. Bake for 55 minutes, when the pastitsio should be covered with a golden-brown crust.

If you want to serve it in neatly cut squares, finish cooking the pastitsio at least 6 hours before you intend to serve it. Let cool for an hour or so, then refrigerate. Cut the casserole into serving portions and reheat in the oven before serving.

STUFFED SHELLS

❧ MAKES 6 TO 8 SERVINGS

This is one of those clean-out-the-refrigerator recipes. It is absolutely delicious when made with cooked chicken. But it can be made as well with leftover beef, ham, or veal, and is a wonderful solution for the very last scraps of the Thanksgiving turkey.

Thirty 2-inch pasta shells, for stuffing

Meat from 2 chicken legs and thighs, or 1½ to 2 cups
    any leftover cooked meat

½ pound mushrooms, roughly sliced

3 large garlic cloves

6 sprigs fresh flat-leaf parsley

2 teaspoons dried tarragon

1 large egg, beaten

1 tablespoon freshly squeezed lemon juice

1 teaspoon kosher salt

1 teaspoon freshly ground black pepper

½ teaspoon Tabasco

Softened butter for the baking dish

2 cups shredded Gruyère cheese

Light Tomato Sauce (page 204)

Bring a large saucepan of lightly salted water to a boil over high heat. Add the pasta and cook according to the package directions until just tender. Drain, rinse under cold running water, and drain well.

Combine the chicken, mushrooms, garlic, parsley, tarragon, egg, lemon juice, salt, pepper, and Tabasco in the bowl of a food processor fitted with the metal blade. Process until the mixture is well blended.

Spoon some of the meat mixture into each of the cooked shells. Lay them in a buttered baking dish, open sides up. Sprinkle with most of the Gruyère, cover with tomato sauce, and then with the rest of the cheese. Bake in a preheated 350°F oven for 30 minutes, until bubbling hot.

VARIATION

SAUSAGE-STUFFED SHELLS: Substitute 2 cups hot Italian sausages, casings removed, for the leftover meat. The sausage is seasoned, so omit the garlic, tarragon, salt, pepper, and Tabasco. Cover the shells with cheese and tomato sauce as suggested, although you may prefer to use an Italian cheese, such as mozzarella or Fontina.

CORNMEAL GNOCCHI

❧ MAKES 6 SERVINGS

These gnocchi are, I admit, somewhat fattening, but I adore their soul-satisfying flavor and texture. Here I use the Italian method of making the basic polenta, but instead of water I prefer milk, which gives a more delicate result. Serve these gnocchi as a first course or as an accompaniment to meat.

5 cups whole milk or water (or a combination of water
    and evaporated milk)

1¼ cups coarse cornmeal (polenta)

1 teaspoon kosher salt

Olive oil, for the pan and baking dish

8 tablespoons (1 stick) unsalted butter, melted

¼ cup freshly grated Parmesan or Romano cheese

Bring the milk to a boil in a large, heavy-bottomed saucepan, taking care not to let it scorch or boil over. While it is boiling, gradually cascade the cornmeal into the liquid in a thin stream, stirring constantly until the polenta thickens, heaves, and bubbles. Stir well to make sure there are no lurking lumps. Remove from the heat, stir in the salt, then pour into a lightly oiled jelly-roll pan, and let stand until cold and firm.

Cut into rounds with a 1½- to 2-inch cutter, and arrange the gnocchi in a lightly oiled baking dish, with the edges overlapping slightly. Pour the melted butter over the gnocchi, sprinkle with Parmesan cheese, and bake in a preheated 350°F oven for 10 to 15 minutes, or until they are hot, soaked with butter, and slightly browned on top.

VEGETABLES

VEGETABLES

Artichokes

Earlier in the (twentieth) century, Italian and Chinese truck farmers raised great quantities of artichokes in Oregon because they grow extraordinarily well in that part of the country. Our itinerant vegetable man, who came by three or four times a week with horse and wagon, grew some himself and would bring us choice globe artichokes throughout the season. Most of them had been picked the same morning. We took them as a matter of course and ate them in great numbers. In later years, I remember driving from San Francisco down through the countryside around Salinas and Big Sur and seeing acres and acres of this glamorous vegetable, ready for budding and soon to be picked. The plants are stunning, with handsome foliage, and when beyond the edible stages, with extraordinary blue flowers.

Globe artichokes vary in size from extremely small, 1 to 1½ inches in diameter, to those which in maturity will be 4 inches across at the widest part. They are most often cooked before eating, although I often use the very tiny artichokes as crudités, simply trimmed and eaten raw. In that case, it is merely the bottom, or the *fond*, which is eaten after the cone of pale leaves and fuzzy tiny fibers in the center, known as the choke, are removed. The larger artichokes are sometimes trimmed by cutting off about 1 inch of the tops and removing the stem and small hard leaves around the base before cooking.

Serve hot artichokes with hot melted butter (seasoned, if you wish, with lemon juice or a chopped herb such as tarragon, rosemary, or dill); Hollandaise or Béarnaise Sauce (pages 353 and 355); or a well-flavored vinegar, such as sherry wine vinegar, if you are dieting.

Serve cold artichokes as an appetizer, or a main dish for a luncheon, followed by a salad, such as crab, lobster, shrimp or scallop, chicken or duck salad, or a finely cut vegetable salad dressed with mayonnaise. Cold artichokes may also be served as a first course or a very light luncheon main course with mayonnaise, vinaigrette dressing, yogurt dressing, or just with the oil and vinegar as a dipping sauce for the leaves. In this case, do not remove the centers, unless you wish to serve the sauce in the artichoke.

To serve artichoke bottoms, after cooling the artichokes, remove all the leaves and choke, leaving only the artichoke bottoms. Use these as a base for hot dishes or as the container in which to serve purées and small vegetables such as fresh peas, whole-kernel corn, or tiny sautéed mushroom caps; or chill and fill with a cold salad or seafood.

To boil artichokes: Stand artichokes upright in a stockpot and cook in plenty of boiling, salted water with a slice of lemon and a clove or two of garlic. Boil from 25 to 40 minutes, according to size, until a leaf from the base can be easily pulled off. Drain upside down on paper towels.

To steam artichokes: Steam in a steamer rack over boiling water for approximately the same length of time as for boiling.

To cook artichokes in a microwave oven: Artichokes cook very successfully in a microwave oven. Stand upright in a nonmetallic dish in a small amount of water and cover with a sheet of plastic wrap, or merely wrap them individually in the plastic wrap. Steam in the oven on full power. According to size, they will take from 9 to 16 minutes.

MINUTE ASPARAGUS

 MAKES 4 TO 6 SERVINGS

Editor: This is a very rapid way to cook asparagus. The recipe is from Beard's Theory and Practice of Good Cooking, *so it is a "teaching recipe" that doesn't leave out a single detail. Essentially, you blanch thinly sliced asparagus and then sauté it in butter.*

2 pounds asparagus

Kosher salt

8 tablespoons (1 stick) unsalted butter

3 to 4 tablespoons soy sauce

1 tablespoon freshly squeezed lemon juice

Freshly ground black pepper

Wash and trim the asparagus and cut into diagonal slices no more than ¼ inch thick—thinner if possible. Place the slices in a colander or frying basket. Place enough water to cover the asparagus in a pot large enough to accommodate the colander of frying basket, add salt to taste, and bring the water to a full, rolling boil. Meanwhile, melt the butter in a large skillet and have the soy sauce, lemon juice, and pepper close at hand. Plunge the asparagus into the pot of boiling water, bring the water to a second boil, and cook the asparagus for just one full minute. Drain the asparagus very well and add it to the melted butter in the skillet along with the soy, lemon juice, and pepper to taste. Toss well over medium heat until the butter has browned and the asparagus is crisp and deliciously flavored.

FRESH ASPARAGUS VINAIGRETTE

 MAKES 6 SERVINGS

Editor: You can pour the vinaigrette over the asparagus, or serve it in small ramekins on the side for dipping the spears.

1½ pounds thick asparagus spears, woody bottoms snapped off

3 tablespoons red or white wine vinegar

1½ teaspoons Dijon mustard

½ cup olive oil

Kosher salt and freshly ground pepper

1 tablespoon chopped fresh flat-leaf parsley

Cook the asparagus in boiling salted water. I use a large skillet, in which the asparagus fit very nicely, and cook it at a fast boil. The spears should be tender but still crisp. About 6 to 8 minutes does the job. Remove the asparagus, drain, rinse under cold water, and cool.

Serve with a mustard-flavored vinaigrette, made as follows: Whisk the vinegar and mustard in a bowl before whisking in the oil. Then season with salt to taste, give it a few grinds of pepper, and add the chopped parsley.

BROCCOLI BEURRE NOIR

Editor: While beurre noir *means black butter in French, it is a misnomer here, as the butter in this recipe should only be colored to a brown the color of hazelnut shells, or* beurre noisette. *This deepens the butter flavor to make it an even better accent to plain vegetables than plain butter.*

8 large broccoli florets

6 tablespoons (¾ stick) unsalted butter

1 teaspoon freshly squeezed lemon juice

Kosher salt and freshly ground black pepper

Cook the broccoli in a large saucepan of lightly salted water over high heat until tender but still crisp, about 4 minutes. Drain, transfer to a serving dish, and cover with aluminum foil to keep hot. Melt the butter in a skillet over medium heat, shaking often until the butter turns nut brown. Add the lemon juice. Pour over the broccoli and season with salt and pepper. Serve hot.

BUTTERED BRUSSELS SPROUTS

❧ MAKES 4 SERVINGS

Brussels sprouts, members of the cabbage family, are underrated because they are usually very badly cooked to a mushy tastelessness with little or no character. Sautéing keeps them crisp and interesting. These are good with broiled or roast meats.

2 pints Brussels sprouts

6 tablespoons (¾ stick) unsalted butter

½ teaspoon freshly ground black pepper

1 teaspoon freshly squeezed lemon juice

Kosher salt

Trim the sprouts, being careful not to cut away too much of the stem end. Remove discolored outer leaves. Put them in a 2-quart saucepan with enough salted water to come one-third of the way up the pan, bring to a boil and blanch, covered, for 5 minutes, or until barely cooked through. Drain well.

Melt the butter in another pan, add the sprouts, and cook, covered, shaking the pan well, for 3 to 4 minutes. Season with the pepper and lemon juice, and a sprinkle of salt.

VARIATIONS

BRUSSELS SPROUTS AMANDINE: Sauté ½ cup thinly sliced almonds in 2 tablespoons unsalted butter until golden and add to the sprouts.

BRUSSELS SPROUTS WITH CHESTNUTS AND BACON: Combine the sprouts with an equal quantity of whole, cooked, peeled chestnuts, heated in butter and seasoned to taste, and a few pieces of crumbled crisp bacon.

RED CABBAGE WITH CHESTNUTS

∾ MAKES 6 TO 8 SERVINGS

Red cabbage goes well with game and red meats. The following recipe, which comes from the central part of France, works as a complete vegetable course—the chestnuts supplying the starch.

4 pounds red cabbage

5 tablespoons (½ stick plus 1 tablespoon) unsalted butter

2 pounds roasted and peeled chestnuts (see Note)

1½ teaspoons kosher salt

1 teaspoon freshly ground black pepper

3 cups Chicken Stock (page 349), as needed

Wash the cabbage, quarter it, and cut out the core, then cut it into very thin shreds with a large chef's knife.

Melt the butter in a heavy skillet over medium heat. Add the cabbage, chestnuts, salt, and pepper, and just enough stock to cover. Bring the liquid to a boil, then reduce the heat to low, cover, and simmer until the cabbage is tender, 40 to 45 minutes.

Editor: To roast chestnuts, using a paring knife, cut an X in the flat side of each chestnut, cutting through the tough outer skin just into the flesh. Spread on a baking sheet and bake in a preheated 400°F oven until the skins are curling and the flesh looks roasted, about 30 minutes. While the chestnuts are still warm, use a paring knife to remove the thick outer skin and the thin brown inner skin.

CHAMPAGNE KRAUT

∾ MAKES 8 SERVINGS

Editor: This isn't green sauerkraut, but fresh cabbage cooked in sparkling wine. It doesn't have to be French champagne; any good sparkling wine from Spain, California, or Australia will do. Bacon drippings are essential for flavor. If you don't keep a can of bacon drippings in the refrigerator, as was the custom of home cooks for decades (if not centuries), just cook a few slices in a skillet over medium heat for about 10 minutes, until crisp, reserve the drippings, and save the bacon for another use.

¼ cup bacon drippings

1 large head green cabbage, cored and shredded

Kosher salt and freshly ground black pepper

One 750-ml bottle champagne or sparkling wine

Heat the bacon drippings in a large saucepan over medium heat. Add the cabbage, cover, and cook, tossing occasionally, until wilted, about 10 minutes. Add salt and pepper to taste, then the champagne. Cover and cook for 10 minutes. Uncover, toss well, and continue cooking until the cabbage is done to your taste. I prefer mine quite crisp.

CARROTS VICHY

MAKES 4 SERVINGS

I'm sure the reason most of us shun carrots is that they are prepared so indifferently in restaurants—boiled to death and combined with canned peas or dressed with a mere sliver of butter. As a result they have no trace of flavor. This classic way of cooking them is certainly a change for the better.

  2 pounds fairly small carrots

  ¼ cup water

  4 tablespoons (½ stick) butter

  1 teaspoon kosher salt

  ½ teaspoon sugar

  ¼ teaspoon dried marjoram

  1 tablespoon chopped fresh flat-leaf parsley

  ¼ cup heavy cream (optional)

Scrape the carrots and cut them into very thin rounds. Put them in a saucepan with the water, butter, and salt. Cook, covered, over medium heat, shaking the pan from time to time and making sure the carrots do not brown or cook too fast, until they are just tender when pierced with the point of a small sharp knife, about 6 minutes. Add the sugar and marjoram and toss well, then sprinkle the carrots with parsley and serve. If you like, add the cream to the carrots just before sprinkling them with the chopped parsley.

PURÉE OF CELERY ROOT

MAKES 6 SERVINGS

Simmer **2 to 2½ pounds celery root** in salted water to cover until it is just tender. Peel it, cut off the little root ends, and cut the bulbs in quarters. Put the bulbs through a food mill or food processor. Whip the purée with **6 tablespoons (¾ stick) unsalted butter**, **1 teaspoon freshly ground pepper**, and **additional salt**, if needed. Spoon it into a heated serving dish, sink **a large piece of butter** in the center, and serve at once.

Or you may combine the **celery root purée** with an **equal quantity of puréed potatoes** and whip them together with **8 tablespoons (1 stick) unsalted butter** and **3 to 4 tablespoons heavy cream**. Spoon the purée into a heated serving dish and top it with **a square of butter** and some **chopped fresh flat-leaf parsley**.

CHARD, SPINACH, AND ZUCCHINI TIAN

MAKES 8 MAIN-COURSE OR 12 BUFFET SERVINGS

Editor: Buffets were Beard's favorite way to entertain, probably necessitated by the cramped quarters in his early New York apartments. He would usually serve a dish like this as part of a menu with meat or seafood salads, but it makes a good vegetarian main course, too.

Olive oil

2 pounds leaf spinach, stems trimmed, leaves well washed and coarsely chopped

2 pounds Swiss chard, well washed and coarsely chopped

6 or 8 small zucchini, finely diced

2 medium yellow onions, coarsely chopped

3 garlic cloves, finely chopped

½ cup finely chopped fresh basil leaves or 2 tablespoons dried basil

Kosher salt

1½ teaspoons freshly ground black pepper

8 large eggs, lightly beaten

1½ cups freshly grated Parmesan cheese

½ cup fresh bread crumbs

Cover the bottom of a large skillet with olive oil and add the spinach and Swiss chard. Cook, stirring often, until just wilted, about 5 minutes. Drain in a colander, let cool, and press out all the liquid. Add the zucchini, onion, and garlic to the skillet with some oil and cook until the zucchini is tender.

Combine the vegetables and the basil in a bowl. Season with the salt and mix in the pepper. Spread in a lightly oiled, heavy earthenware casserole. Pour the eggs over the vegetables and top with the Parmesan cheese and bread crumbs. Bake in a preheated 350°F oven until the eggs are just set and the cheese is melted and bubbly, about 30 minutes. Let cool, and serve warm or at room temperature.

CORN ON THE COB

Corn is certainly one of our most popular vegetables. It's been much spurned by most Europeans, probably because it has never been a standard item of their diet. However, I well remember a delightful bistro in Paris where during corn season it was not unusual to find delicious corn from Alsace presented in a most intelligent way. The corn on the cob was cooked in half milk and half water and served as an hors d'oeuvre, which to me makes great sense. At the beginning of a meal it is delicious, refreshing, and most satisfying, and you are not chewing on an ear while other things on your plate get cold. Naturally, the best way to prepare corn is to rush it from your garden to a pot of boiling water and eat it at once. Few of us can do that anymore.

Everyone has his own opinion as how corn should be cooked. This is my preferred method. Shuck the ears and put them flat in a skillet with cold water. Bring to a boil over rather high heat and remove the corn when the water reaches a full, rolling boil. Serve the corn at once with plenty of melted butter, salt, and a peppermill.

VARIATIONS

CORN WITH BUTTER AND BACON CRUMBS: Roll the cooked corn in melted butter and then in crisp bacon crumbs.

CORN WITH GREEN PEPPER BUTTER: Combine butter with finely chopped peeled green bell pepper.

CORN OFF THE COB

6 to 8 ears corn

8 tablespoons (1 stick) unsalted butter

½ to ¾ cup heavy cream

Kosher salt and freshly ground black pepper

With a sharp knife, remove the kernels from the corn. Melt the butter in a heavy saucepan or skillet over medium heat. Add the corn and shake the pan for about 1 minute, just to heat it through. Add the cream, season with salt and pepper, and heat. Then serve at once.

VARIATIONS

CORN WITH ONION AND GREEN PEPPER:
Sauté 4 tablespoons chopped yellow onion and ½ cup seeded and finely chopped green or red bell pepper in 8 tablespoons (1 stick) unsalted butter. Add the corn kernels and sauté in this mixture until just heated through.

CORN WITH FRESH BASIL: Mix 1 to 2 tablespoons chopped fresh basil leaves into the corn just before serving. This felicitous combination of flavors is Chilean.

CORN OYSTERS

MAKES 6 SERVINGS

Editor: Thanks to their blob-like shape, corn fritters are also known as corn oysters. Some people like them with maple syrup drizzled on top.

12 ears corn

3 tablespoons heavy cream

2 tablespoons all-purpose flour, sifted

1 large egg, well beaten

1 tablespoon unsalted butter, melted

Shuck and clean the corn very well. With a sharp knife make a cut lengthwise in the center of each row of kernels. Scrape with the back of the knife to push all of the pulp out into a bowl. Whisk with the cream and flour, then the egg and melted butter. Drop the batter by spoonfuls on a well-buttered griddle or skillet. Cook until delicately browned on both sides.

BRAISED FENNEL

Certain root vegetables braise very successfully. One is fennel, which takes on a completely different character, losing the strong anise taste of its raw state.

2 fennel bulbs

5 tablespoons (½ stick plus 1 tablespoon) unsalted
   butter

1 cup Chicken Stock (page 349) or Beef Stock
   (page 349)

Kosher salt and freshly ground black pepper

1 tablespoon chopped fresh chives

Fennel has feathery green tops on long white stalks that look rather like dill. These should be trimmed off at the point where the bulbous part of the fennel begins. Also remove any discolored or very tough and stringy outer leaves. Cut the bulbs into quarters.

Melt the butter in a skillet; add the fennel quarters and brown them lightly over medium heat on all sides, about 10 minutes. Add the stock, bring to a boil, then reduce to a simmer. Cover the skillet, and let the fennel cook gently (it should not boil) until just tender when pierced with the point of a knife, 30 to 40 minutes, according to size. Season with salt and pepper to taste, transfer the

Green Beans

The most common variety of green bean is the snap bean, formerly known as a string bean because it invariably needed stringing. This is no longer true, unless the beans are definitely over-age. Buy the smallest, freshest, and crispest you can find—they should snap when you break them. You will occasionally find in specialty vegetable markets the very tiny beans called by the French name, *haricots verts;* these are expensive but well worth buying. Then there is the flat, broad Italian bean and the scarlet runners beloved of the English, which are almost never sold in markets but grown by some gardeners here for their lush vines and brilliant scarlet flowers. They must be picked and cooked when very young as they grow rapidly to tough-skinned inedibility.

There is a lot of controversy about cooking beans. It's very much a matter of taste preference. While they used to be cooked until they were thoroughly limp and soft (some people still like them that way), nowadays there is an equally unfortunate tendency to go to the other extreme and barely blanch them, so they still taste quite raw. Personally, I like green beans cooked until the raw taste disappears but they still retain a fresh taste and a crispness to the bite. The trick is to keep the cooking water boiling rapidly while adding the beans. My friend Julia Child owns an esoteric piece of equipment called a buffalo iron, which is heated until fire hot and plunged into the water to keep it boiling furiously and cook the beans faster. While it might be fun to have, I've always managed to get along without one.

fennel to a hot serving dish, turn up the heat, and let the liquid reduce by about half, about 5 minutes, until it is rather thick. Pour over the fennel and sprinkle with the chopped chives.

COLD GREEN BEANS WITH WALNUT OIL

ॐ **MAKES 6 TO 8 SERVINGS**

Editor: Beard spent many summers in Provence, and often shared the best of simply prepared French country country cooking, with his readers. Use a French walnut oil with lots of character. This oil is only used as a flavoring, and not for sautéing, and should be stored in the refrigerator.

Quick-boiled Green Beans (this page), cooled
4 to 6 tablespoons walnut oil
3 tablespoons freshly squeezed lemon juice
Kosher salt and freshly ground black pepper
¼ cup finely chopped walnuts

Toss the green beans with walnut oil and lemon juice. Season with the salt and pepper. Garnish with the finely chopped walnuts.

VARIATIONS

GREEN BEANS WITH MUSTARD-FLAVORED MAYONNAISE: Season a good rich Mayonnaise (page 355) with 2 to 3 tablespoons Dijon mustard. Mix with the beans. Garnish with crumbled bacon.

GREEN BEANS WITH DILLED VINAIGRETTE: Toss the beans with ½ cup well-dilled Basic Vinaigrette Sauce (page 359). [*Editor: About 2 tablespoons chopped fresh dill should do it.*]

GREEN BEANS WITH SHALLOTS AND GREEK OLIVES: Toss the beans with ¼ cup olive oil, 3 to 4 tablespoons finely chopped shallots, and ¼ cup chopped, pitted Greek olives, such as Kalamata.

QUICK-BOILED GREEN BEANS

ॐ **MAKES 6 TO 8 SERVINGS**

2 pounds green beans
8 tablespoons (1 stick) unsalted butter, cut into tablespoons
Kosher salt and freshly ground black pepper

Wash the beans and trim off the ends. Bring a plentiful amount of salted water to a rapid, rolling boil in a large saucepan. Drop in the beans, a few at a time, so the water never ceases to boil. If it does, replace the cover until it returns to a boil, then take it off and boil the beans uncovered or they will lose their fresh bright color. Boil for 10 to 15 minutes, depending on age and size, tasting from time to time to see if they are done to your liking. Drain immediately. Some people advise plunging the beans into cold water to stop them from cooking further, but if you have drained them while they are still bitey-crisp, this should not be necessary. Return the beans to the pan and toss with the butter for

1 to 2 minutes, seasoning with salt and pepper to taste. Serve at once.

VARIATIONS

GREEN BEANS WITH TOASTED ALMONDS: Toss with the butter and ½ cup toasted sliced almonds.

GREEN BEANS WITH GARLIC AND PINE NUTS: Toss the beans with ¼ cup olive oil, 3 to 4 finely chopped garlic cloves, and ½ cup toasted pine nuts.

GREEN BEANS WITH SWEET ONION RINGS: Toss the beans with ¼ cup olive oil or unsalted butter and garnish with thinly sliced raw sweet onion rings.

GREEN BEANS WITH FRESH HERBS: Toss with ¼ cup unsalted butter, melted, or olive oil and 1½ tablespoons finely chopped herb of your choice, such as tarragon, dill, marjoram, or with chopped garlic and basil.

IMAM BAYILDI

 **MAKES 6 SERVINGS**

This Turkish stuffed eggplant is said to have been given its name, which translates as "the imam fainted," when the imam, or priest, tasted the dish and swooned with pleasure. Whether you believe that or not, there's no denying that this is an utterly delicious way of preparing eggplant. It may be served hot or cold, alone or as a luncheon dish or first course, or with roasted or broiled meat.

3 large eggplants, trimmed

Softened butter, for the baking dish

Kosher salt and freshly ground black pepper

10 tablespoons (yellow) olive oil

3 large onions, finely chopped

1 garlic clove, crushed and peeled

2 ripe tomatoes, peeled, seeded, and chopped

1 tablespoon chopped fresh flat-leaf parsley

1 teaspoon sugar

½ teaspoon ground cinnamon

1 tablespoon finely chopped pine nuts (optional)

Put the eggplants in a large pot and add boiling water to cover. Put a lid on the pot, cook over medium heat for about 10 minutes, until they soften but hold their shape. Drain the eggplants well, plunge them into cold water, and leave for 5 minutes. Cut them in half lengthwise and scoop out most of the flesh, leaving a ½-inch-thick shell. Set aside the scooped-out flesh. Arrange the shells in a buttered baking dish and sprinkle with a little salt and pepper. Pour 4 teaspoons of oil into each shell and cook the shells, uncovered, in the center of a preheated 350°F oven for about 30 minutes, until they are tender. Remove from the oven and cover with aluminum foil to keep warm before stuffing.

While the shells are cooking, heat the remaining 2 tablespoons oil in a skillet, add the onions and garlic, and sauté gently for 5 minutes, then add the tomatoes, parsley, sugar, and cinnamon. Season with salt and pepper. Continue simmering this mixture until the liquid has reduced by half, about 20 minutes. Chop the eggplant flesh and add it to the skillet with the chopped pine nuts, if using, and cook for 10 minutes more. Remove the shells from the oven and stuff them with the tomato mixture.

LEEKS À LA GRECQUE

 MAKES 12 APPETIZER SERVINGS

Editor: Leeks poached and marinated in a flavorful liquid, these can be served as a first course, a buffet salad, or a side dish at a cold meal.

12 leeks, white and pale green parts only

For the Poaching Liquid

½ cup dry white wine, or more if desired for
    poaching (optional)

⅓ cup olive oil

2 tablespoons white wine vinegar

1 garlic clove, finely chopped

1 teaspoon kosher salt

½ teaspoon freshly ground black pepper

1 sprig fresh flat-leaf parsley

Good pinch of dried thyme

Dash of Tabasco

1 tablespoon finely chopped fresh flat-leaf parsley,
    for garnish

Rinse the leeks well under cold running water. Put in a large bowl, add cold water to cover, and place under a faucet of running cold water to loosen any remaining grit. Drain and rinse again.

Place the leeks in a single layer in a large skillet. Add the ½ cup wine, oil, vinegar, garlic, salt,

pepper, parsley sprig, and thyme. Add enough water (or use half water and half white wine, if desired) to cover the leeks. Bring to a boil over high heat. Reduce the heat to medium-low and simmer just until the leeks are tender, about 20 minutes, depending on the size of the leeks. Using a slotted spoon, transfer the leeks to a serving dish. Boil the cooking liquid over high heat until reduced to about ½ cup, about 20 minutes. Season with the Tabasco. Pour over the leeks and refrigerate until chilled. Sprinkle with the chopped parsley and serve.

BRAISED LETTUCE

 MAKES 6 SERVINGS

This leafy vegetable is extraordinarily good braised and served with lamb, beef, game, and roast or braised chicken. I have found that the old recipes for braised lettuce give too long a cooking time, so I have formulated my own somewhat revolutionary way of preparing it, which, to my palate, produces a pleasanter result.

6 heads of Boston or Bibb lettuce

2 leeks or 2 medium yellow onions

2 carrots

8 ounces sliced bacon

3 cups Chicken Stock (page 349), Beef Stock (page
    349), or Veal Stock (page 350), as needed

4 tablespoons (½ stick) unsalted butter

Kosher salt and freshly ground black pepper

Remove the outer leaves from the lettuce, then wash the heads under cold running water, pulling the leaves apart to loosen them and wash away all sand between them (this is especially important with Bibb lettuce, which is usually very sandy). Wrap the heads in paper towels to dry. Trim the root end and all but 1 inch of the green top from the leeks and wash them well under cold running water, separating the leaves to rinse out lurking sand. Dry and cut into fine julienne (matchstick-size) strips. If leeks are not available, use onions, peeled and thinly sliced. Peel the carrots and also cut into julienne strips. Arrange the carrots and leeks or onions in a layer in a heavy skillet and top with 2 slices of bacon, cut into small pieces. Arrange the lettuce heads on top and cover with the remaining bacon slices. Add enough stock to barely cover the lettuce. Bring the liquid to a boil over high heat, then reduce the heat to low, cover the pan, and simmer, covered, for 20 to 30 minutes, or until just tender and pierceable (Bibb lettuce, which is more compact, with heavier leaves, sometimes takes longer to cook than Boston). Carefully remove the lettuce heads with wooden spoons or tongs and drain on paper towels. Strain the stock. It may be saved and used for soups or stews.

Melt the butter in a large skillet, add the drained lettuce, and reheat in the butter for a minute or two. Season with salt and pepper. Transfer the braised lettuce to a heated serving dish and spoon some of the butter over it.

PHILIP BROWN'S ROMAINE SOUFFLÉ

MAKES 6 SERVINGS

This new and different way to cook crunchy romaine was originated by my friend Philip Brown at one of his California cooking classes. The soufflé has an unusual flavor and the little bits of chopped romaine give a pleasant crunchiness. Serve it with roast lamb or beef or a chicken casserole and you will need no green vegetable, starch, or salad to complete the meal, it stands in for all three. Another nice thing about this dish is that you can make the base and fold in the egg whites an hour before you need to bake it, then leave it in the refrigerator until it is time to pop it into the oven.

1 large head of romaine

4 tablespoons (½ stick) butter

3 scallions, white and green parts, chopped

3 tablespoons all-purpose flour

1 cup whole milk, heated

4 large eggs, separated, at room temperature

1 cup shredded sharp Cheddar cheese

1 teaspoon kosher salt

½ teaspoon Worcestershire sauce

Tabasco

Softened butter, for the soufflé dish

¼ cup freshly grated Parmesan cheese

Cut off the coarse bottom of the romaine stalk. Wash the lettuce thoroughly and chop coarsely. Put in a heavy saucepan with a little water and cook over high heat until wilted, about 5 minutes. Drain well and chop finely.

Melt 1 tablespoon of the butter in a skillet

over medium heat and cook the scallions until soft but not brown, about 3 minutes. Add the romaine and cook, stirring, until the excess moisture evaporates. Melt the remaining 3 tablespoons butter in a large saucepan over low heat, whisk in the flour, and cook without browning for 2 minutes, whisking often. Whisk in the milk and cook until simmering and thickened. Remove from the heat. Beat the yolks into the sauce, one at a time, then whisk in the Cheddar cheese. Return to low heat and cook just until thickened a bit more without simmering. Stir in the romaine mixture until well blended. Season with salt, Worcestershire, and Tabasco.

Lavishly butter a 1½-quart soufflé dish, and sprinkle with Parmesan cheese, coating the bottom and sides. Shake out the excess cheese and reserve. Beat the egg whites until stiff but not dry; stir one-third into the romaine mixture, blending thoroughly. Fold in the remaining whites lightly. Pour into the soufflé dish; sprinkle with the reserved Parmesan cheese. Put in a preheated 400°F oven. Immediately reduce the oven temperature to 375°F and bake 25 to 35 minutes, according to how you like your soufflé. At 25 minutes it will still be a little runny in the center.

Editor: Philip Brown was the husband of Helen Evans Brown (see page 283). He sometimes taught tandem cooking classes with Beard.

ONIONS MONÉGASQUE

MAKES 10 TO 12 APPETIZER SERVINGS

Editor: A specialty of Monaco, these glazed onions are wonderful on a buffet table as a rich salad, or as a side dish to grilled pork or chicken. Beard considers the tomato paste optional, but it is a good addition.

To peel the onions: Drop the onions into a large saucepan of boiling water and cook until the skins loosen, about 1 minute. Drain and rinse under cold running water. Trim the tops and bottoms from the onions, and peel.

---

36 to 40 small white boiling onions, peeled

⅔ cup dry white wine

½ cup water

¼ cup olive oil

2 tablespoons tomato paste

1 teaspoon sugar

½ teaspoon dried thyme

1 teaspoon kosher salt

1 bay leaf

1 fresh fennel sprig (optional) or a few fennel seeds

1 cup dried currants or golden raisins

Pinch of saffron threads

Place the onions in a large skillet (not cast iron) with the wine, water, oil, tomato paste (if using), sugar, thyme, salt and bay leaf. Add the fennel, if using. Bring to a simmer and cover with the lid ajar. Cook until the onions are just crisply tender, about 10 minutes. Add the currants and saffron, turn up the heat, and boil, uncovered, until the liquid reduces by half, about 5 minutes. Using a slotted spoon, transfer the onions to a serving bowl. Boil the cooking liquid until it forms a thick sauce, about 2 minutes more. Pour over the onions. Let cool. Serve cold.

crisp, about 2½ minutes. Drain well on paper towels. Keep warm in a 200°F oven. Reheat the oil to 375°F before frying the remaining onions. Serve hot.

FRENCH-FRIED ONION RINGS

〰 MAKES 4 SERVINGS

Editor: Nibble on these as a snack, or serve them as the ultimate accompaniment to steaks or burgers.

3 large yellow onions, peeled
Ice water

For the Batter
1 cup buttermilk
1 large egg
1 cup all-purpose flour
½ teaspoon baking powder
½ teaspoon plain salt

Vegetable oil, for deep-frying

Slice the onions about ¼ inch thick, separate them into rings, and soak in ice water for 3 hours. Drain and dry thoroughly on paper towels.

To make the batter: Whisk the buttermilk and egg in a medium bowl. Sift the flour, baking powder, and salt together. Add to the buttermilk mixture and whisk just until smooth.

Heat the fat to 375°F in a deep fryer. Working in batches, dip the onion rings into the batter and fry in the hot fat, a few at a time, until brown and

FRENCH-FRIED PARSNIPS

〰 MAKES 4 SERVINGS

For the life of me, I cannot understand why so many people dislike parsnips, which are one of our most delicious winter vegetables, if properly treated. There is a good deal of waste on parsnips, because the cores tend to be quite woody. Look for those that are fat around the top, not the long skinny ones. They aren't the easiest of vegetables to peel, so I often cook them in the skins and peel them afterward.

8 parsnips, unpeeled
1 cup all-purpose flour
2 large eggs, lightly beaten
1 cup fresh bread crumbs
Peanut or vegetable oil, for deep-frying

Cook the parsnips in a good amount of boiling salted water for 20 to 45 minutes, depending on the age and size of the vegetables. They are done when easily pierceable with a skewer or the point of a small knife. Plunge the cooked parsnips into cold water and, when cool enough to handle, peel, discarding the tough ends. Cut into fingers 2 inches long by ¼ inch wide.

Put the flour in a shallow bowl, the eggs in another shallow bowl, and the bread crumbs in a third bowl. Dip the parsnip fingers in the flour, then in the beaten egg, and roll in the fresh bread crumbs. Working in batches, deep-fry in a deep fryer or saucepan of deep hot oil (380°F) for about 3 minutes, until golden brown. Using a slotted spoon, transfer to paper towels to drain. Keep warm in a 200°F oven while frying the remaining parsnips. Serve at once.

NEW PEAS

MAKES 4 TO 6 SERVINGS

Editor: New peas are the very first peas of the season. Lacking a garden, you'll find them at your local farmers' market. You can use any fresh peas, adjusting the cooking time as needed until they are tender.

3 pounds new peas

2 to 3 cups water

Kosher salt and freshly ground black pepper

6 tablespoons (¾ stick) unsalted butter, melted

Select the freshest, youngest peas you can buy, and store in the refrigerator until ready for shelling. Do not soak them in water after shelling. Bring the water to a boil in a medium saucepan and add the peas—do not worry if the water does not entirely cover peas. Cook, uncovered, until just tender, about 10 minutes. Drain, season with salt and pepper, and toss with the melted butter.

ROASTED SWEET PEPPERS WITH ANCHOVIES

MAKES 12 APPETIZER SERVINGS

12 red bell peppers

½ cup olive oil

1 to 2 tablespoons wine vinegar or sherry wine vinegar

Kosher salt and freshly ground black pepper

2 dozen anchovy fillets in oil, drained

2 tablespoons chopped fresh flat-leaf parsley

Roast the peppers under a hot broiler, turning them occasionally, until the skins are blackened and blistered, about 10 minutes. Let cool, then remove the skins and seeds. Cut the peppers into halves or quarters. Arrange them in a flat serving dish.

Make a dressing with the oil and vinegar and season with salt (remember the anchovies are salty), and black pepper. Pour this over the roasted peppers and let them marinate several hours.

Remove from marinade, add the anchovies, and sprinkle with chopped parsley. Or serve in the dish with the marinade and pass the anchovies and parsley separately.

STUFFED GREEN PEPPERS

 MAKES 8 SERVINGS

8 green bell peppers

2½ cups (½-inch) cubes of day-old white bread

¾ cup olive oil

2 garlic cloves, finely chopped

½ cup pine nuts

½ cup dried currants

16 anchovy fillets in oil, drained and chopped

2 tablespoons chopped fresh flat-leaf parsley

2 tablespoons dry vermouth

Kosher salt and freshly ground black pepper

Softened butter, for the baking dish

Blanch the peppers in a large pot of lightly salted water for 8 to 10 minutes, until softened. Drain, rinse under cold water, and remove the tops and the seeds.

Sauté the croutons in ¼ cup of oil with the garlic in a skillet over medium-high heat until just golden. Add the pine nuts, currants, anchovies, parsley, and vermouth. Season with salt and black pepper (remember, the anchovies contain a good deal of salt). Stuff the blanched peppers with the bread mixture and place them in a buttered baking dish. Top each pepper with 1 tablespoon oil. Bake in a preheated 350°F oven for 30 minutes.

POTATOES ANNA

 MAKES 6 SERVINGS

Potatoes Anna, a French dish that has become quite the vogue in this country, represents yet another way of baking potatoes. Sliced thinly and well lubricated with butter, they form a kind of cake, crustily brown on the outside and meltingly tender inside. Serve Potatoes Anna with steak, roast meats, or chicken.

6 baking potatoes

About 1 cup (2 sticks) unsalted butter, melted

Kosher salt and freshly ground black pepper

Peel the potatoes and slice them into very thin, even rounds, ⅛ inch thick. You can do this more easily if you use a mandoline or vegetable slicer with an adjustable blade. As the potatoes are sliced, drop them into a large bowl of salted ice water until ready to use.

The best thing to use for baking the potatoes is a heavy 8-inch, cast-iron skillet, 2 inches deep. Lacking this, use a deep 8-inch round pie dish or baking dish of the same dimensions. Brush the bottom and sides of the skillet heavily with melted butter. Drain the potatoes and dry them thoroughly on clean cloth or paper towels. They must be completely dry, as excess moisture would ruin the dish. Arrange a layer of potatoes in the bottom of the skillet: put one slice in the center and arrange overlapping circles of potatoes around it, from center to sides (this will be the top when unmolded). Sprinkle the potatoes very lightly with salt and pepper and spoon a tablespoon or two of melted butter over them.

Continue to make layers of potatoes, seasoning

each layer and spooning butter over it, until the skillet is filled. Spoon another tablespoon or two of butter over the top.

Put the skillet on the center rack of the oven and a baking sheet on the rack below it to catch any butter that might bubble over. Bake in a preheated 400°F oven for 30 to 40 minutes, until the potatoes are crisp and brown around the edges and tender when prodded with a fork or toothpick.

Remove the skillet from the oven. Run a knife around the edge of the potatoes to loosen them. Put a large flat serving platter, big enough to hold the potato cake, on top of the pan and quickly invert it so the cake unmolds itself onto the platter. To serve, cut into wedges.

Twice-Baked Potato Skins

Editor: Beard was very fond of these, and popularized them before they were a staple on bar menus.

Bake potatoes and remove all the pulp and reserve to use in another dish. With scissors cut the skins in strips about an inch wide. Put on a baking sheet; brush generously with melted butter; season with salt, freshly ground black pepper, and a little Tabasco; and put in a 475°F oven or under the broiler until they get brown and quite crisp. Serve with drinks, as an appetizer. These are better than any potato chips.

BAKED POTATOES

∞ FOR EACH SERVING

There is something very satisfying about a perfectly baked potato. Its delicious floury lightness and the earthy flavor of the crisp, chewy skin, intensified by the baking process, needs no dressing up. I prefer to savor that wonderful earthiness with just freshly ground black pepper and a touch of salt—no butter, no sour cream, no chives. Well, maybe a little bit of butter with the skin, but more often just pepper and salt.

The Idaho is surely the finest baking potato. It is said to be grown in a particular soil that has great lava content and that this greatly resembles soil in Peru, where the same type of potato abounds.

Allow **1 baking potato** per person, or, if they are extra large, ½ potato will be ample. Preheat the oven to 375°F. Scrub the potatoes well. (If desired, for a softer skin, rub the potatoes with **oil or butter**, and make a thin slit in each potato.) Place them on a rack in the oven. Bake for approximately an hour, or until the potatoes are soft to the touch. Split at once and serve with **freshly ground black pepper and salt.** They are perfect this way, but you may want to add **butter, sour cream, chives, cooked bacon crumbs, chopped fresh flat-leaf parsley, or paprika.**

STUFFED BAKED POTATOES

Editor: These are hearty enough to be a vegetarian main course for a lunch or light supper.

---

6 Baked Potatoes (see page 241), leave the oven
    turned on
¾ cup heavy cream
8 tablespoons (1 stick) unsalted butter, at room
    temperature
1½ teaspoons kosher salt
1½ teaspoons freshly ground black pepper
1 teaspoon sweet paprika
¾ cup shredded Swiss, Gruyère, or Cheddar cheese

Cut about ¾ inch off the long side of each baked potato with a sharp knife. Scoop the contents into a bowl or saucepan. Beat in the cream, butter, salt, pepper, and paprika. Add ½ cup of the cheese and beat well. Return the potato mixture to the shells and top with the remaining cheese. Put on a baking sheet. Return to the 375°F oven to melt cheese and reheat potatoes, about 20 minutes.

PERFECT FRENCH FRIES

For making French fries, some like the mealy Idaho potato, others the waxier boiling potato. Either one will work, but you might, to amuse yourself, fry different types of potato, such as the long white California, the Idaho, and the Maine and decide which you like best.

Editor: Most cooks prefer large brown-skinned baking potatoes, such as Russets or Burbanks, for French fries.

---

4 medium-to-large Idaho, Maine, or California
    potatoes
Peanut oil or rendered beef fat, for deep-frying
Salt and freshly ground black pepper

Potatoes are best if peeled and cut just before you fry them. If you can't do that, put the cut potatoes into a bowl of cold water, take them out just before frying, spread them out on a double layer of paper towels or a terry towel, and dry thoroughly.

Peel the potatoes and cut them into long strips from ¼ to ½ inch wide and thick. Have ready a baking sheet lined with paper towels. Heat the fat in a deep fryer to 325°F and, if you are using a basket, heat the basket in the fat. See that the potatoes are completely dry; lift out the basket; toss a handful of the potatoes into it and lower them slowly into the hot fat. Cook for 5 to 6 minutes, or until they get rather flabby-looking. They should not brown. During the cooking, lift the basket and shake the potatoes around once or twice to prevent them from sticking together.

Transfer the potatoes, as they are cooked, to a baking sheet lined with paper towels and leave at room temperature from 1 to 1½ hours, until you are ready to do your second frying. Then reheat the fat and basket to 375° or 380°F; lower the partially fried potatoes back into the hot fat, a handful at a time; and fry for 2 or 3 minutes, or until they are as brown as you prefer. Be sure to bring the fat back to the correct temperature after each batch. Keep warm in a 250°F oven, on paper towel–lined baking sheets.

Season your French fries with salt and pepper just before serving.

POTATO GALETTE

✍ MAKES 4 SERVINGS

Peel and slice thinly **4 Idaho (baking) potatoes.** Melt 6 tablespoons (¾ stick) unsalted butter in a heavy skillet over medium heat. [*Editor: A nonstick pan works best here.*] Arrange the potato slices in rosette fashion in the pan. Start with a large slice in center and overlap other slices. **Salt and pepper** each layer and dot with **2 tablespoons unsalted butter, cut into ½-inch cubes.** Cover and cook over medium-low heat for 20 to 25 minutes, until the potatoes are tender. Increase the heat to medium-high and cook, occasionally shaking the pan lightly, to brown the potatoes, about 3 minutes. Invert onto a hot platter.

NOTE: You may also invert potatoes onto a plate, melt 2 tablespoons of butter in the pan, slide the potatoes back into the pan, and brown other side, about 5 minutes more

PURÉED POTATOES

✍ MAKES 6 SERVINGS

Mashed or whipped potatoes, more elegantly known as *purée de pommes de terre*, ideally should be light, fluffy, and creamy and they must be made at the last minute so they won't sit and become soggy. Opinions differ as to whether the potatoes should be cooked in their jackets or not. I believe that if they are floury and mealy they should be peeled.

Peel **2 pounds baking potatoes.** Put in a saucepan of salted water to cover, bring to a boil over high heat, and cook until they are tender, about 20 minutes. Drain them, return them to the saucepan, and let them dry over medium heat, stirring occasionally, for a few minutes. Mash the potatoes with a wire masher or put them through a food mill or potato ricer into a bowl. [*Editor: Never purée mashed potatoes in a food processor—unless they combined with an equal amount of other vegetables, such as celery root.*] Add ½ to ¾ cup boiling milk and about **5 tablespoons (½ stick plus 1 tablespoon) softened unsalted butter** and whip the potatoes with a whisk or an electric mixer. The potatoes must be smooth, very hot, and rather loose in texture. Do not let them get too thick and pasty or they will lose their delicacy. Season them with **kosher salt and freshly ground pepper** to taste and transfer them to a heated serving dish. Add a **dot of butter** and serve them very hot. To keep the potatoes hot, put them in a well-buttered pan set over hot water and cover them with buttered waxed paper.

ROESTI POTATOES

Editor: This is another irresistible variation on the potato cake theme.

Parboil **6 whole baking potatoes** in a saucepan of lightly salted water until almost tender, about 10 minutes. Peel and grate on the large holes of a box grater. Melt **8 tablespoons (1 stick) unsalted butter** in a large skillet over medium heat. Add the potatoes and cook well until they form a crust, about 10 minutes. Press down on the cake with a metal turning spatula. Flip the potato cake and cook on other side. Season with **kosher salt and freshly ground black pepper** to taste and add more butter, if needed. When crisp and beautifully brown, about 10 minutes longer, slide out onto a hot plate. These may be made in small cakes and served individually.

SAUTÉED POTATOES

∽ MAKES 4 TO 6 SERVINGS

This version of sautéed potatoes is made with potatoes boiled in their skins, which hold them together.

    2 to 2½ pounds baking potatoes, scrubbed but
        unpeeled
    6 tablespoons (¾ stick) unsalted butter
    1 teaspoon kosher salt
    Freshly ground black pepper
    1 tablespoon chopped fresh flat-leaf parsley

Boil the potatoes in their skins in a large saucepan of lightly salted water to cover until they are just tender when pierced with a knife, about 20 minutes. Drain, and when cool enough to handle, slice them into rounds about ¼ inch thick.

Heat the butter in a heavy skillet over medium-high heat until foaming. Add the potatoes and sauté them until they begin to brown, about 6 minutes. Turn them carefully with a spatula and cook until browned on the other side, about 6 minutes more. Season them with salt and a few grinds of pepper, carefully transfer to a heated serving dish, and sprinkle with the chopped parsley.

VARIATION

LYONNAISE POTATOES: Make the Sautéed Potatoes and set aside. Melt 4 tablespoons (½ stick) butter in a skillet, add 4 yellow onions, sliced, and sauté over medium heat, turning them frequently, for 10 minutes. Add 1 teaspoon sugar and salt to taste, cover, and cook for 4 to 5 minutes more, or until soft. Add the potatoes to the onions and toss together lightly until well blended and the potatoes are reheated, about 3 minutes. Transfer to a heated serving dish and sprinkle with the chopped parsley.

HOT RATATOUILLE WITH GRATED CHEESE

MAKES 6 SERVINGS

This great dish of Provence may be varied in so many ways. [*Editor: For example, it is often served chilled, although in this recipe, it is hot.*] Here, we add mushrooms in quantity and cheese.

3 garlic cloves, finely chopped

2 medium yellow onions, thinly sliced

⅓ cup olive oil

2 eggplants, trimmed and cut into ¾-inch dice

1 green bell pepper, seeded and cut into thin rounds

6 very ripe tomatoes, peeled, seeded, and diced, or
    2½ cups canned Italian plum tomatoes, coarsely
    chopped

¼ cup fresh chopped basil or 1 teaspoon dried basil

1½ teaspoons kosher salt

1 pound white mushrooms, sliced

Grated Parmesan cheese

Sauté the garlic and onions in the oil in a heavy-bottomed large saucepan over medium heat until soft. Add the eggplant and pepper, and cook for 5 minutes, tossing well and shaking the pan. Add the tomatoes, basil, and salt, and simmer 30 minutes, covered for half that time. Add the mushrooms, correct the seasoning, and continue cooking until the mushrooms are just cooked through, about 10 minutes. Transfer to a serving dish, sprinkle with the Parmesan cheese, and serve.

BRAISED SAUERKRAUT

MAKES 4 TO 6 SERVINGS

Sauerkraut is often overlooked as an accompaniment to meat and poultry, yet its tart, fermented flavor is a perfect balance for any form of pork—from roasts and barbecued spareribs to pigs' knuckles and sausages—or to boiled beef, rich and fatty goose and duck, turkey, and many game birds.

The best buy is the fresh sauerkraut packaged in plastic bags and sold in German pork butcher shops and many supermarkets, but canned sauerkraut is also acceptable. Fresh sauerkraut is very salty and should always be rinsed well before using.

2 pounds fresh sauerkraut

4 to 5 slices salt pork or rindless slab bacon,
    cut ⅛ inch thick

Freshly ground black pepper

Bouquet garni of 4 sprigs fresh flat-leaf parley, 4
    sprigs fresh thyme, and 1 bay leaf, tied in rinsed
    cheesecloth

2 garlic cloves, crushed and peeled

10 crushed juniper berries or 2 tablespoons gin

4 cups Chicken Stock (page 349), dry white wine,
    or lager beer, as needed

Rinse the sauerkraut well in a colander under cold running water, tossing it with your hands. Drain well and squeeze by the handful to remove the excess liquid. Line the bottom of a large heavy pot with the salt pork or bacon (if you use salt pork, soak it in cold water for 30 minutes to remove the excess salt). Put layers of sauerkraut into the pot, grinding black pepper on each layer. Tuck in the bouquet garni, garlic, and juniper berries (or pour in the gin). Pour on enough liquid (I prefer chicken stock, which gives a more delicate flavor) to cover and bring to a boil over high heat. Reduce the heat to medium-low and simmer slowly for 2 to 4 hours. The longer it cooks, the better it tastes.

SPINACH WITH CREAM AND NUTMEG

MAKES 4 SERVINGS

Editor: Here is how to make the steakhouse specialty, creamed spinach, at home.

Two 10-ounce packages frozen chopped spinach, thawed

3 tablespoons unsalted butter

1 tablespoon all-purpose flour

3 tablespoons heavy cream

Kosher salt

¼ teaspoon freshly grated nutmeg

Squeeze the spinach by handfuls to remove the excess liquid. Chop the spinach again. Melt the butter in a skillet, over medium heat. Whisk in the flour, then the cream. Cook until the mixture boils and thickens. Add the spinach and mix. Season with salt and add the nutmeg. Cover and heat over very low heat, stirring once or twice, or heat in a double boiler over hot water, until heated through, about 3 minutes. Serve hot.

SAUTÉED SUMMER SQUASH

MAKES 6 SERVINGS

Summer squash (zucchini, little yellow straightnecks and crooknecks, tiny pattypans, or scalloped squash) have become much more a part of our vegetable lives since we learned that they should be cooked fast so they don't disintegrate to an unappetizing mushiness. Look for the youngest, smallest, and firmest squash you can find and don't on any account peel them.

1½ pounds summer squash

6 tablespoons (¾ stick) unsalted butter, or olive oil or a combination of the two

4 to 5 scallions, trimmed, white and green parts finely chopped

Kosher salt and freshly ground black pepper

2 tablespoons chopped fresh flat-leaf parsley

2 teaspoons freshly squeezed lemon juice

Trim the squash and slice thinly or cut into long fingers (for zucchini or crooknecks). Heat the butter in a heavy skillet over medium-high heat and sauté the scallions until the white parts are just translucent, about 2 minutes. Add the squash and sauté very quickly, tossing well, and seasoning with salt and pepper to taste, until barely tender, about 5 minutes. Just before serving, add the chopped parsley and lemon juice.

BAKED TOMATOES STUFFED WITH MOZZARELLA

◇◇◇ MAKES 4 TO 6 SERVINGS

A versatile and attractive little dish I like to serve as a first course, with Veal Scallops with Lemon (page 96), or as a light luncheon entrée.

4 to 6 large, ripe, firm tomatoes

⅓ cup olive oil, as needed

Kosher salt and freshly ground black pepper

4 to 8 ounces mozzarella cheese, preferably fresh mozzarella (amount depends on size of tomatoes)

2 tablespoons minced fresh basil or 2 teaspoons dried basil

Cut a slice from the top of each tomato. Using a teaspoon, scoop out the pulp and seeds. Turn the tomato shells upside down on a platter and allow them to drain for about 15 minutes. Use some of the oil to brush a baking dish just large enough to hold the tomatoes. Place them in the dish. Season each tomato cavity with salt and pepper, and drizzle 1 teaspoon olive oil into each one. Chop the mozzarella finely and mix it with the basil. Stuff the tomatoes with this mixture. With a pastry brush, brush the outside skin of the tomatoes with the remaining olive oil. Bake in a preheated 375°F oven for about 20 minutes, or until the mozzarella has melted. Serve hot.

VARIATION

BAKED TOMATOES STUFFED WITH CORN: Blend a little of the chopped tomato pulp with 2 cups fresh corn kernels, 6 tablespoons (¾ stick) melted unsalted butter, 2 tablespoons finely chopped onion, 2 tablespoons chopped fresh flat-leaf parsley or basil, 1 teaspoon kosher salt, and ½ teaspoon freshly ground black pepper. Stuff the tomato shells with the mixture, cover the tops with ½ cup fresh bread crumbs, dot with 2 tablespoons cubed unsalted butter, and bake for 25 to 30 minutes, or until heated through.

TOMATOES WITH OKRA

◇◇◇ MAKES 6 SERVINGS

Editor: Beard cooks these in the traditional manner. If you like your okra less well done, cook them just until tender, about 15 mintues.

---

3 to 4 medium yellow onions, coarsely chopped

2 garlic cloves, finely chopped

½ cup olive oil

1 pound small okra, stem ends trimmed, rinsed, and patted dry with paper towels

2 cups canned Italian plum tomatoes with their juices

1 teaspoon ground coriander

Kosher salt and fresh ground black pepper

Lemon wedges, for serving

Sauté the onions and garlic in the olive oil in a large skillet over medium heat, and when they are slightly browned, about 5 minutes, add the okra. Cook for 3 minutes. Add the tomatoes and coriander and season with salt and pepper. Cover and simmer for about 35 minutes, or until the okra is very tender. Serve with lemon wedges.

STEAMED CHERRY TOMATOES

~ MAKES 6 SERVINGS

Editor: A simple recipe that can go with just about any roast meat or grilled steaks or chops, it is best when made with summer tomatoes from the farmers' market.

4 tablespoons (½ stick) unsalted butter

2 pints cherry tomatoes, stems removed

1 teaspoon, or more, chopped fresh dill, basil, or tarragon

1 teaspoon kosher salt

½ teaspoon freshly ground black pepper

Melt the butter in the upper part of a double boiler. Add the tomatoes with the herb of your choice, and the salt and pepper. Cover and cook until they are just tender, about 5 minutes.

SCALLOPED FRESH TOMATOES

~ MAKES 4 SERVINGS

Editor: When Beard was cooking, fresh tomatoes were most often cooked in the summer when they were in season and bursting with flavor. This recipe should be reserved for when you can get great tomatoes.

Softened butter, for the baking dish

8 to 10 ripe tomatoes, peeled and seeded

1 to 1½ cups fresh bread crumbs

8 to 12 tablespoons (1 to 1½ sticks) unsalted butter, cut into ½-inch cubes

1 teaspoon kosher salt

½ teaspoon freshly ground black pepper

Butter a deep baking dish and alternate layers of the tomatoes, bread crumbs, cubes of butter, and salt and pepper. Finish with a layer of crumbs, season with salt and pepper, and dot with the remaining butter. Bake in a preheated 350°F oven for 20 to 25 minutes until bubbling and the crumbs are browned. Serve hot.

GLAZED TURNIPS

~ MAKES 4 SERVINGS

These are a classic accompaniment to roast duck or goose. Often they are basted at the last minute with some of the pan juices from the duck.

6 to 8 small white turnips

8 tablespoons (1 stick) butter

1 teaspoon kosher salt

1 teaspoon or more sugar

Peel the turnips and with a very sharp knife shape each into two ovals about the size of a walnut but slightly longer—you should get two or more ovals from each turnip.

Heat the butter in a heavy skillet, until foaming, add the turnips, sprinkle them with salt, and cook very slowly over medium-low heat, shaking the pan and turning them often, for about 10 minutes. Sprinkle with 1 teaspoon sugar, shake the pan, and keep cooking and turning the turnips until they are lightly glazed and tender but still crisp. For a heavier glaze, add a little more sugar.

MASHED YELLOW TURNIPS WITH BUTTER

❧ MAKES 6 SERVINGS

Peel and slice **2 medium or 1 very large yellow turnip**—called rutabaga or Swede—according to the part of the country in which you live. Cook in boiling salted water until tender. Drain and mash with **8 tablespoons (1 stick) unsalted butter**. Add **kosher salt and freshly ground black pepper** to taste.

VEGETABLE FRITTERS

❧ MAKES ABOUT 8 SERVINGS

Below are suggestions for many kinds of fritters, each item to be dipped in batter and deep-fried.

For the Batter

2 cups all-purpose flour

4 tablespoons (½ stick) unsalted butter, at room temperature

2 large eggs, well beaten

Kosher salt and freshly ground black pepper

Pinch of freshly grated nutmeg

1 cup whole milk, as needed

Suggestions for the vegetables, in bite-size pieces

Marinated buds of cooked cauliflower or raw cauliflower

Cooked and marinated artichoke hearts

Tiny marinated onions

Marinated celery cubes

Marinated celery root (celeriac) cubes

Marinated mushrooms

Marinated Brussels sprouts

Marinated asparagus tips

Tiny raw tomatoes

Vegetable oil, for deep-frying

Editor: The marinated vegetables can be purchased at a supermarket or delicatessen, or marinate the raw or cooked vegetables in Basic Vinaigrette Sauce (page 359).

To make the batter: Work the flour and butter together in a medium bowl with a rubber spatula. Whisk in the eggs. Season with salt, pepper, and nutmeg and add enough milk to make a batter the consistency of heavy cream. Let stand for 30 minutes to 2 hours before using.

Fill a deep pot with enough vegetable oil to come halfway up the sides and heat over high heat to 380°F. Working in batches, without crowding, just before cooking, dip each vegetable in batter and let the excess batter drip back into the bowl. Add the vegetables to the oil and deep-fry until golden, 3 to 4 minutes. Transfer with a slotted spoon to paper towels to drain. Keep warm in a preheated 200°F oven until all of the vegetables have been fried. Serve on a napkin.

SPICED WINTER SQUASH

✎ MAKES 4 SERVINGS

Editor: Winter squash gets a lift from butter and warm spices.

2 pounds Hubbard, banana, or butternut squash, cut into large chunks, seeds removed
6 tablespoons (¾ stick) unsalted butter, plus more for serving
½ teaspoon ground allspice
½ teaspoon ground mace
Kosher salt

Put the squash on a rack or in a steam basket over simmering water and steam until the flesh is just tender, which will depend on the size and age of the squash—but allow at least 20 minutes. Do not overcook. Scrape the pulp from the shell and beat well with a fork or whisk, adding the butter, allspice, and mace, until light and fluffy. Season with salt. Serve in a heated dish dotted with more butter.

WINTER SQUASH WITH BLACK WALNUTS: Omit the spices. Add ½ cup coarsely chopped black walnuts to the purée. Season with salt and freshly ground black pepper.

WINTER SQUASH WITH PECANS AND GINGER: Beat the steamed squash with the butter and add ½ cup chopped pecans, ¼ cup finely chopped candied ginger, and ⅓ cup dry sherry. Put in a deep 9-inch baking dish, dot with butter, and bake in a preheated 350°F oven until the butter is melted and the squash is hot.

WINTER SQUASH WITH PEANUTS: Use ½ cup coarsely chopped salted peanuts instead of black walnuts.

PURÉED WINTER SQUASH WITH RAW ZUCCHINI: Omit the spices. Mix ½ cup shredded raw zucchini into the hot purée for a lovely color, flavor, and texture contrast. Season with salt and freshly ground black pepper.

SAUTÉED ZUCCHINI
WITH WALNUTS

MAKES 6 SERVINGS

This is excellent with roast lamb or with poultry.

6 medium-small zucchini, trimmed and cut into
  ¼-inch rounds
Kosher salt
3 tablespoons unsalted butter
3 tablespoons olive oil
1 garlic clove, unpeeled
Freshly ground black pepper
1 cup coarsely chopped walnuts
Chopped fresh flat-leaf parsley, for garnish

Put the zucchini in a colander, sprinkle with salt to draw out the water, and leave for an hour to drain. Rinse the slices and dry them.

Heat 2 tablespoons of the butter and all of the oil in a heavy skillet over medium-high heat. When foaming, add the zucchini and garlic clove and sauté, shaking the pan constantly, until the slices are tender but still crisp, 3 to 5 minutes. (The unpeeled garlic clove gives a little touch of flavor; discard it after cooking.) While cooking, taste a slice to see if it needs additional salt. If so, salt while tossing and give the slices a few grinds of pepper.

Add ¾ cup of the walnuts to the zucchini, shake the pan to blend them together, and heat the nuts through. Transfer to a heated serving dish, add the remaining tablespoon of butter and ¼ cup walnuts, and garnish with the chopped parsley.

RICE, GRAINS, AND BEANS

RICE, GRAINS, AND BEANS

OLD-FASHIONED BOILED RICE

≈ MAKES 4½ CUPS RICE; 4 TO 6 SERVINGS

Bring **4 quarts of water** and **2 tablespoons of kosher salt** to a rapid boil in a large pot. Throw in **1½ cups of long-grain rice** in small handfuls, making sure that the water continues to boil throughout. Boil the rice rapidly for 15 minutes, uncovered, then drain in a large sieve. Do not overcook. This will give you fluffy rice with well-separated grains, slightly firm to the bite.

If the rice seems a little moist and not fluffy after draining, return it to the pan and dry it out over very low heat for 2 or 3 minutes, stirring it occasionally with a fork to fluff it up. Always stir cooked rice with a fork, or toss it with two forks. Using a spoon bruises the grains and makes them sticky.

This method also works well with the Italian short-grain rice.

Editor: This method takes a lot of guesswork out of cooking rice.

STEAMED CONVERTED RICE

≈ MAKES 3 CUPS; 4 SERVINGS

For converted rice, I prefer to steam it covered. When you steam rice, remember that it will expand to three times its original volume (1 cup raw rice makes 3 cups cooked). [*Editor: Converted rice has been parcooked and dehydrated, which removes some of its starch to ensure fluffy, separate grains. This method works well for regular, nonconverted rice, too.*]

2½ cups water

1 teaspoon kosher salt

2 or 3 tablespoons unsalted butter or olive oil (optional)

1 cup converted rice

Put the water, salt, and 1 tablespoon of the butter, if desired (this is not necessary if you are going to add butter or oil to the cooked rice), in a pan and bring it to a rapid boil. Add the rice, and when the water returns to the boil, cover the pan tightly, turn down the heat, and cook the rice over very low heat, without lifting the lid, for 20 to 25 minutes until the water is completely absorbed. You may, for richer rice, substitute chicken stock for the water. The simplest addition is butter or oil. Add the remaining 2 tablespoons butter or oil to the rice. Toss with a fork until the grains are well coated.

VARIATIONS

HERBED RICE: With the oil or butter add 2 to 3 tablespoons finely chopped fresh flat-leaf parsley and 1 to 2 tablespoons finely cut fresh chives. Other herbs that might be added with the parsley and chives are chopped fresh tarragon and chervil.

RICE WITH PINE NUTS: After adding the butter or oil, toss the rice with ½ cup pine nuts, which give a pleasant crunchiness.

PUNGENT PARSLIED RICE: Add to the cooked rice 6 to 8 chopped shallots that have been lightly sautéed in 2 tablespoons olive oil or butter until just limp and golden, and 2 to 3 tablespoons finely chopped fresh flat-leaf parsley.

SAFFRON RICE: Add ¼ teaspoon crushed saffron threads to the rice with the water.

AROMATIC RICE WITH PEAS

⌒ **MAKES 4 TO 6 SERVINGS**

The whole spices in this dish are for flavoring only and are not to be eaten.

> 3 tablespoons vegetable oil
> 1 stick of cinnamon, about 1½ inches long
> 3 bay leaves
> 4 whole cardamom pods
> 5 whole cloves
> 1 cup peas, either freshly shelled or thawed frozen
> 1½ cups long-grain rice
> 2¾ cups Chicken Stock (page 349)
> ¾ teaspoon kosher salt (use 1¼ teaspoons if the broth is unsalted)

Heat the oil in a heavy-bottomed medium pot over medium heat. When hot, add the cinnamon, bay leaves, cardamom pods, and cloves. Stir the spices for 5 seconds. Now add the peas. Stir and fry for a minute. Add the rice, and turn the heat to low. Stir and fry the rice for about 3 minutes. Now add the stock and salt. Bring to a boil. Cover with a tight-fitting lid, turn the heat to very, very low, and cook, undisturbed, for 25 minutes. Turn off the heat. Let the rice rest, covered and in a warm spot, for 10 minutes. Mix the rice and peas gently with a fork, and serve.

RICE WITH PINE NUTS

⌒ **MAKES 12 SERVINGS FOR A BUFFET**

Editor: For 9 cups of cooked rice, start with 3 cups of raw rice and 6 cups of water.

> 2 cups finely chopped yellow onion
> 2 cups pine nuts
> 1½ teaspoons sweet paprika
> ½ teaspoon Tabasco
> 1 cup olive oil
> 9 cups hot cooked rice
> Kosher salt and freshly ground black pepper
> 6 drained canned pimientos, chopped, for garnish
> Finely chopped fresh flat-leaf parsley, for garnish

Sauté the onion, pine nuts, paprika, and Tabasco in olive oil for 6 to 8 minutes. Toss with the hot rice, using two forks. Season with salt and pepper. Transfer to a serving bowl and garnish with the chopped pimientos and parsley.

RISOTTO

〜 **MAKES 4 SERVINGS**

I like to use a heavy skillet of plain or enameled cast iron or copper and stainless steel for risotto—the Italian rice dish in which the grains, though firm, become creamy like a pudding. A pan that will distribute heat and hold it well aids the bubbling activity and gradual absorption of liquid that a risotto requires.

The next important thing is to have good stock or broth. If making seafood risotto, clam juice may be used, but it is best to use homemade chicken, beef, veal, or fish stock if possible. These stocks keep well in the freezer. There are so many variations of risotto that it is always a pleasure to have the wherewithal on hand to make it at the last minute. I am particularly partial to chicken and fish stock for risottos because I like to use seafood and various meats and vegetables that blend well with those flavors.

The simplest risotto is made with rice, butter or oil, onion, stock, and Parmesan cheese.

> 6 tablespoons (¾ stick) unsalted butter
> 1 small yellow onion, peeled and very finely chopped
> 1½ cups short-grain Italian rice, such as Arborio
> 3 to 4 cups Chicken Stock (page 349) or Beef Stock (page 349), heated
> ½ cup freshly grated Parmesan cheese
> Kosher salt and freshly ground black pepper

Melt 4 tablespoons of the butter in a heavy skillet; add the onion and cook over medium heat, stirring, until light golden. Add the remaining 2 tablespoons butter and, when it has melted, add the rice. Stir the rice around in the butter with a fork until the grains have become coated and almost translucent.

Keep the stock hot in a pan on another burner. When making risotto, the stock is added in increments, not all at once, so it must be kept at a simmer or the rice will not cook properly. When the rice is coated with the butter, pour 1 cup of the stock into a measuring cup and add to the rice. Stir vigorously for a minute with a fork, then let the rice cook over medium-high heat until the liquid is almost absorbed, stirring it now and then so it does not stick to the pan. Add another cup of stock and continue to cook and stir until the liquid is almost absorbed. The rice should bubble and gradually soften and become creamy—at this point, add the stock more cautiously, ½ cup at a time, stirring until it is absorbed. You don't want to drown the rice with liquid, only add as much as it can absorb. You may find you need less, or possibly more, than the amount specified. As it cooks, taste a grain now and then. When the risotto is done, after 25 to 30 minutes, the rice will be creamy and tender, but still al dente in the center, just firm to the bite, with all the liquid absorbed. Keep stirring well in the final cooking to prevent the rice from sticking to the pan. When done, sprinkle with the Parmesan cheese and stir it in with the fork. Season with salt and pepper. Serve at once, on hot plates.

VARIATIONS

SAFFRON RISOTTO: This is the traditional accompaniment to Ossi Buchi (page 94). Stir ½ teaspoon crushed saffron threads into the risotto with the first addition of stock.

RISOTTO VILLA D'ESTE (RISOTTO WITH SMOKED SALMON): Cook the risotto as before, but substitute simmering Fish Stock (page 351) for the chicken stock. When the risotto is almost done, stir in ½ cup heavy cream and let it cook down for 1 minute. Then stir in ⅔ cup finely shredded smoked salmon, distributing it evenly through the rice, 2 to 3 tablespoons finely chopped fresh flat-leaf parsley, and 3 tablespoons freshly grated Parmesan cheese. Serve at once. A tablespoon or two of finely chopped fresh dill may be mixed in for an unorthodox but delicious touch.

RISOTTO AL FRUTTI DI MARE

✑ MAKES 6 SERVINGS

Editor: In this risotto recipe from the 1960s, the rice is long-grain and cooked in the conventional American manner. If you wish, use Italian short-grain rice, such as Arborio, and prepare according to the basic "stirred" risotto recipe on page 257. Stir the cooked shellfish into the risotto.

---

1 pound medium shrimp or scallops

1 pound cooked crabmeat or lobster

12 to 14 littleneck clams or mussels, well scrubbed

4 tablespoons (½ stick) unsalted butter, plus more as needed

1 small yellow onion, finely chopped

2 cups long-grain rice

1 cup dry white wine

3 cups Chicken Stock (page 349) or Fish Stock (page 351), or canned chicken stock or bottled clam juice

Dry sherry or Port

Freshly grated Parmesan cheese

Chopped fresh flat-leaf parsley

Kosher salt and freshly ground black pepper

You may combine any type of seafood for this dish. Use any three of the recommendations above, preparing each variety of shellfish separately: Boil the shrimp until pink, then peel and devein them (or buy ready-cooked); sauté the scallops in a little butter just until seared on the outside; chunk the crabmeat or cut the lobster into bite-size pieces; steam the clams or mussels until they open. Set aside.

Melt 2 tablespoons of the butter in a heavy large skillet, and sauté the onion until just tender. Add the rice, and toss with a fork; do not let the rice brown. Add the wine, and cook until it has almost evaporated. Then add the stock, cover, and cook over low heat for 20 minutes, or until the liquid is absorbed. If rice is not yet tender (to your taste), add more broth, and continue cooking.

Combine the selected seafood and heat over low heat with the remaining 2 tablespoons butter and a dash of sherry or Port just until hot. Fold into the risotto. Add the grated Parmesan and chopped parsley to taste. Season with salt and pepper and serve hot.

PAELLA

MAKES 6 SERVINGS

For this variation of the Spanish paella, try making it with chicken wings rather than the cut-up whole chicken.

Editor: Beard would have probably used long-grain rice because short-grain rice (such as Spanish Calasparra or Bomba or Italian Arborio) weren't commonplace. Short-grain rice is stickier than long-grain, and makes the paella easier to serve. Use either variety for your paella, but as the short-grain isn't hard to find now, it would be more authentic.

---

8 chicken wings, cut apart at the joints, wing tips discarded

All-purpose flour

6 tablespoons peanut oil

Kosher salt and freshly ground black pepper

1 medium yellow onion, finely chopped

2 garlic cloves, chopped

1½ cups long-grain white rice [see Editor's Note]

Chicken Stock (page 347) or water, heated to boiling, as needed

Pinch of saffron threads

1 or 2 links Spanish smoked chorizo, sliced

½ cup drained and chopped canned tomatoes

24 littleneck clams, in their shells, well scrubbed

12 large shrimp, unpeeled

3 pimientos, drained and cut into thin strips

1 cup frozen green peas, thawed

Flour the chicken wings, and brown in oil in a very large skillet or paella pan over medium heat, about 10 minutes. Season with salt and pepper, transfer to a platter, and cover with aluminum foil to keep warm.

Sauté the onion and garlic in the oil in the skillet until soft. Add the rice and stir until well coated with oil and translucent. Pour in enough boiling chicken broth to cover the rice, then season with salt, pepper and the saffron and let the liquid cook down for a minute or two. Add the chicken wings, sliced sausages, tomatoes, and additional liquid, if necessary. Simmer over low heat until the rice is just beginning to get tender, about 15 minutes; add the clams and shrimp. Cook until the shrimp are pink and cooked through and the clam shells open. Nearly all the liquid should have cooked away at this point; if it has not, raise the heat until it evaporates, leaving the rice firm and the grains separated. Garnish with pimiento strips and the peas (the heat from the paella will warm them through).

BARLEY WITH MUSHROOMS

◇◇ MAKES 6 SERVINGS

Editor: Be sure to use pearled barley for this recipe, as hulled barley takes much longer to cook and is quite chewy. To toast the almonds, cook in a skillet over medium heat, stirring often, until lightly browned, about 2 minutes.

4 to 5 tablespoons unsalted butter, plus more for the
    casserole
1 large yellow onion, chopped
8 ounces white mushrooms, sliced
1 cup pearled barley
2 cups Beef Broth (page 349) or Chicken Broth
    (page 349)
Kosher salt and freshly ground pepper
⅓ cup slivered almonds, toasted

In a skillet, melt the butter and sauté the onions and mushrooms until soft. Add the barley and brown it lightly. Pour into a buttered 2- to 3-quart casserole. Before you pour the broth over the barley, taste it for seasoning. If it has enough, the ingredients will need no additional salt or pepper; otherwise, season to taste. Pour 1 cup of the broth over the barley in the casserole and cover. Bake in a preheated 350°F oven for 25 to 30 minutes, then uncover and add the remaining cup of broth. Continue cooking until the liquid is absorbed and the barley is done. Add the almonds just before serving.

BULGHUR (CRACKED WHEAT) PILAF

◇◇ MAKES 4 SERVINGS

Bulghur, or cracked wheat, a staple of Middle Eastern cooking, is light golden brown in color, with a nutty taste and texture. It is an excellent alternative to rice; and may be used, like cooked rice, for stuffings.

2 tablespoons unsalted butter
1 tablespoon finely chopped yellow onion
1 cup medium- or coarse-grind cracked wheat
    (bulghur)
2 cups Chicken Stock (page 349)
½ teaspoon kosher salt
¼ teaspoon freshly ground black pepper

Melt the butter in a skillet; add the onion and sauté over medium heat for 2 or 3 minutes, stirring, until limp and golden. Add the cracked wheat and stir until the grains are well coated with butter. Add the stock, salt, and pepper and bring to a boil. Lower the heat; cover the pan tightly and simmer gently for 15 minutes, or until the liquid is absorbed and the wheat is tender.

TABBOULEH

This Middle Eastern salad is immensely refreshing on a hot day and especially good with broiled chicken or kebabs. Be sure to use the fine grade of bulghur (cracked wheat); the others are too coarse for this salad. You can buy it in Middle Eastern groceries or health-food stores.

½ cup fine-grind bulghur (cracked wheat)

3 ripe tomatoes, peeled, seeded, and finely chopped

1 cup finely chopped fresh flat-leaf parsley

1 cup finely chopped scallions (white and green parts)

⅓ cup freshly squeezed lemon juice

Kosher salt

⅓ cup olive oil

¼ cup finely chopped fresh mint leaves or 2½ tablespoons dried mint, crushed with your fingers

Boston or romaine lettuce leaves, for serving

Soak the bulghur in cold water to cover for 30 minutes. Drain in a wire sieve lined with rinsed cheesecloth to prevent the fine grains from falling through, then twist the cheesecloth into a bag and wring out the remaining moisture from the bulghur. Put the bulghur on a clean, dry dish towel, pat out flat, and leave until fairly dry.

Put the bulghur in a large bowl; add the tomatoes, parsley, scallions, lemon juice, and salt to taste. Mix gently but thoroughly, using your hands or wooden spoons. Just before serving, mix in the oil and mint. Taste, and correct the seasoning, if necessary. Serve on lettuce leaves.

CORNMEAL MUSH (POLENTA)

American cornmeal mush, which is basically the same as Italian polenta, is a good and somewhat different accompaniment to meats, especially pork, game, chicken, sausages, chili and spicy Mexican dishes, or with salt cod, spinach, or just tomato sauce. Mixing the cornmeal with cold water first makes the texture less grainy.

1½ cups yellow cornmeal

4½ cups water

1 teaspoon kosher salt

4 tablespoons (½ stick) unsalted butter

½ cup grated Parmesan cheese

Put the cornmeal in the metal insert of a double boiler and stir in 1 cup of the cold water. Mix well. Bring the remaining 3½ cups water to a boil in a saucepan, and stir into the cornmeal mixture. Bring the cornmeal mixture, still in the metal insert, to a boil over low heat, stirring constantly. Stir the salt into the cornmeal mush. Meanwhile, add enough water to the double boiler to come just below the bottom of the insert, and bring to a simmer. Place the insert in the double boiler, cover, and steam over the simmering water for 1 hour. Stir in the butter and cheese, and serve.

KASHA
(BUCKWHEAT GROATS)

⌖ MAKES 4 SERVINGS

Every once in a while I get a craving for kasha. The crunchiness of the groats makes a nice contrast to foods with a very soft texture, like chicken breasts in a creamy sauce.

1 cup buckwheat groats (kasha)

1 large egg, beaten

2 cups boiling Beef Stock (page 349) or use canned beef stock

4 tablespoons (½ stick) unsalted butter or rendered chicken fat

Kosher salt

Put the buckwheat groats in a preheated skillet over medium heat. Add the egg and stir vigorously over high heat until each grain is separate. Add the stock and salt to taste. Cover the pan, lower the heat, and steam the groats for 30 minutes. Stir in the butter.

VARIATIONS

KASHA WITH MUSHROOMS: Mix ½ cup sautéed sliced mushrooms into the cooked kasha.

KASHA WITH SAUTÉED GIBLETS: Mix ½ cup sautéed chopped chicken gizzards, hearts, and livers into the cooked kasha.

LENTIL SALAD

⌖ MAKES 10 SERVINGS FOR A BUFFET

Editor: When you need a side dish for a buffet where ham is the star attraction, serve this hearty salad.

For the Lentils

2 to 3 pounds brown lentils, soaked overnight in cold water to cover, drained

1 medium yellow onion, stuck with 2 whole cloves

1 tablespoon kosher salt

2 garlic cloves, peeled and left whole

1 bay leaf

1 cup olive oil

For the Salad

1 cup crisply cooked and crumbled bacon

¾ cup finely chopped yellow onion

½ cup finely chopped fresh flat-leaf parsley, plus more for garnish

2 garlic cloves, finely chopped

3 tablespoons red wine vinegar, or more to taste

1 teaspoon freshly ground black pepper

¼ teaspoon Tabasco

Olive oil, as needed

2 thinly sliced scallions, white and green parts, thinly sliced, for garnish

To prepare the lentils: Put the drained lentils in a large saucepan and add fresh water to cover. Add the onion stuck with cloves, salt, garlic, and bay leaf. Bring to a boil, reduce the heat, and simmer until just tender. Drain and discard the onion, garlic, and bay leaf. Transfer the lentils to a large bowl, and add the oil while the lentils are still hot. Let cool.

To assemble the salad: Add the bacon, chopped onion, parsley, and garlic to the cooled lentils and toss well. Stir in the vinegar, pepper, and Tabasco, and more oil, if needed. This salad improves if it is allowed to stand for an hour or so. Garnish with the scallions and more chopped parsley before serving.

BRETON BEANS

MAKES 6 TO 8 SERVINGS

This is the classic accompaniment to roast *gigot*, or leg of lamb, prepared in the Breton style. When serving the beans with roast lamb, you may, if you like, stir 1 or 2 tablespoons of the pan juices from the roast into them. One pound of dried beans equals 6 cups cooked.

    1 pound (2 cups) dried white beans, preferably Great
        Northern
    1 medium yellow onion, stuck with 2 whole cloves
    2 garlic cloves, peeled and left whole
    1 bay leaf
    Kosher salt and freshly ground black pepper
    ¼ cup tomato purée
    Chopped fresh flat-leaf parsley, for garnish

Put the beans in a deep saucepan and add water to cover. Bring to a boil; boil 2 minutes, then remove the pan from the heat and let the beans cool, covered, in the cooking water for 1 hour. Don't let the beans sit in the liquid for longer than 1 hour or they will become too soft. Cook them soon after they have cooled.

After 1 hour, if needed, add some more cold water to cover, the onion, garlic, bay leaf, and 2 teaspoons salt. Bring to a boil, then reduce the heat until the liquid is simmering; cover the pan and simmer for 45 minutes. Then add the tomato purée (don't add it until the beans have had this cooking time, as the acidity of the tomato may harden them). Continue to cook until just tender, another 20 to 30 minutes, checking for tenderness now and then. The beans should be tender when bitten, but not soft, mushy, or broken. During the cooking, check the pan to see that the liquid is simmering, not boiling, as this would break up the beans. If they seem to be getting too dry, add a little more water.

When the beans are cooked, taste them, add more salt if needed, and pepper to taste. Drain the beans and discard the onion and bay leaf. Just before serving, garnish them with a sprinkling of chopped parsley.

VARIATION

WHITE BEAN SALAD: Follow the directions for cooking the beans, but do not add the tomato purée. Drain and cool. Put the beans in a bowl with 1 cup finely chopped scallions (green and white parts), and ¼ cup finely chopped fresh flat-leaf parsley. Add 1 cup Basic Vinaigrette Sauce (page 359) and toss well. Allow to stand 1 to 2 hours before serving to mellow the flavors. If desired, the salad may be garnished with rings of thinly sliced red onion and additional chopped parsley.

NEVADA CHILI BEANS

∽ MAKES 8 SERVINGS

This spicy Southwestern dish is made with the pale pink, brown-speckled pinto beans common to the Western states and Mexico (they were dubbed "pinto," Spanish for "paint," because of the coloring). Pinto beans grow in a very dry climate and so they take longer to cook than some of the other dried legumes. They may be substituted in bean casseroles in place of white beans or red kidney beans. Serve with old-fashioned soda crackers or tortillas and beer.

1 pound (2 cups) dried pinto beans

¼ pound salt pork, rind removed, cut in small pieces

2 cups chopped yellow onion

3 garlic cloves, finely chopped

2 cups tomato purée

3 tablespoons chili powder

½ teaspoon dried oregano

A healthy pinch of ground cumin

Kosher salt and freshly ground black pepper

Put the beans in a large saucepan, cover with water, bring to a boil, boil 2 minutes, remove from the heat, and let stand, covered, for 1 hour. Add more water, if needed. Return to the heat and simmer very slowly until they are not quite cooked, still a bit bitey, 1 to 1½ hours.

Cook the salt pork in a large skillet until the fat is rendered and the pork is crisp. Add the onion and garlic and sauté until soft. Add the tomato purée, chili powder, oregano, and cumin. Season with salt and pepper and bring to a boil. Add the beans with their liquid, reduce the heat, and simmer for 45 minutes. Taste for seasoning, adding more chili powder or salt if you want it spicier or saltier.

VARIATION

COWPUNCHER BEANS: Add 1 pound cooked and diced pork and 1 pound cooked and diced beef to the finished dish. [*Editor: This is especially good made with leftover barbecued meats.*]

WHITE BEANS WITH COGNAC

∽ MAKES 6 SERVINGS

Editor: Serve this as an accompaniment to roast pork or lamb. Or augment with ham and sausages for a main course.

For the Beans

1 pound (2 cups) dried white beans (pea, navy, or Great Northern)

1 medium yellow onion, stuck with 2 whole cloves

1 garlic clove, peeled and left whole

1 sprig fresh thyme or ¼ teaspoon dried thyme

1 bay leaf

4 tablespoons (½ stick) unsalted butter

1 small yellow onion, chopped

2 cups tomato purée

⅓ cup Cognac

¼ cup finely chopped fresh flat-leaf parsley

2 teaspoons kosher salt

To prepare the beans: Put the beans in a saucepan, cover with cold water, bring to a boil, and cook 2 minutes. Remove from the heat and let stand, covered, for 1 hour. Add the clove-studded onion, garlic, thyme, and bay leaf. Bring to a boil, cover, reduce the heat, and simmer until tender, about 2 hours. Strain, reserving 1 cup of the cooking liquid. Discard the onion, bay leaf, and thyme sprig (the garlic will have disintegrated).

Melt the butter in a large skillet and sauté the chopped onion until soft. Add the reserved cooking liquid, tomato purée, Cognac, parsley, and salt. Simmer 30 minutes, then mix with the beans, correct the seasoning, and reheat over low heat in a heatproof casserole suitable for serving.

VARIATION

WHITE BEANS WITH HAM AND SAUSAGE: Serve this as a hearty main dish. Add 1 cup diced cooked ham and 1 pound cooked sausages to the beans and sauce. Correct the seasoning. Bake in a casserole in a preheated 325°F oven until just bubbling. [*Editor: Use smoked, fully cooked sausages, such as kielbasa, andouille, knackwurst, or bockwurst, either left whole or cut into thick slices.*]

YEAST
AND
QUICK
BREADS

YEAST AND QUICK BREADS

BASIC WHITE BREAD

This is my idea of a good, simple loaf of bread—firm, honest in flavor, tender to the bite yet with a slight chewiness in the crust. It is also excellent for toast. Once you have mastered the procedures given here, you can go on to more complex recipes without difficulty.

There are many variables in bread making. As far as flours are concerned, for example, hard-wheat flour produces the best results in wheat breads but it is not always easy to find, so we'll use a common, unbleached (or bleached) all-purpose flour. Compressed or cake yeast is also difficult to find and the active dry variety is everywhere, so we'll use that. (See below.) Water may be used for the liquid; the milk used in this recipe makes a richer bread. The amount of salt may be varied according to taste: my rule of thumb (for this kind of bread) is 1 tablespoon for each pound of flour [*Editor: About 3¼ cups*]. Even the weather has an effect on bread making. The degree

Flour and Yeast

Editor: Beard's original bread recipes often call for hard-wheat, soft-wheat, or all-purpose flours. The type of wheat milled to make flour (hard or soft) is directly related to the amount of protein in the dough. When flour is moistened, the proteins form gluten; high-protein flour makes a dough with a high gluten content. The gluten content affects the texture of the finished baked product. Generally, high-gluten dough results in a chewy, firm texture, and low-gluten dough bakes into a tender crumb.

***Hard-wheat flour** is no longer hard to find, and is sold in every supermarket as bread flour. Its high protein content means it's ideal for yeast bread, whose dough must be strong enough to stand up to kneading. Unbleached flour has fairly high protein content, and although it is sometimes labeled all-purpose, it, too, is really best for yeast breads.* **All-purpose flour** *is a blend of soft- and hard-wheat flours, and is usually chemically bleached to prolong its shelf life. This flour is used for many*

cakes, cookies, and general cooking chores such as coating meat before cooking. **Soft-wheat flour** *is a specialty of Southern mills (see headnote, page 278), and some bakers prefer it for biscuits and pastries where tenderness is important. (The Beard family and their Chinese cooks in Oregon made fine biscuits with Western all-purpose flour.) Cake flour is the softest flour of all, and many cooks use it to ensure cakes with a very tender crumb.*

***Compressed (cake) yeast** is still hard to find and is only manufactured and sold during the winter holiday and Easter seasons. It isn't worth the trouble to locate it. The original recipes often used an envelope of active dry yeast containing a tablespoon of product. Over the years, and thanks to improved processing practices, the current envelope holds 2¼ teaspoons with the same rising power as a tablespoon of the former yeast from Beard's time. The recipes in this edition have been changed to use the modern yeast.*

of humidity and warmth will govern the absorption quality of the flour and the action of the yeast.

One ¼-ounce envelope (2¼ teaspoons) active
    dry yeast
¼ cup warm (110° to 115°F) water
2 teaspoons sugar
1 cup whole milk
1 tablespoon plain salt
3 tablespoons unsalted butter
3¾ cups unbleached or all-purpose flour,
    as needed
Softened butter, for the bowl

For the Egg Wash
1 large egg white
1 tablespoon cold water

To make the bread: In a small bowl mix the yeast and ¼ cup warm water; add the sugar, stir well, and set aside until proofed. It is proofed when fermentation is apparent: the mixture will swell and small bubbles will appear on the surface. (If it doesn't proof at all, it means that the yeast is not fresh). [*Editor: This usually takes 5 to 10 minutes.*]

Meanwhile, heat the milk with the salt in a small saucepan and stir in the butter until it melts. Set aside to cool until it is no warmer than the yeast mixture. Put 2 cups of the flour in a large mixing bowl and stir in the milk mixture. Beat well with a wooden spatula, add the yeast mixture, and continue beating the dough until it is smooth, adding an additional cup of flour to make a firm dough. Turn the dough out onto a floured work surface and begin the kneading process, which evenly distributes the fermenting yeast cells through the dough.

Knead for about 10 minutes, kneading in additional flour as necessary, until the dough is smooth and no longer sticky, and blisters form on the surface. There are several kneading methods, but the basic one is to flour the dough and your hand lightly, then push the heel of your hand down into the dough and away from you. Fold the dough over, give it a quarter-turn, and push down again. Repeat pushing, folding, and turning until the motion becomes rhythmic. If you have a heavy-duty stand mixer with a dough-hook attachment, knead the dough with the hook and finish it off on the board. To test whether the dough has been kneaded enough, make an indentation in it with your fingers; it should spring back. If blisters form on the surface of the dough and break, this is another sign that the kneading is sufficient.

Butter a large bowl, transfer the dough to it, and turn the dough in the bowl until the dough is well coated with butter on all sides. Cover the dough with a dish towel and let it rise in a warm, draft-free place for 1 to 1½ hours, until it has doubled in bulk. To test further if the dough has risen properly, make an indentation in it with two fingers: if the dough does not spring back, then it is ready.

Butter a 9 by 5 by 3-inch loaf pan, or two pans that are about 8 by 4 by 2½ inches. Punch the dough down with your fist to deflate it; transfer it to a floured board and knead well for about 3 minutes. Pat it into a smooth round or oval shape and let it rest for 4 to 5 minutes. Then form into 1 large or 2 small loaves, by shaping the dough into an oval the length of your bread pan, then gently stretching, rounding, and plumping it in the palms of your hands, tucking the edges underneath and pinching them together. Lift carefully; drop the dough into the pan or pans and smooth out. Cover the dough with a towel and let it rise again in a warm, draft-free place for about 45 minutes to 1 hour, until it has doubled in bulk.

Preheat the oven to 400°F. To make the egg wash: In a small bowl, whisk the egg white and water together. Uncover the loaf or loaves, and lightly brush some of the egg wash over the top of the dough. Bake in the center of the oven for 20 minutes; reduce the heat to 350°F and bake for 20 to 25 minutes longer, until the crust is well browned and the bread sounds hollow when removed from the pan and tapped on the bottom with the knuckles.

HOMEMADE WHOLE-WHEAT BREAD

∽ MAKES 1 LARGE LOAF

Editor: With these hearty loaves, Beard uses the professional technique of baking the bread in a steamy oven to create a thick and chewy crust.

Two ¼-ounce envelopes (4½ teaspoons) active
    dry yeast
1 teaspoon sugar
1½ cups warm (110° to 115°F) water
2 cups graham flour
1 tablespoon plain salt
2½ cups unbleached flour, as needed
Vegetable oil, for the bowl
Yellow cornmeal, for the baking sheets

Combine the yeast and sugar in the warm water in a large bowl. Let stand 5 minutes and stir to dissolve. Stir in the whole-wheat flour a cup at a time, then the salt. Add enough unbleached flour to make a stiff dough. Turn out onto a floured board and knead, adding more unbleached flour as necessary, until the dough is smooth but still sticky, about 10 minutes. Shape into a ball, put in a large oiled bowl, and turn to coat the dough with oil. Cover with plastic wrap and let stand in a warm spot to rise until it has doubled in bulk, about 1½ hours.

Turn the dough out onto a floured board and shape it into a long French-style loaf with tapered ends, about 14 inches long. Arrange on a baking sheet heavily sprinkled with cornmeal. Cover loosely with plastic wrap and let rise for about 30 minutes, until almost doubled.

Uncover the loaf. Using a serrated knife, cut 3 long, shallow diagonal slashes down the top of the loaf. Put the baking sheet on the center rack of a cold oven. Put a pan of boiling water on a rack in the lower third of the oven. Preheat the oven to 400°F and bake until crusty, about 40 minutes. Let cool on a wire rack.

Editor: Graham flour is coarse whole-wheat flour that is stone-ground from the entire wheat kernel. With typical whole-wheat flour, the germ (kernel exterior) and endosperm (kernel exterior) are separately processed, and then mixed together. Bob's Red Mill and Hodgson Mill's are good supermarket brands of graham flour.

RAISIN BREAD

MAKES 2 LOAVES

Editor: There are few aromas more enticing than that of raisin bread toasting in the morning. This recipe makes two loaves, so plan to freeze one or give it away to a deserving friend.

1½ cups golden raisins

¾ cup dry sherry or Cognac (optional)

One ¼-ounce envelope (2¼ teaspoons) active dry yeast

2 cups warm (110° to 115°F) whole milk

⅓ cup sugar

6 tablespoons (¾ stick) unsalted butter,
   3 tablespoons at room temperature and
   3 tablespoons melted, plus more for the bowl

1 tablespoon plain salt

5½ cups unbleached flour, as needed

2 teaspoons freshly grated orange zest

½ teaspoon ground mace

Softened butter, for the pans

For the Egg Wash

1 large egg yolk

2 tablespoons heavy cream

Plump the raisins overnight in a bowl with the sherry.

In a large bowl, add the yeast to ¼ cup of the milk, let stand 5 minutes, and stir to dissolve. Add the remaining 1¾ cups of milk, the sugar, the room-temperature butter, and salt. Gradually stir in enough flour to make a stiff dough. Turn out onto a floured work surface and knead for about 10 minutes, until smooth, elastic, and glossy. Clean the bowl, butter it well, return the dough to it, and turn to coat the surface with butter. Cover with plastic wrap and set in a warm, draft-free spot to rise until it has doubled in bulk—1½ to 2 hours.

Punch down the dough and knead for 3 minutes. Return it to the bowl and let rise again for 30 minutes. Divide the dough in half. Working with one half at a time, roll out each piece into a rectangle 7 by 20 inches. Brush with half of the melted butter. Drain the raisins well and mix with the orange zest and mace in a bowl. Sprinkle half over the dough and roll up tightly, tucking the ends under. Fit the roll, seam side down, in a well-buttered 8 by 4 by 2½-inch loaf pan. Repeat with the remaining dough, melted butter, and raisins. Cover the loaves with plastic wrap and let rise in a warm, draft-free spot until the dough just shows above the tops of the pans, approximately 45 minutes.

Preheat the oven to 400°F. In a small bowl, mix the egg yolk and cream together to make the egg wash. Uncover the loaves and brush lightly with some of the egg wash. Bake in the preheated oven for 10 minutes. Reduce the oven temperature to 350°F and continue baking for 20 to 30 minutes, or until the loaves sound hollow when tapped on the top and bottom. If necessary, return the loaves to the oven rack without their pans to brown the bottom crusts. Let cool completely on wire racks.

DARK RYE BREAD

✑ MAKES 1 LOAF

Editor: Make this bread when you want something extra-special for meat sandwiches.

½ cup warm (110° to 115°F) water

One ¼-ounce envelope (2¼ teaspoons) active dry yeast

1 teaspoon sugar

¾ cup warm (110° to 115°F) milk

¼ cup molasses (not unsulfured)

1 tablespoon unsalted butter, melted

1 tablespoon caraway seeds (optional)

1 teaspoon plain salt

2 cups all-purpose flour, as needed

1½ cups rye flour

Softened butter or vegetable oil, for the bowl

Ice water, for brushing the loaf

Pour the warm water into a large bowl; add the yeast and sugar; let stand 5 minutes and stir until dissolved. Cover with plastic wrap and set aside until the mixture has swelled slightly and has surface bubbles, about 5 minutes.

Blend in the milk, molasses, butter, caraway seeds, if using, and the salt. Stir in 1 cup all-purpose flour, ½ cup at a time. Next, stir in all the rye flour, ½ cup at a time. Then beat vigorously until the dough is smooth and elastic. Stir in most of remaining all-purpose flour to make a stiff dough.

Turn the dough out onto a heavily floured board. Knead until dough is not sticky, but smooth and satiny, 8 to 10 minutes. Add more flour while kneading, if necessary. [*Editor: The dough should not stick to the board, but it will feel tacky.*] Put the dough in a greased bowl; grease the top of the dough lightly. Cover the bowl with plastic wrap and set in warm place to rise until it has almost doubled in bulk (1½ to 2 hours).

Punch down the dough, turn out onto a lightly floured board, knead slightly, and form into a loaf.

Put the loaf into a greased 9 by 5 by 3-inch bread pan. Cover with plastic wrap and let rise in a warm, draft-free place until almost doubled in bulk (about 1 hour). Preheat the oven to 425°F. Uncover the bread. Bake in the preheated oven at 425°F for 10 minutes. Brush with ice water, lower the oven temperature to 350°F, and continue baking for 40 to 45 minutes until the bread has turned almost a mahogany color on top. Turn the loaf out of the pan and let cool on a wire rack. If you want the bread very crusty, put the loaf directly on the rack of the oven and let it cool in the turned-off oven.

BLACK BREAD

༄ MAKES 2 LOAVES

There are numerous varieties of what is known as "black bread." I tried out recipes for a great many and finally settled on this one, which is not as dark as the commercial ones but has a flavor that I think is extraordinarily good and a very nice texture. It is rather fun to make, too, and even if you don't achieve the perfect look that one finds in the professional loaves of this kind, the recipe works very well. Thinly sliced, it is a delicious bread with seafood, and it makes extremely good sandwiches. It will hold well if wrapped in plastic wrap and kept in the refrigerator. It has the advantage over many other black breads of not being too sweet.

1½ cups water

⅓ cup plus 1 tablespoon yellow cornmeal

2 tablespoons plus 1 teaspoon light or dark
    brown sugar

1 tablespoon unsalted butter

1 tablespoon unsweetened cocoa powder

1 tablespoon instant coffee

1 tablespoon plain salt

1½ teaspoons caraway seeds

Two ¼-ounce envelopes (4½ teaspoons) active
    dry yeast

¼ cup warm (100° to 115°F) water, as needed

2 cups dark rye flour

2 cups unbleached flour, as needed

1 cup whole-wheat flour

Softened butter, for the bowl

For the Egg Wash
1 egg white
2 tablespoons water

Bring ¾ cup water to a boil in a medium saucepan. Stir the cornmeal into ¾ cup water in a medium bowl. Stir into the boiling water and cook, stirring constantly, until boiling and thickened. Remove from the heat and stir in the brown sugar, butter, cocoa powder, coffee, salt, and caraway seeds. Transfer to a large bowl and let cool.

Add the yeast to the warm water in a small bowl, let stand 5 minutes, and stir to dissolve. Add to the cornmeal mixture and stir well. Stir in the rye flour, 2 cups of unbleached flour, and the whole-wheat flour, adding more liquid if necessary, and stir until you have a fairly sticky dough. Turn out on a floured board and knead, adding more unbleached flour, if necessary, to make a firm, elastic dough. [*Editor: The dough will be tacky, so don't add too much flour.*] Form into a ball and place in a well-buttered bowl, turning to coat with butter on all sides. Cover with plastic wrap. Put in a warm, draft-free spot to rise until doubled in bulk, about 1½ hours.

Punch down the dough and knead for 2 or 3 minutes. Shape into two loaves and fit into two 8 by 4 by 2½-inch bread pans and cover with plastic wrap. Let the loaves rise until almost doubled in bulk, about 45 minutes.

To make the egg wash: In a small bowl, whisk together the egg white and water.

Preheat the oven to 375°F. Uncover the loaves and lightly brush the bread with some of the egg wash. Bake for 50 to 60 minutes, or until the bread bottom taps hollow. If you have doubts about whether it is done, let it bake longer. This loaf is better a little overdone than underdone.

ENGLISH MUFFIN BREAD

✐ 1 LARGE LOAF OR 2 SMALLER LOAVES

As its name suggests, this bread is derived from English muffin batter. Large-grained, with a fairly coarse crumb, it is excellent when sliced and toasted, otherwise, it is rather uninteresting. It may be baked in one large loaf pan, which gives deep slices, or in two small ones.

½ cup warm (100° to 115°F) water

1 tablespoon sugar

One ¼-ounce envelope (2¼ teaspoons) active
    dry yeast

2½ cups unbleached flour

2 teaspoons plain salt

¾ cup plus 2 tablespoons lukewarm whole milk

¼ teaspoon baking soda dissolved in 1 tablespoon
    warm tap water

Combine the warm water, sugar, and yeast in a large bowl. Let stand until the yeast softens, about 5 minutes, then stir to dissolve. Add the flour and salt with the warm milk in alternate portions while stirring vigorously with a wooden spoon. Holding the bowl tightly, beat the dough very hard until it shows some elasticity and looks almost ready to leave the sides of the bowl. (Unlike a kneaded dough, however, it will remain loose and sticky.) When it has an almost gummy quality, cover with plastic wrap and let rise in a warm place for about 1¼ to 1½ hours until doubled in bulk. Stir down with a wooden spoon, add the dissolved soda, and beat vigorously again for about 1 minute, being careful to distribute the soda thoroughly, or else the bread will be streaked. Then butter one 9 by 5 by 3-inch loaf pan or two 8 by 4 by 2½-inch pans and fill with the dough, using a rubber spatula to scrape it from the bowl.

Cover and let rise again in a warm place for about 1 to 1¼ hours. Preheat the oven to 375°F. Uncover the pan(s). Bake for 40 to 50 minutes, until it is golden on top and shrinks slightly from the sides of the pan. [*Editor: The smaller loaves will take less time to bake.*] Cool in the pans for about 5 minutes, then turn out onto a wire rack to cool completely. (If necessary, loosen from edges of the pans with a knife.) Cut into slices about ½ inch thick, toast, and butter well.

BRIOCHE BREAD

3½ teaspoons active dry yeast

2 tablespoons sugar

½ cup warm (110° to 115°F) water

1 cup (2 sticks) unsalted butter, melted and cooled
   to tepid

1½ teaspoons plain salt

4 cups unbleached flour

4 large eggs, beaten

Softened butter, for the bowl

For the Egg Wash

1 egg yolk

¼ cup evaporated milk or light cream

Combine the yeast and sugar with the warm water in a small bowl and allow to proof for about 5 minutes; stir to dissolve the yeast. Mix the melted butter and salt together in another bowl. In a large bowl, combine the flour, melted butter mixture, eggs, and the yeast mixture. Beat with your hand until smooth. [*Editor: A sturdy wooden spoon works just as well.*] Place in a buttered bowl, turning the dough to butter its surface, cover with plastic wrap, and set in a warm, draft-free place until light and doubled in bulk, about 1 to 1½ hours.

Punch the dough down and shape into two loaves. Fit into two buttered 8 by 4 by 2-inch loaf pans and let rise again in a warm place until doubled in bulk, about 1 hour. Mix together the yolk and milk, and brush the loaves with the egg yolk–milk wash. Bake at 400°F for 30 minutes, until the loaves are a deep golden brown and sound hollow when tapped with the knuckles. Cool on a rack.

PISSALADIÈRE

MAKES 8 TO 12 APPETIZER SERVINGS

This is one form of the Provençal version of pizza. It calls for tomatoes, puréed onions, anchovies, and ripe olives and is baked using brioche dough or a plain white bread dough. I prefer the brioche. It makes an attractive, delicious hors d'oeuvre or luncheon dish. I used to buy it in a bakery in St.-Rémy in Provence, where I lived several summers, and found it much to my liking, as I am sure you will.

1 recipe brioche dough (see opposite)

3½ teaspoons active dry yeast

2 tablespoons sugar

½ cup warm (110° to 115°F) water

1 cup (2 sticks) unsalted butter, melted and cooled
   to tepid

1½ teaspoons plain salt

4 cups unbleached flour

4 large eggs, beaten

Softened butter, for the bowl

For the Filling

6 large ripe tomatoes or one 16-ounce can Italian
   plum tomatoes

2 tablespoons tomato paste (optional)

Olive oil, as needed

1 or 2 garlic cloves, crushed under a knife
   and peeled

3 tablespoons unsalted butter

3 medium yellow onions, chopped

Softened butter, for brushing the dough

½ cup freshly grated Parmesan cheese

½ teaspoon crushed dried rosemary

About 30 anchovy fillets in oil, drained, as needed

About 30 pitted Kalamata or Gaeta olives

Olive oil, for the olives

Make the brioche according to the directions on page 276.

While the dough is rising, prepare the filling: Peel, seed, and cut the tomatoes in very small pieces (or, if using canned tomatoes, drain, seed, and chop). Heat 2 tablespoons olive oil in a skillet, add the tomatoes and garlic (and if using canned tomatoes, the tomato paste), and let them reduce over medium heat, stirring occasionally, until broken down and thickened into a sauce, about 20 minutes. In another skillet, melt the butter over low heat. Add the onions, cover, and cook, stirring occasionally, until they form a rather thick golden purée, about 20 minutes.

When the brioche has risen, punch the dough down. Roll the dough out to about ⅜ inch in thickness and line two 9-inch-square cake pans or one 12-inch tart pan. Brush with softened butter, cover with plastic wrap, and put in a warm place to rise slightly, about 20 minutes.

Preheat the oven to 375°F. Uncover the pan(s). Sprinkle the brioche shell(s) with the Parmesan. Spread the onions over the brioche dough, and sprinkle with the rosemary. Cover with the tomato purée. Arrange the anchovies in a lattice pattern on the tomatoes, and place an olive in the center of each opening in the lattice. Brush the olives with a little olive oil. Bake for 25 to 30 minutes until the crust is golden and baked through. Brush the top with more olive oil before serving hot.

CRUMPETS

MAKES 8 TO 10 CRUMPETS

Crumpets, which once could be found all over England and in many places in New York City, have become less and less available. They are flat, about ½ inch thick, and very porous. When toasted, they will absorb vast quantities of butter. Served with raspberry or strawberry jam and Devonshire cream, they are about as habit-forming as any teatime specialty can be.

½ cup whole milk

½ cup boiling water

One ¼-ounce package (2¼ teaspoons) active dry yeast

1 teaspoon sugar

1¾ cups unbleached flour

1½ teaspoons plain salt

¼ cup plus 2 tablespoons warm (110° to 115°F) water

¼ teaspoon baking soda, dissolved in 1 tablespoon water

Unsalted butter, for serving

Combine the milk and boiling water in a medium bowl and cool to lukewarm. Add the yeast and sugar, let stand for 5 minutes, and stir to dissolve the yeast. Sift the flour and salt together. Add to the milk mixture with the warm water to make a batter. Stir several minutes with a wooden spoon. Cover with plastic wrap and let the batter rise in a warm place until almost doubled in bulk and rather bubbly. Stir in the dissolved soda. Cover again and let rise again until doubled in bulk.

Butter four 3½-inch diameter crumpet rings. Place the rings on a moderately hot griddle. Spoon the batter into each ring to a depth of about ½ inch. Cook until the crumpets are dry and bubbly on top. Remove the rings, turn the crumpets, and brown lightly on the other side. Transfer to a wire rack. Repeat with the remaining batter. Let cool. To serve, toast and flood with butter.

Editor: You can purchase crumpet rings at kitchenware shops and online at www.amazon.com or www.kingarthurflour.com. In the past, home cooks would craft rings from tuna cans and the like, but the cans are not the correct size anymore, and it is better to buy the rings.

HARD ROLLS

〰 MAKES 2 DOZEN ROLLS

Editor: A few brushings of ice-cold salt water gives these rolls their shiny, crisp crust. Two choices for soft-wheat flour include White Lily Unbleached Flour (www.whitelily.com) and Bob's Red Mill Unbleached Pastry Flour (www.bobsredmill.com). Do not use whole wheat pastry flour. Imported Italian "00" flour, with various brands available at specialty food stores and online, is another option.

Two ¼-ounce envelopes (4½ teaspoons) active
   dry yeast
1 teaspoon sugar
2 cups warm (100° to 115°F) water
1 tablespoon kosher salt or 2 teaspoons plain salt
1 cup bread flour
4 cups soft-wheat flour, as needed

Vegetable oil, for the bowl
Yellow cornmeal, for the baking sheets

For the Glaze
⅔ cup ice water
1 tablespoon salt

Combine the yeast with the sugar and warm water in a large bowl and let stand until bubbly, about 5 minutes. Stir to dissolve the yeast. Mix the coarse salt with the hard-wheat flour and add to the yeast mixture. Stir in the soft-wheat flour, 1 cup at a time, until you have a firm dough. Transfer to a lightly floured board and knead about 10 minutes, adding soft-wheat flour as necessary, until no longer sticky. Place in an oiled bowl and turn to coat the surface of the dough. Cover with plastic wrap and let rise in a cool place for about 2 hours, or until doubled in bulk.

Punch down the dough. Turn out on a floured board and knead for about 2 minutes. Cut the dough into 24 equal pieces and form each into a ball. Place on 2 baking sheets that have been sprinkled with cornmeal. Slash the tops of the dough with a very sharp knife or single-edge razor blade. Cover each baking sheet with plastic wrap and let rise about 30 minutes, until doubled in size.

Preheat the oven to 400°F. Place four heat-proof baking cups filled with boiling water on the lowest rack of the oven. To make the glaze: In a small bowl, mix the ice water and salt together. Uncover the rolls. Bake the rolls on the center and upper third racks for 25 to 30 minutes, brushing the tops with the salted ice water every 5 minutes, until the rolls are nicely browed and sound hollow when tapped. Transfer to a wire rack to cool.

PITA BREAD

MAKES 8 OR 9 ROUND LOAVES

Pita bread is that flat, round, softish bread called, among other names, Syrian bread, Armenian bread, and Middle Eastern bread. Its two layers are almost separated in the baking, and one can split it very easily to use with shish kebabs and even with hamburgers, as well as all kinds of other sandwiches. It is also extremely good buttered, cut into strips, and baked in a slow oven to get quite crisp, to be served like Melba toast with soup or salads or cold fish dishes. It can be wrapped and stored in the refrigerator or frozen successfully.

The warm bread should be wrapped in aluminum foil to keep it soft after baking. Pita loaves are great fun to make.

Two 1/4-ounce envelopes (4 1/2 teaspoons) active
    dry yeast
1/2 teaspoon sugar
2 cups warm (100° to 115°F) water
1/4 cup olive oil, plus more for the bowl
1 1/2 tablespoons plain salt
6 cups bread flour, as needed
Yellow cornmeal, for the baking sheets

Dissolve the yeast and sugar in 1/2 cup of warm water in a large mixing bowl, let stand 5 minutes, and stir to dissolve. Then add the remaining 1 1/2 cups water. Stir in 1 cup of flour with the oil and salt. Vigorously stir in enough of flour to make a stiff, rather sticky, dough. Turn out on a floured board and knead, working in the remaining flour, as needed, for a good 10 minutes or more until the dough is smooth and elastic. Shape into a ball, place in an oiled bowl, and turn to coat with oil on all sides. Cover with plastic wrap and let rise in a warm, draft-free place for 1 1/2 to 2 hours, or until doubled in bulk.

Punch down the dough, turn out on a floured board, cover again, and allow to rest for 10 minutes. Divide into 8 or 9 equal pieces and shape each piece into a ball. Cover the balls with plastic wrap and let rest for 30 minutes. Flatten each ball with a well-floured rolling pin and roll into 8-inch circles with a thickness of about 1/8 inch. Dust two baking sheets with cornmeal, place 2 circles on each sheet, cover, and let rest again for 30 minutes. (Leave the remaining circles on a lightly floured working surface and transfer them to the baking sheets, dusted again with cornmeal, when the first 4 are baked.)

Preheat the oven to 500°F. Uncover the baking sheets. Put one of the baking sheets on the lowest rack of the oven for 5 minutes. *Do not open the oven door until the 5 minutes are up!* Transfer the sheet to a higher shelf and continue baking 3 to 5 minutes longer until the loaves are puffed like balloons and just very lightly browned. Repeat the procedure with the second baking sheet, unless, of course, you have a large oven so that the baking sheets can go in side by side on the same shelf (or use two ovens, if you are fortunate enough to have two). The loaves should deflate on cooling. After cooling, the pita can be wrapped in aluminum foil and frozen. The loaves will reheat in a 350°F oven in 10 to 15 minutes.

YEASTED CARROT BREAD

◇◇ MAKES 2 SMALL LOAVES

Editor: Note that this is a yeasted bread, and not the typical sweet carrot quick bread.

One 1/4-ounce package (2 1/4 teaspoons) dry yeast

1 teaspoon sugar

3/4 cup warm (110° to 115°F) water

1 1/2 cups grated carrot

1/2 cup vegetable oil

1/2 cup sugar

1 large egg, beaten

1 teaspoon plain salt

3 1/2 cups unbleached flour

1 cup graham flour (see Editor's Note, page 272)

1 teaspoon ground cinnamon

1/2 teaspoon freshly grated nutmeg

1/4 cup chopped candied orange and/or lemon peels

1/4 cup seedless raisins

Softened butter, for the bowl

For the Topping

1 tablespoon honey

1 tablespoon water

Cracked sunflower seeds

Dissolve the yeast with the sugar in the warm water and let stand until bubbling, about 5 minutes. In a large mixing bowl, combine the carrot, oil, sugar, egg, and salt. Add the yeast mixture. Add the unbleached flour and the graham flour, cinnamon, nutmeg, candied citrus peels, and raisins, and mix well.

Turn out onto a floured work surface and knead, adding more flour as needed, to make a soft, smooth dough. Shape into a ball, put into a buttered large bowl, and turn to coat the dough evenly with the butter. Cover the dough with plastic wrap and let it rise in a warm place until doubled in bulk, about 1 1/4 hours. Punch the dough down, cover, then let it rest for 10 minutes.

Preheat the oven to 400°F. Turn the dough out onto a lightly floured work surface and form into 2 loaves. Put the loaves into two 8 by 4 by 2 1/2-inch loaf pans. To make the topping: Mix the honey and water together in a small bowl. Lightly brush the tops of the loaves with some of the honey mixture, and sprinkle with the sunflower seeds. Let the loaves rise in the pans for 10 minutes. Bake for 15 minutes, then lower the heat to 375°F and bake for 40 to 50 minutes until the loaves sound hollow when tapped on the bottoms.

MONKEY BREAD

◇◇ 1 RING LOAF

This is a sensationally good and oddly textured sweet bread or coffee cake. It has been known as monkey bread for as long as I can remember. I have never seen an explanation for the name; perhaps it has stuck because of the bread's silly shape. I have also heard it called bubble bread. It is made in a tube pan, and if you follow directions carefully you will have a very light finished product that can be cooled and sliced or served warm and pulled apart in little clumps. You must, however, take special care in the baking to see that it is thoroughly cooked before it comes out of the oven.

> Two ¼-ounce packages (4½ teaspoons) active
>   dry yeast
> 1 cup granulated sugar
> ½ cup warm (110° to 115°F) water
> 1 cup (2 sticks) unsalted butter, plus more for the
>   bowl and the pan, at room temperature
> 1 tablespoon plus 1½ teaspoons kosher salt
> 1 cup warm (110° to 115°F) whole milk
> 3 large eggs, plus 2 large egg yolks
> 6 cups unbleached flour, plus more as needed
> ½ cup dried currants, soaked in hot water for 1 hour,
>   then drained and patted dry
> ½ cup packed light brown sugar

Combine the yeast, granulated sugar, and water in a large mixing bowl. While this is proofing, stir ½ cup (1 stick) of the butter and the salt into the warm milk. (The butter does not need to melt completely.) Stir the yeast mixture to dissolve the yeast, then add the milk mixture. Stir in the eggs and yolks. Beat with a wooden spoon to blend thoroughly. Add the flour, 1 cup at a time, stirring well after each addition. (After the first 5 cups it will get harder to incorporate the flour and the dough will be very sticky.) Turn out on a floured board, and using a dough scraper or large spatula, scrape under the flour on the board, lift the dough, and fold it over. Continue this procedure, adding more flour until the dough is no longer sticky and can be kneaded with your hands. Knead a full 10 minutes, until the dough is elastic and pliable.

Shape into a ball and put in a buttered bowl,

turning to coat all over with butter. Cover with plastic wrap and set in a warm, draft-free place to rise until doubled in bulk, about 1½ hours. Meanwhile, soak the currants in a bowl with hot water to cover until plumped, about 1 hour. Drain well and pat dry with paper towels; set aside.

Punch the dough down and let rest for 5 minutes. Turn out on a lightly floured board (using about 1 tablespoon flour) and again shape into a ball. Cover with plastic wrap and let rest for another 5 to 10 minutes.

Meanwhile, butter a 10-inch tube pan. [*Editor: If your tube pan has a removable bottom, wrap the bottom of the pan with aluminum foil to avoid leakage.*] In a saucepan, melt the second stick of butter with the brown sugar and drained currants; let cool until tepid. Pinch off the dough to make golf ball–size balls. Roll the balls in the butter mixture, line the bottom of the tube pan with them, and continue to arrange them in loose layers. Pour what is left of the butter mixture over the top. Cover loosely with an aluminum foil tent and let the dough rise to the top of the tube pan, about 45 minutes.

Preheat the oven to 375°F. Bake the monkey bread, covered with the foil, for about an hour; it may take a minute or two more. Tap the top: it will sound hollow when the bread is ready. (If the top browns a little too much don't worry, because this will be served inverted.) Unmold and let cool thoroughly before slicing, or serve warm and pull apart.

MRS. MAYNARD'S CINNAMON ROLLS

∽ MAKES 12 ROLLS

If you make it by hand, it is wise to begin the kneading with the aid of a dough scraper, which looks something like a paint spatula, until you have a slightly firm dough.

For the Dough

Three ¼-ounce packages (6¾ teaspoons) active
   dry yeast
½ cup plus 2 teaspoons granulated sugar
1 cup warm (110° to 115°F) water
8 tablespoons (1 stick) unsalted butter, at room
   temperature
2 teaspoons plain salt
3 large eggs, beaten
3 cups all-purpose flour, as needed, plus more for
   rolling the dough

For the Filling

1 cup golden raisins
¼ cup dark or golden rum
3 tablespoons granulated sugar
1 tablespoon ground cinnamon
3 tablespoons unsalted butter, melted
½ cup chopped pecans
Softened butter, for the baking sheet

For the Icing

1 cup confectioners' sugar
1 to 2 tablespoons water

To make the dough: Dissolve the yeast and the 2 teaspoons granulated sugar in the warm water in a small bowl. Let stand for 5 minutes, then stir to dissolve.

Using an electric stand mixer, cream together thoroughly the softened butter, the remaining ½ cup granulated sugar, and salt for 2 minutes. Gradually beat in the eggs. Add the yeast mixture and blend well. Stir in enough flour, mixing it in thoroughly, so that the dough is soft and tacky, but not sticky. Cover the bowl with a kitchen towel, put it in a warm place, and let the dough rise until double in bulk, about 1½ hours.

Meanwhile, make the filling: In a small bowl, soak the raisins in the rum. Mix the granulated sugar and cinnamon in another bowl. Set both aside while the dough is rising.

Punch the dough down. Roll on a lightly floured board into an 18-inch-long rectangle about ¼ inch thick. Spread with the melted butter and sprinkle with the cinnamon-sugar mixture. Drain the raisins, distribute them evenly over the top, and sprinkle with the chopped pecans. Roll up the rectangle lengthwise so that you end up with a long cylinder, and pinch the long seam closed. Cut the cylinder into 1½-inch slices and place them on a buttered cookie sheet, not touching. Cover with a kitchen towel and let rise again for 30 minutes. Preheat the oven to 350°F. Bake the rolls for 20 to 30 minutes, or until they are nicely browned.

To make the icing: Mix the confectioners' sugar and water into a thick paste in a bowl. Spread on top of the hot rolls. Serve warm or cooled.

CORNBREAD

MAKES 6 SERVINGS

There are innumerable recipes for corn bread, which is leavened by baking powder. This one, which is very moist and rich, happens to be my favorite.

Softened butter, for the pan
1½ cups yellow cornmeal
½ cup all-purpose flour
1 tablespoon baking powder
1 teaspoon sugar
1 teaspoon plain salt
1 cup whole milk
3 large eggs, well beaten
¼ cup heavy cream
5 tablespoons (½ stick plus 1 tablespoon) unsalted butter, melted

Preheat the oven to 400°F. Butter an 11 by 8½-inch baking pan. Sift the cornmeal, flour, baking powder, sugar, and salt together in a large bowl, to mix the ingredients thoroughly and distribute the baking powder evenly. Beat in the milk and eggs with a wooden spoon until well mixed. Beat in the cream and, lastly, the melted butter. Pour into the buttered pan and bake for 18 to 20 minutes, until risen and golden brown. While still hot, cut into squares and serve wrapped in a napkin.

HELEN EVANS BROWN'S CORN CHILI BREAD

9 TO 10 SERVINGS

The late Helen Evans Brown was a specialist in California's traditional foods. This recipe of hers is an extremely moist, rich bread that is delicious with plenty of butter. It can be served with such things as roast pork or a roast turkey or even with a good stew. It is one of my oldest bread recipes, and one of my very favorites. As a matter of fact, I have often served it for large parties, doubling the recipe, which is very simple.

3 ears of corn, husks and silks removed
1 cup yellow cornmeal
1 cup sour cream
12 tablespoons (1½ sticks) unsalted butter, melted, plus more for serving
2 large eggs, well beaten
1 tablespoon baking powder
2 teaspoons plain salt
1 cup very finely diced Gruyère or Monterey Jack cheese
One 4-ounce can diced green chilies, drained

Preheat the oven to 350°F. Scrape the kernels from the corn cobs. Put in a large bowl. Add the cornmeal, sour cream, melted butter, eggs, baking powder, and salt and stir to combine. Fold in the cheese and chilies. Pour into a well-buttered 9-inch square baking dish or 2½-quart soufflé dish. Bake for 1 hour. Serve with melted butter.

CLAY'S CORNSTICKS

Cornsticks are different in their way from cornbread. They are baked in a mold shaped like a row of corn ears. The mold is heated as hot as possible after you have greased it with bacon fat, goose grease, or homemade lard, which will give a good flavor and won't burn the way butter will. The cornsticks usually bake to a golden color and are puffy inside and deliciously crunchy on the outside. For a variation, add 2 tablespoons of fresh grated corn.

This recipe will make about 14 sticks. Most cornstick molds make 7 or 8, so you can bake one batch, quickly regrease the mold, and bake another batch during the meal. Before using a new mold it is wise to follow the rules for curing it, generally given on the label. Then try these very good, simple-to-make cornsticks.

"Clay" is Clayton Triplette, who has been my assistant and housekeeper for many years, and who is no mean cook himself.

1 cup yellow cornmeal, preferably stone ground

1 cup all-purpose flour

1 tablespoon baking powder

½ teaspoon plain salt

1 cup whole milk or buttermilk

2 large eggs, beaten

2 tablespoons unsalted butter, melted

Rendered bacon or pork fat, lard, or vegetable shortening, for the molds

Preheat the oven to 400°F. Sift the cornmeal, flour, baking powder, and salt together into a medium bowl. Stir in the milk, eggs, and melted butter to make a light batter. Generously grease the mold with the fat and heat in the preheated oven until very hot. Spoon the batter into the molds, filling them three-quarters full. Bake at 400°F for 18 to 20 minutes until the cornsticks are brown and puffy. Remove at once, regrease the mold, and refill with the remaining batter. Serve the cornsticks hot with plenty of butter.

Editor: If you want to serve all of the cornsticks at once, keep the first batch warm by loosely wrapping in aluminum foil and returning to the oven with the second batch for the last few minutes of the baking time.

IRISH WHOLE-WHEAT SODA BREAD

Traditionally, soda bread is baked over a peat fire in a three-legged iron pot that can be raised or lowered over the fire in the old-fashioned way [*Editor: That is, with a chain*]. Soda bread is very different from any other bread you can find in the world. It's round, with a cross cut in the top, and it has a velvety texture, quite unlike yeast bread, and the most distinctive and delicious taste. Sliced paper thin and buttered, it is one of the best tea or breakfast breads I know, and it makes wonderful toast for any meal.

3 cups whole-wheat flour

1 cup all-purpose flour

1 tablespoon kosher salt or 2 teaspoons plain salt

1 teaspoon baking soda

¾ teaspoon baking powder

1½ to 2 cups buttermilk

Preheat the oven to 375°F. Combine the flours, salt, baking soda, and baking powder and mix thoroughly to distribute the soda and baking powder. Stir in enough buttermilk to make a soft dough, similar in texture to biscuit dough but firm enough to hold its shape. Knead on a lightly floured board for 2 or 3 minutes, until quite smooth and velvety. Form into a round loaf and place in a well-buttered 9-inch cake pan or on a well-buttered cookie sheet. Cut a cross on the top of the loaf with a very sharp, floured knife.

Bake for 35 to 40 minutes, until the loaf is nicely browned and sounds hollow when rapped with the knuckles. (The cross will have spread open, which is characteristic of soda bread.) Let the loaf cool before slicing very thinly; soda bread must never be cut thick.

VARIATION

WHITE SODA BREAD: Use 4 cups unbleached flour, and decrease the baking soda to ¾ teaspoon. Otherwise, the bread is prepared in exactly the same way as in the master recipe.

CREAM BISCUITS

ABOUT 10 BISCUITS

We had a reputation at home for very special biscuits, which were made by our Chinese cook, who was with us for many years. After he left us they became a standard item in our household, and I still make them very often. The secret of their unique quality is this: They use heavy cream instead of butter or shortening.

4 tablespoons (½ stick) unsalted butter

2 cups all-purpose flour

1 tablespoon baking powder

2 teaspoons sugar

1 teaspoon plain salt

¾ to 1 cup heavy cream

Softened butter, for the baking pan

Preheat the oven to 375°F. Melt the butter in a small saucepan, pour into a small bowl, set aside to cool until tepid. Sift the flour, baking powder, sugar, and salt together in a medium bowl. Fold in the cream until it makes a soft dough that can be easily handled. Turn out on a floured board, knead for about 1 minute, and then pat to a thickness of about ½ to ¾ inch. Cut in rounds or squares, dip in the butter, and arrange on a buttered baking sheet or in an oblong baking pan. Bake for 15 to 18 minutes until golden brown. Serve very hot.

Editor: If you cut the dough into rounds, gather up the scraps of dough, and gently knead them together. Pat out the dough and cut out more biscuits until all of the dough has been used. The biscuits made from the scrap dough will be a bit tougher because the gluten has been activated more than the first batch. Square biscuits have an advantage—there will not be any scraps.

GIRDLE SCONES

Among the breads baked on a griddle (the Scots insist on saying "girdle"), scones seem to run high in popularity. They are rather sour-flavored because of the buttermilk content, and their delicate texture makes them excellent when hot, split, buttered well, and spread with raspberry jam. Cold, they are best cut in half, toasted, and served swimming in butter. Exceptionally easy to make, they are apt to be a novelty to some people.

2 cups all-purpose flour, plus more for dipping

1 teaspoon cream of tartar

1 teaspoon baking soda

1 teaspoon granulated sugar

½ teaspoon plain salt

¾ cup buttermilk or sour cream, as needed

Sift the flour, cream of tartar, baking soda, sugar, and salt together. Combine it with enough buttermilk or sour cream to make a soft dough. Pat it with the hand on a floured board and form into a circle ½ inch thick. Cut into 8 equal wedges. Dip each wedge in flour. Cook on a heated griddle over medium heat until lightly browned. Turn to brown the other side. Serve hot or cold.

NUT RUM BREAD

Editor: This not-too-sweet quick bread would be a good holiday gift.

4 tablespoons (½ stick) unsalted butter, at room temperature, plus more for the pan

3 tablespoons light or dark brown sugar

2 large eggs, lightly beaten

1½ cups all-purpose flour

1½ cups whole-wheat flour

1 tablespoon baking powder

½ teaspoon plain salt

1¼ cups whole milk

½ cup dark rum

1 teaspoon vanilla extract

½ cup golden raisins

1 cup coarsely chopped walnuts

Preheat the oven to 375°F. Beat the butter and sugar with an electric mixer in a medium bowl until smooth, add the eggs, and beat well. Stir together the all-purpose and whole-wheat flours, baking powder, and salt. Add to the butter mixture, along with the milk, rum, and vanilla. Stir briefly to moisten the dry ingredients and stir in the raisins and walnuts. Spoon into a buttered 8½ by 4½ by 2½-inch loaf pan. Bake for 50 to 60 minutes until a straw comes out clean when inserted in the center. Cool in the pan for 10 minutes, then turn out onto a wire rack to cool.

CARL GOHS'S ZUCCHINI BREAD

MAKES 2 LOAVES

This rather unusual loaf has a very pleasant flavor, a little on the sweet side, and a distinctive texture. The built-in moisture provided by the zucchini makes it a very good keeper. If you wish, substitute 1 cup whole-wheat flour for an equal amount of all-purpose flour, or walnuts for the hazelnuts.

Editor: Beard explains: "Carl Gohs is a fellow Oregonian who has done much research on early foods, as well as on pioneer and Indian cooking."

3 large eggs, at room temperature

2 cups peeled and shredded zucchini

2 cups sugar

1 cup vegetable oil, plus more for the pans

1 tablespoon vanilla extract

3 cups all-purpose flour

1 tablespoon ground cinnamon

1 teaspoon baking soda

1 teaspoon plain salt

¼ teaspoon baking powder

1 cup toasted, skinned, and coarsely chopped hazelnuts

Preheat the oven to 350°F. Beat the eggs with an electric mixer in a large bowl until light and foamy. Add the zucchini, sugar, oil, and vanilla and mix lightly but well. Add the flour, cinnamon, baking soda, salt, and baking powder and stir well. Stir in the hazelnuts. Pour into two 9 by 5 by 3-inch oiled loaf pans. Bake for 1 hour. Cool in the pans on a wire cake rack for 10 minutes.

Turn out onto the rack, turn right sides up, and let cool completely.

WHOLE-WHEAT BRAN MUFFINS

MAKES 12 MUFFINS

Editor: Make these to freeze and have on hand for breakfast when you are on the go.

1 cup wheat bran

½ cup whole-wheat flour

½ cup all-purpose flour

1 teaspoon baking soda

¼ teaspoon baking powder

½ teaspoon plain salt

2 large eggs, separated

1 cup buttermilk

2 tablespoons unsalted butter, melted

1 tablespoon honey

Preheat the oven to 375°F. Butter a standard 12-cup muffin pan or line with paper liners.

Combine the bran, whole-wheat, and all-purpose flours, baking soda, baking powder, and salt in a bowl. Stir to mix.

Lightly beat 2 egg yolks in a bowl. Add the buttermilk, melted butter, and honey and mix well. Beat the egg whites in a separate bowl with an electric mixer until stiff but not dry. Add the buttermilk mixture to the bran mixture and stir only until moistened. Fold in the egg whites. Fill the muffin cups two-thirds full with the batter. Bake for 15 to 20 minutes, until a wooden toothpick inserted in a muffin comes out dry. Let cool 5 minutes, then serve warm.

SOUR MILK PANCAKES

✍ **MAKES 2 TO 3 SERVINGS**

I am quite aware that we do not have the opportunity to get sour milk these homogenized, pasteurized days. One must content oneself with buttermilk—and cultured buttermilk at that. However, it does have the same rather pleasant sour quality. If you want to quicken this process of making the batter, I find the buttermilk pancake mixes on the market to be pretty good.

Beat **2 large eggs** very well—they should be foamy and light-colored. Add **2 cups buttermilk or sour milk** and beat. Add **1 tablespoon sugar, 1 teaspoon baking powder, ½ teaspoon baking soda,** and **½ teaspoon salt.** Gradually stir in enough **all-purpose flour** (2 to 3 cups) to make a batter the consistency of very heavy cream, and add **5 tablespoons unsalted butter, melted.** Spoon the mixture onto a buttered griddle and cook the pancakes until they are nicely browned on both sides. Serve them with **melted butter** and **hot syrup** and **lemon juice.**

Editor: These days, pasteurized milk does not sour—it just goes rotten and is unusable as a cooking ingredient. However, you can create a substitute for sour milk (and buttermilk) by combining 2 cups milk with 2 teaspoons vinegar, and letting the mixture stand until clabbered, about 5 minutes.

YEAST GRIDDLE CAKES OR PANCAKES

✍ **MAKES 12 TO 14 CAKES**

These are simply wheat-flour pancakes made with a starter. In earlier times people kept a starter going especially for pancakes. Nowadays we usually make the starter the night before, which is what we are doing in this case. It makes light, puffy, absolutely delicious pancakes. Serve with melted butter, syrup, or honey, and bacon, ham, or even a little steak.

> One ¼-ounce package (2¼ teaspoons) active
>   dry yeast
> 1 cup warm (100° to 115°F) water
> 2 to 3 tablespoons sugar
> 2 cups all-purpose flour
> 1 large egg
> 3 tablespoons unsalted butter, melted
> ½ teaspoon plain salt
> Whole milk or evaporated milk, as needed

The night before making the pancakes, combine the yeast, water, 1 tablespoon sugar, and 1 cup of flour in a mixing bowl. Cover with a cloth and leave overnight to rise. The next morning beat the egg well in a mixing bowl and add 1 to 2 tablespoons sugar. Beat again, add the yeast mixture, and stir in the butter, salt, and remaining 1 cup flour; add milk if the mixture seems too thick. However, the batter should be a little thicker than is customary. The pancakes should be cooked as usual on a well-buttered griddle. Serve at once.

FRUITS

FRUITS

APPLE CHARLOTTE

Editor: The perfect warm dessert for cold weather, a charlotte is fruit baked in a case of bread slices. A charlotte mold is a round, deep metal pan made specifically for the purpose, but a loaf pan works, too.

Softened butter, for the mold

8 tablespoons (1 stick) unsalted butter, as needed

6 tart apples, peeled, cored, cut into ½-inch wedges

¼ cup plus 1 tablespoon sugar

1 teaspoon vanilla extract

About 12 slices firm white sandwich bread, preferably day-old, crusts trimmed

½ cup heavy cream

1 tablespoon dry sherry

Melt 2 tablespoons of the butter in a large skillet over medium-high heat. Add half of the apples and cover. Cook, stirring occasionally, until lightly browned, about 5 minutes. During the last minute, stir 2 tablespoons of the sugar and ½ teaspoon of the vanilla into the apples. Transfer to a bowl. Repeat with the remaining apples and 2 more tablespoons of the butter. Clean the skillet.

Melt 2 tablespoons of the butter in the skillet. Working in batches, add the bread and cook until crisp and brown on both sides, about 3 minutes, adding more butter as needed. Transfer to a plate.

Butter a 1-quart charlotte mold or an 8 by 4 by 3-inch bread pan. Line the mold with overlapping pieces of bread on the bottom and sides, trimming the bread as needed. Fill with the apple mixture and top with more overlapping bread.

Bake in a preheated 375°F oven for 25 minutes, or until golden brown. Let stand 5 minutes. Whip the cream, the remaining 1 tablespoon sugar, and sherry in a bowl with an electric mixer until the cream is stiff. Unmold the charlotte and serve warm with the sherried whipped cream.

HOT FRUIT COMPOTE

In the winter, substitute the dried versions of the fresh fruit in the compote. The compote (with either fresh or dried fruit) is also very good served chilled.

2 cups water

1 cup sugar

½ teaspoon vanilla extract

4 ripe apricots, peeled, pitted, and halved

4 ripe plums, pitted and halved

3 ripe peaches, peeled, pitted, and halved

2 firm but ripe figs, cut into quarters

1 pear, peeled, cored, and cut into sixths

Heavy cream, for serving

Bring the water and sugar to a boil in a large saucepan over medium heat, stirring to dissolve the sugar. Stir in the vanilla. Add the apricots, plums, peaches, figs, and pear and reduce the heat to medium-low. Simmer just until the fruit is tender, about 10 minutes. Spoon the fruits and some of the cooking liquid into bowls, and serve hot, with heavy cream to pour over each serving.

FRUIT FRITTERS

These are the dessert equivalent of the batter-dipped shrimp, meat, and vegetables, and they make a light and delicious end to a meal. If you want a sauce for the fritters, serve them with Crème Anglaise (page 293) flavored with 2 tablespoons of the spirit you use to marinate the fruit.

For the Batter

2 cups all-purpose flour

1 cup lager beer, at room temperature

2 large eggs, beaten

2 tablespoons unsalted butter, melted

1 tablespoon kirsch or Cognac

Pinch of plain salt

Vegetable oil for, deep-frying

Flavored fruit (see choices below)

1 to 1½ cups stale almond macaroon crumbs or
    sponge cake crumbs

Superfine or confectioners' sugar

To make the batter: Sift the flour into a bowl. Add the beer, eggs, melted butter, kirsch, or Cognac and salt and whisk until smooth. Or whirl until smooth in an electric blender. Let the batter stand at room temperature for 2 hours before using.

When you are ready to fry, stir the batter with a spatula in case the flour has sunk to the bottom of the bowl. Heat the oil in a deep fryer to 350°F. Roll the fruit in the crumbs, then dip into the batter and lower into the hot fat with a slotted spoon, a few pieces at a time. Deep-fry until golden brown on all sides, about 2½ minutes. Remove with the slotted spoon and transfer to paper towels to drain. Dust with sugar and serve hot.

VARIATIONS

APRICOT FRITTERS: Drain 12 pitted canned apricot halves. Marinate them in ⅓ cup kirsch for 1 hour; drain again.

APPLE FRITTERS: Peel, core, and quarter 4 apples and poach gently in syrup (see Hot Fruit Compote, page 291) until just tender when pierced with a fork, about 5 minutes. Drain. Marinate for 30 minutes in applejack; drain.

PEAR FRITTERS: Poach 6 small, peeled, cored, and halved pears in syrup (see Hot Fruit Compote, page 291) until just tender when pierced with a fork, about 5 minutes. Drain. Marinate for 30 minutes in eau-de-vie de poire or kirsch; drain.

PINEAPPLE FRITTERS: Marinate 12 slices of canned, drained pineapple or fresh pineapple in ⅓ cup kirsch for 1 hour; drain.

BROILED GRAPEFRUIT

For each serving, allow **half a grapefruit**. Remove the seeds with the point of a knife or spoon. Cut around the membranes and between the outer peel and the pulp with a grapefruit knife to loosen the sections. Arrange the halves on a baking sheet and sprinkle them lightly with about **2 teaspoons brown sugar.** Add about ½ teaspoon Grand Marnier to each one. Dot with **1 teaspoon unsalted butter** cut into small pieces. Preheat the broiler. Broil the grapefruit with the surface 5 inches from the heat until the topping is brown and bubbly—about 5 minutes. If you serve these for breakfast, omit the Grand Marnier.

MELON WITH PORT

⌒ MAKES 1 SERVING

Cantaloupe, honeydew, or Crenshaw melons are all perfect for this dish. Be sure the melons are fully ripe and sweet. **Cut them into halves or slices,** depending on type and size, and make 2 or 3 gashes in the flesh of each piece with a spoon. Add **2 ounces of Port** to each piece and let it chill half an hour to mellow. Serve a half cantaloupe or a slice of a larger melon per person.

SUGARED ORANGES

⌒ MAKES 1 SERVING

Sometimes people forget how satisfying good oranges can be when served as a dessert. In Spain and Mexico the oranges are peeled and sliced as below and arranged in layers in a serving dish. Each layer is sprinkled with confectioners' sugar and ground cinnamon. Extra orange juice is sometimes added.

For each serving peel **1 or 1½ oranges** very carefully with a sharp knife, removing all the white pith, and cut them into ⅜-inch slices. **Sugar** them lightly, sprinkle them with **Grand Marnier** or other **orange-flavored liqueur,** and chill them.

Crème Anglaise

Makes about 2⅓ cups

½ cup sugar
4 large egg yolks
Pinch of plain salt
1 cup whole milk
1 cup heavy cream
2 teaspoons vanilla extract

Whisk the sugar, egg yolks, and salt in a heavy-bottomed saucepan until pale and creamy. Heat the milk and cream together in another saucepan. Gradually whisk the hot milk mixture into the egg yolk mixture. Cook over low heat, stirring constantly with a wooden spoon, until the custard thickens enough to heavily coat the back of a spoon, about 5 minutes. The sauce should not be allowed to boil. Strain the sauce through a wire sieve into a bowl, stir in the vanilla, and cool. Cover with plastic wrap and refrigerate until chilled. Serve chilled. (The crème anglaise can also be served warm, right after it is strained, or keep warm over hot water in a top insert of a double boiler.)

PEARS *CONDÉ*

MAKES 6 SERVINGS

Editor: Condé means "earl" in French, and these poached pears served with rice pudding are truly fit for the nobility.

For the Rice Pudding

1½ cups boiling water

¾ cup raw medium-grain rice

2 cups whole milk

½ cup sugar

3 tablespoons unsalted butter

1½ teaspoons vanilla extract

Pinch of plain salt

4 large egg yolks, slightly beaten

For the Poached Pears

2 cups sugar

1 cup water

1 teaspoon vanilla extract

6 medium pears, peeled, cored, and halved

Candied fruit, chopped pistachio nuts, and Whipped Cream (page 300) for serving

To make the rice pudding: Bring the water to a boil in a saucepan over high heat. Stir in the rice and remove from the heat. Let stand for 10 minutes; drain. Heat the milk in the saucepan over medium heat until tiny bubbles appear around the edges of the milk. Combine the drained rice, milk, sugar, butter, vanilla, and salt in a bowl. Pour into a buttered shallow baking dish. Bake at 325°F, stirring occasionally, until the rice is tender, about 30 minute. Remove from the oven, stir in the beaten egg yolks, and bake until the rice is lightly thickened, about 5 minutes.

Meanwhile, poach the pears: Bring the sugar and water to a boil in a large skillet over medium heat, stirring to dissolve the sugar. Stir in the vanilla. Add the pears, reduce the heat to medium-low, and simmer until just tender, about 10 minutes. Set the pears in the syrup aside.

To serve, spoon equal amounts of the rice pudding in a ring onto each plate. Place 2 pear halves in the center of each ring, and garnish with candied fruit, pistachios, and whipped cream.

FRESH PEARS AND CHEESE

The delicious **Oregon pears** are at their peak at the beginning of the year. Most of us seem to get them as early as Christmas. Look for them at a good fruiterer's. Serve ripe with **Roquefort, a fine Camembert, or even with cream cheese** and preserves.

Editor: The superiority of Oregon pears has not changed, and if you don't find them at the best produce store where you live, look for a mail-order purveyor online, such as www.harryanddavid.com.

STRAWBERRY FOOL

Editor: Nothing more than fruit and cream, this dessert needs to be made with the very best in-season produce and top-notch (i.e., nonpasteurized or organic) heavy cream.

Hull **1½ pints ripe strawberries** and process into a purée in a food processor. Stir about **½ cup sugar** (or to taste) into the purée, and add a drop or two of **freshly squeezed lemon juice** to accent the flavor. Whip **1 cup heavy cream** in a bowl with an electric mixer until stiff. Fold into the strawberry purée. Chill until serving.

VARIATION

RHUBARB FOOL: Cook about **1 pound rhubarb,** trimmed and cut into ½-inch pieces, with **1 cup sugar** in a saucepan over very low heat until it is quite soft, about 15 minutes. Substitute for the strawberry purée.

RICH STRAWBERRY SHORTCAKE

MAKES 8 TO 10 SERVINGS

Editor: To most Americans, strawberry shortcake represents summer on a plate. In this version, Beard does not use whipped cream, and instead pours cream over each serving. Look for a thick heavy cream at a local dairy or farmer's market and skip over the ultra-pasteurized version. If you wish, substitute sweetened whipped cream for the poured cream.

For the Shortcake

4 cups all-purpose flour

6 tablespoons sugar

1 tablespoon plus 2 teaspoons baking powder

2 teaspoons plain salt

12 tablespoons (1½ sticks) cold unsalted butter, cut into ½-inch cubes

1½ cups heavy cream

2 tablespoons unsalted butter, melted and cooled

2 quarts fresh, ripe strawberries, washed and hulled

Sugar, to taste

1 pint heavy cream, for serving

To make the shortcake: Preheat the oven to 425°F. Sift the flour, sugar, baking powder, and salt together in a large bowl. Add the cold butter pieces and rub them into the dry ingredients with your fingertips until the mixture resembles coarse meal with some pea-size pieces of butter (or pulse a few times in a food processor and transfer to a bowl). Add the cream and mix thoroughly until a soft dough is formed. Gather it into a compact ball and place on a lightly floured board. Knead briefly, then divide into two pieces, one a third larger than the other.

Press the larger piece of dough into a 9-inch round about ½ inch thick on a greased cookie sheet. On another greased cookie sheet, press the second piece into an 8-inch round about ½ inch thick. Brush each with melted butter. Bake about

15 minutes or until firm to the touch and golden brown. Let cool slightly.

Set aside the most attractive strawberries to garnish the shortcake. Coarsely chop the remaining strawberries. Place the larger shortcake on a serving platter. Spread the chopped strawberries on the larger shortcake layer, sprinkle with sugar, and gently slide the smaller layer on top. Garnish with the whole strawberries. Cut the shortcake into wedges and serve with the cream poured over each serving.

STRAWBERRIES ROMANOV

〰 MAKES 4 SERVINGS

If there is one satisfactory version of strawberries Romanov, there are twenty-five. The classic is probably that of the great Escoffier. As served at the Carlton in his day, it was a simple but extraordinarily good dish notable for the interesting contrast of flavors.

1 quart large, ripe strawberries, washed and hulled

4 tablespoons sugar, or as needed

1 cup freshly squeezed orange juice

⅓ cup Grand Marnier or other orange-flavored liqueur

1½ cups heavy cream

Candied violets, for garnish

Put the strawberries into a bowl, taste, and sweeten with 1 or 2 tablespoons of the sugar, if necessary. Add the orange juice and the liqueur and let the strawberries macerate for 1 hour. Transfer the berries to a chilled serving dish, draining off some of the liquid. Using an electric mixer, whip the cream and 2 tablespoons of the sugar in a medium bowl until stiff. Spread the cream over the berries and decorate the dish with candied violets. Serve chilled.

DRUNKEN WATERMELON

〰 MAKES ABOUT 12 SERVINGS

Cut a deep plug about 2 inches square out of the top of **a ripe watermelon**. Remove the plug and slowly pour in as much **light rum, brandy, or champagne** as the melon will absorb. Replace the plug and seal with masking tape. Refrigerate the melon for 24 hours, turning it 4 or 5 times to allow the liquor to seep through the pulp. Serve in slices, like ordinary watermelon.

HOT, COLD, AND FROZEN DESSERTS

HOT, COLD, AND FROZEN DESSERTS

SOUFFLÉ FRITTERS
(BEIGNETS SOUFFLÉS)

~ MAKES 6 SERVINGS

Beignets are simply tablespoons of sweetened and flavored cream puff dough (*pâte à choux*) fried in deep hot fat until they rise into air-filled puffs—the eggs in the dough are the leavening agent. Serve with Crème Anglaise (page 293) or Raspberry Sauce (below).

1 cup water

8 tablespoons (1 stick) unsalted butter, cut into
   ½-inch pieces

½ teaspoon granulated sugar

⅛ teaspoon plain salt

1 cup all-purpose flour

4 large eggs

2 tablespoons golden rum or brandy

Vegetable oil, for deep-frying

Confectioners' sugar, for dusting

Combine the water, butter, granulated sugar, and salt in a heavy-bottomed medium saucepan. Cook over medium heat the water is just until boiling and the butter is melted. Remove the saucepan from the heat. Dump in the flour all at once and beat vigorously with a wooden spatula until well blended. Return the saucepan to the burner over medium heat and beat the mixture with a wooden spatula or spoon for about 1 minute, or until the mixture forms a mass that clings to the spatula and comes away from the sides and bottom of the pan.

Remove the pan from the heat and let it stand for 5 to 6 minutes. (If you have an electric stand mixer, transfer the dough to a bowl.) The dough should have time to settle and cool slightly before the eggs are added, or the eggs will curdle when added.

Make a well in the center of the dough with the spatula; drop in one egg and beat into the dough until thoroughly absorbed. Beat in the other eggs in the same way, one at a time, until the dough is smooth and glossy and the eggs are completely absorbed. When adding the last egg, also beat in the rum. (Or, with the mixer on low speed, add the eggs one at a time, then, as the eggs become absorbed, increase to high speed, and add the rum with the last egg. Beat only until the dough is smooth and glossy—it should not be overbeaten.)

Heat the oil in a deep fryer with a basket to 370°F. Drop the dough into the hot oil by tablespoons, a few at a time, and fry for about 3 minutes, or just until the beignets puff up and brown. When one side browns, the beignets will turn themselves over. Transfer to paper towels to drain. Just before serving, sift the confectioners' sugar through a fine sieve over the beignets. Serve hot.

Raspberry Sauce

Makes ¾ cup

Editor: Vibrant red raspberry sauce adds color and flavor to many desserts. Superfine sugar works best, as it dissolves quickly.

Purée in a blender, or push through a fine wire sieve, **two 6-ounce baskets of fresh raspberries.** (If you use a blender, strain the purée through a sieve.) Taste and add **sugar**, if necessary.

CHOCOLATE SOUFFLÉ

MAKES 6 SERVINGS

Like the Grand Marnier Soufflé on page 302, this is made without flour. It is much lighter and more delicate than a chocolate soufflé made with a béchamel base. [See Editor's Note, page 302.] The basic mixture may also be baked as a Chocolate Roll (page 317) or as "fallen soufflé."

Editor: As Beard notes, "fallen" is a convenient way to serve this dessert, because you don't have to rush it into the dining room before it deflates. Let the soufflé cool slightly and deflate for about 5 minutes. Run a dinner knife around the inside of the mold, and invert and unmold the fallen soufflé onto a serving dish. Sift confectioners' sugar on top. The soufflé won't look very impressive, but with the addition of whipped cream, it will taste fantastic.

For the Soufflé

Softened butter and sugar, for the soufflé dish

6 ounces semisweet chocolate, finely chopped

6 large eggs, separated, at room temperature

½ cup granulated sugar

1 teaspoon vanilla extract

¼ teaspoon plain salt

¼ teaspoon cream of tartar

For the Whipped Cream

1 cup chilled heavy cream

2 tablespoons sifted confectioners' sugar

1 tablespoon Cognac, Grand Marnier, dark rum, or 2 tablespoons kirsch

Position a rack in the center of the oven and preheat the oven to 375°F. Butter a 1-quart soufflé dish. Sprinkle with sugar, tilt to coat the inside, and tip out the excess sugar.

To make the soufflé: Melt the chocolate in the top of a double boiler over hot water. Remove the boiler top from the bottom and let the chocolate cool slightly.

Beat the yolks in a large bowl with an electric mixer on high speed until light and lemon-colored, then gradually beat in the granulated sugar and salt until the mixture is very thick, pale yellow, and ribbony, about 3 minutes. Beat the chocolate and vanilla into the egg yolk mixture.

In a clean bowl using clean beaters, beat the egg whites until foamy; add the salt and cream of tartar and continue to beat until they hold soft, unwavering peaks. Fold into the chocolate mixture, first folding in one-fourth of the egg whites to lighten the mixture and then lightly folding in the rest. Pour into the prepared soufflé dish. Bake for 45 minutes—this soufflé needs a longer baking time because of the density of the chocolate.

To make the whipped cream: Just before the soufflé is ready to come out of the oven, beat the cream in a chilled bowl until it has doubled in volume and holds its shape when the beater is lifted. Gently fold in the confectioners' sugar and Cognac. Put in a serving bowl and serve with the soufflé as a sauce.

GINGER SOUFFLÉ

⁓ MAKES 4 TO 6 SERVINGS

Editor: Preserved ginger in syrup was often used in desserts in the days before fresh ginger was available at every supermarket in our nation. If you wish, substitute chopped crystallized ginger, but not fresh ginger, which is too tough for this recipe. Note that this soufflé does not require a collar on the baking dish.

Softened butter and sugar for the soufflé dish

3 tablespoons unsalted butter

3 tablespoons all-purpose flour

¾ cup whole milk, heated

Pinch of plain salt

5 large eggs, separated, plus 1 large egg white,
    at room temperature

½ cup sugar

½ cup drained and finely cut preserved ginger
    in syrup

Whipped Cream (page 300), for serving

Position a rack in the center of the oven and preheat the oven to 400°F. Butter a 1½-quart soufflé dish. Sprinkle with sugar, tilt to coat the inside, and tip out the excess sugar.

Melt the butter in a medium saucepan over medium-low heat. Whisk in the flour, and cook for a minute without browning. Slowly whisk in the milk. Whisk until the sauce comes to a boil. Cool slightly. Whisk the egg yolks and sugar together in a small bowl, then whisk into the sauce. Cook over low heat, stirring constantly, until the sauce is lightly thickened. Stir in the ginger, and cool slightly again. Beat the egg whites until stiff but not dry. Stir one-fourth of the whites into the sauce, then fold in the remaining whites. Pour into a the prepared soufflé dish. Bake at 400°F for 25 to 30 minutes, or until puffed and golden brown. Serve the soufflé with whipped cream.

NOTE: If you wish, prepare the soufflé before dinner, except for beating and adding the egg whites. Butter and sugar the dish; have the oven heated to the proper temperature. Then take time to clear the table and prepare it for the dessert course while the soufflé cooks.

Editor: This made-ahead advice applies to all soufflés, including the Grand Marnier and Chocolate versions on pages 302 and 300. Also, note that this soufflé uses a larger dish than the other two recipes, and therefore does not need a waxed paper or aluminum foil collar.

GRAND MARNIER SOUFFLÉ

✎ MAKES 8 SERVINGS

This type of dessert soufflé is made without a bécha-mel base and with a great many eggs, to produce a very light, delicate, and high-rising result. In this case, it is advisable to use a paper collar on the soufflé dish.

Editor: Some dessert soufflé recipes use a thick white sauce as the base. Beard learned this technique ob-serving the chefs at the venerable Restaurant Allard in Paris, while lunching with Alice B. Toklas. This picture-perfect bistro is still in operation.

Softened butter and sugar, for the soufflé dish

8 large eggs, separated, plus 1 large egg white,
   at room temperature

1¼ cups sugar

⅓ cup Grand Marnier

Grated zest of 1 large orange

¼ teaspoon cream of tartar

Pinch of plain salt

Take a piece of waxed paper, or aluminum foil, long enough to fit around a 2-quart soufflé dish with a little overlap. Wrap the waxed paper around the dish, and fold lengthwise so it rises 3 to 4 inches above the rim of the dish. Butter one side heavily. Using kitchen twine, tie the paper around the soufflé dish, buttered side inward. Butter the in-side of the soufflé dish, sprinkle it with the sugar, and tilt the dish so the sugar rolls around and coats the bottom and sides completely. Tip out any excess sugar. This helps the soufflé to rise and gives it a crusty, sugary exterior. The butter and sugar coating is standard for dessert soufflés.

Position a rack in the center of the oven and preheat the oven to 375°F.

Beat the egg yolks in a large bowl with an elec-tric mixer on high speed until the yolks are light and lemon-colored. Gradually beat in 1 cup of sugar and continue beating for about 3 minutes, or until the mixture is very thick, pale and rib-bony, which means that when the beater is lifted the mixture falls from it in a thick, broad ribbon. Beat in the Grand Marnier and orange zest.

In a clean bowl, using clean beaters, beat the egg whites, adding the cream of tartar and salt when they are foamy. Beat until they reach the soft-peak stage, then gradually beat in the re-maining ¼ cup sugar and continue to beat until the egg whites form stiff, glossy peaks. Fold one-fourth of the egg whites into the egg yolk mixture to lighten it, then lightly fold in the rest of the whites.

Pour the mixture into the prepared soufflé dish, smoothing the top with a rubber spatula. Bake in the center of the preheated oven for 25 to 30 minutes, according to how cooked you like your soufflé. This type of soufflé is best if baked 25 minutes—the center will be slightly liquid and creamy and will form a little sauce for the crustier, firmer part of the soufflé.

Remove from the oven and untie the paper col-lar. Very gently peel it away from the risen soufflé, being careful not to puncture the crust, or the soufflé will collapse. Serve immediately.

FIVE-DAY PLUM PUDDING

∾ MAKES 12 TO 16 SERVINGS

Editor: Plum pudding was a specialty of Beard's British mother, Elizabeth, and was served with pride at Christmas dinners during his childhood in Portland. Beef suet will probably have to be ordered from your butcher, but today, even many British cooks now substitute butter. A pudding bowl, made from ceramic with fairly straight sides to help the bowl fit easily into a stockpot, is the traditional cooking vessel. In a pinch, pour half of the batter into a buttered 12-cup fluted tube pan, cover tightly with aluminum foil, and steam for about 3 hours; repeat with the remaining batter. The pudding (or puddings, if you have used the tube pans) can be cooked, cooled, covered, and refrigerated in its bowl a few days ahead, and reheated in the oven or in the pot before serving.

½ pound beef suet, finely chopped

2 cups all-purpose flour

1 cup golden raisins

¾ cup dark seedless raisins

½ cup dried currants

1 pound mixed, finely chopped candied orange peel, lemon peel, and citron

6 or 7 tart apples, cored, peeled, and chopped

3 cups fresh bread crumbs (made in a food processor or blender from day-old white sandwich bread)

1 cup packed light brown sugar

½ cup toasted, skinned, and finely ground hazelnuts

2 teaspoons ground cinnamon

1 teaspoon ground ginger

1 teaspoon ground mace

½ teaspoon ground cloves

1 teaspoon plain salt

Grated zest and juice from 1 orange

Grated zest and juice from 1 lemon

About 2 cups Cognac, rum, or brandy, as needed

6 large eggs, lightly beaten

Dark or lager beer, if needed

Softened butter, for the mold and aluminum foil

Cognac Sauce (see Box, page 305)

Toss the suet in a very large bowl with 2 tablespoons of the flour. Add the golden and seedless raisins and the currants, add a few more tablespoons of flour, and toss again. Add the candied fruits, add about ½ cup flour, and toss again. Stir in the remaining flour, apples, bread crumbs, brown sugar, hazelnuts, cinnamon, ginger, mace, cloves, and salt. Add the grated zests and juices from the orange and lemon, and ½ cup of Cognac. Stir well.

Cover and refrigerate for 5 days, adding ¼ cup more of Cognac each day and stirring the mixture well. On the last day, stir in the lightly beaten eggs. If the batter is too thick, thin it with a little beer.

Pour the batter into a well-buttered 3½- to 4-quart heatproof pudding mold or ceramic bowl and cover tightly with buttered aluminum foil, buttered side down. Place on a trivet or steamer rack in a large pot, and pour in boiling water to reach halfway up the bowl. Cover the pot and steam the pudding over medium-low heat until the pudding is a glossy dark brown, about 6 hours, adding more boiling water to the pot if necessary. Remove the bowl from the pot and let stand 10 minutes. Unmold and serve with the Cognac Sauce.

APPLE TAPIOCA

 MAKES 6 SERVINGS

Often damned, this rather gelatinous pudding is sometimes referred to as fish eyes. To those who, like me, love it, it is indeed a treat.

Editor: Small pearl tapioca, available online and at many supermarkets, is neither instant tapioca (pearl tapioca that has been crushed into granules for faster cooking) nor large tapioca pearls. Be sure to purchase the correct tapioca for this dessert.

¾ cup small pearl tapioca, soaked in cold water to cover for 2 hours, and drained

2 cups boiling water

½ teaspoon plain salt

1 cup granulated sugar

6 tart apples, peeled and thinly sliced

3 tablespoons cold unsalted butter

1 teaspoon vanilla extract

½ cup fresh bread crumbs (preferably pumpernickel or whole wheat, made in a food processor or blender)

⅓ cup packed light or dark brown sugar

Vanilla ice cream or heavy cream, for serving

Put the drained tapioca in the top of a double boiler over simmering water and add the boiling water and salt. Cover and cook until the tapioca is transparent, approximately 50 minutes.

Place the granulated sugar in a heavy skillet and cook over medium heat, until melted, dark amber, and caramelized. Add the sliced apples (they will splatter, so be careful) and cook until the apples are tender. Stir in 2 tablespoons of the butter and the vanilla.

Preheat the oven to 350°F. Alternate layers of apples and tapioca in a buttered 9 by 7-inch baking dish, ending with apples. Combine the bread crumbs with the brown sugar and sprinkle over the top. Cut the remaining butter into small cubes and dot over the top of the pudding. Bake for 30 minutes. Serve hot, with ice cream or heavy cream.

VARIATION

TAPIOCA WITH APPLES AND PEARS: Use half apples and half pears.

FLAN

 MAKES 6 SERVINGS

This is a typical Spanish dessert, beautiful to look at and simple to make. Flans are best when made hours before serving and thoroughly chilled.

1¾ cups sugar

3 large eggs, separated, plus 5 large egg yolks

Two 12-ounce cans evaporated milk

2 teaspoons vanilla extract

¼ cup plus 2 tablespoons Cognac or rum

Put 1 cup of the sugar into a 8 by 2-inch round metal cake pan in which you can bake the custard. Place this over low heat, and stir constantly until the sugar melts and turns a golden color. Tilt the pan, and allow the caramel to coat it entirely. Set this aside to cool while you make the custard.

Preheat the oven to 350°F. Beat the eggs and yolks together in a medium bowl. Add the evaporated milk, the remaining ¾ cup sugar, and vanilla. Mix well. Strain into the caramel-coated pan, and place the pan in a larger pan. Add enough hot water to come halfway up the sides of the custard-filled pan. Bake for about an hour, or until a knife inserted in the center comes out clean. Cool slightly, and turn out on a flameproof platter while it is still warm (or else the caramel will stick to the sides). Refrigerate until chilled, at least 4 hours or overnight.

When you are ready to serve, heat the Cognac or rum until warm in a small saucepan, pour over the flan, and ignite with a long kitchen match. Bring to the table blazing. To serve, cut into wedges and transfer to plates, spooning the caramel and Cognac on top.

Cognac Sauce

Makes 2 cups

This sauce adds great contrast to steamed puddings and very rich desserts. It is one of the sauces used for the traditional Christmas pudding.

6 tablespoons (¾ stick) unsalted butter, at room temperature
⅔ cup confectioners' sugar
2 large egg yolks
¾ cup heavy cream
3 tablespoons Cognac or brandy

Beat the butter with the sugar in a medium bowl with an electric mixer until the mixture is light and fluffy, about 3 minutes. Beat in the egg yolks, one at a time. Pour into a heavy-bottomed saucepan and stir in the cream. Cook over medium-low heat, stirring constantly, until the mixture thickly coats a wooden spoon. Do not let boil. Remove from the heat and strain into a bowl. Flavor with the Cognac. Serve warm or cold.

CHOCOLATE MOUSSE

MAKES 6 SERVINGS

Editor: Beard advises to make the mousse the day before your dinner party, but a few hours will suffice. You can use your favorite bittersweet or semisweet chocolate, finely chopped, instead of the chocolate chips. Note that this recipe uses raw eggs, which have been known to carry the potentially harmful salmonella *bacterium, and should not be served to the elderly, very young, or anyone with a compromised immune system.*

One 6-ounce package semisweet chocolate chips
6 large eggs, separated, at room temperature
2 tablespoons Cognac
Dash of plain salt

Melt the chocolate in the top of a double boiler over hot water. Add the egg yolks and cognac and whisk well. Remove the insert from the double boiler. Whip the egg whites in a medium bowl with an electric mixer on high speed until foamy, then add the salt and beat until stiff but not dry. Stir one-fourth of the whites into the chocolate mixture, then fold in the remaining whites. Pour into individual pots or a glass dish, cover, and chill at least 4 hours or overnight. Serve cold.

IRISH WHISKEY TRIFLE

꩜ MAKES 6 TO 8 SERVINGS

Editor: For a make-ahead dessert, trifle is hard to surpass. If you have the time, let the ladyfingers stand out overnight, uncovered, so they stale slightly before using.

10 to 12 ladyfingers

½ cup Irish whiskey, as needed

½ cup raspberry preserves

2½ cups Crème Anglaise (page 293), chilled

1 cup heavy cream

2 tablespoons superfine sugar

⅓ cup coarsely chopped pistachios

Line the bottom of a 9-inch trifle bowl or soufflé dish with the ladyfingers. Liberally sprinkle them with the whiskey, but do not make them soggy. Let stand for 15 minutes.

Spread the ladyfingers with a thick layer of raspberry preserves. Cover with the crème anglaise and chill for 3 to 4 hours.

Just before serving, whip the cream in a chilled bowl until it stands in soft peaks, then beat in the sugar and 1 or 2 tablespoons Irish whiskey. Cover the surface of the crème anglaise with the whipped cream, smoothing it evenly with a rubber spatula. Sprinkle the chopped nuts over the top. Serve chilled, but do not let stand in the refrigerator for more than 30 minutes, or it will become soggy.

ICE-TRAY APRICOT ICE CREAM

꩜ MAKES 6 SERVINGS

If you are making ice cream in an ice-tray, I find it advisable to use a slightly different mixture and to whip the cream, the result of which is nearer a frozen cream or a very rich, creamy version of sherbet. As it is very difficult to get luscious, ripe apricots these days, I made this ice cream with apricot preserves, which works beautifully.

Editor: In this recipe, Beard shows how to make ice cream without an ice cream machine. You can use a metal 13 by 9-inch baking pan instead of the old-fashioned ice trays with removable ice cube molds.

1½ cups apricot preserves

1 cup water

⅓ cup sugar

1½ cups heavy cream

Rub the preserves through a wire sieve with a wooden spoon or put through a food mill.

Boil the water and sugar together for 5 minutes to make a simple syrup, then cool until cold.

Combine the apricot purée and the syrup, mixing well.

Whip the heavy cream in a chilled bowl with an electric mixer until it is doubled in volume and holds its shape when the beater is lifted. Fold the cream thoroughly into the apricot mixture with a rubber spatula, then pour the mixture into metal ice trays. Freeze until frozen around the edges and mushy in the center. Remove, turn into a bowl, and beat with a wooden spatula until smooth. Return to the trays and freeze again. Repeat the freezing and beating process 1 or 2 times. This will take a few hours. Cover with plastic wrap, return to freezer, and freeze until hard enough to scoop, about 2 hours more. The beating process keeps the ice cream from forming ice crystals and makes it smooth.

FROZEN LEMON MOUSSE

∽∾ **MAKES 6 SERVINGS**

This very simple form of frozen dessert mousse is made with a thick, cooked lemon mixture, which the English call "lemon curd," lightened by whipped cream, that can also be used, unfrozen, as a filling for a jelly roll. As this mixture is not quite as firm as one containing gelatin, it is advisable not to unmold it.

  8 tablespoons (1 stick) unsalted butter
  1½ cups sugar
  Grated zest of 1 large lemon
  Juice of 3 large lemons
  ¼ teaspoon plain salt

  3 large eggs plus 3 large egg yolks
  1 cup heavy cream

Melt the butter in the top part of a double boiler over barely simmering water (the water should not touch the bottom of the insert). Whisk in the sugar, lemon zest and juice, and salt. Beat the eggs and yolks together with a whisk in a medium bowl, and add to the ingredients in the double boiler. Cook over the barely simmering water, whisking constantly, until the mixture is smooth and glossy, and very thick, 3 to 5 minutes. Do not let the curd boil, or it will curdle. Strain into a bowl, press a piece of plastic wrap directly on the curd to keep a skin from forming, and let cool in the refrigerator.

When the lemon curd is cold, whip the cream in a chilled bowl with a whisk or electric mixer until it holds soft peaks. Fold the whipped cream into the lemon curd with a rubber spatula until thoroughly combined. Pour into a metal serving bowl, cover with plastic wrap, and freeze until firm and set, about 6 hours. Serve from the bowl.

FROZEN MOCHA PARFAIT

MAKES 4 TO 6 SERVINGS

Editor: Another "too-easy-to-be-true" dessert that is, nonetheless, elegant enough to serve to company.

½ cup sugar

½ cup water

1½ teaspoons instant coffee

One 6-ounce package semisweet chocolate chips

2 large eggs, at room temperature

1½ cups heavy cream

Combine the sugar, water, and instant coffee in a saucepan and bring to a boil. Boil for 3 minutes. Put the chocolate chips in a blender or food processor and add the coffee mixture. Blend for 6 seconds to start to melt the chocolate. Add the eggs and blend for 1 minute, until the mixture is light and fluffy. Transfer to a bowl and let cool without setting. Whip the cream in another bowl with an electric mixer until the cream forms soft peaks. Fold in the chocolate coffee mixture. Pour into a 13 by 9-inch metal baking pan, cover with plastic wrap, and freeze for about 4 hours, or until firm. Scoop into dessert dishes and serve.

RAISIN AND CHESTNUT ICE CREAM

MAKES 8 SERVINGS

Editor: Be sure to purchase unsweetened chestnuts. You might want to use vacuum-packed chestnuts instead of the canned variety.

1 cup dark seedless raisins

¼ cup Scotch

1 cup sugar

6 large egg yolks

⅛ teaspoon plain salt

2 cups whole milk

1 quart heavy cream

½ vanilla bean, split lengthwise, or 4½ teaspoons vanilla extract

½ cup cooked and finely chopped unsweetened chestnuts or drained canned chestnuts

In a small bowl, soak the raisins in the Scotch until they plump up, about 1 hour. Drain well.

Whisk the sugar, egg yolks, and salt together in a heavy-bottomed medium saucepan until the mixture is pale and creamy. Meanwhile, in another pan, heat the milk to the boiling point. First mix a bit of the hot milk into the egg mixture to temper the eggs, stirring constantly. Then add the remaining milk. Cook over medium heat, stirring constantly with a wooden spatula, until the custard is thick enough to lightly coat the spatula. Strain the custard into a bowl and let cool. Stir in the heavy cream and the tiny seeds from the vanilla bean. Pour the mixture into an electric ice cream maker and churn according to the manufacturer's directions. During the last few minutes of churning, add the drained raisins and chestnuts. Transfer to an airtight container and freeze until firm enough to scoop, at least 2 hours.

VARIATION

GINGER AND MACADAMIA NUT ICE CREAM:

Omit the soaked raisins, vanilla bean, and chestnuts. Drain a 10-ounce jar of preserved candied ginger in syrup, reserving the syrup. Chop the ginger; you should have about 1 cup ginger and ½ cup syrup. Flavor the custard-cream mixture with 2 teaspoons vanilla extract and ¼ teaspoon ground ginger. Churn until frozen. During the last few minutes of churning, add the chopped ginger, syrup, and 1 cup toasted and coarsely chopped macadamia nuts. Transfer to an airtight container and freeze until firm enough to scoop, at least 2 hours.

FROZEN ZABAGLIONE

∽ MAKES 8 SERVINGS

Editor: You will not *need an ice cream maker to create this smooth frozen dessert.*

½ envelope (about 1 teaspoon) unflavored gelatin

2 tablespoons cold water

8 large egg yolks

1 cup Marsala, Cognac, or Port

⅔ cup sugar

Grated zest of 1 large lemon

3 tablespoons Grand Marnier or other orange-flavored liqueur

2 cups heavy cream, whipped

Sprinkle the gelatin over the cold water in a ramekin and set aside to soften, about 5 minutes. Meanwhile, whisk the egg yolks very well in the top part of a double boiler until thickened. Whisk in the Marsala, sugar, and lemon zest. Whisk over slightly boiling water (the water should not touch the bottom of the insert) until hot and fluffy. Remove the insert from the water, add the gelatin, and whisk until dissolved. Transfer the boiler insert to a bowl of iced water. Add the Grand Marnier and whisk until the mixture is cool but not set. Fold in the whipped cream. Spoon the mixture into individual dishes or a metal mold. Cover with plastic wrap and freeze for several hours before serving. If frozen in a mold, dip the mold in a bowl of warm water for a few seconds. Dry the outside of the mold, and invert and unmold the dessert onto a platter.

CAKES

CAKES

ANGEL FOOD CAKE

MAKES ONE 10-INCH TUBE CAKE; 12 SERVINGS

Editor: Angel food cake is a beloved American dessert, but Beard gives it sophistication with a splash of Cognac. Be sure to use a tube pan that does not have non-stick coating, as the batter will not rise if it is touching a slick surface. Delicate angel food cakes are cooled upside-down so they hold their shape. Most angel food pans have legs or an especially long central tube to lift the crown of the cake above the cooling surface.

1¼ cups egg whites (from about 10 large eggs), at room temperature

1 teaspoon cream of tartar

¼ teaspoon plain salt

1½ cups sugar

1 cup all-purpose flour, measured and then sifted three times

1 tablespoon Cognac

½ teaspoon vanilla or almond extract

Beat the egg whites with an electric mixer on high speed until they form soft peaks. Add the cream of tartar and salt and beat until stiff but not dry—firm peaks and a glossy surface. Gradually beat in the sugar, a few tablespoons at a time.

Sprinkle the flour over the surface and fold it in very carefully but well. Add the Cognac and vanilla and fold lightly. Pour into a 10-inch ungreased tube pan. Bake in a preheated 375°F oven about 40 minutes, or until the cake has browned. It will spring back when tested with your finger.

Cool the cake in the pan, upside down, on the pan legs. If there are no legs on your pan, rest and balance the cake pan's central tube on a bottle or funnel until cool.

Editor: There are two methods for measuring flour by volume: Dip-and-sweep and sift-and-sweep. The most common way to measure flour is the dip-and-sweep method, where the measuring cup in dipped into the flour container, and the excess is swept off to level the cup. But many professional bakers eschew this method because it compacts the flour, and could result in a heavy cake.

Beard preferred the sift-and-sweep method for fine-textured cakes. Sift the flour into a bowl. Put the measuring cup on a piece of waxed paper. Lightly spoon the sifted flour into the cup, letting it overflow onto the waxed paper. Do not pack the flour into the cup. Use a knife to sweep off the mounded flour so the flour in the cup is level with cup's top edge. The excess flour can be returned to the container and resifted.

DON FARMER'S FRESH APPLE CAKE

MAKES ONE 9- OR 10-INCH TUBE CAKE; 12 SERVINGS

With the crunch of the raw apple and an almost pudding-like texture and spiciness, this has a distinction not often found in cakes.

For the Cake

2 cups granulated sugar

1½ cups vegetable oil

3 large eggs

3 cups all-purpose flour

2 teaspoons ground cinnamon

1 teaspoon baking soda

½ teaspoon freshly grated nutmeg

½ teaspoon plain salt

3 cups diced tart raw apples, such as Granny Smith, Pippins, or Greenings

1 cup coarsely chopped black walnuts or English walnuts

2 teaspoons vanilla extract

For the Glaze

2 tablespoons unsalted butter

2 tablespoons light or dark brown sugar

2 tablespoons granulated sugar

2 tablespoons heavy cream

¼ teaspoon vanilla extract

Softened butter and flour, for the pan

To make the cake: Combine the granulated sugar and oil in a bowl. Beat very well with an electric mixer until pale, about 1 minute. Add the eggs, one at a time, beating well after each addition. Sift together the flour, cinnamon, baking soda, nutmeg, and salt. Sift these again into the oil-egg mixture and combine thoroughly. Add the diced raw apples, walnuts, and vanilla. Mix well with a spoon or spatula. Pour the batter into a buttered and floured 9- or 10-inch tube pan. Bake in a preheated 325°F oven for 1¼ hours, or until the cake tests done when pierced with a bamboo skewer. Remove from the oven and let rest in the pan while you prepare the glaze.

To make the glaze: Mix and melt the butter, brown and granulated sugars, heavy cream, and vanilla in a heavy-bottomed saucepan. Boil for 1 minute. Remove from the heat and spoon over the warm cake. Let it cool in the pan before removing.

VARIATION

FRESH PEAR CAKE: Instead of apples, use 3 cups firm Anjou or Bartlett pears. Proceed as above.

BRIDE'S CAKE

MAKES ONE 2-TIERED CAKE;
AT LEAST 20 SERVINGS

Editor: A tall, apricot-filled layer cake with a thick white frosting, this was a popular dessert to serve at bridal showers. For the decoration, use flowers whose edibility is well documented, and do not guess at their toxicity. Roses, nasturtiums, and Johnny jump-ups are known to be safe, but be sure to use ones that have not been sprayed with insecticides or fertilizers. Some specialty grocers carry edible flowers in the produce department.

For the Cake

Softened butter and flour, for the pans

4½ cups all-purpose flour

1½ teaspoons baking powder

½ teaspoon plain salt

1½ pounds (6 sticks) unsalted butter, at room temperature

3 cups sugar

12 large eggs, separated, at room temperature

3 tablespoons freshly squeezed lemon juice

Freshly grated zest of 1 lemon

For the Filling

1½ pounds dried apricots

4 cups water

1 cup sugar

⅓ cup kirsch

For the Frosting

1½ cups sugar

⅔ cup water

⅛ teaspoon cream of tartar

3 large egg whites

1 teaspoon vanilla extract

⅛ teaspoon plain salt

Unsprayed edible flowers, for garnish

To make the cake: Lightly butter one 9 by 2-inch round pan, and one 8 by 2-inch round cake pan. Line the bottoms of the pans with waxed paper. Dust with flour and tip out the excess.

Sift the flour, baking powder, and salt together three times. Beat the butter with an electric mixer until it is very light and fluffy, about 2 minutes. Then slowly beat in 1 cup of the sugar. Beat in the egg yolks until the mixture is light and lemon-colored, then add the lemon juice and zest. Gradually fold in the sifted flour mixture. In a separate bowl beat the egg whites with clean beaters until they hold soft peaks. Very gradually beat in the remaining 2 cups sugar into the whites. Gently fold the whites into the batter until completely smooth, but do not overmix.

Divide the batter between the prepared cake pans. Bake in a preheated 350°F oven for 45 minutes for the smaller cake, and 1 hour for the larger cake. The cakes are done when the edges of the cakes begin to pull away from the sides of the pans. Let the cakes cool on a rack for 15 to 30 minutes. Loosen the sides very gently and invert the cakes onto racks to finish cooling. Remove and discard the waxed paper.

To make the filling: In a medium saucepan soak the apricots in the water for 1 hour. Add the sugar and bring to a boil, stirring until the sugar has dissolved. Boil for 30 to 45 minutes until the mixture is slightly thickened. Cool. Put in a blender or food processor, add the kirsch, and process to make a smooth purée.

Slice the cakes in half horizontally. Place the bottom of the larger cake on a platter and spread with one-third of the apricot filling. Add the top layer and spread the center with another third of the filling, leaving about an inch of the circumference untouched; it will be frosted. Add the bottom half of the smaller cake and spread with the last third of the apricot filling. Place the remaining layer on top.

To make the frosting: In a heavy-bottomed saucepan, combine the sugar, water, and cream of tartar. Bring the mixture slowly to a boil, stirring well once or twice to dissolve sugar. Cover and boil 3 minutes, then uncover and boil to the soft-ball stage (240° to 245°F on a candy thermometer). Reduce the heat to its lowest setting. Beat the egg whites in an electric mixer at medium to high speed until stiff. Remove the pan from the heat, and pour the syrup in a thin stream into the whites as you continue beating. Add the vanilla and salt and beat until the frosting cools a bit and is firm enough to spread. If too firm, beat in about ¼ teaspoon boiling water.

Spread the frosting on the sides and top of the cake, fluffing it into peaks with a spatula or back of a spoon. Decorate with the flowers.

FRENCH CHOCOLATE CAKE

≈ **MAKES ONE 8-INCH CAKE; 8 TO 10 SERVINGS**

This chocolate cake is very rich and gooey, and the center will appear to be undercooked. Don't worry, that's how it's meant to be—hence the soft texture and exceptional flavor. The cake both refrigerates and freezes perfectly, but should be brought to room temperature before serving so the glaze will become shiny again. It will be easier to cut if refrigerated before serving.

For the Cake

8 tablespoons (1 stick) unsalted butter, at room temperature

1½ cups blanched sliced almonds or toasted and skinned hazelnuts

4 ounces semisweet chocolate, coarsely chopped

⅔ cup sugar

3 large eggs

¼ cup very fine fresh bread crumbs (from about 1 slice firm white bread)

Freshly grated zest of 1 large orange

For the Glaze

2 ounces unsweetened chocolate, finely chopped

4 tablespoons (½ stick) unsalted butter, at room temperature, and cut into tablespoon-size pieces

2 teaspoons honey

Toasted slivered almonds or skinned whole hazelnuts (see page 344)

Use a little of the butter to butter the bottom and sides of an 8-inch round cake pan. Line the bottom with parchment or waxed paper; if you use waxed paper, butter it too.

To make the cake: Grind the almonds as finely as possible in a food processor blender. Melt the chocolate for the cake in the top part of a double boiler over hot—not boiling—water. Remove the insert from the water and let the chocolate cool slightly. Beat the remaining butter in a bowl with an electric beater until light and fluffy, about 2 minutes. Gradually beat in the sugar. Add the eggs, one at a time, beating well after each addition. At this point the batter will look curdled, but it will all come together when the remaining ingredients are added. Add the melted chocolate, ground almonds, bread crumbs, and orange zest and stir thoroughly with a rubber spatula. Spread the batter into the prepared pan. Bake in a preheated 375°F oven for 25 minutes. Cool the cake on a wire rack for about 30 minutes, then run a spatula around the edge and turn it out onto the rack. Remove and discard the paper. Cool completely, upside down on the rack, before glazing.

To make the glaze: Combine the chocolate, butter, and honey in the top of a double boiler, and let the mixture melt, whisking occasionally over hot—not boiling—water. Remove the insert from the double boiler and let the chocolate mixture cool until it is beginning to thicken. Place the cooled cake on a rack over waxed paper and pour the glaze over it. Tip the cake so the glaze runs evenly over the top and down the sides. Smooth the sides, if necessary, with a metal spatula. Garland the rim of the cake with the nuts, placed fairly close together. Refrigerate to set the glaze.

CHOCOLATE ROLL

〰️ MAKES ONE 15-INCH JELLY ROLL; 8 SERVINGS

Editor: Here is a true story of Beard's generosity: When John Ferrone, Beard's longtime editor, admired this light but chocolate-intense dessert, Beard wrote the recipe down on his torn shirt sleeve. The sleeve was ripped off and presented to Ferrone.

For the roll

Softened butter, for the pan

Chocolate Soufflé (page 300)

Unsweetened cocoa powder or confectioners' sugar, for sifting

For the Whipped Cream Filling

1 cup heavy cream

2 tablespoons confectioners' sugar, sifted

1 tablespoon Cognac, Grand Marnier, or dark rum, or 2 tablespoons kirsch

To make the chocolate roll: Butter a 15 by 11 by 1-inch jelly-roll pan, then line the pan with waxed paper, leaving an overhang of about 2 inches at each end. Butter the waxed paper, to prevent the cake from sticking. Or, line the pan with parchment paper, which does not need to be buttered. Preheat the oven to 350°F with the shelf positioned in the center of the oven.

Spread the soufflé mixture evenly in the prepared pan, smoothing it with a rubber spatula so it is the same overall thickness. Bake for 15 minutes, or until the top feels firm and springy when touched.

Sift the cocoa over a large sheet of waxed paper or aluminum foil. Remove the jelly-roll pan from the oven and, holding it carefully with pot holders, very quickly invert the pan onto the paper or foil so the cake falls onto it, top side down. Carefully peel the waxed or parchment paper from the cake, loosening it, if necessary, with a small, sharp knife. If some of the surface sticks, this is not too important as the filling will go on this side. Cool completely.

To make the filling: Whip the cream in a chilled bowl with an electric mixer until it has doubled in volume and it holds its shape when the beater is lifted. Gently fold in the confectioners' sugar and Cognac. Spread the cake with the whipped cream, not quite to the cake's edges. Lift one long edge of the waxed paper and raise it so the cake rolls inward. Then, with the aid of the waxed paper, roll the cake onto a long, narrow chocolate-roll board, or flat serving tray. To serve, cut on the diagonal into slices.

VARIATION

NUT ROLL: Substitute 1 cup finely ground nuts (pecans, walnuts, hazelnuts) for the melted chocolate in the soufflé, folding them into the egg-and-sugar mixture before folding in the egg whites.

CHOCOLATE CHEESECAKE

Alice Petersen, long the food editor of the New York *Daily News*, perfected this cheesecake, which is almost overpoweringly rich. It's well worth the trouble to buy natural cream cheese without additives when you make cheesecake, as the gummy commercial super-market version is a travesty. [*Editor: You can find cream cheese without gums in natural food stores and specialty cheese shops.*]

For the Crust

Softened butter, for the pan

2 cups graham cracker crumbs

8 tablespoons (1 stick) unsalted butter, melted

¼ cup sugar

For the Filling

4 large eggs, separated, at room temperature

⅔ cup sugar

1 pound cream cheese, cut into cubes, at room temperature

Two 6-ounce bags semisweet chocolate chips

½ cup hot strong coffee

2 tablespoons dark rum

1 teaspoon vanilla extract

⅛ teaspoon plain salt

For the Topping

½ cup heavy cream

2 tablespoons sugar

Chocolate curls, for garnish

To make the crust: Preheat the oven to 350°F. Butter the bottom and sides of a 9-inch spring-form pan. Blend the graham cracker crumbs, butter, and sugar in a bowl and pat the crumb mixture onto the bottom and sides of the pan. Set aside while preparing the filling.

To make the filling: Beat the egg yolks and ⅓ cup of the sugar in a bowl with an electric mixer until thick and lemon-colored. Gradually beat in the cream cheese, being sure the mixture is smooth. Melt the chocolate in the top of a double boiler over hot but not boiling water. Add the hot coffee, rum, vanilla, and salt and whisk together. Beat into the cream cheese mixture.

In a clean bowl, using clean beaters, beat the egg whites until they hold soft peaks. Gradually beat in the remaining ⅓ cup sugar until you have a rather stiff meringue mixture, with glossy, up-right peaks. Fold this gently into the chocolate mixture and pour into the prepared crumb crust. Bake in a preheated 350°F oven for 1 hour. Turn the oven off, but leave the cake in the oven until it has completely cooled. Run a knife around the inside of the pan, and remove the sides of the pan. Wrap the cheesecake in plastic wrap and refriger-ate until chilled, at least 2 hours.

To make the topping: Whip the cream with the sugar. Spread on the cheesecake and decorate with chocolate curls.

Editor: Chocolate curls can be shaved from a block of chocolate with a vegetable peeler. To facilitate mak-ing the shavings, either slightly warm the chocolate in a microwave oven or dip the peeler in hot water and dry before using.

COFFEE CAKE

You may use a coffee cake from a good bakery, if you wish, but if you prefer to do your own, try this quick version.

1⅓ cups plus 1 tablespoon all-purpose flour

½ cup plus 1 tablespoon sugar

2 teaspoons baking powder

½ teaspoon plain salt

½ teaspoon ground mace

½ cup whole milk

1 large egg, well beaten

3 tablespoons unsalted butter, melted

Softened butter, for the pan

2 tablespoons cold unsalted butter, cut into ½-inch cubes, for topping

¼ teaspoon ground cinnamon or additional ground mace, for topping

Sift the flour, ½ cup of the sugar, the baking powder, salt, and mace together. Combine with the milk, egg, and melted butter and beat until smooth. Pour into a buttered 8 by 8-inch pan. Dot with the cold butter that has been rolled in 1 tablespoon of sugar, and sprinkle the remaining sugar over the top. Dust with cinnamon. Bake in a preheated 400°F oven for 25 minutes, or until brown and puffy. Serve hot.

GINGERBREAD

The special gingerbread one has for tea in England and occasionally in this country is very different from the gingerbread we are used to, which really is a bread. English tea gingerbread is a cake, and it has a rather different texture and flavor. Serve it warm with butter.

3 cups all-purpose flour

2 teaspoons ground ginger

1 teaspoon baking soda

⅔ cup dried currants

⅔ cup coarsely chopped slivered blanched almonds

½ cup vegetable shortening, plus more for the pan

½ cup Lyle's golden syrup (available at British grocers and many supermarkets)

½ cup molasses (not blackstrap)

⅓ cup sugar

⅓ cup whole milk

1 large egg

Sift the flour, ginger, and baking soda into a bowl. Mix in the currants and almonds. In a saucepan, gently heat and stir the shortening, golden syrup, and molasses with the sugar until the shortening is melted and the sugar dissolved. Let the mixture cool. Using a wooden spoon, work it into the flour mixture with the milk. Then beat in the egg.

Grease an 8-inch square baking pan with vegetable shortening, cover the bottom with waxed paper, and grease the paper. Spread the batter in the pan. Bake in a preheated 375°F oven for 35 minutes, or until a cake tester or wooden toothpick inserted in the center comes out clean. Let cool in the pan for 10 minutes, then turn out on a wire cake rack. Remove the waxed paper.

GLENNA McGINNIS' LANE CAKE

↪ MAKES ONE 4-LAYER 9-INCH CAKE; 12 SERVINGS

Editor: This fruit-packed invention of Alabaman Mrs. Emma Rylander Lane grew in fame after winning the grand prize at a county fair in 1898. Beard's recipe is attributed to Glenna McGinnis, a food editor at Woman's Day *magazine. Beard remarks Lane Cake is a great keeper, and, well-wrapped and frozen, it keeps indefinitely.*

For the Cake

1 cup (2 sticks) unsalted butter, at room
    temperature

2 cups sugar

1 teaspoon vanilla extract

3¼ cups sifted all-purpose flour

1 tablespoon plus ½ teaspoon baking powder

1¼ teaspoons plain salt

1 cup whole milk

8 large egg whites

For the Frosting

12 large egg yolks

1¾ cups sugar

12 tablespoons (1½ sticks) unsalted butter,
    cut into tablespoons

½ cup bourbon or rye whiskey

1½ cups coarsely chopped pecans

1½ cups chopped dark seedless raisins

1½ cups shredded fresh coconut

1½ cups quartered candied cherries

To make the cake: Lightly butter four 9 by 1½-inch round cake pans. Line the bottoms with waxed paper and butter the paper. Dust with flour and tip out the excess flour. If you only have two pans, simply fill and bake two cake layers at a time.

Beat the butter in a large bowl with an electric mixer until pale, about 1 minute. Gradually add the sugar and beat until the mixture is fluffy, about 2 minutes. Add the vanilla, and beat until the mixture is as light and fluffy as whipped cream, about 2 minutes more.

Sift together the flour, baking powder, and ¾ teaspoon of the salt. Reduce the mixer speed to low. In three additions, alternating with two equal additions of the milk, beat in the flour mixture, scraping down the bowl as needed. In a clean bowl using clean beaters, beat the egg whites to stiff, but not dry, peaks. Fold the whites into the batter.

Divide the batter evenly among the prepared pans. Place on two oven racks so that one pan is not directly beneath another—one rack set in the middle of the oven, the other in the top third. Bake in a preheated 350°F oven for about 25 minutes, or until the cake shrinks from the sides of pan and springs back to light pressure of the finger. Let the pans stand on cake racks for 10 minutes. Carefully loosen edges and turn out the cakes, upside down, onto the racks. Slowly peel off the waxed paper. Turn right side up and let cool before filling and frosting.

To make the frosting: Put the egg yolks in the top part of a double boiler, and whisk them slightly. Add the sugar, butter, and remaining ¾ teaspoon salt. Cook over simmering water, whisking constantly until the sugar is dissolved, the butter is melted, and the mixture is slightly thickened. Do not overcook, or the eggs will scramble. Remove from the heat. Add the whiskey and beat with an electric mixer for 1 minute. Mix in the pecans, raisins, coconut, and cherries and let cool until thick enough to spread.

Spread the filling between the cake layers, then on the top and sides. After an hour, if any has dripped off, just spread it back on the sides. Repeat if necessary. Cover with a cake cover or loosely with aluminum foil and refrigerate overnight.

1-2-3-4 CAKE

✎ MAKES ONE 3-LAYER CAKE; 12 SERVINGS

This layer cake was a standard in our house. This recipe is a very old one that people could keep in their heads because of the utter simplicity of the formula that gave the cake its name—1 cup of butter, 2 cups of sugar, 3 cups of flour, and 4 eggs. The juice mixture will give the cake a lovely, fresh, fruity flavor and it is not rich like an icing.

For the Cake

Softened butter and flour, for the pans

3 cups sifted cake flour (not self-rising)

4 teaspoons baking powder

½ teaspoon plain salt

½ pound (2 sticks) unsalted butter, at room temperature

2 cups sugar

4 large eggs, separated, at room temperature

1 cup whole milk, at room temperature

1½ teaspoons vanilla extract

For the Filling and Topping

¾ cup freshly squeezed orange juice

2 tablespoons freshly squeezed lemon juice

¾ cup sugar

1 tablespoon finely grated orange zest

Butter and flour the bottom and sides of three 8 by 1½-inch cake pans with the softened butter, tipping out the excess flour.

Sift the flour, baking powder, and salt together. Beat the butter in a large bowl with an electric mixer on high speed until it is light, creamy, and fluffy, about 1 minute. Gradually add the sugar into the butter, and beat until the mixture is very light and fluffy, about 2 minutes more. As the sugar blends in it will change the color of the butter to a much lighter color, almost white.

Whisk the egg yolks in a small bowl until they are well blended. Gradually beat into the butter mixture, mixing well after each addition. With the mixer on low speed, starting with the flour mixture, add the flour mixture in thirds, alternating with two equal additions of the milk, scraping down the sides of the bowl as needed. Beat in the vanilla. In a clean bowl using clean beaters beat the egg whites until they form firm, glossy peaks. Do not overbeat until they are stiff and dry. Fold the whites into the batter.

Pour and scrape the batter into the prepared

pans, dividing it equally among them. Give the filled pans a little knock on the countertop to level the batter. Bake in the center of a preheated 350°F oven for 25 minutes, or until each cake springs back when touched in the center. Remove the pans from the oven and put them on wire cake racks to cool for a few minutes, then loosen the layers by running the flat side of a knife blade around the sides of the pans, put a rack on top of each pan, and invert so the cake comes out onto the rack, top side down. Then reverse the layers so they are top side up.

Mix the orange juice, lemon juice, sugar, and orange rind together and drizzle the mixture over the still warm cake layers, being careful not to let it all soak into one spot; then pile the layers on top of each other. Let the cake cool.

POUND CAKE

MAKES ONE 12-INCH TUBE CAKE; 12 SERVINGS

Editor: Beard was the spokesperson for the Cognac industry for many years, and he found myriad ways to sneak Cognac into dishes that might not typically include liquor. However, liquor does enhance flavor, so don't leave out the Cognac, as it adds an unexpected dimension to this old-fashioned cake.

Softened butter and flour, for the pan
1 pound (4 sticks) unsalted butter, at room temperature
2 cups sugar
10 large eggs, separated, at room temperature
¼ teaspoon plain salt
4 cups sifted all-purpose flour
½ teaspoon ground mace
2 tablespoons Cognac

Butter and flour a 12-cup tube pan. Preheat the oven to 300°F. Beat the butter in a large bowl with an electric mixer until pale, about 1 minute. Add the sugar and continue beating until light and very fluffy, about 2 minutes more. Beat the egg yolks in another bowl until they are light and lemon-colored, about 2 minutes. Add to the butter mixture. In a clean bowl using clean beaters, beat the egg whites and salt until they form stiff peaks. Fold into the butter mixture. Add the sifted flour, mace, and Cognac, and mix until combined. Pour into the prepared tube pan. Bake until golden brown and a bamboo skewer inserted in the cake comes out clean, about 1½ hours. Let cool on a wire cake rack for 20 minutes. Loosen the cake from the sides and center tube of the pan, and invert onto the cake rack. Turn right side up and let cool completely.

VARIATION

FRUIT OR NUT POUND CAKE: Dark seedless or golden raisins or chopped walnuts or pecans may be added to this basic recipe. Mix about 1 cup of either with ¼ cup of the flour and fold into the finished batter.

PIES
AND
TARTS

PIES AND TARTS

APPLE PIE

If I am to enjoy apple pie at all, it must be made with juice-laden apples of good flavor and crunchy fresh texture, preferably left in their natural state, apart from sugaring, and it must have a fine, crisp crust. Simple enough, but these qualifications are rarely achieved by the standard two-crust pie served in this country, which is generally nutmeged and cinnamoned to the point where the fruit hardly matters, and it invariably has a soggy bottom. [*Editor: Beard fixes these blemishes in this recipe, which uses lard pastry, a minimum of nutmeg, and bread crumbs to soak up the apple juices to prevent the dreaded soggy bottom.*]

For the Filling

8 tart apples, cored, peeled, and cut into
    ½-inch-thick slices

1 cup granulated sugar

2 tablespoons freshly squeezed lemon juice

2 tablespoons vanilla extract

¼ teaspoon freshly grated nutmeg

Lard Pastry (page 333)

⅓ cup dried unflavored bread crumbs

4 tablespoons (½ stick) unsalted butter, cut into
    ½-inch pieces

For the Egg Wash

1 large egg

1 tablespoon heavy cream

To make the filling: Combine the apples, sugar, lemon juice, vanilla, and nutmeg in a bowl, and toss well.

Roll out the larger ball of pastry into a 12-inch round to make a bottom crust for a 9-inch pie pan. Ease it into the pan, fitting it in loosely but firmly. Sprinkle the bottom of the pie shell with bread crumbs. Fill the crust generously with the apple mixture, spooning it in with a slotted spoon so as to drain off any excess liquid, which would otherwise make the crust soggy. Dot the layers of apple with the butter. Roll out the remaining pastry ball into a 10-inch round for the top crust. Brush the rim of the pie shell with cold water, put on the top crust, and trim, seal, and crimp the two crusts. Cut vents in the top crust to allow the steam to escape.

To make the egg wash: Beat the egg and cream together in a small bowl with a fork. Lightly brush the top crust with the egg wash. Bake in a preheated 425°F oven for 45 minutes, or until the crust is nicely browned and the juices are bubbling through the vents. Cool for at least 1 hour before cutting and serving.

BLUEBERRY DEEP-DISH PIE

Editor: Beard believed that the beginning cook could learn a lot from making pastry dough by hand. This was meant literally, without a pastry blender or spoon, as it is only when working the dough with your hands that you can really judge the texture of the dough, which should be moist and malleable, but not dry or crumbly. Try it this way at least once as an exercise.

For the Pastry

2¼ cups all-purpose flour

¼ teaspoon plain salt

8 tablespoons (1 stick) cold unsalted butter, cut into
  ½-inch cubes

4 tablespoons cold vegetable shortening, cut into
  ½-inch cubes

¼ cup ice water, as needed

For the Filling

Softened butter, for the pie dish

6 cups fresh blueberries

3 tablespoons all-purpose flour

1 cup sugar

6 tablespoons (¾ stick) cold unsalted butter,
  cut into ½-inch cubes

1 large egg yolk, beaten

Maple or vanilla ice cream, or whipped cream,
  for serving

To make the pastry: Sift the flour and salt into a mound on a wooden cutting board or marble slab. Add the butter and shortening, and quickly rub them into the flour with your fingertips until crumbly. Then add just enough ice water to hold the pastry together. Pull off lemon-size bits, smear on the work surface with the heel of your hand, and form into a ball. Wrap in plastic wrap and refrigerate for 1 hour.

Butter a 10-inch deep-dish pie plate lightly. Pour in the blueberries, keeping them higher in the center. Dust with the flour, then add sugar (use more or less depending on the sweetness of the berries) and dot with butter.

Roll out the pastry slightly larger than the pie dish, and cover the berries with the crust. Trim away the excess pastry. Flute the edges, and cut a vent in the top. Brush the pastry with the beaten egg yolk. Bake in a preheated 450°F oven for 10 minutes. Reduce the heat to 350°F and continue to bake until the crust is browned, about 40 minutes more.

RICH PUMPKIN PIE

MAKES TWO 9-INCH PIES; 8 SERVINGS EACH

I prefer to serve this pie on the warm side with Cognac-flavored and sweetened whipped cream.

Editor: This recipe is a variation on Beard's mother's pumpkin pie. She would use steamed Hubbard squash, rubbed through a sieve, instead of canned pumpkin.

Plain Pie Pastry for two 9-inch pie shells (page 334)

2 cups mashed pumpkin, (canned pure pumpkin
  purée is ideal)

6 large eggs, lightly beaten

2 cups heavy cream

⅔ cup sugar

½ cup Cognac

½ cup drained and finely chopped preserved ginger
  or ¼ cup finely chopped crystallized ginger

1 teaspoon ground cinnamon

¼ teaspoon ground cloves

¼ teaspoon ground mace

¼ teaspoon plain salt

Line two 9-inch pie pans with the pastry and crimp the edges. Line the pastry shells with aluminum foil, and fill with dried beans. Bake in a preheated 425°F oven for 12 minutes until the pastry edges are slightly browned. Remove the pie shells from the oven, then lift off the foil and beans. Reduce the oven temperature to 375°F.

Place the pumpkin in a large bowl and make a well in the center. Add the eggs, cream, sugar, Cognac, chopped ginger, cinnamon, cloves, mace, and salt and whisk well. Pour into the partially baked pie shells. Bake about 40 minutes, until the custard is just set. Let cool on a wire rack for about 1 hour. Serve warm.

PECAN PIE

 MAKES ONE 9-INCH PIE; 8 SERVINGS

Editor: Many people think that pecan pie is a Southern dessert, but actually, it was devised as a promotional recipe for corn syrup in the 1920s. It eventually became an American classic.

Plain Pie Pastry for one 9-inch pie shell (page 334)

1 cup pecan meats, either halves or broken pieces

2 large eggs

1 cup dark corn syrup

½ to 1 cup packed light brown sugar

1 teaspoon vanilla extract or 2 tablespoons dark rum

¼ teaspoon plain salt

2 to 4 tablespoons (¼ to ½ stick) unsalted butter, cut into small pieces

Roll out the pastry into a ⅛-inch-thick round. Line a 9-inch pie pan with the pastry and crimp the edges. Sprinkle the pecans in the pastry shell. Whisk the eggs in a medium bowl, and stir in the syrup, brown sugar, vanilla, and salt. Pour over the pecans and dot with the butter. Bake in a preheated 450°F oven for 10 minutes. Reduce the heat to 325°F, and bake until the filling is almost firm in the center, about 25 to 30 minutes. Cool the pie on a wire rack.

SHOOFLY PIE

ᏓᏜ MAKES ONE 9-INCH PIE; 8 SERVINGS

Editor: A very old recipe known both in Pennsylvania Dutch and Southern cooking, shoofly pie is almost candy in a pie shell. Serve it with whipped cream.

Plain Pie Pastry for one 9-inch pie shell (page 334)

1 cup all-purpose flour

½ cup packed light brown sugar

1¼ cups vegetable shortening

1 cup boiling water

1 teaspoon baking soda

⅔ cup light corn syrup

⅓ cup dark molasses (not blackstrap)

Line a 9-inch pie pan with the pastry, crimp the edges, and refrigerate. Prepare a crumb topping by mixing the flour and brown sugar in a bowl. Add the shortening and cut it into the flour mixture with a fork or pastry blender to form a coarse, mealy texture.

In a deep bowl, whisk the boiling water and baking soda. Stir in the corn syrup and molasses. Let cool and pour into the pastry shell. Sprinkle the crumb mixture evenly over the top.

Bake in a preheated 375°F oven for 10 minutes. Reduce the temperature to 350°F and continue baking 30 to 35 minutes, or until the filling is just firm when the pan is gently shaken. Do not overbake. Cool on a wire rack before serving.

PEAR TARTE TATIN

ᏓᏜ MAKES ONE 9-INCH TART; 8 SERVINGS

Editor: Tarte Tatin is the famous upside-down tart, usually made with apples. Beard shows that it also works well with pears. He suggests serving the tart with goat cheese.

For the Filling

¾ cup plus 3 tablespoons sugar

6 ripe but firm pears, peeled, halved, cored, and cut into quarters or sixths

4 tablespoons (½ stick) unsalted butter, cut into small pieces

Freshly squeezed juice of 1 lemon

2 teaspoons vanilla extract

Rich Tart Pastry (page 334)

To make the filling: Melt ¾ cup of sugar in a heavy 9-inch ovenproof skillet (preferably cast iron) over medium heat until it turns a delicate brown. Remove the pan from the heat. Arrange the pears on the melted sugar, and mound up in the center. Sprinkle them with the 3 tablespoons of sugar, and dot with the butter. Sprinkle with the lemon juice and vanilla.

Carefully roll out the chilled pastry into a 10-inch round about ⅛ inch thick. Fit the pastry into the skillet, trimming away excess pastry. Make 3 holes in the top with a skewer or sharp knife. Bake in a preheated 350°F oven for about 45 minutes, until the crust is brown and firm to the touch and the pears are bubbling up a bit around the edges. Remove from the oven and let it stand

2 minutes. Run a sharp knife around the edge of the skillet, and invert the *tarte* onto a platter somewhat larger than the skillet. This must be done quickly and deftly so the hot pears and their juices don't burn you. [*Editor: Place the platter over the skillet. Hold the platter and skillet together, and quickly invert them to let the pears and crust fall onto the plate.*] Should the pears shift position, push them back into place with a spatula. Serve warm or tepid.

PEAR AND CHOCOLATE TART

〜 MAKES ONE 9-INCH TART; 8 SERVINGS

Editor: This sophisticated tart is something that Beard might have been served in a French restaurant.

Tart Rich Tart Pastry (page 334)

For the Filling

2 cups water

1 cup sugar

One 1-inch piece vanilla bean, split lengthwise, or 1 teaspoon vanilla extract

4 to 6 pears, peeled, halved, and cored

6 ounces semisweet chocolate, coarsely chopped

2 tablespoons unsalted butter

For the Glaze

1 cup apricot preserves

2 tablespoons Cognac

To make the tart: Following the instructions on page 334, roll out the pastry and fit into a 9-inch tart pan with a removable bottom. Line the shell with aluminum foil and raw rice or dried beans. Bake in a preheated 425°F oven until the edges of the pastry are golden brown, about 15 minutes. Remove the foil and rice and continue baking until fully baked, about 2 minutes more. Cool completely.

Meanwhile, bring the water, sugar, and vanilla to a boil in a heavy skillet over medium heat. Cook for 5 minutes to make a syrup. Add the pears and simmer them in the syrup until just cooked through but still firm, about 10 minutes. Do not overcook. Cool in the syrup. Remove the pears with a slotted spoon and drain them on paper towels. (The syrup may be reserved for poaching other fruits.)

Melt the chocolate and butter in a small saucepan over very low heat. Brush the bottom of the tart shell with the chocolate mixture and let it cool. Arrange the poached pear halves in the flan shell.

To make the glaze: Melt the apricot preserves in a pan and bring to a boil. Stir in the Cognac and boil for 2 minutes. Strain into a small bowl. Brush the hot glaze over the pears. Let cool on a wire rack. Remove the sides of the pan and serve.

THE COACH HOUSE QUINCE TART

≈⁄ MAKES ONE 12-INCH TART; 12 SERVINGS

Editor: New York's The Coach House, not far from Beard's brownstone in Greenwich Village, and quite possibly his favorite restaurant, celebrated the very best of American cooking. This tart, made with quince—a sadly overlooked autumn fruit—was one of its specialties. See also the Black Bean Soup and Pastitsio for a Party on pages 38 and 218.)

For the Pastry

2½ cups all-purpose flour

½ pound (2 sticks) unsalted butter, cut into ½-inch cubes, at room temperature

3 large egg yolks

2 tablespoons sugar

½ teaspoon ground cinnamon

Freshly grated zest of 1 lemon

For the Filling

6 large quince

1 stick cinnamon

2 whole cloves

3 cups water

3 cups sugar

Freshly squeezed juice of 1 lemon

2 tablespoons chopped almonds, roasted lightly

Whipped cream (page 300), crème fraîche, sour cream, or vanilla ice cream for serving

To make the pastry: Place the flour in a large bowl. Make a well and add the butter, yolks, sugar, cinnamon, and lemon zest. Mix with your fingertips until well mixed and you can shape the mixture into a ball. Wrap in plastic wrap and refrigerate until firm.

To make the filling: Peel and core the quince, saving the seeds. Wrap the quince seeds, cinnamon, and cloves in a piece of rinsed cheesecloth and tie into a sachet with kitchen twine. Cut the quince into strips about 2 inches long and ½ inch wide. Meanwhile, in a heavy skillet, bring the water, sugar, and lemon juice to a boil. Add the quince and the cheesecloth sachet. Bring the mixture to a boil, lower the heat, and simmer for 1½ hours, or until the juice is thickened. (The pectin in the seeds acts as a thickener.) Stir the mixture from time to time, being careful that it doesn't stick or burn. Discard the cheesecloth sachet and let the mixture cool.

Preheat the oven to 375°F. Roll out two-thirds of the pastry between 2 pieces of wax paper, and fit into a 12-inch tart pan with a removable bottom. Line with aluminum foil and fill with raw rice or dried beans. Bake for 10 minutes, or until the edges of the pastry are set. Remove the foil with the rice.

Fill the shell with the quince mixture. Roll out the remaining pastry to ⅛ inch thickness, cut into ¼- to ½-inch strips, and use to make a latticework top. Bake for about 30 minutes, or until the pastry is golden brown and the quince filling is bubbling. Remove the tart from the oven and sprinkle the almonds on top. Let cool at least 2 to 3 hours, but do not refrigerate. Remove the sides of the tart pan. Serve with whipped cream.

SIMPLE STRAWBERRY TART

☙ MAKES ONE 9-INCH TART; 6 TO 8 SERVINGS

Rich Tart Pastry (page 334)

1 large egg yolk, beaten

One 12-ounce jar red currant jelly

2 tablespoons kirsch

1½ to 2 pints perfect ripe strawberries, of more or less even size, washed and hulled

½ cup heavy cream

Roll out the pastry and fit it into a 9-inch tart pan with a removable bottom. Line the pastry with aluminum foil and raw rice or dried beans. Bake the tart shell blind (see page 336) in a preheated 425°F oven until the edges are browned and crisp, about 18 minutes. Remove the foil and rice. Brush the pastry shell with the egg yolk and return to the oven for 2 minutes to bake and set the egg yolk. Let cool completely.

Heat the currant jelly in a heavy-bottomed saucepan over moderate heat until it comes to the boiling point; add 1 tablespoon of the kirsch and let it cool slightly. Brush the bottom of the cooled pastry shell with 1 to 2 tablespoons of the currant glaze.

Arrange the strawberries, tips up, in the pastry shell, building from the sides toward the center. You may make a double layer in the center to give a feeling of elevation. Spoon the warm currant glaze over the berries. Beat the heavy cream and remaining kirsch together in a bowl with an electric beater until the cream is stiff. Remove the sides of the pan. Serve the tart with the kirsch-flavored whipped cream.

LARD PIE PASTRY

☙ MAKES ENOUGH PASTRY FOR ONE 9-INCH DOUBLE-CRUST PIE OR TWO 9-INCH PIES

The old-fashioned method of using lard in piecrust instead of butter is one I favor, as the result is much flakier and tenderer. The purer the lard, the better. Buy leaf lard (pork kidney fat); this is the best lard you can use. To render the lard, cut up a 3- or 4-pound piece of the leaf fat and render it (let it melt slowly) in a shallow pan in a 300°F oven, pouring off the fat as it melts and transferring it to a jar. When all the fat is rendered and only the crispy bits of crackling remain, chill the fat in the refrigerator until firm and set.

2½ cups all-purpose flour

½ teaspoon plain salt

¾ cup chilled leaf lard, cut into ½-inch cubes

About ⅓ cup plus 1 tablespoon ice water

Mix the flour and salt in a large bowl. Add the lard and cut it into the flour with 2 knives or a pastry blender just until the mixture resembles coarse cornmeal; the texture will not be uniform but will contain crumbs and bits and pieces. Sprinkle water over the flour mixture, a tablespoon at a time, and mix lightly with a fork, using only enough water so the pastry holds together when pressed lightly into a ball. Divide the dough into 2 balls. (If you are making a double-crust pie, make one ball slightly larger than the other.) Wrap each in plastic wrap and refrigerate 30 minutes or more. [*Editor: The dough can be refrigerated overnight, or frozen for up to 1 month. Defrost the frozen dough overnight in the refrigerator before using.*]

PLAIN PIE PASTRY: If you prefer not to use lard, substitute 12 tablespoons (1½ sticks) cold unsalted butter or 6 tablespoons each cold unsalted butter and vegetable shortening, cut into ½-inch cubes, for the lard.

Editor: Lard can mean both raw pork fat and rendered pork fat, and Beard uses the same word for both. Raw pork fatback (used to make pâté and rillettes) can occasionally be found at supermarkets, but raw leaf lard is only available at artisan butchers. Leaf lard is preferred for rendering because it is harder than fatback; lard made from fatback can be too soft and make greasy pastry. You can purchase rendered leaf lard fat at D'Angelo Bros. in Philadelphia (www.dangelobros.com) and Dietrich's Meats in Krumsville, Pennsylvania (www.dietrichsmeats.com).

RICH TART PASTRY

〰️ MAKES ONE 9-INCH PIE OR TART SHELL

This classic French pastry dough, *pâte brisée*, can be prepared well in advance and refrigerated or frozen. The dough, formed into a ball, is wrapped airtight in waxed paper, plastic wrap, or aluminum foil, or it may be rolled out, fitted into a pie or tart pan, covered, and stored either unbaked or partially or fully baked, according to your needs.

1¾ cups sifted all-purpose flour

¼ teaspoon plain salt

2 tablespoons sugar (optional, for dessert pastry only)

8 tablespoons (1 stick) cold unsalted butter, cut into ½-inch cubes

2 tablespoons ice water

1 tablespoon freshly squeezed lemon juice

1 large egg yolk

Put the flour and salt in a mixing bowl (add the sugar if you are making a sweet pastry). Make a well in the center and put the butter in the well. Work the butter and flour together quickly with the fingertips (do not let the warm palms of your hands come near pastry—they cause the butter to soften, melt, and become very difficult to work with) until the mixture forms small, flaky granules, like oatmeal. Mix the ice water, lemon juice, and egg yolk together in a small bowl. Gradually stir in enough of the liquid mixture to make a dough that holds together when pressed.

Cupping your hands tightly, gather the dough into a rough ball, pulling in any crumbs from the sides and bottom of the bowl. The dough should feel moist but not sticky. If it seems too sticky, sprinkle with 2 to 3 teaspoons flour and blend in; if it feels dry, sprinkle with a few drops of water and knead in. Turn the dough out onto a board. Break off small pieces, about 2 to 3 tablespoons each, and smear them across the board by pushing hard with the heel of your hand. This process, called the *fraisage*, ensures the complete blending of the butter and flour. When all the dough has been worked this way, gather it together with a pastry scraper or spatula, form it into a ball, wrap in plastic wrap, and chill for 30 minutes, or until firm, but not so firm that it cracks at the edges when rolled out. (The dough can also be frozen for up to 4 weeks. Defrost the dough in the refrigerator overnight. Let stand for a few minutes at room temperature before rolling out.)

To roll out the pastry: Select as cool a surface as possible: a marble slab is ideal, but a countertop almost as well, as long as it is in a cool part of the kitchen. If the dough gets too warm, the butter melts and the pastry becomes extremely difficult to work with. To prevent this, work as quickly as possible on a cool surface. Roll the pastry out on the lightly floured marble slab or other smooth surface. Rub the rolling pin lightly with flour and begin by flattening the ball of dough into a disk. Starting in the center of the dough, roll in one direction, not back and forth, smoothly, evenly, and quickly, rotating the pastry a quarter-turn each time and stopping just short of the edge so that you get a fairly even round. While rolling, lift the pastry occasionally to see if it is sticking to the board; if it is, sprinkle the board lightly with flour. Also flour the rolling pin if the pastry is sticking to it. Roll the pastry out about 1/8 inch thick, until you have a circle 11 to 12 inches in diameter, or large enough to fit into a 9-inch pie or tart pan without skimping. There should be a little overhang at the edge of the pan. To check, hold the pan over the rolled-out pastry and gauge with your eye. Use this method of gauging the size of your pastry whatever type of pan you are using.

Another good way to roll out a rich pastry such as this is between sheets of waxed paper: roll smoothly and evenly, and turn dough over often. With every turn, loosen the top paper to prevent it from sticking to the dough and wrinkling.

To line a pie or tart pan: The method for lining a removable-bottom tart pan or standard pie pan is much the same. If the dough has been rolled on a board, roll it loosely but carefully over the rolling pin, lift, then unroll carefully over the pan. Lift the edges of the dough and let it fall gently into place, patting it lightly into the bottom, without forcing or stretching it. If the pastry is stretched, it will shrink during baking. Press it snugly into the sides.

If the dough has been rolled between sheets of waxed paper, remove the top sheet, slip one hand under the bottom sheet, and lift up the rolled dough, inverting it over the pan. Lift the edges of the dough and let it fall gently into place in the mold or pan without forcing or stretching it. Peel off the waxed paper and let the dough sink into place in the mold, then pat it snugly into place.

Trim the pastry edges with a sharp knife or scissors, allowing an overlap of about 1/4 to 1/2 inch—you need the excess because the pastry will shrink. For a pie, crimp the edges of the pastry by pinching it between two fingers, making a firm edge. For a tart pan, using the flat of a paring knife, press the dough gently against the sides in an even pattern so it adheres. Be sure the pastry is pushed well (without being stretched) into the fluted sides of the pan. Also be certain it is completely sealed and free of cracks or the filling will run out of the bottom.

Should the pastry break while you are lining the mold or pan (this can happen, as this short pastry is very fragile), don't worry. Just patch it by pressing the broken edges together with your fingertips. Patch any holes in the pastry with some of the trimmings.

If the pastry shell is to be baked and has become quite soft after rolling and fitting into the mold or pan, refrigerate or freeze it for 10 to 15 minutes, until firm.

To bake a pastry shell: Baking an unfilled tart shell is called "baking blind." Prick the dough lightly, line the shell with aluminum foil, weigh it down with raw rice or dried beans (they may be kept in a jar and used repeatedly), and bake it in a preheated 425°F oven for about 15 minutes, until the bottom is set and the edges lightly browned. Remove the shell from the oven, and remove the lining and weights. If you wish, brush the bottom with beaten egg yolk (or Dijon mustard for a savory tart), and return to the oven and bake until the yolk looks dry, about 2 minutes. This seals the bottom and prevents a soggy crust.

The timing of 14 to 16 minutes and the 2-minute period with the yolk glaze is for a partially baked shell; the pastry will finish cooking when it is baked with its filling. For a fully baked shell, bake it for about 20 minutes, then brush on the egg-yolk glaze and dry out for 2 minutes in the oven.

COOKIES AND BARS

COOKIES AND BARS

CHINESE CHEWS

MAKES ABOUT 30 COOKIES

I have no idea why these are called Chinese Chews, but I've been making them for over fifteen years and I've yet to find anyone who doesn't find the combination of flavors irresistible.

2 cups all-purpose flour
½ pound (1 cup) unsalted butter, at room temperature
1 cup packed light or dark brown sugar

For the Topping

1½ cups packed light or dark brown sugar
1 cup coarsely chopped pecans
2 tablespoons all-purpose flour
½ teaspoon baking powder
¼ teaspoon plain salt
2 large eggs
1 teaspoon vanilla extract

Mix the flour, butter, and brown sugar in a bowl until crumbly, and spread this in a buttered shallow 13 by 9-inch baking pan. Bake in a preheated 300°F oven for 10 minutes, until the edges are set, then remove from the oven.

Beat all of the ingredients for the topping together in a bowl with an electric mixer and spread the mixture evenly over the prepared crumb crust. Return it to the oven and bake until lightly browned, 30 to 40 minutes. Cool. Cut into fingers.

CINNAMON STARS

MAKES ABOUT 5 DOZEN SMALL COOKIES

5 large egg whites
Dash of plain salt
2 cups sifted confectioners' sugar, plus more for sprinkling
2 teaspoons ground cinnamon
Grated zest of ½ lemon
1 pound sliced unblanched almonds, finely ground in a food processor

Beat the egg whites with salt in a large bowl with an electric mixer until they hold soft peaks, then gradually beat in the confectioners' sugar and continue beating until the mixture holds stiff peaks when you lift up the beater. Stir in the cinnamon and lemon zest. Take about one-third of the egg white mixture and place it in a separate bowl to use later on as a glaze. Fold the ground almonds into the remaining two-thirds of the egg white mixture and mix in thoroughly. Let the dough stand for 30 minutes.

Lightly sprinkle the work surface or a wooden cutting board with confectioners' sugar. Take half the mixture at a time and pat it to a thickness of ⅜ inch on the work surface. If mixture seems sticky, dust the palms of your hands frequently with confectioners' sugar. Cut with a 2½-inch star cookie cutter and place on a greased cookie sheet. Brush the tops of each cookie with a generous coating of the reserved egg white mixture and bake in a preheated 300°F oven for 20 minutes, or until the edges begin to get firm. Baking does not change the color, you will notice. Let cool for a few minutes on the baking sheet, then transfer to a wire rack to cool completely. Take the other half of the batter and repeat the operation, gathering up and cutting out the scraps, as well.

GINO'S MACAROONS

⚮ **MAKES 20 MACAROONS**

Editor: Gino Cofacci was Beard's partner for over a decade. A trained architect, for a time, Gino delivered his homemade baked goods to New York restaurants. Here is his recipe for Italian-style almond cookies.

8 ounces almond paste

⅓ cup plus 2 tablespoons superfine sugar

¼ cup confectioners' sugar

⅓ cup (about 2 large) egg whites

Freshly grated zest of 1 lemon or orange

Granulated sugar, for sprinkling

Line a baking sheet with parchment paper. Break the almond paste into pieces and process in a food processor until finely ground. Add the superfine and confectioners' sugars and mix until thoroughly blended, about 1 minute. Transfer to the bowl of a heavy-duty stand mixer fitted with the paddle attachment. Gradually beat in the egg whites to make a soft paste that is thick enough to pipe. Mix in the lemon zest. Beat at high speed for 3 minutes.

Put the mixture into a pastry bag fitted with a ½-inch plain pastry tube. Pipe 1½-inch rounds on the parchment paper, about 1½ inches apart.

Or use a teaspoon and drop the mixture onto the parchment, spreading it out 1½ inches in diameter. Brush the tops with a pastry brush dampened with cold water, then sprinkle them lightly with granulated sugar. Bake in a preheated 350°F oven for 30 minutes, or until lightly browned. These can be stored in an airtight container for up to 6 months.

MERINGUE KISSES

⚮ **MAKES 5 DOZEN COOKIES**

These are dropped cookies made with a meringue mixture and are therefore very sticky. Preferably they should be baked on a cookie sheet lined with parchment paper. If you don't have parchment paper, the cookie sheets should be both buttered and floured.

3 egg whites

½ teaspoon cream of tartar

1 cup superfine sugar

1 teaspoon vanilla extract

These meringues are most easily made with an electric mixer. Prepare 3 cookie sheets, either by lining them with parchment paper or by buttering them well, then dusting them lightly with flour.

Beat the egg whites in a bowl until foamy, add the cream of tartar, and beat until white, fluffy, and just beginning to hold their shape when the beater is lifted. Gradually beat in the sugar, 3 or 4 tablespoons at a time, adding the vanilla when half the sugar has been added. Beat until the sugar is dissolved and the whites are smooth, glossy, and stand in stiff, upright peaks—the meringue stage.

Take up a teaspoon of the meringue mixture and push from the tip of the teaspoon with the back of another teaspoon into the prepared cookie sheet. Space the meringues at least 1 inch apart to allow for expansion. Bake in a preheated 275°F oven, one sheet at a time, on the center shelf, for about 20 minutes, or until the meringues are set and very lightly colored. Remove from the oven and cool slightly, then remove them from the sheets to a wire rack to cool, sliding a flexible metal spatula under them. Cool completely. Store in an airtight container between sheets of waxed paper or aluminum foil.

OATMEAL CARROT COOKIES

∽ MAKES 24 COOKIES

Editor: A cross between two favorite desserts, a carrot cake and an oatmeal cookie.

12 tablespoons (1½ sticks) unsalted butter

¾ cup sugar

1 cup grated raw carrot

1 large egg

Freshly grated zest of ½ lemon

1¼ cups sifted all-purpose flour

2 teaspoons baking powder

½ teaspoon plain salt

1 cup old-fashioned (rolled) oats

Beat the butter in a medium bowl with an electric mixer. Beat in the sugar and mix until combined. Add the carrot, egg, and zest and mix well. Sift the flour, baking soda, and salt together, and stir into the carrot mixture. Stir in the rolled oats. Place about 1 teaspoonful of dough on a greased teaspoon and push off with the back of another onto a well-oiled or buttered baking pan or sheet. Continue with all the cookie dough. Bake in a preheated 375°F oven 10 to 12 minutes, or until the cookies are a delicate brown around the edges. Loosen from the pan while still warm, cool on a rack, and store in airtight containers. These freeze well, as does the unbaked dough.

SAND TARTS

∽ MAKES ABOUT 2½ DOZEN COOKIES

One of the most popular kinds of rolled cookie is sand tarts. Make sure the dough is thoroughly chilled before rolling.

For the Cookies

8 tablespoons (1 stick) unsalted butter

1 cup sugar

1 large egg

¼ teaspoon plain salt

2 cups sifted cake flour (not self-rising)

½ teaspoon vanilla extract

For the Topping

2 large egg whites

2 tablespoons sugar

½ teaspoon ground cinnamon

To make the cookies: Beat the butter in a medium bowl with an electric mixer until creamy and fluffy, then beat in the sugar, egg, and salt and continue to beat until very light, fluffy, and pale. Beat in the sifted flour and vanilla until thoroughly combined. When the dough is well blended, form it into a ball, wrap in waxed paper, and chill in the refrigerator for at least 3 hours.

Roll out the dough between sheets of waxed paper until very thin, less than ¼ inch, and cut into 3- or 3½-inch rounds with a plain or fluted cookie cutter.

Butter 3 cookie sheets. Arrange the cookies on the sheets, lifting them from the paper with a flexible, thin-bladed metal spatula. Beat the egg whites lightly with a fork and, using a pastry brush, brush the tops of the cookies with the beaten egg white. Sprinkle the tops with the sugar and cinnamon, to taste. Do not overdo either sugar or cinnamon.

Bake the cookies in a preheated 375°F oven until they turn a deep yellow around the edges, 10 to 12 minutes. Remove from the oven and cool slightly, then remove from the pans with a metal spatula and put on wire racks to cool. These cookies are better used within a week, but they will stay crisp 3 or 4 weeks if stored in an airtight tin in a cool place.

"MONSTER" PEANUT BUTTER COOKIES

MAKES TWELVE 6-INCH COOKIES

I've always had great fun baking outsize cookies as big as a small plate. This recipe makes about a dozen 6-inch cookies, but you can increase the number by doubling or tripling the ingredients. You may use any favorite recipe for oatmeal, chocolate chip, or sugar cookies. Just follow the rule of using ⅓ cup dough for each cookie.

Editor: For the best results, use a large rimmed baking sheet (a half sheet pan, measuring 18 by 13 inches), and allow two cookies per pan. Do a test run to see how much the cookies spread on your baking sheet.

½ pound (2 sticks) unsalted butter, at room
    temperature
1 cup sugar
1 cup smooth or chunky peanut butter
2½ cups all-purpose flour

Beat together the butter and sugar in a large bowl with an electric mixer until light and fluffy, then add the peanut butter and the flour. When well mixed, scoop up ⅓ cup measures of the mixture and place on a well-buttered cookie sheet, being sure to leave lots of room between the mounds. Dip the bottom of a 9-inch pie plate in sugar and press the mounds firmly, flattening them to 6-inch circles. Bake in a preheated 375°F oven for 15 minutes. Remove the cookies from the oven but leave them on the cookie sheets for at least 5 minutes before lifting them with a spatula. This is essential, as they are thin. Repeat with the remaining dough on cool baking sheets.

SUGAR COOKIES

 MAKES ABOUT 48 COOKIES

Editor: Looking for a rolled sugar cookie appropriate for icing? These work well for that purpose, but they are just as good in an unadorned state.

8 tablespoon (1 stick) unsalted butter, at
    room temperature
1 cup sugar
2 large eggs
1¼ teaspoons vanilla extract
2½ cups sifted all-purpose flour
2 teaspoons baking powder
½ teaspoon plain salt
Sanding or granulated sugar, for
    sprinkling

Beat the butter and sugar in a large bowl with an electric mixer until fluffy, then beat in the eggs and vanilla. Sift the flour, baking powder, and salt together, and stir into the butter mixture. Chill the dough for easier handling; if you are in a hurry, spread it out on aluminum foil in 2 portions, wrap, and place in the freezer for 10 to 30 minutes.

Use only half the dough at a time for rolling and cutting. Roll between sheets of waxed paper to ¼ to ⅓ inch thick. Peel off the waxed paper: Peel it off the top of the rolled dough, flop the dough over onto a slightly sugared board, and peel off the other sheet.

Cut the cookies with a sugared 3-inch round cookie cutter. Lift with a spatula onto a lightly buttered baking sheet. Allow about 1 inch between them for expansion. Sprinkle the cookies with sugar, preferably the sanding sugar. Bake in a preheated 375°F oven for 8 to 10 minutes, or until very lightly browned around the edges. Loosen from the pan while still quite warm. When they have cooled on a rack to room temperature, store in airtight containers.

TUILES

 MAKES ABOUT 2 DOZEN COOKIES

A classic French almond cookie that takes its name from its shape, similar to curved terra-cotta roof tiles. It is delicate and crisp, a lovely partner for sherbet. You'll sometimes find it made in a very large size. Be sure to shape the cookies while they are hot and pliable.

6 tablespoons (¾ stick) unsalted butter, at room
    temperature, plus more for the cookie sheet
½ cup sugar
1 cup sliced almonds
2 large egg whites
⅓ cup sifted all-purpose flour
Pinch of plain salt

Beat the butter and sugar together in a medium bowl with an electric mixer until well blended. Mix in the almonds, egg whites, flour, and salt.

Working with one cookie sheet at a time, butter a heavy cookie sheet and drop the batter by teaspoonfuls 1½ inches apart, leaving enough room to allow the cookies to spread. Bake in a preheated 400°F oven for about 10 minutes, or until golden brown around the edges and slightly yellow in the center. Remove the cookies from the sheet with a spatula and drape and press them over a rolling pin while they are still hot and pliable. Leave to set for a few minutes and remove to a cake rack to cool completely. Repeat with a cool baking sheet and the remaining batter until all of the cookies are made.

BUÑUELOS

∞ **MAKES ABOUT 36**

Similar forms of this deep-fried pastry are found in Europe and in Latin America. In France they are known as *galettes à l'huile,* and in Italy, where they are shaped into bow knots, they are called *farfallette dolci.* Paper-thin and crisp, they are absolutely marvelous when sprinkled well with cinnamon and confectioners' sugar. Sometimes they are made into a dessert by adding a cream or a syrup to them. This version comes from Mexico.

  4 cups all-purpose flour, plus more for kneading
  2 tablespoons granulated sugar
  1 teaspoon baking powder
  1 teaspoon plain salt
  2 large eggs
  1 cup whole milk
  4 tablespoons (½ stick) unsalted butter, melted
  Vegetable oil, for deep-frying
  Confectioners' sugar, for sprinkling
  Ground cinnamon (optional)

Sift 4 cups of the flour, the granulated sugar, baking powder, and salt together into a bowl. Whisk the eggs thoroughly and then beat the milk into the eggs. Gradually combine the egg-milk mixture and the dry ingredients, and finally add the melted butter. Turn out on a floured board and knead until quite smooth and elastic, about 10 minutes. (I then like to divide the dough into about 36 tiny balls and roll them out individually, but you can roll the dough and cut it into 4- to 6-inch rounds or squares.) Fry the pieces in deep oil heated to about 370°F. When done they will curl somewhat and become golden brown and crispy. Drain well on paper towels, and sprinkle with confectioners' sugar and ground cinnamon or just with confectioners' sugar.

BLOND BROWNIES

⌀ MAKES ABOUT 24 BROWNIES

Editor: White chocolate is the secret ingredient in these moist and chewy "blondies." Be sure to use a top-notch brand that has cocoa butter in the ingredients, and skip any white chocolate that contains palm oil.

5 ounces white chocolate, coarsely chopped

8 tablespoons (1 stick) unsalted butter, cut up

2 cups sugar

2 large eggs, at room temperature

1 teaspoon vanilla extract

1 cup sifted all-purpose flour

1 cup coarsely chopped walnuts, pecans, or unsalted
   macadamia nuts

½ teaspoon plain salt

Softened butter, for the pan

Melt the white chocolate and butter together in a medium saucepan over very low heat. [*Editor: Be careful, as the chocolate is very delicate, and scorches easily.*] Remove from the heat and stir well. Stir in the sugar, then beat in the eggs and vanilla. Add the flour, nuts, and salt and stir just to lightly mix. Spread in a well-buttered 11 by 8-inch or 13 by 9-inch baking pan. Bake in a preheated 325°F oven, 35 minutes for the smaller pan, 30 for the larger. Do not overbake or they will lose their nice chewy texture. Remove the pan to a wire rack to cool. While slightly warm, cut into squares with a buttered knife.

LEMON MERINGUE BARS

⌀ MAKES ABOUT 2 DOZEN BARS

This rather rich cookie, good with tea or with ice cream, is not difficult to make.

1 cup all-purpose flour, sifted

½ cup confectioners' sugar

8 tablespoons (1 stick) unsalted butter, cut into
   tablespoons, at room temperature

2 large eggs, separated, at room temperature

Freshly grated zest of 1 lemon

½ teaspoon plain salt

½ cup granulated sugar

1 tablespoon freshly squeezed lemon juice

Put together in a bowl the flour, confectioners' sugar, butter, egg yolks, lemon zest, and salt. Rub together with your fingertips until the mixture is smooth and the color evenly distributed. Press into a 9-inch-square baking pan. Bake in a preheated 350°F oven for 10 minutes, until the edges of the dough look dry. Remove from the oven and allow to cool while making the meringue.

Beat the egg whites with an electric mixer until stiff. Gradually add the granulated sugar and beat until very stiff and shiny. Beat in the lemon juice. Spread on the dough. Return to the oven and bake for 20 to 25 minutes, or until nicely browned. Cool completely on a wire rack. Cut into bars.

LINZER BARS

〰 MAKES ABOUT 30 BARS

Editor: There are many recipes for jam-filled Linzer bars, all based on the famous specialty torte of Linz, Austria, although most, unlike Beard's authentic version, leave out the nuts, cocoa, and spices. These are beautiful additions to the holiday cookie tray.

---

8 tablespoons (1 stick) unsalted butter, at room temperature

½ cup granulated sugar

½ cup packed light brown sugar

1 cup toasted and very finely chopped sliced almonds or skinned hazelnuts (see Note)

1 large egg, beaten, at room temperature

½ cups all-purpose flour

1 tablespoon cocoa

1 teaspoon baking powder

1 teaspoon ground cinnamon

¼ teaspoon ground cloves

¼ teaspoon ground mace or nutmeg

1 cup raspberry jam

Freshly grated zest of 1 lemon

Beat the butter and sugars together in a medium bowl with an electric mixer until smooth, about 2 minutes. Beat in the chopped almonds and the egg.

Sift together the flour, cocoa, baking powder, cinnamon, cloves, and mace. Gradually beat into the butter mixture. Press two-thirds of the dough into a 13 by 4½-inch tart pan with a removable bottom or an 8-inch square baking pan. Combine the jam and lemon zest in a small bowl, and spread over the dough in the pan.

Roll out the remaining dough between 2 pieces of waxed paper into a square about ¼ inch thick. Refrigerate the dough in the waxed paper and the dough-filled pan for 30 minutes. Remove from the refrigerator. Discard the top sheet of waxed paper and cut the rolled dough into ½-inch-wide strips. Place diagonally on the jam, creating a lattice top. Bake in a preheated 375°F oven until the lattice dough is lightly browned, about 30 minutes. Cool completely on a wire rack. Cut into squares.

NOTE: To toast the almonds, spread out on a baking sheet, and bake in a preheated 350°F oven, stirring occasionally, until they are fragrant and toasted, 10 to 12 minutes. To toast the hazelnuts, spread on a baking sheet, and bake in a preheated 350°F oven, stirring occasionally, until the skins are cracked and the flesh underneath is lightly toasted, 10 to 12 minutes. Transfer the hazelnuts to a kitchen towel, let stand 5 minutes, and then rub off the skins with the towel while the nuts are warm. Let both nuts cool before chopping in a food processor or blender.

BASIC
STOCKS
AND
SAUCES

BASIC STOCKS AND SAUCES

CHICKEN STOCK

≈ MAKES 2½ QUARTS

Editor: Chicken stock is one of the most essential ingredients of good cooking, and no canned broth will ever be better than the homemade version. If you wish, substitute chicken wings, cut apart at the joints, for the gizzards.

2 pounds chicken gizzards

2 pounds chicken necks and backs

1 medium yellow onion, peeled and stuck with 3 whole cloves

1 leek, white and pale green part only, well washed to remove grit

1 carrot, scraped

2 garlic cloves, peeled

1 teaspoon dried thyme

1 bay leaf

1 sprig fresh flat-leaf parsley

6 whole black peppercorns

Kosher salt

Put all of the ingredients except the salt in a stockpot. Add enough water to cover by 1 inch—about 3 quarts—and bring to a boil over high heat. Reduce the heat to low and simmer for 15 minutes. Skim off the scum that forms on the surface, using a wire skimmer or large spoon. Cover the pot and simmer for 2 to 2½ hours. Season with the salt.

Strain the stock through a colander lined with several thicknesses of rinsed cheesecloth into a large bowl and cool thoroughly. Save the gizzards (they are good eating) and discard the other chicken parts and vegetables. When the stock is cool, refrigerate until chilled. Before using, remove the layer of fat that has formed on the surface. [_Editor: The stock can be stored in airtight containers and frozen for up to 3 months._]

BEEF STOCK

≈ MAKES ABOUT 2½ QUARTS

Editor: Although canned broth has improved much over the years, it is still difficult to find a good-tasting beef broth. It is worth making homemade beef stock and freezing it in one-quart containers.

2 to 3 pounds veal or beef marrowbones

3 tablespoons all-purpose flour

5 pounds beef shin

1 large yellow onion, peeled and stuck with 2 whole cloves

1 carrot, scraped

1 leek, white and pale green part only, well washed to remove grit

1 small white turnip, peeled

2 garlic cloves, peeled

1 teaspoon dried thyme

1 bay leaf

1 sprig fresh flat-leaf parsley

6 whole black peppercorns

Kosher salt

Dust the bones with flour and place on the rack in a broiling pan. Place under a broiler (or in a preheated 500°F oven), and cook, turning once, until nicely browned, about 10 minutes (or about 20 minutes in the oven). Put the bones and the remaining ingredients, except the salt, in a stockpot. Add enough water to cover by 1 inch—about 3 quarts—and bring to a boil over high heat. Reduce the heat to low and simmer for 15 minutes. Skim off the scum that forms on the surface, using a wire skimmer or large spoon. Cover the pot and simmer for 2 to 2½ hours. Season with the salt.

Strain the stock through a colander lined with several thicknesses of rinsed cheesecloth into a large bowl and cool thoroughly. Discard the solids. When the stock is cool, refrigerate until chilled. Before using, remove the layer of fat that has formed on the surface. [*Editor: The stock can be stored in airtight containers and frozen for up to 3 months.*]

VARIATION

VEAL STOCK: Substitute 4 pounds meaty veal bones for the beef bones and beef shin.

Stock or Broth

Editor: The difference between stock and broth can be semantics; both are cooking liquids based on meat and bones. Some cooks feel that a stock is unseasoned and used only as a recipe ingredient, but broth is fully seasoned and can be eaten like a soup. Here is Beard on the subject:

"The other morning my old friend Helen Mc-Cully [*Editor: Food editor of* House Beautiful] called me at an early hour and said, "Now that you're revising your fish book, for heaven's sake, define the difference between a stock, a broth, and a bouillon."

"The reason no book does is that they are all the same thing. A stock, which is also known as a broth or a bouillon, is basically some meat, game, poultry, or fish simmered in water with bones, seasonings, and vegetables. Food writers have been known to wax nostalgic about the thrifty French housewife who, according to them, kept a stockpot permanently simmering on the stove, putting in leftovers from other meals. If this ever happened, which I very much doubt, it would have resulted in a ghastly mess of hot garbage. No one in his right mind would throw picked-over chicken and lamb bones, vegetable scraps, and all the other bits and pieces from the dinner table into the pot.

FISH STOCK

If you can't buy fish bones and heads, use an inexpensive bony white fish such as whiting but not an oily fish. I like to add salt to taste after the stock has cooled, as the fish throws off a good deal of natural salt. Stock may be frozen until needed.

Editor: Porgy is another good option if you are buying whole fish. Do not simmer this stock for more than 30 minutes, as the thin bones of fish give off their flavor quickly, and overcooking yields a bitter stock.

2 pounds fish bones and heads or 2 pounds bony fish

3 cups water

3 cups dry white wine

1 lemon slice

1 small yellow onion, stuck with 2 whole cloves

1 teaspoon fennel seeds

4 sprigs fresh flat-leaf parsley

6 crushed black peppercorns

Kosher salt

Wash the fish well and remove the gills from the heads. Combine in a large saucepan with all of the other ingredients except the salt. Bring to a boil over high heat. Reduce the heat to a simmer and simmer 20 to 30 minutes. Strain and discard the solids. Taste the stock and add salt as needed. Cool, cover, and refrigerate until needed. [*Editor: The stock can be stored in airtight containers and frozen for up to 1 month.*]

VEGETABLE BROTH

For certain vegetable soups, a delicately flavored broth is preferable to a strong, rich beef stock. As vegetables contain their own natural sodium, season with salt after making the broth.

3 quarts water

3 carrots, finely chopped

6 celery ribs, finely chopped (3 cups)

3 medium yellow onions, finely chopped

½ pound white mushrooms or mushroom stems, sliced

3 leeks, white and pale green parts, thinly sliced

1 bay leaf

Kosher salt

Combine all of the ingredients except the salt in a large saucepan. Bring to a boil over high heat. Reduce the heat to medium-low and simmer, covered, for 2½ hours. Strain the broth, discarding the vegetables. Season with the salt. [*Editor: The stock can be stored in airtight containers and frozen for up to 3 months.*]

BÉCHAMEL SAUCE

Editor: Every cook should know how to make this basic white sauce, which can be spun off into many variations.

2 tablespoons unsalted butter
2 tablespoons all-purpose flour
1 cup whole milk, heated
Kosher salt and freshly ground black pepper
Pinch of freshly grated nutmeg (optional)

Melt the butter over low heat in a heavy-bottomed medium saucepan. Whisk the flour into the butter and cook slowly, whisking all the time, for 1 to 3 minutes, or until the roux is well blended. Gradually whisk in the hot milk. Increase the heat to medium and cook, whisking all the time, until the sauce is smooth, thick, and at the boiling point. Let the sauce simmer over low heat, whisking often, for 3 to 4 minutes, then season with salt and pepper, and the nutmeg, if desired.

If you are not using the sauce right away, butter a piece of waxed paper large enough to fit inside the pan and lay it on the surface of the sauce, buttered side down, to prevent a skin from forming.

VARIATIONS

CAPER SAUCE: Add 1 to 2 tablespoons drained nonpareil capers, according to your taste, to the finished sauce.

MUSTARD SAUCE: Stir 2 tablespoons Dijon mustard into the finished sauce. Simmer for 2 to 3 minutes. This makes a fairly hot sauce. For a milder sauce, use less mustard.

SAUTÉ VELOUTÉ: Substitute 1 cup Chicken Stock (page 349) or canned chicken broth for the milk. Add ½ cup heavy cream to the finished sauce, and continue simmering for about 5 minutes, until the sauce has returned to its original thickness.

SAUCE SUPRÉME: Substitute 1 cup Chicken Stock (page 349) or canned chicken broth for the milk. Whisk 1 cup heavy cream with 3 large egg yolks in a small bowl. Gradually whisk in half of the hot finished sauce. Return to the saucepan and cook over low heat, whisking constantly, until heated through and lightly thickened, but do not boil.

QUICK BROWN SAUCE

This is an easy, economical brown sauce, not as time-consuming as the classic version. It will keep in the refrigerator for a week or two.

One ½-inch slice of ham, fat removed, diced
2 medium yellow onions, sliced
2 carrots, sliced
2 tablespoons unsalted buter
1 quart Beef Stock (page 349)
½ bay leaf
1 sprig fresh thyme or ¼ teaspoon dried thyme
1 large ripe tomato, peeled, seeded, and chopped, or
   1 tablespoon tomato paste

Kosher salt and freshly ground black pepper

½ cup dry red wine (optional)

2 tablespoons unsalted butter, at room temperature (optional)

3 tablespoons all-purpose flour (optional)

Sauté the ham, onions, and carrots in the butter in a large saucepan over medium heat until the onion is browned, about 10 minutes. Slowly mix in the stock. Add the bay leaf and thyme. Simmer gently for 1 hour over medium-low heat. Add the tomato and the wine, if you like. Season with salt and pepper to taste. Simmer for a further half hour, then strain through a wire sieve. If the sauce does not seem thick enough, boil down to the required consistency. (Or thicken with beurre manié: Mash the butter and flour together in a small bowl with a rubber spatula until smooth. Whisking quickly, add bits of the butter mixture into the strained, simmering sauce, and let cook until thickened as desired. Simmer for 5 minutes to remove any raw flour taste.)

VARIATIONS

BORDELAISE SAUCE: Reduce 1 cup of dry red wine (preferably a Bordeaux or American Cabernet Sauvignon) in a small saucepan over high heat to ½ cup. Sauté 2 finely chopped shallots in 2 tablespoons unsalted butter in a medium saucepan over medium heat until golden, 3 to 5 minutes. Add 1 cup Quick Brown Sauce and the reduced wine. Simmer 3 or 4 minutes to amalgamate the flavors; correct the seasoning. Strain, if you wish. [*Editor: This is a fine sauce for roast beef and grilled steaks.*]

MADEIRA BROWN SAUCE: Add 3 or 4 tablespoons Madeira to taste to the finished sauce.

SAUCE DIABLE: Sauté 2 finely chopped shallots in 2 tablespoons unsalted butter in a medium saucepan over medium heat until golden, 3 to 5 minutes. Add 1 cup Quick Brown Sauce. Season with ½ teaspoon freshly ground black pepper, 1 teaspoon hot dry English mustard (or prepared Dijon mustard), ¼ to ½ teaspoon Tabasco, according to your palate, plus 1 teaspoon fresh lemon juice. Simmer 3 or 4 minutes to amalgamate the flavors; correct the seasoning. Strain, if you wish.

HOLLANDAISE SAUCE

✐ MAKES 1 CUP

This rich, suave butter and egg sauce, which tastes so elegant with freshly cooked asparagus, artichokes, poached fish, or eggs Benedict, takes care and patience unless you make it in a blender or food processor, in which case it is practically foolproof. When you make hollandaise by hand, over direct heat or hot water, you have to be very careful that the sauce doesn't overheat or you'll end up with scrambled eggs.

Editor: Hollandaise is another essential French sauce that is the base for many useful adaptations.

---

3 large egg yolks

1 tablespoon freshly squeezed lemon juice

½ teaspoon kosher salt

Pinch of cayenne pepper or dash of Tabasco

8 tablespoons (1 stick) unsalted butter, cut into

½-inch pieces, at room temperature

To make your sauce by hand: Use a small, heavy-bottomed saucepan (enameled cast iron is ideal) or the top of a double boiler over, but not touching, hot (not boiling) water. If you use the saucepan, make the sauce over low heat.

Put the egg yolks, lemon juice, salt, and cayenne in the saucepan over low heat. Beat with a wire whisk or electric hand mixer until the eggs and seasonings are well blended and the egg yolks have thickened to the consistency of heavy cream. You should be able to see the bottom of the pan between strokes. The egg yolks must be beaten until thick or they will not absorb and hold the butter properly and the sauce will not thicken as it should.

Have the pieces of butter at your elbow, on a plate. The minute the yolks are thick, drop one piece of butter into them and stir rapidly with a wire whisk in a circular motion until it has been absorbed by the eggs. Then stir in another piece. Continue to add the butter, one piece at a time, each time stirring until absorbed, until you have the sauce of a consistency that coats the whisk heavily.

If by chance the sauce seems to be thickening too fast, add a tablespoon of cold water to slow the process. If it is too thin, you are adding the butter too quickly.

As soon as the sauce is made, remove it from the heat and serve. If you have to keep it for a short time, cover the pan with plastic wrap and let it stand over warm water, then reheat slowly over the water until the sauce is just warm. Hollandaise should not be served hot. However, it is my contention that hollandaise should be served freshly made and not reheated, because there is always the chance that the warm sauce will develop harmful bacteria.

Should your sauce break and curdle because you have let it get too hot, try stirring a tablespoon of hot water or an ice cube into it, which often works. If it doesn't, start over again with a clean saucepan and 1 egg yolk. Beat the yolk until thick and then gradually beat in the curdled sauce until it smooths out (this will be the same technique you use for saving a curdled mayonnaise).

To make the sauce in a blender: Combine 4 egg yolks, the lemon juice, and the salt and cayenne in the container of a blender and turn the blender on and off, at high or "blend" setting, just to blend the mixture. Heat the butter until it is bubbling and very hot, but not browned. Remove the insert from the lid of the blender, turn the blender to high or "blend," and pour in the hot butter in a thin, continuous stream—do not pour too fast or the eggs will not absorb the butter properly. When the butter is absorbed and the sauce thick, turn off the machine. If the sauce should start curdling while you are adding the butter, pour 1 tablespoon hot water into the sauce while the blender is running.

To make the sauce in a food processor: Add 4 large egg yolks, 2 tablespoons fresh lemon juice, the salt, and the cayenne to the bowl of a food processor fitted with the metal blade for 3 seconds. Heat the butter until it is bubbling and very hot, but not browned. With the machine running, pour the bubbling melted butter through the feed tube in a thin, continuous stream. It is essential that the butter be bubbling hot or the sauce will not thicken. If the sauce curdles, add 1 tablespoon hot water.

VARIATIONS

ANCHOVY HOLLANDAISE: Add 4 very finely drained and chopped anchovy fillets, 1 finely chopped or crushed garlic clove, and 1 teaspoon drained capers to the finished Hollandaise Sauce. Serve with steak.

BÉARNAISE SAUCE: Put ¼ cup white wine vinegar, 1 tablespoon finely chopped shallots or scallion, 1 tablespoon chopped fresh tarragon or 1 teaspoon dried tarragon, and 1 teaspoon chopped fresh parsley into a small saucepan; bring to a boil and boil until it is reduced practically into a glaze—about 2 tablespoons. Cool. Press this through a strainer into the beaten egg yolks before starting to add the butter. Serve with steak, broiled liver, chicken, or fish.

MUSTARD HOLLANDAISE: Add 1 or 2 tablespoons Dijon mustard or 1 teaspoon hot dry English mustard to the seasonings for the Hollandaise. Serve with steak or fish.

SAUCE MOUSSELINE: Fold 1 cup whipped cream [Editor: That is, ½ cup heavy cream, whipped to stiff peaks] into the finished Hollandaise Sauce. Serve with fish, asparagus, or soufflés.

TOMATO HOLLANDAISE (Sauce Choron): Add 1 to 2 tablespoons of your favorite cooked tomato sauce to Béarnaise Sauce. Serve with steaks, fish, or chicken.

MAYONNAISE

⌒ MAKES 1¾ CUPS

I learned to make mayonnaise when I was just about tall enough to reach the work table. I would stir the mixture constantly with a fork in a deep plate to the slow drip, drip, drip from the oil cruet. Later, I made the sauce with a Dover beater (now called a rotary beater), which was to me a much trickier process than the slow, sure, productive technique of the fork. Nowadays I prefer to make mayonnaise in a food processor or blender. Or if a large quantity is needed, I use an electric mixer with a whisk attachment. I start the mixer on a rather slow speed and increase it as the mixture becomes a true emulsion.

I have always, since childhood, preferred mayonnaise made with a good, fruity olive oil. However, I'm aware that many people do not like the definite flavor of olive oil and would rather have a bland and tasteless oil, in which case I consider peanut oil as good as anything else. [Editor: Do not use extra-virgin olive oil to make mayonnaise; its acidity will curdle the mayonnaise. A good quality gold-colored oil (formerly called pure) is fine, but it makes a thicker sauce than one cut with peanut oil.]

In making mayonnaise, it is imperative that both the eggs and the oil be at room temperature. Often mayonnaise made with refrigerated eggs and warm oil will curdle. Here, then, is the traditional way of making mayonnaise by hand.

  2 large egg yolks
  1 teaspoon kosher salt
  ½ teaspoon dry or Dijon mustard
  1½ cups good, fruity olive oil or half olive oil and
     half peanut oil [Editor: You can also use canola or
     vegetable oil.]

1 tablespoon freshly squeezed lemon juice or white
    wine vinegar
Dash of Tabasco (optional)

Put the egg yolks, salt, and mustard into a mixing bowl and beat with a wire whisk or electric hand mixer until the yolks become thick and sticky. Begin adding the oil, drop by drop, beating it in thoroughly after each addition.

Should the mayonnaise start to curdle, this indicates you have added the oil too fast. Start over again in a clean bowl. Beat 1 egg yolk until thick, then beat in a few drops of oil. Gradually beat in the curdled mixture until it becomes thick and smooth. This method also works if the mayonnaise does not thicken properly but remains liquid.

As the mayonnaise begins to thicken, stiffen, and become light in color, which means it has emulsified, you can beat in the remaining oil more rapidly, but be sure it is all incorporated before adding the next batch. When thick and stiff, beat in the lemon juice, which gives a nice tartness and thins it out slightly. Season with Tabasco, if using. Transfer the mayonnaise to a bowl or jar, cover, and refrigerate. You can safely keep it for a week under refrigeration.

To make the mayonnaise in a blender: Put 2 whole eggs, the salt, mustard, and lemon juice in the blender and mix for just 5 seconds at the blend or high setting, then, with the machine still running, remove the cover insert and dribble the oil in very slowly until the mayonnaise starts to thicken, then add the rest of the oil more quickly. The minute the mayonnaise is thick and smooth, stop blending.

To make the mayonnaise in a food processor: Use the metal blade of the processor when making mayonnaise. Put 1 whole large egg and 1 large egg yolk, the salt, mustard, and lemon juice in the processor bowl and process until blended, about 2 or 3 seconds. Then, with the machine still running, gradually pour in the oil, as you would if using the blender, until thick and smooth, and then stop processing.

VARIATIONS

GREEN MAYONNAISE: Purée ½ cup very dry raw spinach leaves in a food processor or blender. Combine with 1½ cups Mayonnaise and 2 tablespoons finely chopped fresh flat-leaf parsley, 2 tablespoons finely cut fresh chives, and 2 tablespoons finely chopped dill or tarragon. Serve with poached fish.

RÉMOULADE SAUCE: Mix 1 finely chopped hard-boiled egg, 2 tablespoons finely chopped capers, 1 tablespoon finely chopped flat-leaf parsley, and 1 teaspoon freshly squeezed lemon juice into 1½ cups Mayonnaise. Check for seasoning and add kosher salt and freshly ground black pepper. Or omit the salt and add ½ teaspoon anchovy paste. Serve with poached fish.

MUSTARD MAYONNAISE: To each cup of mayonnaise add 1 tablespoon Dijon mustard. Serve with poached or grilled fish or chicken.

TARTAR SAUCE: Mix 1½ tablespoons finely chopped onion, 1 tablespoon finely chopped dill pickle, 2 teaspoons finely chopped flat-leaf parsley, and 1 teaspoon freshly squeezed lemon juice into 1 cup Mayonnaise. Serve with grilled, fried, or poached fish.

AÏOLI

MAKES ABOUT 3¼ CUPS

Aioli, the headily garlicky Provençal mayonnaise, does something wonderful for bland fish fillets. The traditional way to make aïoli is to pound the garlic and egg yolks in a huge mortar with a pestle and then gradually work in the olive oil is very stiff. I find this arduous, time consuming process can be considerably simplified if you use a food processor or blender.

Editor: Aïoli adds punch to sandwiches and is often served as a dip for crudités. Aïoli is served with other foods (salt cod, shrimp, new potatoes, and more) to make a meal called le grand aïoli, *described on page 177. In Provence, many community organizations still organize* grande aïoli *feasts as fundraisers much in the same way that American churches give bake sales or chicken barbecues.*

---

4 large garlic cloves

3 large egg yolks

2½ cups fruity olive oil, but not extra-virgin olive oil

1 tablespoon freshly squeezed lemon juice

Kosher salt

Put the garlic and egg yolks in a blender and blend at high speed until combined, about 30 seconds. If you use a food processor, process the garlic and yolks for about 2 to 3 seconds, just until blended. With the machine running, very slowly pour in the olive oil, in a thick trickle at first until the mayonnaise starts to thicken, then more rapidly. When stiff, add the lemon juice and season with the salt.

TAPENADE MAYONNAISE

MAKES ABOUT 1½ CUPS

---

*Editor: Tapenade is a classic recipe of Provence, and this mayonnaise-based recipe is different from the version that is currently popular, which resembles an olive purée. In Beard's recipe, the key ingredient is capers (*tapéno *in Provençal dialect), not olives. As he spent many summers in St. Remy-de-Provence, and also with Julia and Paul Child in their home near Grasse, he knew his tapenade. Use it like Aïoli (opposite), a dip, spread, or sauce for grilled fish, chicken, and lamb.*

---

1 cup Mayonnaise (page 355), made without salt or pepper

½ cup drained and finely chopped capers

Juice and finely chopped zest of 1 lemon

1 garlic clove, crushed through a press

2 tablespoons chopped fresh flat-leaf parsley

Blend all together thoroughly in a bowl, cover, and chill in the refrigerator.

BASIC STOCKS AND SAUCES   355

SAUCE GRIBICHE

MAKES ABOUT 2 CUPS

Editor: Serve thick and chunky Sauce Gribiche with poached, fried, or grilled fish or poached meats.

3 hard-boiled eggs, shelled

1 teaspoon dry mustard

1 teaspoon kosher salt

½ teaspoon freshly ground black pepper

1 cup olive oil

2 tablespoons finely chopped mixed herbs (chives, parsley, chervil, and/or tarragon)

1 tablespoon red or white wine vinegar

1 tablespoon finely chopped dill pickle

1 teaspoon drained and finely chopped capers

Clarified Butter

Makes about ¾ cup

This is something that you make, rather than buy. Melt **1 cup (2 sticks) unsalted butter** in a heavy-bottomed saucepan over low heat, to prevent it from browning. The white froth that rises to the top should be skimmed off with a spoon, and the clear yellow "clarified" liquid butter carefully poured off into a container, leaving the curdlike dregs in the pan. Cover and refrigerate the clarified butter. You may make it in quantity and use as needed. Use it for sautéing when you need high heat.

Remove the yolks from the whites, put the yolks in a bowl, and crush with a fork. Finely chop the egg whites. Mix with the mustard, salt, and pepper. Gradually stir in the oil. When it is all absorbed, add the herbs, vinegar, chopped whites, pickle, and capers. Let stand for 1 hour or more to blend the flavors.

MANTEQUILLA DE POBRE (POOR MAN'S BUTTER)

MAKES ABOUT 2 CUPS

Editor: This guacamole-like mixture is delicious served with grilled fish fillets.

2 large tomatoes, peeled

2 ripe medium avocados, pitted

12 scallions, white and green parts, finely chopped

3 tablespoons red wine vinegar

1 tablespoon vegetable oil

Kosher salt

Cut the tomatoes and avocados into small cubes. Toss gently in a bowl with the scallions, vinegar, and oil until well mixed. Season with salt. Cover tightly with plastic wrap and let stand at room temperature for about 30 minutes before serving.

PESTO

MAKES 2 CUPS

I have basil plants growing in pots in the garden behind my house. I chop the fresh leaves onto summer tomatoes, and every so often I harvest a lot of leaves and make pesto. With pesto in the freezer, I can recover the fragrance of summer in my kitchen all winter long. Use it on plain noodles (you'll need about ½ cup for 1 pound), or to flavor soups, stews, and salad dressings. For an extraordinary treat, combine it with pasta and new potatoes.

> 4 cups packed fresh basil leaves
> ½ cup pine nuts
> ½ cup packed fresh flat-leaf parsley leaves
> 3 garlic cloves
> 1 teaspoon kosher salt
> ½ to 1 cup extra-virgin olive oil
> ½ cup freshly grated pecorino or
>   Parmesan cheese

Put the basil, pine nuts, parsley, garlic, and salt into the food processor or blender with ½ cup oil. Process, adding enough additional oil to make a smooth paste. Add the cheese and process a few seconds longer.

VARIATIONS

FREEZER PESTO: To make pesto for the freezer, just process the basil, parsley, garlic, salt, and oil. Freeze it in 1-cup portions. When you are ready to use it, defrost the sauce and put it back into the processor with the nuts and cheese. If you want to use it as a seasoning, you can eliminate the nuts and cheese and simply chip off teaspoonfuls of puréed pesto from the frozen mass.

PESTO WITH WALNUTS: Instead of the pine nuts, use ½ cup walnuts and omit the cheese.

PESTO WITH PARSLEY: Instead of basil, use 3 cups packed fresh flat-leaf parsley leaves for a midwinter pesto.

BASIC VINAIGRETTE SAUCE

MAKES ½ CUP; ENOUGH FOR 8 CUPS OF MIXED GREENS

You can't make a good salad without a good vinaigrette sauce. A true vinaigrette is as simple as one, two, three—oil, vinegar, salt, and pepper—and the success depends on the quality of the ingredients.

First, a good oil, preferably a rich, fruity, and flavorful olive oil. Other oils don't have enough flavor to make a good vinaigrette.

Second, a vinegar that is not sharp or acid, either red or white wine vinegar (white tends to be milder). There are some fine imported French wine vinegars available and a few excellent ones from California. If you can't find a good wine vinegar, use cider vinegar or lemon juice. I don't recommend that you buy an herb-flavored vinegar—if you want an herb flavor in your salad it's better to use real herbs, fresh or dried.

Third, salt and pepper. I like to use coarse (kosher) salt for salads, as for other cooking, because it has more flavor and guts than iodized table salt, and a better texture. Freshly ground black peppercorns have more spiciness and taste than ready-ground pepper which, as far as I'm concerned, is worse than useless.

As to proportions, after years of experimenting I find that I prefer to use 3 or 4 parts of oil to 1 of vinegar, depending on the heaviness of the oil and the sharpness of the vinegar. This is something you must learn to adjust so there is a perfect balance. Start with less vinegar than you think you will need, then taste and see if you need more. You can always add, but you can't subtract.

6 tablespoons fruity olive oil

1½ to 2 tablespoons wine vinegar

1 teaspoon kosher salt

½ teaspoon freshly ground black pepper

Blend the ingredients together in a bowl with a wooden spatula or a fork, using 1½ tablespoons vinegar. Then taste, and add more if you feel the dressing needs it.

Never add sugar to a vinaigrette. If the vinegar is mild, as it should be, no sweetening is necessary. Always mix your vinaigrette just before you intend to use it. The fresher it is, the better. Don't follow that reprehensible practice of making the vinaigrette days ahead and keeping it in a jar in the refrigerator. For that matter, don't store oil in the refrigerator. It gets cloudy, thick, and sluggish. If you are afraid of opened oil going rancid in hot weather, buy a small quantity at a time and use it up quickly.

VARIATION

MUSTARD VINAIGRETTE: Whisk ½ teaspoon Dijon mustard with the vinegar, salt, and pepper in a bowl. Gradually whisk in the oil. This dressing is thicker than the Basic Vinaigrette.

INDEX

Brown sauce 200